THE GOOD HOUSEKEEPING
ILLUSTRATED
BOOK OF
HOME
MAINTENANCE

THE GOOD HOUSEKEEPING
ILLUSTRATED
BOOK OF
HOME
MAINTENANCE

John McGowan & Roger DuBern

HEARST BOOKS

New York

The Good Housekeeping Illustrated
Book of Home Maintenance
was conceived, edited and designed
by Dorling Kindersley Limited,
9 Henrietta Street,
London WC2E 8PS

Project Editor
Rosanne Hooper
Editor
Phil Wilkinson
Project Art Editor
Neville Graham
Art Editor
Derek Coombes
Designer
Roger Priddy
Managing Editor
Alan Buckingham
American editor
Michael Stowers

Library of Congress Catalog Card Number: 85-80003

ISBN: 0-688-04315-1

First U.S. Edition
1 2 3 4 5 6 7 8 9 10

Filmsetting by
Chambers Wallace Limited, London
Reproduction by
Reprocolor Llovet, Barcelona
Printed and bound in Germany by
Mohndruck Graphische Betriebe GmbH,
Gütersloh

William Morrow & Company, Inc.,
105 Madison Avenue,
New York, NY 10016

Contents

Home contents

Home maintenance

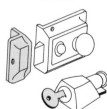

The home tool kit

Introduction

Your house is more than a home – it is likely to represent your largest investment and the basis of your financial security. If that investment is to remain sound, the house has to be protected by regular maintenance – inside and out. Anticipating problems and defects before they arise and redecorating before rot and rust set in, are the best policies.

What causes the problems?
Human beings impose the stresses of normal wear, tear, use and abuse on a home. But most problems are caused by nature, in the form of the elements, parasites and natural decay. Moisture rising from below ground and rain, snow and sleet attacking from above lead to dampness and rust. The wind penetrates gaps in windows and door frames, disperses dirt and dust, may dislodge slates on roofs, and encourages movement in the structure of the house. Even the sun can be harmful: cracking and blistering paintwork, and discoloring curtains, wallpaper and paint.

Termites in woodwork, birds nesting under the eaves and rodents in the basement or attic cause problems if left for long Small shifts or subsidence in the under-lying land can result in movement and cracking in the structure of a house.

What are the solutions?
Most situations take years to develop into a major problem, but the sooner you take action, the easier and cheaper the work. There are two possible solutions: either call in a professional or undertake to do the work yourself.

The rewards of doing it yourself
The most obvious advantage of undertaking your own home care, maintenance and decoration is the saving in cost. The amount saved on professional fees will pay for further home improvements. These in turn help to make your home more comfortable, more attractive and more saleable. There is also the convenience of being able to do the work at a time to suit yourself and any other inhabitants. You can plan to vacate areas of the house to suit your lifestyle and do not need to supervise the progress of the work. But perhaps the greatest advantage is the satisfaction of seeing the results of your own work, and the knowledge that you can make your home as you want it, without relying on

outside help. The more you do yourself, the more skilful you become, and so the greater your satisfaction with the results.

It is important, however, to know when to call in the professional. By following the advice in this book, you will soon gain the confidence to cope with anything from putting up a shelf to dealing with a burst pipe. The more experienced you become, the less daunting you will find apparently complex, but in fact quite simple, jobs. In an emergency or if you are in any doubt about the safety of a particular job, it is often worth calling in expert help. Likewise, heavy structural work, such as building an extension, knocking through a wall or re-tiling a roof might be best left to a professional builder.

How this book can help
This book is for anyone with a home to maintain and the desire to improve it. It offers clear, easy to follow instructions for the willing, but inexperienced handy person. The book is divided into five self-contained parts – three main practical sections on "Home decorating", "Home maintenance" and "Home contents" – and two photographic reference sections: "Choosing materials" and "The home tool kit". Each section is identified by its individual colored thumb tag and symbol. The sections are divided into individual subject areas, such as Painting; Electricity; Storage and shelving; Choosing furnishing fabrics; Measuring and marking tools. In the three practical sections these chapters are further organized into numbered jobs, which consist of illustrated step-by-step instructions on how to tackle the work.

Each chapter is introduced with an invaluable guide to the amount of time, the quantities of materials and the specific tools you will need before you start work, together with a list of jobs contained within the chapter. Where one basic technique is relevant to a variety of jobs you will find a self-contained "Basic technique" box, which serves the entire chapter. Many jobs involve similar steps, so cross-references to specific job and page numbers are to be found in bold type for quick, easy reference. You will also find references to specific pages in the "Choosing materials" and "The home tool kit" sections. The "Home decorating" and "Home contents" sections also include advice on color and design and suggest

List of household terms

The following selected definitions are an introductory guide to commonly-used terms, to denote the parts of a house, decorating jobs and essential fittings. Other specific words relating to repairs are explained in the main body of the book.

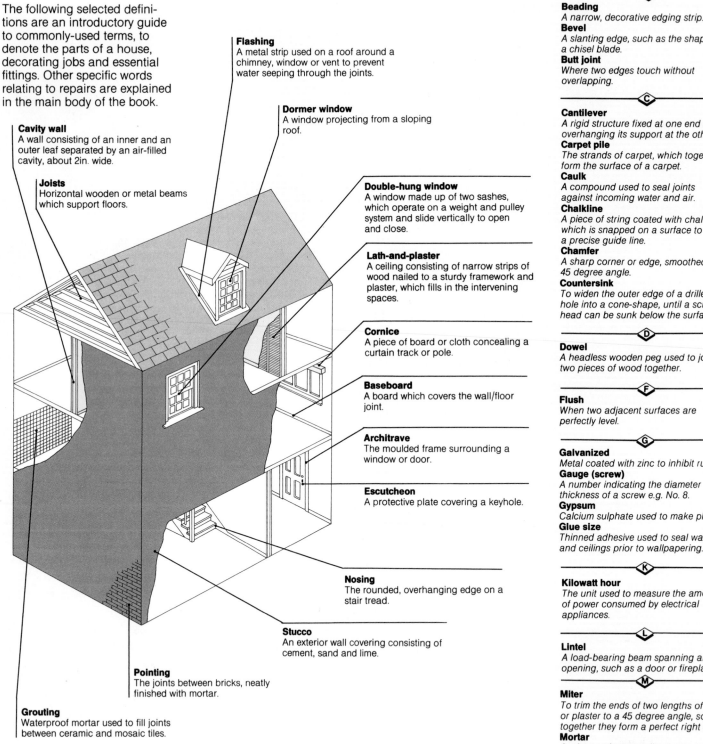

Cavity wall
A wall consisting of an inner and an outer leaf separated by an air-filled cavity, about 2in. wide.

Joists
Horizontal wooden or metal beams which support floors.

Flashing
A metal strip used on a roof around a chimney, window or vent to prevent water seeping through the joints.

Dormer window
A window projecting from a sloping roof.

Double-hung window
A window made up of two sashes, which operate on a weight and pulley system and slide vertically to open and close.

Lath-and-plaster
A ceiling consisting of narrow strips of wood nailed to a sturdy framework and plaster, which fills in the intervening spaces.

Cornice
A piece of board or cloth concealing a curtain track or pole.

Baseboard
A board which covers the wall/floor joint.

Architrave
The moulded frame surrounding a window or door.

Escutcheon
A protective plate covering a keyhole.

Nosing
The rounded, overhanging edge on a stair tread.

Stucco
An exterior wall covering consisting of cement, sand and lime.

Pointing
The joints between bricks, neatly finished with mortar.

Grouting
Waterproof mortar used to fill joints between ceramic and mosaic tiles.

B

Beading
A narrow, decorative edging strip.
Bevel
A slanting edge, such as the shape of a chisel blade.
Butt joint
Where two edges touch without overlapping.

C

Cantilever
A rigid structure fixed at one end and overhanging its support at the other.
Carpet pile
The strands of carpet, which together form the surface of a carpet.
Caulk
A compound used to seal joints against incoming water and air.
Chalkline
A piece of string coated with chalk, which is snapped on a surface to leave a precise guide line.
Chamfer
A sharp corner or edge, smoothed to a 45 degree angle.
Countersink
To widen the outer edge of a drilled hole into a cone-shape, until a screw-head can be sunk below the surface.

D

Dowel
A headless wooden peg used to join two pieces of wood together.

F

Flush
When two adjacent surfaces are perfectly level.

G

Galvanized
Metal coated with zinc to inhibit rusting.
Gauge (screw)
A number indicating the diameter thickness of a screw e.g. No. 8.
Gypsum
Calcium sulphate used to make plaster.
Glue size
Thinned adhesive used to seal walls and ceilings prior to wallpapering.

K

Kilowatt hour
The unit used to measure the amount of power consumed by electrical appliances.

L

Lintel
A load-bearing beam spanning an opening, such as a door or fireplace.

M

Miter
To trim the ends of two lengths of wood or plaster to a 45 degree angle, so that together they form a perfect right angle.
Mortar
A mixture of cement, lime putty and sand, used to bind bricks together in a masonry wall.

Mortise
A recess cut in the edge of a door to house the protruding tongue of a lock.
Molding
A length of wood, shaped to form a decorative strip.

Plumb bob
A small, cone-shaped weight attached to a line, which when held against a wall gives a true vertical.
Primer
A paint used to seal and key a surface before undercoat is applied.

Screed bead
A straight or angled strip or wire mesh, used to reinforce corners before plastering or to cover holes in plaster walls.
Scriber
A tool used to trace off the edges and contours of an area on to decorating materials.
Shim
A tapered piece of wood, used to correct levels.
Sole plate
A horizontal length of wood, which forms the bottom rail of a stud partition framework.
Stud partition
A wall made out of a wooden framework covered with plasterboard.

Template
A pattern cut to specific dimensions, used as an outline for cutting the same shape from another material.
Thread
The spiral grooves in a screw.
Tongue and groove
Wooden boards or blocks with a groove down one edge and a protruding tongue down the other. The tongue slots into the groove of an adjacent piece, for a secure fixing.
Toggle
A small metal screw with a hinge or wings which open when pushed through a hole in a partition wall and so secure the screw in place.

UL (Underwriter's Laboratory)
An independent agency that checks electrical and other safety standards.

Veneer
An outer layer of decorative wood applied to a core of stronger but less attractive lumber.

Wallplug
An expandable plastic or fiber encasement for a screw, inserted into a hole drilled in a solid wall to provide a gripping surface for the screw. It can be cut to length.

ideas for the decorative effects you can achieve by carefully following the jobs in the book. Throughout the book, additional boxes on safety, cleaning tips, points to remember, and charts on quantities and qualities of materials offer immediate, easy to absorb information. Each job has been carefully selected to give you the information, know-how and confidence to become your own painter, decorator, electrician, plumber and interior designer – an all-round home maintenance person, capable of tackling essential jobs around the house.

Getting to know your home

A good understanding of the geography of your home, how the plumbing, electrical and heating systems work and how the fixtures and fittings are assembled is an essential starting point for home maintenance. Emergencies, such as flooding, blown fuses and burglaries always come at the most inconvenient moments, and it is only through a good knowledge of the systems in the house that you can take the right action to handle and prevent such crises. Within the section on "Home maintenance", you will find "maps" of all the basic systems and clear explanations of how they work, together with detailed advice on specific tasks. With this knowledge, home maintenance will become a simple, routine matter.

Investing in the right tools and materials

Your first priority is to choose a good tool kit. In "The home tool kit" at the back of the book you will find a complete, illustrated guide to the tools you are likely to need, with detailed information about how and when to use each item, the range of types and sizes within each group, and tips on care and safety. You may wish to begin with a skeleton tool kit and gradually add to it as you tackle more jobs. Large and expensive tools, which you may only need once, are often available for rent from tool suppliers.

A knowledge of the range of decorating materials is as important as a good set of tools. The central section of the book, "Choosing materials", is a visual catalog of the materials available for decorating walls, floors, ceilings, and for furnishings. It is backed up with a thorough comparison of types: their individual qualities, their relative costs, their ease of handling and so on, together with an analysis of the

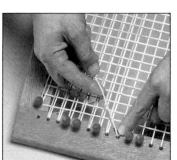

most suitable materials to choose for individual rooms and situations. It is worth buying the best quality you can afford; it will last longer and produce better results. Prices and qualities vary dramatically, so an exploration of your local hardware store and home-center will probably reveal the best buys.

Planning and preparation

The main ingredients of successful home maintenance are time and patience. Since many jobs in the home are "one-offs", it is vital to take the time to work steadily toward perfect results. Laying a parquet floor, plastering a wall or paneling a ceiling, for example, may be jobs you only ever need to attempt once. Mistakes and materials are expensive, so serving your apprenticeship on the job leaves little or no margin for error. Your best insurance against mistakes is careful planning and preparation. Each section in the book and each job within it is presented in a clear, logical sequence, beginning with planning and preparation, followed by the detailed stages of the work to be done. The time you take in the early stages is always well rewarded in the final results.

Enjoying your home

Improving your home is an enjoyable experience if you know what to do. The more you do to encourage the services of the house to run smoothly, to improve the standard of the decoration and to make the furniture and furnishings as good as new, the more you will appreciate your home. And the more you practise, the better the results will be.

The future

Once you have successfully completed a few maintenance jobs, you will find you develop the confidence and experience to undertake a wider range of jobs. Once learnt, these skills are never forgotten, but you may need reminders and new challenges. We hope this book will prove a continual source of help, ideas and reference both in the day-to-day running of your home, and when you decide to redecorate or move house.

Safety tips

◇ Use all power and cutting tools with great caution, keep cords well clear and lock all tools away immediately after use.
◇ Avoid drilling into walls if you suspect pipes or electrical wires lie behind.
◇ If you smell gas, call the gas company immediately.
◇ Always install a fire extinguisher in a workshop and a kitchen.
◇ Repair cracked pipes immediately or call in an expert.
◇ Only use ladders that you know to be completely safe.
◇ Wear goggles to shield your eyes when stripping paint or scratch brushing; gloves to protect your hands from chemicals; and a mask if there is a lot of dust.
◇ Pour any left-over chemicals back into the original container or into a clearly labelled jar.
◇ Keep chisels, saws and other cutting tools sharp. Blunt blades slip easily and can cause accidents.
◇ Whenever you rent equipment from a store or from friends, make sure you know exactly how to use it.

Home decorating

Painting ◇ Wallpapering ◇ Tiling ◇ Carpeting
Wooden flooring ◇ Sheet vinyl ◇ Paneling
Plastering ◇ Windows ◇ Curtains, blinds and
shutters ◇ Doors

Decorating the interior of your home is rewarding only if the results are good. And to be sure of the best return on your investment of time, enthusiasm and materials, it is important to take each job stage by stage and to use the correct equipment. This section outlines the tools and materials you will need, explains how to estimate quantities of paint, wallpaper, tiles or wood, for your size of room and suggests how much time to put aside, *before* you begin work. It tells you how to plan out the job, how to prepare the surface, and how to undertake necessary repairs. It then moves on to detailed step-by-step coverage of specific jobs and basic techniques. Relevant advice on dealing with tricky areas, and diagnosing problems and faults are also included. And within each section you will find ideas on effects you can achieve through the imaginative use of color, texture and individual design, in conjunction with the techniques covered in the section.

Painting

Estimating time and quantities ◇ Tools and equipment ◇ How to fill cracks and holes
Preparing bare wood ◇ Stripping old paint
How to apply paint ◇ Using ladders safely
Fault-finding ◇ Textures and finishes

Good paintwork is to a house what a good complexion is to a human face. It reflects the general condition and attitudes of the owner, it provides a background for more striking features and highlights, and lends an individual quality to the whole appearance.

Choice of paint is the first major decorating decision, and it is worth taking time to choose the most suitable color. It is also important to select the right type of paint for each job to avoid repeating the work before you are ready for a change. Modern materials give better and faster results than ever before and a competent repainting will last for many years with new, hard-wearing paints. Although paints are now sold under various descriptions such as semigloss or low-luster finish, latex is still used for walls and ceilings and alkyd for woodwork and metalwork. In spite of the slightly higher cost of these materials, it is still usually cheaper to paint than to paper.

Preparation of surfaces before painting is all-important, since untreated cracks and flaws will rapidly appear through new paintwork and may even be exaggerated. Any time "saved" in preparation is counter-productive, for you will treble your working time by soon having to strip off new paint to redecorate properly.

Points to remember

◇ Make sure you have enough paint before you start work.
◇ Prepare ceilings first, then walls, and finally, wood and metalwork. Repaint in the same order.
◇ Test paints on a small area of wall before buying the full quantity.
◇ Use the undercoat or primer recommended for the color you have chosen for the top coat of alkyd.
◇ Fill cracks and remove dust before painting.

For more information on types of paint, see Choosing materials, pp. 114-5.

Planning

New decoration will only be as good as the planning and preparation of the work. The first step in any redecoration job is to decide on the extent of the initial structural and repair work required, before estimating time, costs and quantities of materials needed. This work will depend on the age of the house and its condition.

Modern houses
In a post-1950's house, the lumber is unlikely to be well seasoned, so, when heating is turned on, there may be some cracking and shrinking that produces minor problems in the finished wall. Many modern homes however, do have the advantage of low-maintenance accessories, such as plastic gutters and downspouts, and anodized aluminum windows that do not need paint.

Older houses
Different problems arise in older houses. The walls often encourage dampness which must be corrected before decorating can begin. If the laths are deteriorating, the lath and plaster must be stripped and replaced with wallboard before painting or wallpapering.

On the woodwork a thick layer of paint is likely to have built up over the years. If the paintwork tends to chip badly, it is best to strip back to bare wood and start again.

Estimating time

Home decorating invariably takes longer than you think. The times (right) give an estimate of the number of hours needed to paint a 10ft × 13ft room in average condition. Convert this into your own room sizes and allow more time for any extra coats. Remember, however, that your skill and experience, the care you take in your workmanship, the speed at which you work and the number of hours a day you actually work, including meal breaks, will all influence the total time needed to complete the work. Try to arrange three to four uninterrupted hours for each session and, if possible, avoid changing from natural to artificial light. Remember to build in a little extra time for cleaning brushes and equipment at the end of each session. When adding up the total number of days needed to complete the whole room, allow for the time needed for the paint to dry between coats. As a rough guide, latex takes about four hours to dry, but alkyd should be left overnight.

Ceilings

Washing and filling
(1)-(1½) **hours**

Applying stabilizing primer
(1)-(1½) **hours**

Applying latex
(¾)-(1) **hour**

Walls

Preparing and priming
(2)-(3) **hours**

Applying latex
(¾)-(1) **hour**

Doors, windows, baseboards

Sanding and filling (allow more time if stripping to bare wood)
(2)-(3) **hours**

Priming patches
(¼)-(½) **hour**

Applying undercoat
(3½)-(4) **hours**

Applying alkyd
(3½)-(4) **hours**

Estimating quantities

To estimate the amount of paint you need, first calculate the area of each surface to be covered by multiplying the height or length by the width. Then total your surface areas. Some types of paint go further than others, so consult the table (right) for the area covered by specific paints. Brands may also differ so, if in doubt, refer to the estimated covering rate specified on the label. To find the quantity in gallons needed for each type of paint, *per coat*, divide the area by the covering rate.

When measuring the area of walls, include windows and doors as part of the surface, unless they are significantly large. This will allow a little extra paint in case the walls prove highly absorbent. A wall measuring 6ft high by $11\frac{1}{2}$ft wide has a total area of 23yd^2 If it was to be painted in latex semigloss with a covering rate of 30yd^2 per $\frac{1}{2}$ gal., the area (23yd^2) divided by the covering rate (30yd^2) would give the number of $\frac{1}{2}$ gals. required: $\frac{3}{4}$ of a $\frac{1}{2}$ gal. can per coat. Windows are difficult to estimate, but as a guide, allow $21\frac{1}{2}$ft^2 for a small window, 43ft^2 for a medium-sized window, and 54ft^2 for a large one. For doors, allow $21\frac{1}{2}$ft per side; this includes the frame and the trim. For baseboards, measure the length by the height and multiply the figures. Remember to allow for any extra space taken up with alcoves and chimneys.

Ceilings
Multiply the widths of two adjacent walls and allow for any alcoves.

Doors, windows and baseboards
An average window measures 43ft^2. Most doors measure 43ft^2 ($21\frac{1}{2}$ft^2 per side) including frame and trim. For the baseboard area, multiply total length by height.

Walls
Measure the height and width of each wall, without deducting window and door areas, and add the multiples together for the total wall area.

Covering rates of paints

The covering power of paints varies with the type of paint, the porosity of the surface and the thickness of the coat applied. Non-drip alkyd paints, for example, will not cover such a large area as liquid alkyd or latex but since the coating is thicker, fewer coats may be required. Most stains and varnishes will go farther than paint while primers will not stretch so far. Bare plaster and textured surfaces absorb more liquid, so it is often more economic to add water to a first coat than to apply an extra top coat.

Paint type	Covering area (in yd^2 per $\frac{1}{2}$ gal.)
Latex primer	7-8 (wood)
	9-11 (metal)
	5-9 (plaster)
Aluminum primer-sealer	11-13
Alkyd primer/undercoat	15-16
Alkali-resistant primer	9-11
Primer/sealer	10
Stain-blocking primer	6-12
Metal primer	9-11
Undercoat	15
Alkyd (liquid)	17
Alkyd (non-drip)	12
Alkyd gloss (oil-based)	12
Eggshell latex	15
Latex, flat (dripless solid)	14
Latex, semigloss	15
Aluminum paint	12-14

The number of coats
The type of paint, the color and the surface determine the number of coats to be applied. You will need an extra coat, for example, when covering a dark color with a lighter one, but not when using a dark final color. When decorating previously unpainted wood, use primer and an undercoat before one or two coats of alkyd. If painting over old alkyd you may need to apply one or two coats of undercoat, to leave a good base for the alkyd.

A third coat of latex is sometimes needed to obliterate a dark background. High-gloss latex may also need an extra coat.

Tools and equipment

Cheap tools produce poor results. However tempting it is to save money, this is always a false economy, because good-quality equipment lasts longer, even improving with age; is more satisfying to use; and, most important, promotes a finer finish. Always choose brushes well packed with boar's bristle; use new pads and brushes for undercoats until they stop shedding hairs, and reserve cheap brushes for priming. Clean tools thoroughly and store them in a cool, dry, well-ventilated place. Before using any equipment, check that it is thoroughly dry. (*For more information, see The Home Tool Kit, pp. 230-1.*)

Strippers and scrapers
To soften old paint, you will need either an electric hot-air gun, a gas blowtorch or chemical stripper; and two scrapers to strip the paint off flat surfaces – one narrow, one broad. For clearing irregular areas, such as window frames and moldings, choose a shavehook with a combination of straight, convex and concave sides, it will prove more versatile than the straight-sided, triangular type.

Large scraper

Small scraper

Shavehooks

Hot-air gun

Gas blowtorch

Chemical stripper

Cleaning and storage
Wash and dry scrapers and shave-hooks or scrub with steel wool, before wiping with a lightly oiled rag or petroleum jelly, and store in a dry place. If shavehook edges have become blunt, sharpen with a file or grindstone.

Clean shavehooks and scrapers with steel wool then wipe with petroleum jelly or a lightly oiled rag.

Sanders and fillers
To repair cracks and nicks, a putty knife, filler and tray are all that is needed. Many surfaces need abrading before receiving paint. Sandpaper comes in grades from 150 (fine) to 40 (coarse) and the medium or fine grades are the most useful. A longer-lasting, though more expensive alternative is aluminum oxide paper. A range of medium-grade silicon carbide papers (240 and 180) will also help to provide a good key for new paint on smooth surfaces. It is tough, durable, creates less dust and produces a smoother finish than sandpaper. It can be used dry, but lasts longer when wet, since it will not clog. A cork, wooden or rubber block used as a "hand hold" for abrasive paper will ease the work on flat surfaces. For large areas, electric finishing sanders help to speed up the work. An orbital sander, which can be rented, provides the best finish, although a disk sander or mesh disk attached to a power tool can be useful. if care is taken.

Orbital sander

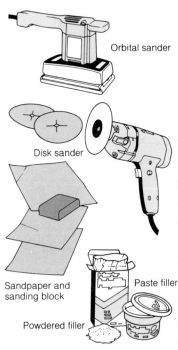

Disk sander

Sandpaper and sanding block

Powdered filler

Paste filler

Cleaning and storage
Remove dried filler with emery paper or steel wool. Store unused filler in a dry place. Wash silicon carbide paper thoroughly to remove particles and store all equipment in a cool, dry place.

Brushes
A range of brushes will be needed for painting an average room, in addition to a priming and dusting brush. The smallest, a ¾in. cutting-in brush with angled bristles, is useful for painting window frames without smudging the glass. A 1in. size is also suitable for window frames and moldings; a 2in. for baseboards; and a 3in. for flush doors and similar large areas of alkyd. If you prefer not to use a roller or pad for large areas of latex, use a 5in. brush. For small jobs, such as touching up old paintwork, disposable foam brushes are available in a range of sizes. Choose brushes with good length well-packed bristles.

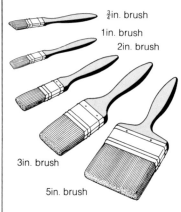

¾in. brush

1in. brush

2in. brush

3in. brush

5in. brush

Cleaning and storage
During short breaks of up to half an hour, wrap bristles tightly in cling wrap or foil, but clean thoroughly every night, immediately after use. Scrape off excess water-based paint with a knife blade on to newspaper, then wash in hot water and dishwashing liquid. Rinse, shake and hang up to dry. For long-term storage, wrap in newspaper, taking care not to bend the bristles, and secure around the base (ferrule) with a rubber band. A brush used for oil-based paint should first be cleaned in turpentine or a proprietary brush cleaner. Work up and down on clean newspaper and manipulate in hot dishwashing liquid, until all traces of paint disappear. Oil-based paints that prove particularly sticky can be removed by rubbing bristles with linseed oil after the initial cleaning in turpentine. Soften old hard brushes by agitating in paint stripper. Brush cleaners and turpentine can be used repeatedly if kept in a screw-top jar, but must be discarded when sediment builds up.

Rollers and pads
These allow large areas to be covered quickly and easily, but are more suit-able for latex than for oil-based alkyd paint. Solid latex is supplied in a block, but liquid paints need a roller tray or pad trough for an even coating. For a smooth finish, use a roller with a short pile; for a lightly textured look, a medium pile; and for a deeply textured finish, a long pile. Foam rollers with an indented pattern are available for tex-tured paints, but for general use, lambswool and mohair produce a better result. Choose a paint pad that will fit into a ½ gal. paint can.

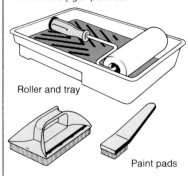

Roller and tray

Paint pads

Cleaning and storage
Scrape off extra paint. Then, if used with water-based paints, wash in warm detergent and rinse in cool water, or turpentine if oil-based paints have been used. Rinse, squeeze and shake out before hanging up to dry. When dry, cover the roller and tray to protect from dust. If lined with cooking foil, the tray will not need cleaning. Clean pads in the same way as rollers, and store flat and unwrapped.

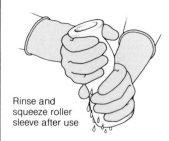

Rinse and squeeze roller sleeve after use

Other equipment
Additional essential items include a paint bucket for decanting the paint, a bucket and sponge, and dropcloths.

The effects of color on a room

Color has the power to transform a room. It can raise and lower ceilings, it can expand and reduce walls, it can disguise and highlight individual features, and it can soothe or excite. A dark room can be lightened with a light-reflecting sheen, and warm, dark colors can make a large, cold room feel more cosy. Your decision may be influenced by existing furnishings, and in many rooms the paintwork may need to act as a neutral backdrop to more vibrant accessories. Remember that when applied, the accumulated color will intensify the shade of the color chart.

Using color to disguise room shapes

Color can influence the apparent size and shape of a room. Light shades will bring space to a small room and dark tones foreshorten a large one. A low ceiling will appear higher if it is painted a paler shade than the walls. For a more complete disguise of the room shape, a single dark background color over the ceiling and walls can be applied, and can then be broken up with spotlights (above). The reflections produced by the luster of a high-gloss paint deepen and enlarge a room, as well as adding pattern. A paler, receding background shade will lighten and open out a small, dark room (right) and will help to conceal pipes, radiators and irregular window shapes. A co-ordinating furnishing color will contribute to the enlarging effect.

Using color to establish moods

Temperament and lifestyle influence choice of color as much as the intended purpose of the room. Those who demand a stimulating home environment, for example, probably enjoy strong primary colors, broken up with neutrals; others who need a restful, relaxing atmosphere may prefer natural and more muted tones. The aspect of the room should also be considered when selecting paint color. A burnt orange shade (top) on the wall – picked up in the furnishings – gives warmth to a large room with harsh light coming through the windows, and promotes an air of relaxation. Cool shades, such as the frosty blue, monochromatic color scheme (above) lends a cool feeling of light and space to a sunny room. This crisp and vibrant effect is accentuated by the sparkling white woodwork and silver chrome accessories.

1
Preparing ceilings

First remove any light fixtures that may impede the work, not forgetting to turn off the electricity at the fuse box first and to tape any exposed wires afterwards. Then assess the condition of the existing paint and plasterwork. If it is sound, wash down the surface with diluted ammonia solution and rinse thoroughly with clean water, taking care not to allow any drips to penetrate fixed light fixtures.

If the paint is discolored by nicotine stains, apply a coat of aluminum sealer paint. Dried water stains, caused by a leaking roof or pipes, will show through latex, so these need to be coated with an oil-based primer sealer. Kitchen ceilings are often coated with accumulated grease, which will prevent the paint from sticking if it is not removed. Likewise, soot or dust deposited on the ceilings above fireplaces must be thoroughly cleaned to prevent it

discoloring subsequent layers of paint. Fill any small cracks with spackle compound. If deep cracks persistently develop between the wall and the ceiling, they are probably caused by the normal movement of the house and will re-open if filled, so consider fixing molding to conceal them. In an old house, if mineral deposits remain, scrape off the flakes and either wash off the rest or coat the ceiling with primer sealer before repainting.

Papered ceilings
Loose ceiling paper should be stripped off but any which is firmly attached can be left and painted. When removing paper, always wash off any remaining adhesive. If existing paper bubbles when washed, make a small slit when dry and re-stick the edges. Remember that a ceiling may have been papered because it is badly cracked though structurally sound or, in the case of a plasterboard ceiling, because the joints are conspicuous. (For ladders, see Job 11, p. 24 and Job 14, p. 32.)

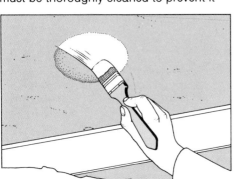
Cover nicotine stains with sealer paint

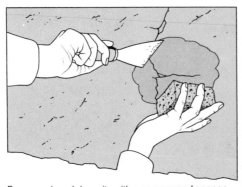
Remove mineral deposits with a scraper and sponge

2
Preparing walls

More preparation is needed if a wall is to be painted than if it is to be concealed with wallpaper. Even a small hairline crack will show through paint, if it is not filled and carefully sanded first. Where an otherwise sound wall has become a network of small cracks, try covering it with lining- or wallpaper for overpainting. (For chips and small cracks, see opposite; for more extensive damage, see p. 93; and for stripping off old paint, see Job 6, pp. 18-19.)

Sound surfaces
A new plaster wall should be left to dry for several weeks before sealing with a primer or a thin coat of latex prior to painting and fresh plasterboard should be given a coat of plasterboard primer sealer. A previously painted wall must be washed thoroughly from the bottom up with diluted ammonia solution, then rinsed.

Clearing the room

◇ Remove anything you may need from drawers, and move small pieces of furniture into another room.
◇ Take down curtains and pictures and remove door and window handles.
◇ Move large furniture to the center of the room.
◇ Roll up the carpet and cover the floor with a polythene or cloth dropcloth, secured at the corners.

3
Preparing metal

Rust is the enemy of ferrous metals (those that contain iron and steel) and must be kept at bay with a rust-inhibiting primer and a sound coat of alkyd. Even small chips in the surface paint can allow moisture to seep below the paint film and encourage corrosion, especially in window frames. First locate the areas of rust and remove all traces with an emery cloth or a scratch brush. For larger areas, a disk sander or a drum sander will save time, but

always protect your eyes with safety goggles. Holes caused by rust can be repaired using a glass fiber repair kit.

Primers
Rust re-forms rapidly, even overnight, so apply rust-inhibiting primer immediately. Zinc chromate is the most useful substance in primer, since it can also be used for aluminum and galvanized surfaces, but red lead and zinc phosphate are also suitable. Non-ferrous metals such as aluminum and copper should be washed down with alcohol, abraded and primed.

Treating rust
Scrape off any rust and flaking paint with a scratch brush, 1. When no trace of rust remains, apply rust-inhibiting

primer, 2, before rust has time to re-form and give vulnerable points an extra coat. If the surface is sound and rust-free, simply wash it down.

1 Remove rust of flaking paint with a scratch brush

2 Seal metalwork with primer to inhibit the formation of rust

---

Basic technique

How to fill cracks and holes

Time spent filling cracks and holes will be well rewarded in the final result. Standard interior-grade cellulose putty is suitable for most inside plaster or wooden surfaces to be repainted. They come as ready-to-use paste in tubs or tubes, or as a powder to be mixed with water to a creamy consistency. Most small holes can be simply built up with filler and smoothed off. Corners of walls can be easily chipped when moving furniture. Apply thin layers of filler and when the surface is slightly raised, allow to harden, then sand down. Small, superficial chips in otherwise good paintwork can be filled with a fine surface filler, which is worked into the surface and spread with a broad putty knife, then sanded to produce an ultra-smooth finish. Badly cracked plasterboard ceilings can be concealed with thick, textured paint, which stretches with the normal movement of the ceiling to keep the crazing covered. (*For information on more serious cracks and holes, see Jobs 104-6, p. 93.*)

Applying filler

*First score the crack with the side of a putty knife to widen the cavity for filler, and brush away any debris, **1**, then moisten the crack, **2**. Prepare the filler and pack it tightly into the crack. Push in the filler by drawing the filling knife across at right angles, **3**. If the crack is deep, allow to dry and apply another layer. Then smooth off. If it will not lie flush, leave the filler slightly proud of the surface and leave for a few hours to harden. Finally rub with sandpaper, for a smooth finish, **4**. To avoid waste when preparing paste, try not to make up more than you can apply within the setting time marked on the packet (usually about 30 mins). cellulose filler, resin-based fillers will not shrink as they dry and harden. This means they can be applied flush with the surface, instead of proud, and will produce a smooth surface with less abrasion.*

1 *Widen the crack below surface and brush out debris*

2 *Dampen the crevice with a water-soaked brush*

Pour powdered filler on to a board for mixing

3 *Apply filler and smooth it down with a knife*

4 *When dry, sand to a flush finish*

4

Using wood-colored putty

Where wood is to be given a clear varnish or lacquer finish, instead of a coat of paint, waterproof filler that comes in a variety of wood colors can be used. One type of filler comes as a putty-like material; another, which also dries to a natural wood color and can later be stained to any shade, is sold as paste and separate hardener to be mixed together. Both fillers should be worked well into the surface with a putty knife and allowed to set before sanding down and applying an oil- or spirit-based stain. Take care not to spread the filler into the grain beyond the immediate split or nail hole. Small gaps that tend to form in window frames and at joints can be packed with putty and pushed down with a finger before smoothing off with a damp cloth. Always use an oil-based filler on particleboard, since it is very porous.

Use wood-colored filler under clear varnish

5
Preparing bare wood

Whether it is brand new or stripped of old paint, all bare wood to be painted needs a coating of primer, undercoat and alkyd. To ensure a smooth finish, the surface should be first rubbed down with sand-paper or a power sander. Rough surfaces may call for coarse paper, but a final smoothing with a fine grade will ensure a good finish.

Sealing the surface
After filling any cracks with wood putty, knots in the wood will need a coating of shellac to prevent resin staining the paint-work. To seal the pores in the wood and to provide a sound, stable base for under-coat, a coat of primer is applied. Most woods will take a standard white or pink wood primer, but particularly resinous woods need aluminum primer. Latex primer may be used, although wood primer gives a better result.

Undercoat
Since undercoat is heavily pigmented for hiding power, always select the color recommended by the manufacturer for use under the chosen alkyd. It might be necessary to apply more than one coat of undercoat, in order to leave a smooth finish for the alkyd coat.

For a natural wood finish, use a trans-parent varnish or a varnish stain if the color of the wood is to be changed.

Before applying gloss to wood
Sand and wipe the surface and fill any cracks before soaking wood knots and resinous patches with shellac. Dab the liquid on to each knot with a clean brush, 1, taking care to cover the edges. Leave to dry for a couple of days, then apply primer, 2. Brush in the direction of the grain and give end grain a second coating, before applying a coat of well-stirred undercoat, 3.

1 Brush a layer of shellac liquid on to wood knots

2 When the shellac is dry, brush on primer

3 Finally paint on a layer of undercoat

6
Stripping old paint

It is not always necessary to strip off old paint, for if the alkyd on woodwork is sound and smooth, it will form an ideal base for fresh paint. Old whitewash and mineral deposits on walls can often be removed by washing, but if the paint is loose and chips off easily, it is better to strip it off. Test the surface with masking tape; if it pulls paint away, strip the affected area.

Choosing the method
Dry scraping is hard work and can leave score marks, so unless the paint peels off readily, it is best to use heat or chemicals to loosen the coat. Heat stripping is the most economical way of clearing a large area, but a gas blowtorch, may scorch the surface. Chemical strippers, although expensive, are useful on intricate surfaces.

Peel-off stripper
This new generation of chemical strippers can be a great time- and labor-saver. Apply a thick layer of paste over the paintwork, 1, and leave it to eat through the layers of paint. After several hours, the layer can be peeled off, 2, leaving a clean sub-surface.

1 Apply the paste with a putty knife

2 Peel off the dried paste with gloved fingers

Cleaning paintwork

◇ Before applying a fresh coat to exist-ing paintwork, the surface must be free from stains, dust, or mildew or the new finish will look pimpled and will soon start to flake prematurely.

◇ Remove surface dirt by brushing, washing or vacuuming and use a pointed handle or knife to clear dust particles from awkward corners.

◇ When washing down the area, use ammonia solution or a mild solution of detergent, and prevent water dripping down behind electric fittings.

◇ Before painting window frames from inside, always ensure that outside frames are thoroughly clean, so that dirt is not picked up on the brush. Wipe down sills and other wooden surfaces with a lint-free rag moistened with alcohol.

◇ Allow all surfaces to dry before applying paint.

Chemical stripper

Chemical solvents are most useful for removing paint from intricate moldings or tight corners where the wood could be scorched by heat. They can be used on latex, cellulose and most oil-based paints, but a specialized type is needed for removing varnish. Dab on the liquid thickly with an old brush, 1, and after a few minutes the paint will shrivel and can be stripped off, 2. Scrape off any remnants, 3. Follow the instructions and consult the safety tips (below).

1 *Brush on a thick layer of stripper*

2 *Scrape off the shriveled paint*

3 *Remove remnants with steel wool and alcohol*

Gas blowtorch

Modern blowtorches are simple to use and most suitable for removing large areas of alkyd. Avoid using lead-based paints, which release toxic fumes; and take care around windows where the glass may crack, the draft may dissipate the heat, and billowing curtains may be a hazard. Hold the torch about 6 to 8in. from the surface and, starting at the top, play it across the paint until it starts to melt. Using a sharp scraper, quickly peel it off into a tin tray, before it hardens. Gently sweep the flame over any remaining paint until it slides off, taking care not to scorch the wood.

Remove softened paint with a scraper on flat areas

Use a shavehook for peeling paint off moldings

Hot-air gun

Operating like an immensely powerful electric hair dryer, a hot-air gun blasts out a stream of heat which will melt the paint in its path. Direct the gun at an area of paint and when it softens after a few seconds, peel off the coat with a scraper. For stripping paint around windows and awkward areas, special nozzle attachments are available (below). Although effective, some hot-air guns are noisy and heavy to use, and all need an electricity supply.

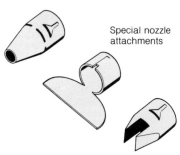

Special nozzle attachments

A nozzle attachment will shield the glass around windows

Safety tips

With chemical stripper
◇ Always wear goggles, gloves and protective clothing, to avoid skin burns, and don't smoke.
◇ Cover furnishings that may be splashed.

With heat stripper
◇ Keep buckets of water to hand.
◇ Never place fingers in the air stream.
◇ Catch burning peelings in a tin tray, never in newspaper.
◇ Always switch off the stripper when not in use.

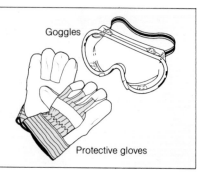

Goggles

Protective gloves

How to apply paint

Before you start work, check that you have: enough paint for the first coat; a spare brush and some brush cleaner; a rag and old clothes or an apron. Latex and other water-based paints will usually brush straight from the can, but half-full cans of oil-based paints develop a skin. To remove this, score around the inside of the can and lift off the layer of solidified paint, then stir thoroughly. Dripless paints, however, should never be stirred. Before dipping the brush into the paint, flick the bristles to dislodge dust and loose bristles. Alkyd and latex paints demand slightly different techniques as shown below. Thixotropic paints, designed to go on in one coat, should be brushed sparingly. There is no need to scrape off surplus paint, but try

Brushing on alkyd
For a smooth, shiny finish, free from brush marks and runs, do not over-load the brush. First flick the bristles to dislodge dust and loose bristles, dip the ends into the paint, and wipe any excess on the side of the can or paint bucket, 1. Avoid dipping in too deep or the paint will trickle down the handle on to your hand. Begin with two or three strokes in the direction of the wood grain, covering a small area, 2. Without re-loading, change direction and spread the paint lightly to cover the surface. Then work back again with the grain, finishing with an upward stroke. Re-load the brush and, leaving a gap the width of the brush, move on to paint a parallel strip. Then paint across to fill in the area between strips, 3. At the join, allow the brush tips to gently skim the line, to avoid a thick ridge forming at each overlap.

Finally, brush vigorously over the whole area and lay off with vertical strokes, 4. Alkyd takes several hours to dry, so leave surfaces clear until the paint no longer feels tacky. Sand the surface with fine-grade sandpaper after each coat, to make a key for the next one.

Brushing on latex
Since latex is used for large surfaces and dries faster than alkyd, select a wide 4in. or 5in. brush, for quick application. Stir the paint thoroughly and pour enough into a paint bucket to cover half the length of the bristles. Coat the brush in a generous layer of paint and apply in horizontal bands, about 2ft wide, 1. Work away from the light and cover the area quickly to con-ceal joints before the edge of the painted section dries. High gloss latex paints dry more quickly than flat, so if you find it is drying faster than you can paint, you may have to modify the band system and work radially from a top corner. With flat latex paint finish off with criss-cross strokes, and with high-gloss paint finish off with light, upward strokes, 2.

1 *Dip the bristle tips into the paint and squeeze off the excess on the inside of the paint bucket*

2 *Begin with downward strokes*

1 *Apply latex in horizontal bands*

3 *Then spread the paint across*

4 *Finish with vertical strokes*

2 *Finish with light upward strokes*

(brush icon)

not to load too much paint on to the brush initially. Before applying a second coat of paint, dust the surface with a lint-free rag to make sure no specks spoil the finish. Complete each surface in one session to prevent dried paint lines forming.

Using a roller
The fastest way of applying latex is with a roller .Pour some paint into the well of the roller tray, dip in the edge of the roller and run it up and down the slope to ensure an even layer of paint on the roller sleeve. Run the roller over the surface in a random, criss-cross pattern, 1, taking care to fill any gaps and to keep the joins well merged. Be careful not to overload the roller or to jerk it, or a spray of paint will spatter the area. Finish off the edges with a small brush.

With a roller, apply paint in a criss-cross pattern

Using a pad
Dip lightly into the paint and wipe away the excess on the side of the can or paint bucket or use a special applicator to load the paint evenly on to the pad. Smooth on the paint in random directions, 2, and re-load as soon as the layer begins to thin.

Use a paint pad quickly in random directions

7
Painting flat surfaces

The first consideration when preparing to paint a large area is the light. Try to avoid starting in natural light and finishing in artificial, or you may find yourself covering the same area twice. You should also complete ceilings and individual walls in one session since, if you stop mid-wall for a meal-break or for the night, the dried paint line will show conspicuously through the final finish.

Working conditions
Before applying latex, close the windows to stop the paint drying too quickly and so give you time to join up the wet edges of each section. When the room is finished, open the windows to accelerate drying time. For ease of working, try to get as close as possible to the ceiling. Bare walls need a diluted coat of latex to prime the surface, before applying a first coat, but pre-painted surfaces need no primer. If the paint does not cover well, do not try to thicken the coat, but leave it to dry and apply an extra coat. For a perfectly smooth finish, you may need two or three coats. While painting, keep a damp cloth handy for removing dust or blobs. As a general rule, paint a room from top to bottom, so that disturbed dust does not fall on to wet paint and so that drips can be painted over later. If using a roller complete corners with a small brush.

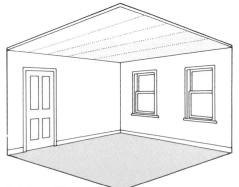

Painting ceilings
Always plan to complete a ceiling in one uninterrupted session, to prevent dried paint lines forming. Start at the window end, in a corner and work away from the light. Paint systematically from wall to wall in 2ft strips and ensure the edges are wet when joined.

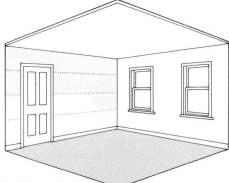

Painting walls
Start at the top corner of a wall nearest the window. Cover the wall in broad, horizontal bands and work down to the baseboard. Cut in with a narrower brush around windows and door frames. If using a roller, first coat the edges with a narrow brush.

Painting a mural

First design your image on grid paper, then divide the wall area into the same number of squares, but enlarged in proportion, to fill the allocated space. Sketch the outline on the wall, floor, ceiling or furniture in pencil, one square at a time, then fill in the colors, using masking tape and a thin brush for the edges.

Using masking tape
Fix masking tape to the outlines, then, apply the color (right). Start with the paler shades and let each section dry before moving on to the next. Brush on the paint thickly to reduce the number of coats required. Finally, remove the masking tape, fill in any gaps in the color and apply a thin, black line to the edges (far right).

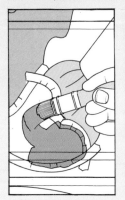

8
Painting doors

Always remove door handles, keyhole plates, hooks and other hardware before painting, to avoid smudges and runs and to speed up the work. Store them carefully with their screws and loosely refit between coats, to allow doors to be opened and closed. Give keyholes and the top edges of doors a thorough clean, so that specks are not picked up on bristles and spread over the surface. Complete any necessary repairs, such as fixing hinges and sanding down a sticking door before painting. (For preparing surfaces, see Jobs 5/6, pp. 18-19.)

Achieving a good finish

Aim to paint doors after walls and windows, but before baseboards, and in one continuous session to prevent dried-paint lines forming. Doors need an oil-based alkyd finish for protection against normal wear and tear; they represent the largest area of alkyd in most homes. An undercoat is necessary – even if the existing paint surface is sound and the new color is darker than the old. Use two undercoats, however, when covering a dark or strong color with a paler shade and sand between coats. There is no need to paint the top edge of a door, unless it is visible from stairs above. However, a painted edge will collect less dust than bare wood. If the door is to be painted in different colors each side, paint the hinge edge the same color as the outer face and the lock edge the same color as the inner face if the door opens into the room.

Painting baseboards

Use a 2in. brush for painting baseboards. At corners, dab a lightly loaded cutting-in brush into the crevice and draw away the excess paint. Use masking tape or cardboard to prevent paint smudging on to the walls.

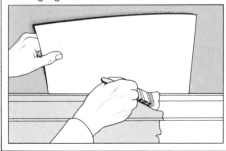

Paneled doors

The following working sequence is designed to minimize the number of "wet edges" and so avoid ugly ridges. Using a 1in. brush, begin by painting the moldings, **1**. Take care not to overload the brush or runs will spoil the finish. Then paint the panels, **2**, with a 2in. or 3in. brush, before moving on to the vertical center sections, **3**. Next, cover the top, middle and bottom horizontal bands, **4**, then complete the vertical outside sections and edges, **5**, and finally the frame.

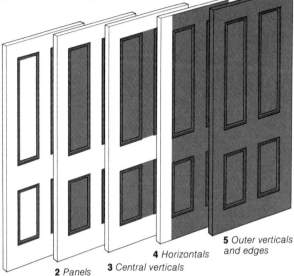
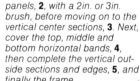

5 Outer verticals and edges
4 Horizontals
3 Central verticals
2 Panels
1 Moldings

Paint the panels from the top down

Flush doors

To cover the area quickly, use a 3in. brush. Start at the top corner of the hinge side and work in 9in.^{2} sections until you reach the bottom corner on the handle side. Begin with vertical strokes, then cross-brush to spread the paint and finish with light, upward strokes, before moving on to the next section. When painting the edges, take care not to allow the paint to build up into ridges, and where possible, take the paint over the corners. You will find a small 2in. brush easiest for the edges (below). Try to avoid the common mistake of applying too much paint to the top of the door and too little to the sides. Work quickly so that the edge of each 9in.^{2} painted section can be covered before it dries.

Which direction to paint

Begin with vertical strokes, then cross-brush the paint to fill in gaps. Finish each section with upward strokes.

Use a small brush for edges to prevent ridges forming

Jamming the door open

Jam a flush or paneled door open by tapping a wedge under it. This exposes both the hinge and handle edges for painting. Allow each coat to dry thoroughly before closing the door.

9

Painting windows

Window frames. which suffer both condensation and changes of temperature, are subjected to the worst conditions of all interior woodwork, so it is worth taking the time to ensure a good result. Repair any damage and prepare the surface before painting (see Job 5, p. 18). Paint any open-able windows as early in the day as possible, to allow enough time for them to dry before closing in the evening. You will need a 1in. brush and, for precision work, a cutting-in brush; also, if you choose, a paint shield.

The order of working for individual parts of a window is determined by its construction. For the best results, follow the order given below for double-hung and casement windows, and always finish painting in the direction of the grain.

Cutting in

It is worth practising the cutting-in technique to get a fine line on glazing bars, frames and edges. Place a loaded brush about $\frac{1}{8}$in. from the edge and carefully push it toward the join. Press lightly down and draw the brush swiftly along to make a long, clean line. Until you have acquired this skill, however, it would be wise to use a more foolproof method for painting around glass, such as a paint shield or masking tape.

Double-hung windows

Push the bottom sash up and the top sash down, until there is a 8in. over-lap. First paint the bottom meeting rail of the top sash, followed by the accessible vertical sections, 1. Almost close both windows and paint the rest of the top sash, 2, before covering the bottom sash, 3. Leave to dry with the sashes almost closed and matchsticks inserted between them to prevent them sticking together, then paint the frame, 4. Finally close the windows and paint the exposed parts of the runners, taking care not to get paint on the sash cords. Then paint the sill.

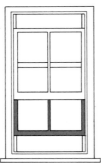
1 *Bottom of top sash*

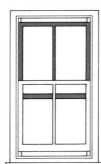
2 *Rest of top sash*

3 *Bottom sash*

4 *Frame*

5 *Runners*

Casement windows

First remove catches and handles and store in a safe place. If one window is fixed, begin with the opening one. Paint the rabbet first, 1, next the crossbars, 2, then the crossrails, 3. Move on to the side verticals and edges, 4, then the frame, 5, and finally the sill. Always paint the sill last, or sleeves and clothing will smudge the wet paint. If paint overlaps on to the hinges, wipe it off before it dries and becomes more difficult to remove. Leave the stay until last to allow the window to be adjusted during painting.

1 *Rabbets*

2 *Crossbars*

3 *Crossrails*

4 *Sides and edges*

5 *The frame*

Tips on keeping paint off glass

To guarantee a neat edge around window panes, try protecting the glass with a paint shield (right) as you work, or apply masking tape (far right), before you begin. Press the tape firmly down to prevent paint creeping under the edges, and remove it before the final coat of alkyd is dry, to avoid peeling a layer of paint off the frame. Alternatively, with experience and a steady hand, a clean line may be drawn using a cutting-in brush. Splashes and smudges can be scraped off when dry with a razor-blade and the surface cleaned with alcohol on a clean rag. Always allow the paint to overlap $\frac{1}{8}$in. on to the glass to prevent moisture seeping through the join between the putty and the glass, and causing the wood to rot.

Hold the paint shield firmly against the glass

Alternatively, paint over masking tape

10

Painting stairs and stairwells

If you have a two story house the stair area should be painted last, since halls and landings are likely to be scuffed when moving furniture from room to room; and, as the nucleus of the house, forms the main color link between individual rooms and upper and lower floors. First set up a secure working platform for reaching even the least accessible parts of the stairwell (below). Remove carpet and fittings, clean the entire staircase and cure any faults such as creaking and uneven stairs, cracks, dents or splits. Follow the usual order of work, beginning with the landing ceiling, then the walls of the stairwell, working from the top down, and finally the stairs, banisters and the handrail. Throughout the work, keep the movement of doors and people to a minimum until the paint has dried, to reduce dust. If the wood is to be varnished and its color changed, first fill any holes or splits and coat it with a woodstain.

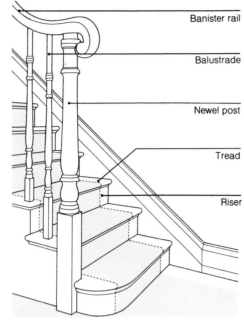

Stairs and banisters
Staircases attract a great deal of dust, so when painting the treads and risers, ensure that working conditions are spotless. Wash the banister thoroughly and, working from the top, clean each tread and riser immediately. If carpet is to be fitted, paint the border only, allowing a 1 in. carpet overlap.

11

Using ladders

Painting stairwells can prove perilous, so make sure your ladders are safe. A variety of convertible step ladders are now available, which will either slide or swing out into a straight ladder, for using against the wall (right). Ensure, however, that the connections will not allow the ladder to slip when extended and check for loose screws and jammed parts. If you are buying a new ladder, the aluminum types (right) are generally lighter and cheaper than the old wooden sort. Always ensure that it reaches at least 3ft above the highest level at which you wish to stand, and never stand above the third highest rung. Face the ladder as you climb and do not lean over too far either side while painting. For larger areas, use a working platform (*see Job 14, p. 32*).

Convertible ladders

Clip-on shelf

A clip-on shelf
If your ladder does not have a built-in shelf, consider buying a clip-on one. It will serve as a useful platform for equipment.

Non-slip ladders
Ladders which will stand on two different levels are useful on stairs, provided there are suction pads on the feet.

12

Painting kitchens and bathrooms

Steam and condensation are the main problems to be solved when redecorating these rooms. Good ventilation in the form of efficient extractor fans will help to minimize the effect of moisture and a layer of latex on walls and ceilings will provide an easily washable surface, especially if it has a slight sheen. Anti-condensation latex paints containing insulating material are now available to help offset some of these problems. Cream-colored, these paints can be overpainted to match a color scheme. Avoid alkyd on walls and ceilings since it exaggerates condensation.

Pipes
Copper pipes can be given a coating of undercoat and alkyd and will not need primer. Normal alkyd will withstand temperatures up to 194°F, although white and pale colors may yellow at over 158°F. Alternatively, a metallic paint can be used. These are corrosion and heat resistant and give luster to hot and cold pipes. Avoid water-based paints, since they tend to soften and crack when heated. Never paint connections or fitting nuts on pipes; they could prove difficult to undo if they are sealed with a layer of paint. If you are repainting sound paint, simply wash down the surface and abrade it to improve the adhesion of the new paint.

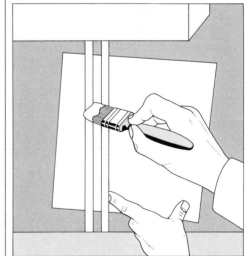

Painting behind a pipe
When pipes lie close to the wall, hold a card behind to shield the wall paint from smudges and splattering and start painting at the top.

Banister rail

Balustrade

Newel post

Tread

Riser

13

Painting radiators

Radiators should always be painted when cold and allowed to dry thoroughly before the heating is turned on again, or the finish will be impaired. A strong smell usually emanates from a newly painted surface when heated but it soon fades. Old radiators may need to be treated for rust and primed, but new ones are delivered pre-primed, ready for undercoat and gloss. Any copper pipes connecting with the radiator can be painted in the same way. Use a 1in. brush for a panel radiator. Work carefully to avoid runs, and do not paint the connections or they may prove difficult to undo if the radiator needs to be removed. Ordinary paints are usually satisfactory, but avoid paints with a metal pigment, since this will reduce radiating power.

Painting exterior walls

◇ Start at the top of the house and work down, to avoid dripping on to new paintwork.
◇ Divide the house into sections using natural breaks as demarcation lines. Begin with fascia boards, gutters and eaves, then tackle the walls, downspouts and finish with the windows and doors.
◇ Work in horizontal strips one block at a time.
◇ Do not apply masonry paint in frosty weather, it may damage the paint.
◇ Porous surfaces, such as masonry and stucco absorb about 50 per cent more paint than wooden surfaces.
◇ Try to work in the shade. and move around the house in the same direction as the sun.

Fault-finding

Painting faults can always be traced back to an error in preparation, poor working conditions, or incorrect application. Inadequate cleaning and abrading of surfaces, over-brushing or overthinning the paint, and over-loading the brush are some of the most common mistakes made by amateurs. In addition to surface textural problems, the paint color may deteriorate. Lack of light will make some white paint yellow, and some red and orange pigments will bleed into a new coat if a barrier coat is not applied.

Brushmarks
A poor-quality brush will leave tell-tale marks. Other possible causes include overloading the brush and applying too thick a coat of paint, or failing to sand down an old surface sufficiently.

Loss of sheen
If a coat of alkyd fails to retain its sheen, insufficient drying time between coats may be the cause. Overbrushing or overthinning the paint may also contribute.

No hiding power
Where a previous coat is still visible, either the wrong undercoat has been used or there are insufficient under-coats. Overthinning, overbrushing or understirring may also dilute the paint and cause transparency.

Flaking off
On woodwork, paint will peel if the surface is not correctly prepared. On latex, painting over dust, dirt or distemper is the cause.

Runs, sags and wrinkles
Unsightly tears and ridges form if the paint is applied too thickly or if it has not been adequately brushed out,
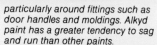
particularly around fittings such as door handles and moldings. Alkyd paint has a greater tendency to sag and run than other paints.

Specks and pimples
Dust in the paint, either blown by the wind or transferred from the brush, or a badly sanded surface may leave a speckled finish.

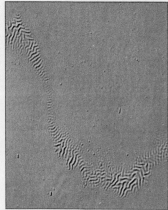

Blisters
Surface bubbles are caused by painting on a damp surface or on to old, soft or lifting paint.

Remedies

For all the above
*Allow paint to harden for a week
Rub down with sandpaper
Clean the surface
Cure damp if necessary.
Apply fresh alkyd or latex.*

For blisters on woodwork
*Cut out the bubble and fill with fine surface filler
Sand down, dust off
Apply fresh alkyd
If excessive, strip off the paint and start again*

Textures and finishes

A wide range of attractive paint finishes can be achieved by brushing, sponging, rolling or dabbing a design into a colored glaze or stenciling on a shape, while textured paints can be rollered or combed into a raised pattern. These effects need no special skill and in many cases can be completed more rapidly than a standard painting job.

Decorative finishes

No specialized tools are needed beyond normal painting equipment, but you must use the correct paint for the base coat and the right glaze. For the ground coat, an oil-based paint with an eggshell finish produces the best results. Ordinary latex can be used, but it is more absorbent and so produces a less crisp finish. Glazes can be shiny, matt or transparent. Transparent oil glazes can be bought ready-made, to be tinted with universal stainer or artist's oil colors. Alternatively, a glaze can be made up from: one part linseed oil, one part turpentine, one part drying agent, a little whiting and some color. Extra whiting will reduce the sheen. A third type of glaze is made from oil-based paint, thinned with alcohol.

Textured paints

Textured paints create a subtle decorative finish and, some are also flexible, so that if a ceiling or wall "moves", the cracks remain covered. They are available in both a ready-to-use and powdered form for mixing to a gluey consistency. Some automatically leave a raised pattern when applied, while others are textured by hand after application, with combs, brushes or rollers.

Sponging
A mottled or stipple pattern can be produced with a large natural sponge and a little patience. Unlike dragging and ragging, sponging usually involves adding color to a neutral background, instead of removing patches of color. First apply a coat of paint to the wall and leave it to dry for 24 hours. Then pour some thinned, colored glaze into a shallow bowl. Dampen a sponge, dip it lightly into the glaze and dab on to a sheet of newspaper to absorb the excess. When the pattern becomes a delicate speckle on the paper, begin work on the wall. As the design begins to fade, refill the sponge with glaze. Allow the coat to dry, then fill in any gaps. For a softer effect, apply a second glaze color (below).

Dragging
A fine, striped pattern is achieved by "dragging" a brush through a superficial coating of transparent oil glaze. First brush on the background coat to allow it to dry. Then brush on an even coating of colored oil glaze in a broad band. While it is still wet, run the dragging brush down through the glaze to score straight lines. Then glaze and drag the next band of wall. You may find it easier to work with another person, so that one applies the glaze, while the other uses the dragging brush.

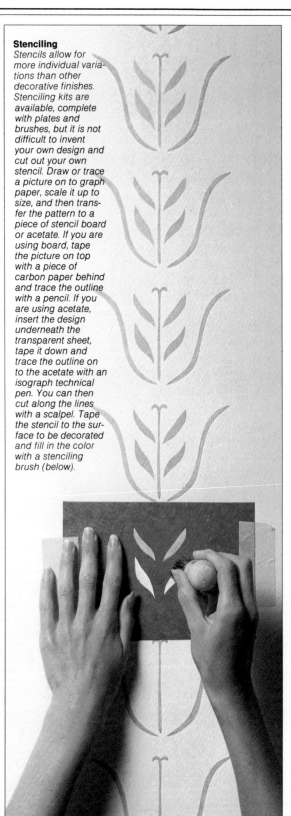

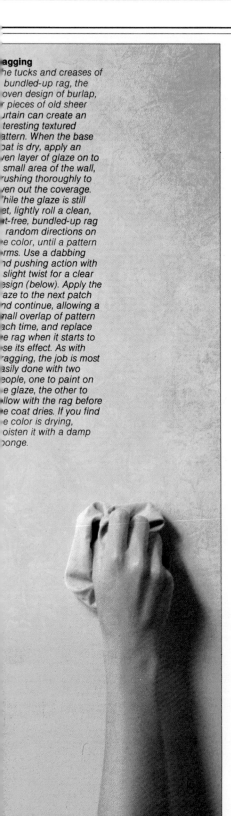

agging

he tucks and creases of
bundled-up rag, the
oven design of burlap,
r pieces of old sheer
urtain can create an
teresting textured
attern. When the base
oat is dry, apply an
ven layer of glaze on to
small area of the wall,
rushing thoroughly to
ven out the coverage.
hile the glaze is still
et, lightly roll a clean,
nt-free, bundled-up rag
random directions on
e color, until a pattern
rms. Use a dabbing
nd pushing action with
slight twist for a clear
esign (below). Apply the
aze to the next patch
nd continue, allowing a
mall overlap of pattern
ach time, and replace
e rag when it starts to
se its effect. As with
agging, the job is most
asily done with two
eople, one to paint on
e glaze, the other to
llow with the rag before
e coat dries. If you find
e color is drying,
oisten it with a damp
ponge.

Stenciling
Stencils allow for
more individual varia-
tions than other
decorative finishes.
Stenciling kits are
available, complete
with plates and
brushes, but it is not
difficult to invent
your own design and
cut out your own
stencil. Draw or trace
a picture on to graph
paper, scale it up to
size, and then trans-
fer the pattern to a
piece of stencil board
or acetate. If you are
using board, tape
the picture on top
with a piece of
carbon paper behind
and trace the outline
with a pencil. If you
are using acetate,
insert the design
underneath the
transparent sheet,
tape it down and
trace the outline on
to the acetate with an
isograph technical
pen. You can then
cut along the lines
with a scalpel. Tape
the stencil to the sur-
face to be decorated
and fill in the color
with a stenciling
brush (below).

Applying textured paints
Ensure the surface is
clean, dry, sound and
free from flaking paint
and mineral deposits. If
you are applying self-
texturing paint, it will
automatically create its
own texture as you roller
or brush it on. With
ordinary textured paint,
apply a coat first, then
work the textured pattern
into the smooth layer of
paint. A variety of effects
can be created with
different implements,
such as a plasterer's
comb, a swirl brush
(below), a stipple brush,
and patterned rollers.
Experiment on a piece of
cardboard before com-
mitting the pattern to the
wall.

Wallpapering

Estimating time and quantities ◇ Types of paper
Tools and equipment ◇ Setting up safe
workstations ◇ Stripping off old wallpaper
Measuring and cutting ◇ Pasting and booking
Hanging lining paper and wallpaper
Papering awkward areas

Modern wallpaper is no longer simply paper – but includes a wide choice of synthetic and fabric materials, designed to wash, wear, strip and hang more easily than old-fashioned papers. Vinyls and washable papers are as easy to clean as paintwork, and "dry-strip" papers, that can be removed without water, make preparation quick, clean and simple when redecorating. New, slower-acting adhesives also give more time to position the paper accurately. Improved designs, colors and finishes have introduced a wider range of choice and most manufacturers change their collections every two years.

Once you have decided on the type of wall covering, measure the areas carefully, double check the figures and calculate quantities. Choice of pattern and color will, to some extent, be determined by local availability, existing furnishings and price. Prices vary widely for the same paper, so it is worth comparing prices in the stores in your area.

Unlike painting, wallpapering can be done gradually and will conceal minor cracks. Thorough preparation, however, is important to ensure a smooth finish.

Points to remember

◇ When using unpasted paper, always buy the type of adhesive recommended for the wall covering you have chosen.
◇ Check lot numbers on rolls before unwrapping them.
◇ Always paper ceilings before walls.
◇ Finish any paintwork before papering.
◇ Wear overalls or an apron with large pockets for holding scissors, a smoothing brush and other equipment.

For more information on types of wallpaper, see Choosing materials, pp. 118-21.

Estimating time

The figures below are a guide to the time needed to prepare and wallpaper an average 10ft × 13ft room with a normal number of windows, doors and other obstacles. If the surface needs extra preparation, allow an additional $\frac{1}{4}$–$\frac{1}{2}$ hour for sizing and 1-1$\frac{1}{2}$ hours for applying primer sealer.

Ceilings

Stripping old paper
(2)-(3) hours

Washing down a sound ceiling
(1) hour

Filling cracks and holes
($\frac{1}{2}$)-(1) hour

Hanging lining paper
(4)-(6) hours

Hanging paper
(4$\frac{1}{2}$)-(6$\frac{1}{2}$) hours

Walls

Stripping old paper
(2)-(3) hours

Filling cracks and holes
($\frac{1}{2}$)-(1) hour

Hanging lining paper
(6)-(8) hours

Hanging pre-pasted paper
(6)-(8) hours

Hanging wallpaper
(12)-(16) hours

Estimating quantities

Wallpaper quantities can be calculated more accurately than paint, since there are fewer variable factors. Use the chart (right) to calculate the number of rolls required, and remember to add on 10 per cent for waste, especially with a large or "drop" pattern. When completing a room, note down the number of rolls used as a guide for next time. Either jot down measurements and quantities in an unseen place, such as the top of the door frame, or keep a house "log book". Wallpapers are priced by the roll and sold in bolts of two or three rolls. Standard wallpapers come in rolls of approximately 33ft × 21in. Lining paper rolls are usually slightly wider and are available in both standard and economical large roll sizes.

Lot numbers
Never skimp when ordering paper, since running out can cause considerable problems. Although you may be able to buy another roll with the same design, the colors in the pattern might be a remarkably different shade, which will show in bright light. This discrepancy occurs when the amount of ink used varies from lot to lot during printing. Each lot is marked on the label supplied with each roll, so check that each roll you buy bears the same batch number. To avoid running out, consider buying a spare roll on a sale or return basis, but remember to keep the cellophane wrapper intact.

Unfortunately, the lot system is not infallible, since rolls of the same lot sometimes differ in shades of color. If there is a variation, hang darker colors nearer the window, but where possible avoid using lengths of differing shades on one wall.

Types of paper

When selecting wallpaper, it is important to match the color, pattern and texture to the size, shape and general style of individual rooms (*see Color and pattern for effect, pp. 30-1*). It is, however, equally important to choose a suitably practical material for the job. Some areas, for example, will need resilient papers, others demand easily sponged surfaces. Ease of hanging may also influence your choice, particularly if you lack experience.

Ready-pasted papers

Ready-pasted wall coverings, which are backed with a dry, crystalline paste, save the time and trouble of mixing and applying paste (*see Job 18,*

p. 36). They are easy to hang and their only drawback is that the pasted edges may dry out and need extra paste, where the paper has to be cut to fit around fixtures.

Ease of handling

The hardest papers to hang are the thin, cheap types which tear easily when wet with paste, particularly when pulling round corners. Medium, heavyweight, washable and vinyl papers are stronger, so tolerate rougher handling. Paste smudged on the decorative side of the paper can leave a stain, so the easily wiped vinyl-coated papers and paper-backed vinyls can be an advantage in this respect. Since they are non-porous, these

papers are ideal for steamy rooms, such as kitchens and bathrooms, while heavy vinyls which resist stains and scuffs, are suitable for hallways, stairs and landings.

Lining paper

Usually hung beneath specialty wall coverings, lining paper forms a smooth base for foils, burlap and fabrics. It is also useful as a sort of paper primer to camouflage the outline of carefully filled cracks and pits. On an old plaster wall, lining can also be added to create a smooth surface for paint. There are several grades of lining paper, including a pure white type – where the walls are to be painted later

Choosing patterns

Complicated patterns are usually best avoided by the beginner, especially in a room with lots of alcoves and corners. Simple, repeat patterns are equally problematic, since the eye will quickly pick up any mis-matching. These usually fall into two types; straight "set" patterns which have horizontal repeats, and "drop" patterns with diagonal repeats (below). There are, however, many "free match" designs now available, which will match automatically.

Patterns for problem areas

Vertical stripes emphasize out-of-true corners and a horizontal pattern should be avoided on a sloping ceiling, since the motif will gradually "disappear" as the ceiling line slopes down. In any difficult situation, a small, random pattern is the best solution.

Calculating the number of rolls

Measurement round walls in feet, including doors and windows	Height from baseboard in feet							Ceilings
	8	9	10	11	12	13	14	
	Number of rolls required							
30	8	9	10	11	12	12	12	2
34	10	11	12	12	13	13	13	4
38	11	12	13	13	14	15	15	4
42	12	13	14	14	15	17	17	4
46	13	14	15	16	16	18	18	6
54	15	17	18	18	20	21	22	6
58	16	18	20	19	21	23	23	8
62	17	19	21	20	23	25	25	8
66	18	20	22	22	24	26	26	10
70	19	21	24	23	26	28	28	10
74	20	23	25	24	28	30	30	12
78	21	24	26	26	29	31	31	14

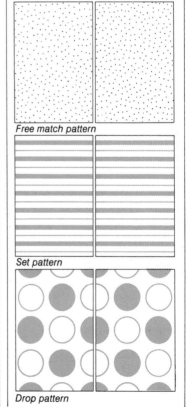

Free match pattern

Set pattern

Drop pattern

Tools and equipment

A full set of wallpapering tools is not a large investment, particularly since some general household items form part of the collection. The only expensive piece of equipment you might need would be a steam stripper for removing difficult papers; and this can be rented. Choose painter's smocks with pockets large enough to hold brushes, scissors and a sponge.

Pasting tools
Essential wallpapering tools include a paste brush or an old 4in. or 5in. paint brush that does not shed bristles; a paste bucket, with a taut piece of string tied across it for resting the brush on, and a disposable plastic liner to save cleaning it; also a paper-hanging brush for smoothing down the paper. A 6½ft × 2ft fold-away paste table is a good investment; it is cheap, takes up little space and serves as a work surface for cutting lengths and matching patterns. For pre-pasted paper, you will need a plastic water trough, instead of paste, a bucket and a pasting brush. A sponge is also recommended instead of a smoothing brush.

Scraping and cutting tools
You will need a straight and, possibly, a serrated scraper for removing wallpaper, and a pair of shears about 10in. long for making straight, accurate cuts. A utility knife and a smaller pair of household scissors are also handy when making intricate cuts around complicated shapes.

Measuring tools
For marking an accurate guide line before hanging, you will need a plumb bob and a pencil for walls, and a chalked stringline for ceilings (or walls). When measuring out the paper, use a steel tape, a 2ft × 3ft folding boxwood rule or a straight-edge ruler.

Finishing tools
Finally, use a sponge for removing unwanted paste and, if necessary, a wooden seam roller for pressing down edges on untextured wallpapers.

Care and storage
A kit of decorating tools should last a lifetime. Just ensure that, at the end of the job, everything is cleaned of paste in warm, soapy water, dried and stored safely away. To save cleaning the paste bucket, simply insert a disposable plastic liner, which can be thrown away and replaced. Always store paper rolls on their side and leave them in their wrappers to keep them clean. Never stand them on their ends, since this can crumple the edges.

Pastes
Always choose the paste recommended by the manufacturer for both lining and top paper or use a universal paste which can be mixed up to suit different types of wall covering. Modern cellulose paste is suitable for all types of wall covering except vinyl, which must be hung with a paste containing fungicide, to prevent mold forming on the wall. Ready-mixed pastes are only economical for heavy textiles, and cold-water paste is best used on heavier papers. Remember to buy sufficient quantities.

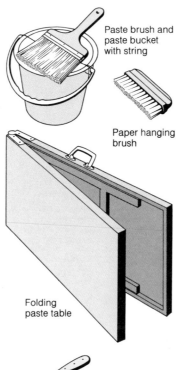

Paste brush and paste bucket with string

Paper hanging brush

Folding paste table

Straight scraper

Serrated scraper

Shears

Seam roller

Steel tape

Sponge

Plumb bob and line

Pattern, like color, influences the mood and shape of a room. Florals, for example, tend to be restful, while geometrics may create a more stimulating atmosphere. Designs can be used to play visual tricks: vertical lines help to "raise" a ceiling; horizontal lines "lengthen" a room; three-dimensional geometrics give the impression of depth; small designs give a feeling of space; large motifs diminish the size of a surface. Motifs have the power to focus interest on a feature or disguise irregularities when taken over an entire room. Try to avoid too many patterns in one room, do not combine florals with geometrics and always set off a pattern with a plain background, floor or furnishings.

Floral patterns
Fresh spring colors lend warmth and character to a bleak, angular room (above). Large sprigs have the effect of opening out a room and raising a ceiling, particularly when arranged in vertical strips. If the pattern is carried on to the blinds or furnishings, the warming and softening effect increases. In a small room with irregular shapes – an attic for example – a miniature floral in random sequences would be more suitable, since a regular line will highlight crooked walls or ceilings. The type of floral design may also suggest an era, a national style or the purpose of a room; a conservatory, for instance (right).

Large motifs
A large design continued over the walls and ceiling will help to conceal strangely shaped corners and will soften a series of harsh or irregular angles (right). A big motif, however, will only look comfortable if the room is broad or tall enough to accommodate it. It is not easy to mix floral designs, particularly if a floral forms a main feature or contains large shapes. The best effects are created by picking up the main color of the pattern in other parts of the room, and using a neutral second color, such as white, as a backdrop and to co-ordinate accessories.

Color and pattern for effect

Geometric patterns
A geometric pattern instantly gives a room a clean and modern feel — particularly suitable for a bathroom (below). Ideally, the lines should complement any other verticals and horizontals, such as the grouting lines in tiles or the slats of blinds. The angles of the room, however, must be straight or the geometric lines will exaggerate any irregularities. A tiny motif within the geometric will help to soften lines and one or two colors should be repeated in other parts of the room.

A printed collage
Menus, wine labels, newspapers, magazines, catalogs and other printed matter, arranged into a collage, will form an unusual wall covering. This sort of montage is best pasted on to a small area to form a feature in a study, a bathroom, or a child's bedroom.

14
Setting up safe workstations

Always set up a safe working platform before attempting to decorate ceilings and stairwells. In most houses, this can be improvised using a combination of ladders and boards. If the stairwell is particularly high, however, a narrow scaffold tower, rented locally, may be the best solution. When using step ladders always ensure that they are fully open and that the shelf is pushed well down. When climbing ladders to reach the platform, remember to empty pockets of scissors and knives.

Stairs and stairwells
The exact arrangement of ladders, steps, boards and boxes will depend on your staircase, but the system shown (right) can be adapted for most stair shapes. Put a step ladder on the top landing and lean a straight ladder against the head wall with its foot firmly lodged against a stair riser. Then link them with boards. For the lower levels, put a step ladder in the hall and form a platform with planks resting on a ladder step and a stair. Keep equipment handy on the stepladder shelf or in a bucket hung from a ladder rung.

Ceilings and walls
Arrange a strong working platform across the room in the direction the paper is to be hung. Use two step ladders, some trestles or heavy packing crates, and a plank or a series of boards which span the complete room from wall to wall. In this way, the platform will only need to be moved once for each wall. Make sure you can reach comfortably, since stretching is dangerous.

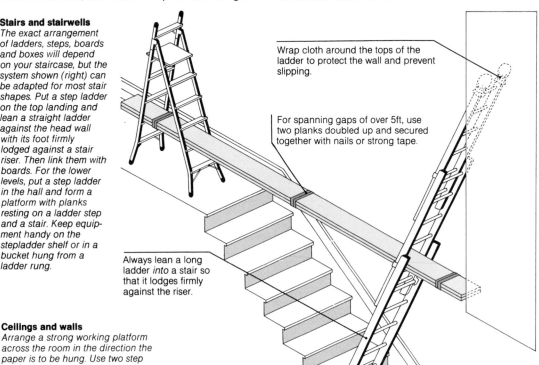

Wrap cloth around the tops of the ladder to protect the wall and prevent slipping.

For spanning gaps of over 5ft, use two planks doubled up and secured together with nails or strong tape.

Always lean a long ladder *into* a stair so that it lodges firmly against the riser.

Ensure that step ladders are fully opened to avoid sudden jarring or toppling.

A single plank spanning more than 5ft will need additional support.

Preparing the room

◇ Clear furniture away from the walls and leave space for the pasting table. If papering ceilings, remove *all* furniture to another room.
◇ Remove light fixtures, curtains and, if necessary, picture rails.
◇ Spread a dropcloth or newspapers over the floor to catch drips, debris and paste.
◇ Lock any doors obstructed by ladders and keep dogs and children away from the work area.

Any existing wall covering should be stripped off to leave bare walls, since joins, peeling, blistering and a strong pattern in the old paper may show through the new. The fresh adhesive may also pull the old covering away from the wall, together with the new paper you have just hung. The key to stripping wallpaper is to take time and care over the job. The paper should not be scraped off too vigorously or lumps will be gouged from the plaster, leaving more holes to fill in later. Be patient with stubborn areas and continue soaking and scraping until the paper loosens. Standard wallpapers are removed by sponging with warm water until the paper is soft enough to scrape off. Easy-strip papers are simply peeled off. Washable papers which hold fast may need to be removed with a steam stripper.

Marking screw holes
When a fixture, such as a picture or shelf, is taken off the wall, put a toothpick in each screw hole, leaving about $\frac{1}{4}$in. protruding. When the new paper is brushed on, the toothpicks will pop through to indicate the exact location of the screw hole.

15
Preparing surfaces

When all old paper has been removed, wash down the walls with hot water, to remove any traces of old paste and to loosen any final traces of paper. Then fill any holes or cracks (*see Basic technique, p. 17*). When a wall covering comes

Basic technique

How to strip off old wallpaper

1 *Soak the paper with warm water using a large sponge or brush*

2 *Scrape off the softened paper while it is damp*

Stripping normal wallpaper

*Most wallpaper is removed by soaking with warm water, **1**, using a large brush or a sponge, and then by scraping. Thicker papers may need an extra soaking: go right round the room once, so that by the time you get back to the starting point, the water will have started to loosen the old paste. Another soaking and the paper should scrape off easily as you work around the room. A little soap powder or liquid detergent added to the water will speed up the soaking process, and a handful of wallpaper paste will both thicken it enough to give it more time to soak through the paper, and will prevent water running down the wall. While scraping, keep the scraper as flat as possible, to avoid gouging out plaster, **2**.*

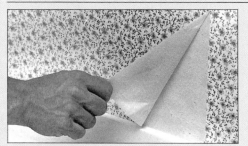

1 *Gently peel back the bottom corner of vinyl paper*

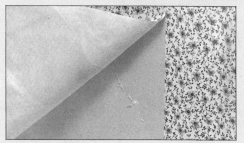

2 *Remove the backing paper if it is damaged*

Stripping vinyl wallpapers

*Easy-strip wall coverings, now widely available, can be removed simply by releasing the bottom edge of the paper with your fingernail or a stripping knife, **1**, and pulling each length straight off the wall. Pull carefully upward, not outward, to avoid ripping the backing in uneven strips. With vinyls, a layer of thin white paper will remain on the wall as each length is removed. This is backing paper and can remain in position to act as lining paper for the new wall covering. If, however, the backing paper comes away in places, it must be removed completely, **2**.*

1 *Score the paper with a steel brush or serrated scraper*

2 *Hold the steam stripper plate to the wall, then scrape off the paper*

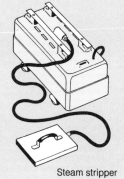

Steam stripper

Stripping difficult papers

*Washable and overpainted papers are made to withstand water, so soaking the surface will have little effect. First score the surface using a steel brush, **1**, a serrated scraper or a sharp implement; this will break down the surface and allow the water to infiltrate and loosen the old paste. If the job proves hard going try renting a steam stripper; it is simple to use and creates less mess than soaking and scraping. Steam generated by the machine passes through a plate held close to the wall, **2**. This loosens the paper so that it can be scraped off immediately with your other hand.*

away easily – assuming it is not an easy-strip type – it indicates a flaking, dusty or damp surface. Scrape away any flaking paint then check and cure the cause of any dampness in the wall (*see pp. 205-7*) and apply a coat of oil-based primer sealer to provide a sound surface for the new wall covering. If papering over sound paintwork, wash down the wall first.

Applying glue size
Glue size is a gelatinous sealant that prevents a wall absorbing water from the paste. Diluted paste will serve the same purpose. Although it is not always necessary, it is wise to simply brush a coat over a wall to ensure that the wall covering sticks well, and to avoid ruining expensive paper. It also leaves the surface slippery, which makes it easier

to slide the paper over the wall when butting up adjoining lengths. Special formulations of glue size can be obtained, although it is now customary for diluted wallpaper paste to be used as size. Normally, a weak mixture of paste is made up according to the instructions on the packet and applied generously with a large brush. Within minutes, it will be dry and papering can begin.

Apply glue size liberally to the surface

16
Measuring and cutting

Measure the height of each wall to give you a maximum length for your strips of paper and allow an additional 4in. before cutting. This gives an extra 2in. at both ceiling (or picture rail) and baseboard for neat trimming. Measure ceilings in the same way, and allow an excess of 2in. for trimming on to the side and window walls. Trim off the end of the roll, use a measure to mark out lengths then cut the paper. When using a plain or random-patterned paper, work from one roll and cut equal lengths. With a diagonally matching pattern, work from two or three rolls at a time, to minimize waste in pattern matching. Mark consecutive numbers on the back and make a note of which end is the top.

Measure out lengths with a tape measure, allowing 4in. extra for trimming

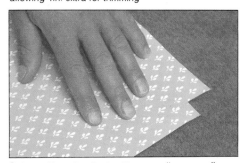

Cut equal lengths of set patterns or allow a small margin where necessary

Carefully match up drop patterns before measuring and cutting lengths

17
Marking guide lines on ceilings and walls

Corners, door architraves and window frames rarely form true verticals. So, the first step when papering walls is to mark a vertical line on the wall as a guide to

Where to begin on ceilings
The starting point for hanging ceiling paper is generally parallel with the main window, so that, as with painting, you will be working away from the light. In this way, accidental overlaps will not be caste in shadow. Draw your first guide line, to allow for about 1in. of paper to be turned on to the window wall for final trimming.

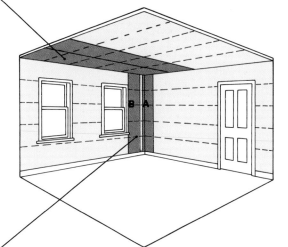

Where to begin on walls
*When papering any room, the aim is to work outward from the largest window, away from the light in both directions. The normal starting point is in the corner adjacent to the window wall (**A**). Draw your first guide line at a point which will allow a ½in. margin of paper to turn on to the window wall. Having papered the first side wall, go back and paper the window wall, then the other side wall and finally, the far wall. Alternatively, the first length can be hung next to the window (**B**) and from there to paper the rest of the window wall, followed by the side walls, working away from the light, then the end wall. Starting beside the window may prove easier, since it usually removes the need to cut awkward lengths around the window.*

Where to begin on chimney breasts
A chimney breast forms a focal point in any room, so special planning is needed to create a balanced effect. If the paper has a large pattern, centralize the motif on the chimney breast (right). If the paper has a random design, mark a vertical line at the center of the chimney breast and hang a length each side, so that two full widths can be used (far right).

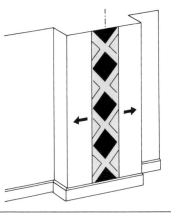

hanging the first length. The most effective method is to suspend a plumb bob on a chalkline from the top of the wall and snap it to leave a vertical line. Draw a new guide line as you come to each wall and after hanging a few lengths, use the plumb bob to check the alignment. Straight guide lines on ceilings are made by measuring equal distances from the wall at each end of the ceiling and snapping a chalkline between the two points.

Using a plumb bob and chalkline
When the plumb bob stops swinging, press the chalkline into the base of the wall and pluck it, to leave a vertical line.

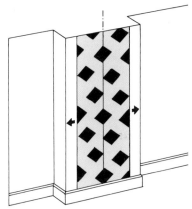

Basic technique

How to hang pre-pasted paper

The secret of successful wallpapering is to be sure that the surface is sound, and to be thorough, methodical and careful when matching patterns. It is best to paper ceilings before walls, to prevent paste splashing on to finished walls and woodwork. When you have prepared the surface (*see Job 15, p. 32-3*), cut lengths, and marked straight guide lines, the paper is ready to hang. Pre-pasted paper has a coating of dried paste on the back which is activated by immersing the paper in a waterbox. Before you start work, lay plenty of newspaper or plastic sheeting over the floor. The waterbox is placed under the first guide line, a length of paper is rolled in the water, removed, lined up precisely against the guide line, smoothed into place, then trimmed. Subsequent lengths are brushed into place to form neat pattern matches and butt joints.

Activating the paste
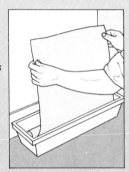
Loosely roll up a length of paper, with the pattern facing inward to expose the pasted back. Make sure the free end is the top edge, then immerse the paper in the waterbox for a full minute. Slowly pull the paper out by the top edge, allowing the water to run back into the box then apply it to the wall.

Applying paper to a wall
*Open the step ladder close to the wall by the waterbox and as you pull the first length out of the water, mount the ladder. Stand square to the wall, and position the edge of the paper against the first vertical guide line marked on the wall, **1**, leaving a 1 in. trimming edge at the top. Run the wallpaper brush firmly down the center of the aligned length. Brush outward to expel any air bubbles and smooth the paper neatly on to the wall, **2**. If the top half of the paper is correctly aligned with the guide line, the lower half will follow it automatically. If it does not lie straight, peel the length off and reposition it. At the ceiling angle or molding and baseboards, run the back of the shears lightly along the paper, **3**, peel back the edge of the paper and cut carefully along the crease line, **4**. Brush the paper back into place to leave a neat finish, **5**. Take the second length to the top of the wall, align the pattern where necessary and position the edge close to the first length. A slight push with your fingers will encourage the paper to slide across the wall until both edges touch and buckle slightly, **6**. As the paper shrinks a little this will form a neat "butt" joint. Go over the joints with a wallpaper brush and seam roller.*

1 *Align the first length of paper with the vertical line*

2 *Brush the paper flat to expel air bubbles*

3 *Mark a crease line at the ceiling angle*

4 *Trim along the crease line with wallpaper shears*

5 *Smooth back the trimmed edge*

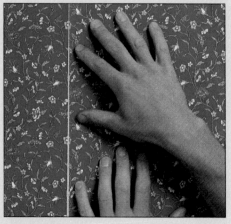

6 *Slide the new edge to form a butt joint*

18

Pasting and folding lining paper

It is advisable to use lining paper under heavy and slippery wallcoverings, such as unbacked fabric or grasscloth and foil, and under ordinary wallpaper if the surface is uneven. A lining speeds adhesion and thus prevents shrinkage; it helps to prevent creasing and conceals any surface roughness. You will need to paste each cut length (see Job 23, p. 39) and arrange it into accordion folds.

Folding long lengths
Lining paper is usually applied in long lengths, so for ease of handling, fold each pasted length into a manageable stack. Carefully arrange the pasted sections into accordion folds, pasted- *side to pasted-side, 1, taking care not to allow any paste to smudge on to the top side. Handle the lengths gently and do not crease the folds, 2, since this will leave unsightly marks when the paper is hung.*

1 Fold the paper pasted-side to pasted-side

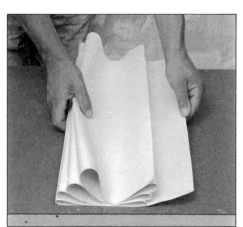

2 Arrange the accordion folds into a pile

19

Hanging lining paper on ceilings

Lining paper is normally hung at right angles to the top covering on both ceilings and walls, so that the joins in the two layers do not coincide. The first essential is to set up a safe working platform (see Job 14, p. 32).

Marking guide lines
Having prepared the surface of the ceiling (see Job 15, p. 32-3), a guide line should be marked on the ceiling for the first length of paper. This is best made with a chalkline. The line is secured taut to the top of the walls and is then plucked to snap against the ceiling and leave a chalked impression. Alternatively, you could use a pencil and a long straight-edge. (For positioning, see below right.) The lengths can be hung immediately after pasting and folding. However, once hung, leave the lining to dry for 48 hours before pasting on the top covering. When learning the art of paper hanging, it is worth practising with lining paper, even if you choose to paint rather than paper over the layer of lining.

Applying the lining paper
Mark a chalk or pencil guide line on the ceiling, 1, unfold the first portion of the paper and align it with the guide line. The remainder of the paper can be supported with a spare roll, 2, or by an assistant standing on the floor and using a clean sweeping brush. Gravity is the enemy of papering ceilings. The paper will want to drop down, so brush each fold quickly, 3, and keep the remainder of the length close to the ceiling so that it does not pull down the part already brushed into place. When the length is smoothed down, push the edges neatly into the wall-ceiling joint, 4, and trim, 5. If the walls are to be papered, leave a $\frac{1}{4}$in. margin of paper on each wall. Hang successive lengths in the same way, ensuring that the edges of all lengths are neatly butt-joined.
To paper round a ceil-ing light fitting, cut a hole *in the paper, pull the fitting through and hang the rest of the length. Then make release cuts, press back the flaps and trim (see Job 29, p. 41).*

Cleaning shears
For neat trimming, stand paste-clogged shears and scissors in a jar of hot water from time to time to dislodge the adhesive and so guar-antee clean cuts. If the paste hardens, it may need to be washed off in clean, soapy water.

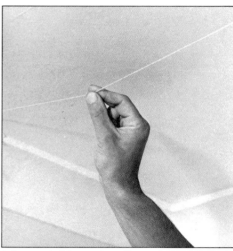

1 Snap a chalkline on the ceiling and align the first length with it

3 Smooth the paper into position, eliminating air bubbles

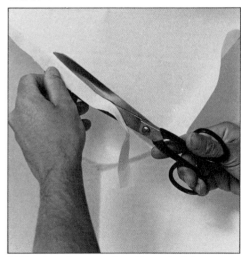

5 Trim along the crease line with a pair of sharp, clean shears

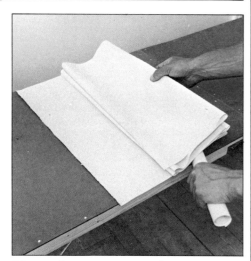

2 *Support the paper on a spare roll*

4 *Mark a crease line with a scraper*

Where to begin on ceilings
The first length of lining paper is usually hung at right angles to the main window. In this way, the lining will also lie at right angles to the top layer of wallpaper, which is usually hung parallel with the window (see Basic technique, p. 39). Begin lining in a corner and allow about 2in. of paper to be turned on to the window wall for trimming. Also allow an extra 2in. for trimming on to the side walls.

20
Hanging lining paper on walls

Lining paper is hung horizontally, so each length must be as long as the wall's width. Joining short lengths is not advisable, since it is difficult to get a perfect join. You will need to make a guide line for the first horizontal length, in the same way as on a ceiling (*see Job 19, left*). The first length should overlap on to the ceiling by about 1in. before you trim off. Each length should also overlap around the corner on to the next wall by about ½in. As you work down the wall, make neat butt joints (*see Basic technique, p. 35*) between lengths as any overlaps, except at corners, will show under the top covering.

Gradually unfold the paper and smooth it on to the wall

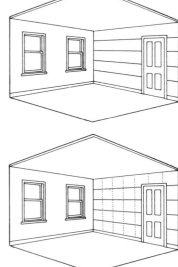

Where to begin lining on walls
Lining paper should be hung in horizontal layers on walls (top) unless the surface is bad enough to need a double layer of lining paper, known as cross-lining (above). The first layer is hung vertically and the second layer horizontally, so that the top wall covering will lie vertically. You could hang the lining paper vertically if the joins in the layers do not coincide.

21
Patch lining

Where only a small part of the wall needs to be lined, try patch lining. Hang enough lining paper to cover the poor area with an overlap of about ½in., but do not stick down the edges. Allow the paste to dry, then tear off a rim of paper, to leave a feathered edge to the patch, which should not show through the wall covering. Alternatively, gently rub the edges with a medium-grade sandpaper.

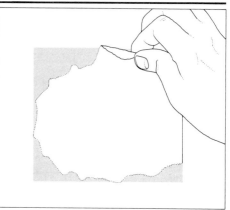

Tear around the patch for a soft line

Borders and friezes

Borders and friezes add an inexpensive finishing touch to a newly decorated room. Although traditionally fitted at ceiling or picture rail level, they can be used to good effect as a vertical wall surround or to trim a sloping ceiling, for example. A well-placed decorative strip can affect the apparent dimensions of a room. It may reduce the apparent height of a tall ceiling, elongate a short room or highlight an unusual structural feature and will mimic the effect of a cornice, picture molding or dado cap. It can also play a role in the color scheme, co-ordinating disparate colors, toning down a bright color combination or enlivening a quiet room. With some geometric patterns, you can create a scalloped or serrated effect by cutting around the outline at the top or bottom edge. Borders and friezes can be bought by the roll, sometimes in pre-pasted form, to match your wallpaper, or you can cut and paste your own from a roll of suitably patterned or plain paper.

A softening effect
In a simple, neutral room (right) a soft frieze adds a warm and friendly touch, particularly if it picks up a color in the furnishings. In a room without pattern, a frieze can become a feature in its own right. It is important, however, to choose a design that is in tune with the mood of the room. A horizontal line will take the eye sideways and can help to broaden a narrow room, or lower the ceiling line in a tall one, particularly if the line is echoed by the arrangement of the furniture.

A co-ordinated effect
On a vibrant wall, the border needs to link with either the pattern or the color of the wallpaper for a unified effect (far right). A patterned border, for example, can look stylish against a patterned wallpaper, provided the colors are co-ordinated and other surfaces or furnishings form a neutral background. A border design can give a splash of interest between two plain surfaces, and a single strip of color can divide two different patterns and so quieten the effect. Many wallpapers come with an integrated border.

22
Hanging narrow strips

Borders and friezes will only adhere to a smooth, dry surface, so should be applied at least 48 hours after hanging wallpaper.

To look good they need to be perfectly straight, so the first task is to establish a true horizontal or vertical. You will need to measure the width of the strip and mark guide lines using a carpenter's level and pencil or a chalkline and plumb bob. The strip can then be cut to length. If you are joining strips, match patterns carefully. Pre-pasted strips are immersed in water before hanging (*see p. 35*). If you are pasting the back, be sure to apply an even coating and to cover the edges, because if the adhesive is not well applied, the strip will peel at the edges. Once the border or frieze is in place on the wall, go over the edges with a seam roller.

Pasting and joining borders
Cover the pasting table with newspaper and place the long strip face down on top. Ensure that the remainder of the strip falls on to clean floor. Brush an even coating of wallpaper paste over the strip, allowing it to spread over the edges. Fold the pasted section into neat accordion folds (see Job 18, p. 36) and paste the rest of the strip. Then hang the border. To join two strips, overlap the ends, align them accurately for a good pattern match and make a single cut through both strips, then smooth down the ends.

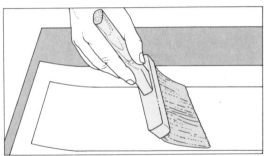
Cover the pasting table with newspaper and paste the strip

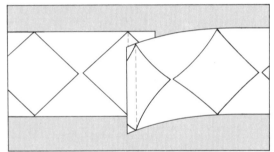
To make a join, overlap the ends of the two pieces, match the pattern and cut through both strips

---

23
Pasting and booking ordinary wallpaper

If you are not using pre-pasted paper (*Basic technique, p. 35*), you will need to apply a coating of wallpaper paste to each length after it has been cut to size. Paste should be mixed until all the lumps are dissolved and allowed to stand for a couple of minutes. If you are using thin paper, you will have to add extra water for a more dilute mixture. To ensure a good covering of paste, coat the brush generously, then paste systematically and in good light. Dry patches will form "bubbles" when the length has been hung. After pasting, each length is folded into a "book", for ease of handling and to speed the "soaking" process.

Soaking
Some papers need to be left to soak or soften for a few minutes before they are hung. Medium-weight papers should be left for about 5 minutes, and heavyweight papers for about 10 or 12 minutes. If no exact guidance is given on the label, the best approach is to soak long enough to ensure that the paper is supple before it is hung. To soak the paper, simply leave the booked length on a clean, dry surface after you have applied the paste, and continue pasting more lengths. Always keep the soaking time constant between lengths, to avoid variations in stretching and the resulting pattern-matching problems. Each pasted length is taken to the wall, draped over one arm. The top half is unfolded and the length is hung against a guide line, as for pre-pasted paper (*see Basic technique, p. 35*).

Applying the paste
Place a length of paper decorative side down on the paste table. Allow the short edge of the paper to overlap the end of the table by 1 in. and let the long edge nearest to you overlap the table edge by about $\frac{1}{4}$ in. Divide the paper into three imaginary long bands. First load the brush and paste the central portion, 1, then work toward the edge nearest to you – the one that overlaps the edge of the paste table. Push the paper across to the farther edge, again allowing the paper to overlap by about $\frac{1}{4}$ in., then brush the paste outward toward that edge, herringbone style (see above right), 2. This should prevent the paste smearing on to the table. Keep the brush well coated with paste and continue feeding the paper along the table until about half the length has been pasted. Then fold the top edge over to the center line, 3. Paste the second half of the length, following the same sequence, then fold the other short edge over to meet the first in the middle, 4. taking care not to crease the book. Put this length aside to soak while you paste the next or hang a soaked length. If you need to paste long lengths for a ceiling or a stairwell, fold the lengths in the same way as for lining paper (see Job 18, p. 36).

1 *Paste the central portion of the paper, then the long edge nearest to you*

2 *Brush the paste over to the opposite long edge*

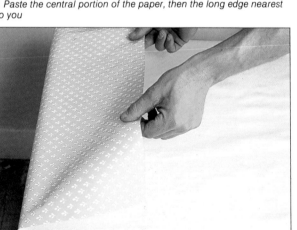

3 *Fold over the pasted half of the paper*

4 *Paste the second half then fold it over and leave the whole strip to soak*

The order of pasting
First paste the central band of the paper, then the strip nearest to you and finally, the far strip. When coating an edge strip, ensure that it overlaps the edge of the table, to avoid smearing paste on to the table and from there on to the decorative side of the paper. When half the sheet is completed, book it and paste the other half.

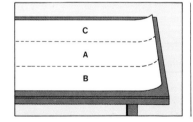

How to carry a length of pasted paper
Drape the length over one arm, with the two ends uppermost. This will prevent you smearing paste on to your clothes, allow you to mount the ladder easily and will protect the paper from crushing.

24
Papering stairwells

The height of most stairwells poses the problem of how to reach the top of the walls and how to handle very long lengths of paper. The first essential is therefore to set up a safe work-station (*see Job 14, p. 32*).

Although it runs against the normal procedure of working away from the light, it is easiest to hang the longest length first and work away from it in both directions.

When measuring lengths, mark the paper to allow for the slope of the stairs (see below). After pasting, fold each length accordion-style for ease of handling (*see Job 18, p. 36*) and, if possible, enlist a helper to support the length of paper as it is hung.

If you use a pre-pasted paper, always roll each length twice in the trough to ensure that water reaches all parts of the dried paste on the back of these long strips of paper. First immerse the length, pattern outward, in the trough, so that the bottom end extrudes, then re-roll it until the end which will lie at the top of the wall emerges.

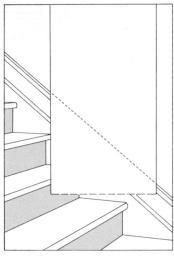

Measuring for the stair angle
Allow for the slope of the stairs when measuring lengths, so that the paper falls below the longest drop. Crease the paper along the baseboard and trim.

25
Papering corners

Joins are less noticeable if they fall in a corner, so unless a width of paper conveniently ends in a corner, you will need to cut it into two strips. Internal and external corners are treated in much the same way. When less than a full width is needed to reach a corner, you should measure from the edge of the last length into the corner. Turn the paper face down to mark off the width needed, and double check that the strip is being cut from the correct edge, or the pattern will not match. Pencil guide marks to indicate which edges are to fall in the corner. When the first strip is in place, the off-cut is hung on the new wall, its edge covering the join.

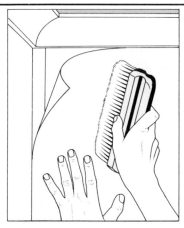

Internal corners
Hang complete lengths until a cut width is needed to reach the corner. Measure from the edge of the last length into the corner. Take three measurements, one at the top, one in the middle and one at the bottom, in case the corner is not true. Then add $\frac{1}{8}$in. to the largest dimension for turning on to the next wall. Cut a strip this wide and paste it down. Then hang the offcut, ensuring that the "good" edge is vertical and overlaps for a good pattern match.

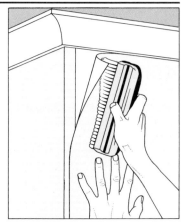

External corners
Measure from the edge of the last full width into the corner, as for internal corners. This time, however, add 1in. instead of $\frac{1}{2}$in. to the largest dimension. Cut a strip this wide, paste it and hang it, smoothing the paper carefully round the corner. Use your judgement to decide where the offcut should lie for the best pattern match. Mark a vertical line on the next wall, the width of the offcut from this point, before pasting and hanging.

26
Papering around fireplaces

The way to tackle a fireplace surround depends mainly on the mantelshelf. If it reaches right across the chimney breast wall or to within about 1in. of the corners, treat the wall above and below the shelf as two separate areas. Hang the paper down to the mantelshelf and make a neat horizontal cut. Then hang the lower half of the length and make a neat butt joint where the pieces meet.

If the mantelpiece spans only a part of the wall, hang the length as one piece. Brush on the top half of the paper and cut along the rear edge of the mantelshelf. Then cut carefully round the contours of the fire-place surround, using sharp household scissors for intricate shapes (top right). When papering chimney breasts, try to make joins and overlaps on the side, recessing walls (bottom right).

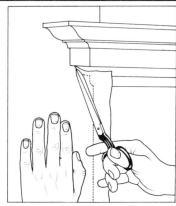
Use sharp scissors for intricate cuts

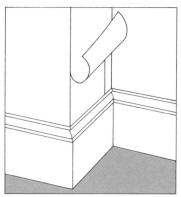
On chimney breasts make joins on the side walls

27
Papering doorways

Hang complete lengths until less than a full width of paper is needed to reach the door frame. Cut out an L-shaped piece of paper, leaving about 2in. excess all around for trimming. Hang the paper from the ceiling down to the top of the frame and trim along the line. Make a diagonal cut, about 1in. long, working away from the top corner of the frame to allow the rest of the length to be smoothed into place, then crease and cut.

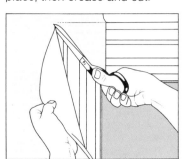
Cut diagonally up to the frame edge

28
Papering around windows

The shape of the window surround will determine the papering technique. In a window reveal, paper the inside walls first, cutting the paper to align exactly with the edge of the outer wall. Then hang a length on the outer wall, with a small margin overlapping into the papered reveal, and match the pattern carefully (top right). The trickiest rooms to wallpaper are in attics and lofts where there are unusual angles. Where dormer windows have triangular-shaped wall reveals, turn a 1in. margin of paper from the outer wall into the reveal. Cut triangular-shaped pieces to cover the reveal walls precisely and so overlap the margin (bottom right).

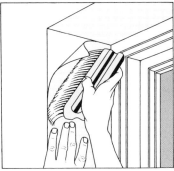

In a window reveal, paper the inside walls first.

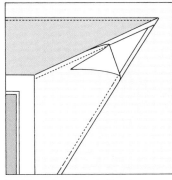

Cut triangular pieces to fit a dormer window exactly

29
Papering around light fittings

First switch off the electricity supply at the fuse box. Modern, flush-fitting outlets and switches are simple to trim around neatly. First loosen the cover plate, then hang the length of paper up to the electrical fitting. Cut a hole in the paper, about $\frac{1}{4}$in. smaller than the size of the plate. Then smooth the paper on to the wall, and replace the plate.

To fit paper around a ceiling light, make a series of radial release cuts from the center to the edges of the fixture and gently press the paper flat around the edges to remove the "tongues" and brush the paper flat. If you are using pre-pasted paper, you may need to add a little pre-mixed adhesive to the edges.

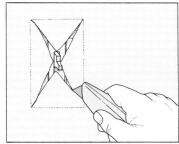

Remove the cover plate to fit paper around the edges

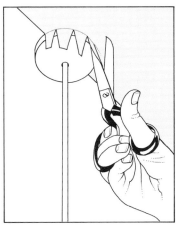

Make a series of radial cuts and trim

30
Papering arches

Paper the outer wall first and turn a 1in. margin into the arch. Make small cuts in the edge to allow for the curve of the arch. Fold the flaps around the corner and smooth them down. Paper the inside of the arch in two pieces, the exact width of the arch, making a neat butt joint at the top.

Carefully align the edges of the paper with the arch.

31
Papering around radiators

Some radiators can be tilted or removed for decorating, but others are fixed permanently in place. Either remove the radiator or tuck enough paper behind it to leave a "fully papered" look. If the paper is visible below the radiator, butt join the strips at the base of the wall and trim carefully along the top of the baseboard. If not, simply trim the strips so that they lie about 6in. below the top of the radiator. Make sure the edges are well glued.

Fault-finding

Symptom	Cause	Cure
Bubbles below the surface	Failure to brush out well.	If paste is wet, peel back the paper and rebrush. If dry, cut a cross through the bubble with a sharp knife and paste down flaps.
Failure to adhere	A damp wall, an unsized porous wall, the wrong paste, pasting too sparsely, insufficient soaking time.	Strip off paper and hang new material on a suitably prepared surface.
Loose edges	Insufficient paste or brushing.	Apply more paste and smooth edges with a brush or seam roller.
Pattern mis-matching	Stretching caused by differing soaking times or allowing lower half of roll to drop suddenly. Over-vigorous brushing.	Rehang, aligning design at eye level.
Open joints	Stretching then shrinkage caused by over-vigorous brushing.	Hang new length immediately if possible; re-paper if necessary.
Tears	Carelessness with thin paper.	Try to smooth down the torn edge to make an invisible join or hang a new length.
Bumpy surface	Poor preparation.	Strip off paper, smooth wall or hang lining paper.

Textured wallcoverings

Texture in furnishing fabrics influences the atmosphere of a room. Shiny surfaces, such as foils, reflect light and are cool to the touch and to the eye. Lustrous finishes, such as silks and satins, are elegant and cool but soft. Heavier, mat textures, such as burlaps, tweeds and linens, absorb the light and give a warmer, more muted and relaxed effect. Many materials also act as heat or sound insulators and most wear better than paper.

Wall coverings are made in a wide range of textures and are sold by the roll or by the foot. Burlaps, grasscloths and paper-backed types come in 36in. widths. Silks, foils and unbacked types come in 27in. and 30in. widths. Alternatively, a suitable fabric can be bought by the foot from a store.

Preparing the wall

Thick fabrics, such as burlap, linen and grasscloth, help to disguise irregularities in a wall, but thinner materials, such as foils, tend to exaggerate them. So, with the latter, thorough preparation is even more important than with traditional wallpaper. It is best to hang lining paper and then, if the covering is semi-transparent, apply a coat of neutral latex before hanging.

Hanging techniques

Coverings with a paper backing are usually easier to hang than those without and can be pasted like normal wallpaper. (*See Job 18, p. 36.*) With fine materials, such as silks, it is best to paste the wall not the fabric. Great care is needed when hanging any fabric to avoid stretching or staining it, even though many coverings are now made for easy hanging and can be spot cleaned.

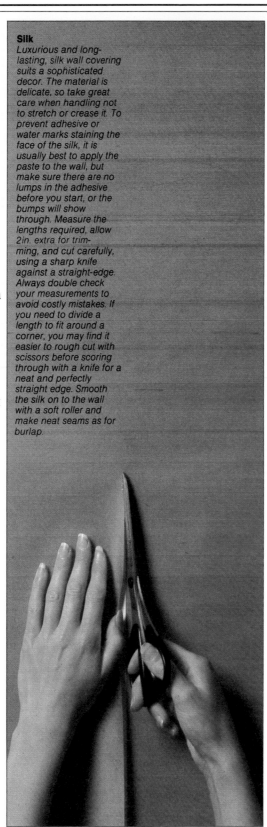

Silk
Luxurious and long-lasting, silk wall covering suits a sophisticated decor. The material is delicate, so take great care when handling not to stretch or crease it. To prevent adhesive or water marks staining the face of the silk, it is usually best to apply the paste to the wall, but make sure there are no lumps in the adhesive before you start, or the bumps will show through. Measure the lengths required, allow 2in. extra for trimming, and cut carefully, using a sharp knife against a straight-edge. Always double check your measurements to avoid costly mistakes. If you need to divide a length to fit around a corner, you may find it easier to rough cut with scissors before scoring through with a knife for a neat and perfectly straight edge. Smooth the silk on to the wall with a soft roller and make neat seams as for burlap.

Burlap
This resilient fabric is available with or without a paper backing and in a wide range of colors and patterns. Paper-backed burlap is pasted and hung like traditional wallpaper with a layer of adhesive on the back. With unbacked burlap, you paste the wall before hanging cut lengths. Flatten each strip into place with a roller, and take care not to pull the material or it will stretch and leave an uneven surface. Overlap successive strips and complete all the walls before trimming, in case the burlap shrinks. Trim top and bottom with a sharp knife against a wide-bladed scraper. Make neat seams by cutting through each overlap with a very sharp knife held against a steel straight-edge. Remove the offcut and press down the join.

Fabric

Fabrics designed as wall coverings have a paper backing, but you can buy material off the roll from furnishing stores. Choose a color-fast shrink- and stretch-proof fabric and avoid ones that will attract dust – a slightly shiny finish, for example. Choosing an easily-matched pattern will make the job simpler, too. With most fabrics, it is best to paste the wall and then gently smooth the fabric into place with a paint roller. When the adhesive is dry, trim the edges with a sharp knife against a straight-edge, and make seams in the same way as for burlap.

Foil

Made from metallized plastic film on a paper backing, foil provides a reflective surface. This makes it an ideal covering for bathrooms, but only on walls that are perfectly smooth, as any irregularities will be exaggerated. Two types of foil are available; ordinary and ready-pasted. With the ordinary type, each length is pasted with a foam roller. The ready-pasted type is immersed in a trough of water to activate the paste. Hang the foil from the top down and smooth it on to the wall with a clean sponge. Take care to match the pattern accurately and to get the design straight, since any mis-matching will show up glaringly. Trim the top and bottom edges, butt join the lengths and flatten the joints with a seam roller.

Grasscloth

Oriental in origin, this woven fabric is made from natural grasses woven with cotton and glued to a paper backing. To hang grasscloth, paste it in the same way as normal wallpaper, but cover the face of the pasting table first with a strip of lining paper, to protect the face of the fabric from adhesive and scratching. Do not fold the cloth or you will be left with hard crease lines. Apply lengths directly to the wall and smooth them down with a clean roller. Crease a trimming line at the wall-ceiling angle and at the baseboard, using a piece of cardboard. When the adhesive is dry, but not before, trim each length with a sharp knife against a steel straight-edge.

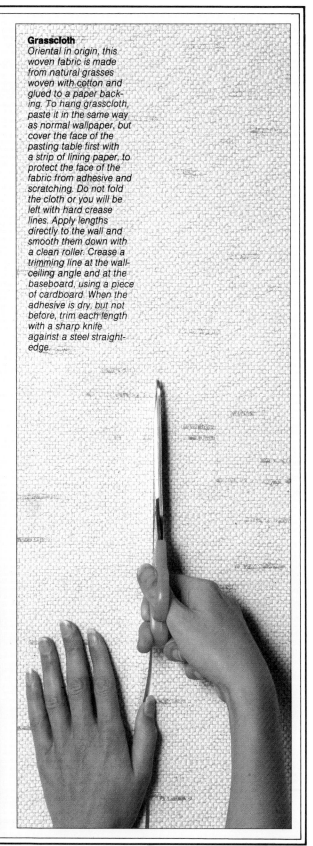

Tiling

Estimating time and quantities
Tools and equipment
Working out the tiling sequence
Fixing ceiling tiles
How to apply ceramic wall
tiles ◇ Fixing mosaic, mirror
and cork tiles ◇ How to lay
ceramic floor tiles

Tiles are resistant to water, heat and most household chemicals. They are hard-wearing, easy-to-clean and demand little maintenance. Although time-consuming, the laying of tiles requires no special skill, particularly with modern adhesives and lightweight tiles. In many cases, tiles prove easier to lay than material from the roll and, since they may be bought in small quantities, result in less wastage.

Beyond the wide range of ceramics, tiles are now produced in a variety of materials. Cork, brick, mirrored glass, vinyl, fiberboard and steel tiles offer new textures and can be fitted in much the same way as ceramic. Transfer, mural and mosaic tiles have opened up new individual design possibilities, and heat-, frost-resistant and other special-purpose tiles have broadened their practical value.

Points to remember

◇ Always take time to plan the job carefully before laying tiles. The position of the first tile determines the end result.
◇ Remember to allow for grouting joints when mapping out the tiling area.
◇ Choose adhesives and grouting to suit both the tiles and room conditions.

For more information on types of tile, see Choosing materials, pp. 122-5.

Estimating time

The time needed to tile a surface depends on the size of the area to be covered, the size of the tiles, the amount of preliminary preparation needed and, to some extent, your experience. A good result can only be achieved by careful planning, so always take the time to work out the best starting point and laying sequence. The times below give an approximate guide to the amount of time needed for each job. Remember to allow time for the adhesive to dry before grouting can be applied. The preparation time in each case will depend on the condition of the surface.

Fiberboard ceiling tiles
(10ft × 13ft)

Installing furring strips

(4) - (6) **hours**

Hanging full tiles

(3) - (4) **hours**

Replacing a damaged tile

($\frac{1}{2}$) **hours**

Wall tiles (6½ft long × 8ft high wall)

Ceramic tiles
Planning and installing furring strips

(1) - (2) **hours**

Laying tiles (incl. an average number of tiles to be cut)

(3) - (4) **hours**

Grouting

($\frac{1}{2}$) **hour**

Finishing (beading, filling or edge pieces)

(1) - (1½) **hours**

Cork tiles
Planning

(1) - (2) **hours**

Laying tiles (incl. an average number of tiles to be cut)

(1½) - (2) **hours**

Varnish (2 coats)

(1) **hour**

Wall tiles contd

Mirror tiles
Planning

(2) **hour**

Laying tiles (incl. an average number to be cut)

(1) **hour**

Brick tiles
Planning

(1) - (2) **hours**

Laying (incl. an average number of tiles to be cut)

(2) - (3) **hours**

Filling joints

(2) - (3) **hours**

Floor tiles (10ft × 13ft)

Setting out the floor (for all types of tile)

(1) **hour**

Laying (self-adhesive vinyl plastic tiles, incl. an average number of tiles to be cut)

(3) - (4) **hours**

Laying (ceramic tiles, incl. average number to be cut)

(8) - (10) **hours**

Grouting joints (for ceramic tiles)

(3) - (4) **hours**

Estimating quantities

The same method of calculating the number of tiles required can be used for all types of tile. First make a plan of the area to be covered and measure the length of each edge, then work out how many tile widths will fit into each. For example, a 10ft × 13ft room with 12in. square tiles will need 13 tiles along the 13ft wall and 10 along the 10ft wall, so 13 × 10 = 130 tiles are needed in total. For large areas with obstructions, divide the area into smaller squares, then add up a total. Since tiles are usually sold in boxes of a set amount, this may allow for wastage. If you are buying them loose, however, you should add an extra 5 per cent for accidental damage.

Tile size

4in. × 4in.

Mirror wall tiles
Ceramic wall tiles

6in. × 6in.

Mirror wall tiles
Ceramic wall tiles
Ceramic floor tiles

4in. × 6in.

Ceramic floor tiles

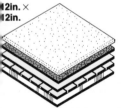

12in. × 12in.

Fiberboard ceiling tiles
Cork wall/floor tiles
Vinyl wall/floor tiles
Mosaic floor tiles
Mirror wall tiles

Calculating the number of tiles

Area to be tiled (sq ft)	Number of tiles needed			
	4 × 4	6 × 6	4 × 6	12 × 12
3	27	12	18	3
6	54	24	36	6
9	81	36	54	9
12	108	48	72	12
15	135	60	90	15
18	162	72	108	18
21	189	84	126	21
24	216	96	144	24
27	243	108	162	27

Tools and equipment

For a good result, the correct tiling tools are essential; they cannot be improvised. Always ensure that you have the correct adhesive and grouting (if needed) for the type of tile and situation, and in sufficient quantities. A flexible waterproof sealant is useful to fill gaps around baths or sinks. Plastic spacer lugs are also available for ceramic wall tiles that are not already self-spacing.

Fiberboard tiles
Tools for preparation work include graph paper for drawing a plan to scale, and $2\frac{1}{2}$in. nails and a hammer for pinning furring strips to the joists. A 12in. strip of wood is also useful as a spacer bar when installing furring strips and you may need some wooden shims. To cut border tiles, you will need a straight-edge and a utility knife and for securing tiles to the furring strips and joists, you will need a staple gun and $\frac{9}{16}$in. staples. For cutting around obstructions you may need a compass and a keyhole saw or a saber saw. For replacing a damaged tile, use a knife and a prybar to remove the old tile, pliers to take out old staples and install the new tile with a synthetic latex mastic adhesive for a secure fixing. If you want to pin up molding to fill gaps at the edges, you can use the same $2\frac{1}{2}$in. nails as for nailing the furring strips.

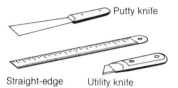

Putty knife
Straight-edge   Utility knife
Hammer
Staple gun
Small handsaw

Ceramic wall and floor tiles
The essential tools for ceramic tiling include a trowel or spatula for applying adhesive to the wall or floor, and a notched spreader which is drawn evenly through the adhesive to leave a series of ridged lines on which to bed the tiles. Many types of tile cutter are available, some incorporating a measuring gauge for marking an accurate cutting line. For fitting around pipes and other awkward areas, tile clippers, pincers or a tile saw (see p. 218) should be used. A tile file is also available for smoothing rough edges. Finally, you will need a rubber grouter or sponge for filling the joints with grout, and a large sponge for wiping the tiles clean. With wall tiles, you will need a hammer, screwdriver and carpenter's level for fixing the battens.

Adhesives
Always choose waterproof adhesive in damp situations, such as shower cubicles and sink splashbacks, where ceramic tiles are likely to be soaked regularly with water. There is no need to change adhesives halfway through a job, so continue with waterproof adhesive if this proves more convenient. Thin-bed adhesive, which is spread about $\frac{1}{8}$in. thick, is normally used in preference to the thick-bed type, which is more difficult to use.

Grouting
Cement grout is supplied as powder to be mixed with water into a creamy paste. For color add a powdered pigment, or use a ready-mixed colored grout.

 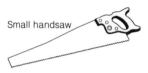

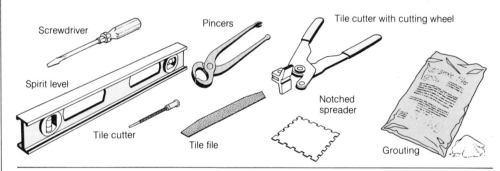

Screwdriver   Pincers   Tile cutter with cutting wheel
Spirit level
Tile cutter   Tile file   Notched spreader   Grouting

Mirror tiles
Since they are supplied with adhesive tabs, no equipment is needed beyond the basic measuring and cutting and leveling tools.

Cork wall and floor tiles
Measuring, marking and cutting tools are required in addition to a cork wall- or floor-tile adhesive.

Brick tiles
These tiles are difficult to cut so use an electric grinder, a circular power saw fitted with a masonry disc, or a tungsten-carbide rod saw fitted in a hacksaw frame. Use brick tile adhesive; and for pointing the joints, a dry mortar mix or a pointing compound and a brick jointer.

Vinyl and plastic
You will need stringlines for marking out the floor, and a sharp knife or scissors and a straight-edge for cutting the tiles. Use vinyl flooring adhesive if the tiles are not self-adhesive. As with cork floor tiles, no grouting is needed, since the tiles butt up closely against each other.

32

Preparing the surface

All surfaces must be sound, level and dry before tiling begins. Strip off any wall or floor covering material and flaking paint. Rub down sound alkyd to take off the shine and roughen the surface for tile adhesive. If a layer of old ceramic tiles is flat, firmly fixed and well abraded, new ceramic tiles can be applied on top.

Stripping off old tiles

If you choose to remove existing ceramic tiles, use a brick chisel and club hammer or a small hammer with a chasing tool – all usually obtainable for rent from a local builder's supply store.

If necessary reline the surface with concrete composition backerboard with fiberglass lining.

Testing for level surface

It is difficult to align tiles unless the wall or floor is perfectly flat. Hold a long, flat piece of wood against the surface vertically, horizontally and diagonally to test for "see-sawing".

33

Marking out a center point on floors

A well-planned room will have equal-sized tiles at edges and corners, to give the area a symmetrical look. To achieve this effect, you should start in the center of the area to be tiled. If you simply begin from a corner, you may end up with whole tiles one side and narrow slivers the other. So the first task is to find the center of each side of the square or rectangle to be tiled, then snap a chalked stringline between both pairs of sides, to form a cross. Where the two lines intersect is the central starting point. (*For a starting point on walls, see Job 41, p. 50.*)

Dealing with crooked areas

If the work area is an irregular shape, it is usually better to line up the first row of tiles parallel with the wall opposite the main door. Snap a chalked stringline parallel with this wall, then, using a compass to scribe arcs, snap a second at right angles to the first. Finally, snap a third at right angles to the second, in the center of the room. This cross gives the position of the first tile.

Where to place the first tile
Once the center point has been marked, the first tile may be laid in one of four positions (below). Before applying adhesive, plan out two rows of tiles at right angles to each other. If you are left with less than a half-tile gap at the edge, reposition the first tile at the center point, using one of the other options, and try again. When the correct position is established, re-strike the stringlines before starting to tile, to clarify the guide lines.

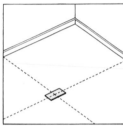
Centered on the cross

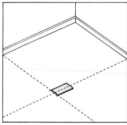
Centered on a guide line

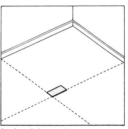
In the right angle

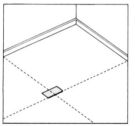
Centered on the other line

34

Working out the tiling sequence

It is best to tackle an area by dividing the job up into four segments sketched out by the chalklines. Fix the tiles diagonally across the square, to ensure that an equal number of cut tiles of the same size will be needed at each border. Work outward in both directions from the first tile, to form a right angle and fill in the gaps as you go. If, however, the area is irregular, you may need to use a piece of wood to mark off the tile widths (*see Job 41, p. 50*).

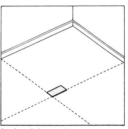
Work outward in squares from the center point

Tiles offer countless opportunities for individual style and pattern, since they are laid individually and come in a vast array of colors, shapes, textures and patterns. However, it is important not to 'overdo' it. The best effects are usually created with the clever combination of plain or textured tiles in one or two colors. In most cases, patterned tiles should be restricted to a single wall in an otherwise plain-tiled room, or interspersed individually or in rows among complementary plain tiles. Murals can be effective if the style and scale are well chosen.

Decorative effects with tiling

Soft and sophisticated hallways

Cool to the touch, but warm to the eye, quarry tiles (top left) comple- ment the soft neutral colors of an entrance hall and the natural pine finish of a kitchen, giving a warm continuity to the entire area. Traditional quarry and brick tiles in earth colors look par- ticularly apt in country- style kitchens and patios. Stark black and white vinyl tiles (left), can look important, especially if laid diagonally. A bold, black and white floor, however, needs to be offset by low-key walls.

Increasing the space

An all-over mosaic design (above) taken over the floor, the walls and the side of the bath adds a touch of class to a simple bathroom, and gives a feeling of space. The muted effect helps to offset the white of the bath and basin and allows changeable accessories to create a splash of color. In a small room, like a bath- room, use a single back- ground color, to avoid dividing the room into disparate blocks of color. With patterned mosaic tiles, choose small designs for a small room.

Reducing the space

Warm, advancing colors help to make a large, airy bathroom feel more cozy (left). The cherry floor color taken a short way up the walls helps to reduce the height of the room; and blue tiles interspersed in the tiled area help to break up the spread of color and soften the monochrome effect. If a large expanse of single-colored tiling is to be used, colored grouting can relieve the effect and complement or contrast the basic color.

35
Marking out a ceiling for fiberboard tiles

Fiberboard tiles can be cemented directly on to a wallboard or plaster ceiling if it is perfectly sound and level. But if the ceiling is not in perfect condition or if the joists are exposed, it is best to install parallel rows of 1in. × 2in. furring strips, nailed at right angles to the joists. These are spaced at 12in. intervals, so that they form a grid network with the joists to support the 12in. tiles. Unless your ceiling is an exact and even number of feet in both directions, you will need to allow for border tiles. To ensure a symmetrical result, it is important to plan out the job carefully, so that the border tiles are the same size at opposite ends of the ceiling. This means that the edge furring strips are positioned to accommodate these border tiles. Before you start work you will have to locate the joists by tapping the ceiling until you hear a solid sound. To detect the direction of the joists, continue tapping in a straight line in front of you. If the sound is in turns hollow and solid at 16in. intervals, the joists are running at right angles to you. If the sound is continuously solid, you are tracing a joist. When you have mapped out your ceiling plan, make a note of the position of any light fixtures.

Planning out a ceiling
First measure the ceiling, make a plan, drawn to scale on graph paper and mark on the position of the joists. To establish the position of the furring strips, first work out the border tiles. If, for example, the ceiling is 8ft 10in. wide by 13ft 6in. long, you will need 8 full tiles on the width with 5in. border tiles at each end; and 12 full tiles on the length with 9in. border tiles at each end. Mark on the first furring strip flush with a wall and at right angles to the joists, then the second, the size of the border tile from the first strip. Space the rest of the strips at 12in. intervals, but again allow for a border tile at the far end. Follow this plan closely as you work.

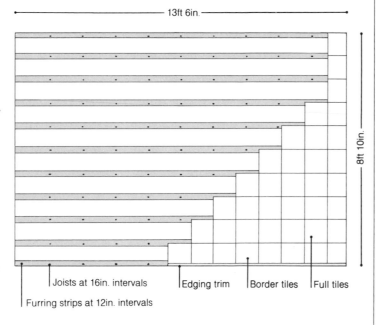

Joists at 16in. intervals | Edging trim | Border tiles | Full tiles
Furring strips at 12in. intervals
13ft 6in.
8ft 10in.

36
Installing furring strips

The furring strips are cut to size and positioned as calculated on the plan – the first and last against the wall, the second and second-to-last allowing for a border tile and the rest at 12in. intervals. Each strip is nailed to the joists with 2½in. nails. To ensure even spacing between the strips, you could cut a 12in. strip of wood to use as a spacer bar. When all the strips are in place, you should check that they are level, and pack them with shims if necessary.

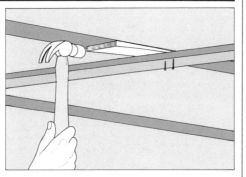

Packing with shims
If the furring strips are not level, insert shims at appropriate points between the joists and the strip and nail through the three layers.

37
Applying fiberboard border tiles

Border tiles are fitted first, so that the work begins in a corner and continues first along one wall, then along the adjacent one. Before you start, you will need to snap one chalkline down the second furring strip and another at right angles to it, a border tile width away from the wall. These provide guide lines to ensure that the border tiles are positioned accurately. Fiberboard tiles need time to adjust to the temperature and humidity of the room, so remove them from their packaging 24 hours before you start work. The tiles are then cut to the size established on the plan, allowing for a small space next to the wall for edging trim, before they are secured into position.

Cutting and securing a border tile
Refer to the plan for the required tile measurements, and deduct a fraction of an inch to allow for a small space next to the wall. Transfer these measurements on to the tile and, using a steel straight-edge and a utility knife, cut off the tongued edge, 1. Position the tile with the cut edge towards the wall and nail it to the first furring strips with 1¼in. nails, 2, then staple the flange of the groove to the second strip.

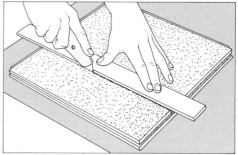

1 Cut the border tile with a sharp utility knife

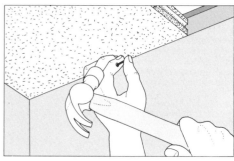

2 Nail the cut edge of the tile to the first furring strip

38
Applying uncut fiberboard tiles

When border tiles are in position along two walls, the full tiles can be added. The tongues of the full tiles slot into the grooves of the border tiles, and the full tiles are secured on the other edge by stapling through the groove flange into the next furring strip. The next row of full tiles will then slot into the grooves of the previous row and so on until the ceiling is covered. At the far end, border tiles will have to be fitted along the last two walls to complete the job (*see Job 37, left*). You will find, however, that the groove edge instead of the tongue edge will have to be cut off these last two rows of border tiles, so that the tongues will slot into the last row of full tiles. When tiling is complete, a narrow trim of pre-stained wooden molding can be added around the perimeter of the ceiling for a neat finish and to conceal the nail heads in the border tiles. This trim is pinned to the joists or wall studs with $2\frac{1}{2}$in. nails.

Stapling a tile into place
*Slide the tongue of the tile into the groove of the border tile, check that it is well lodged, then staple through the flange of the grooved edge into the furring strip, using coated staples, **1**. Insert three evenly-spaced staples on the leading edge of the tile and a fourth in the back corner, **2**, for added support. To fit subsequent tiles, follow the same principle, sliding the tongued edges into the grooved edges. Always check that the tiles in one row are all facing the same way and check that the rows are straight as you work.*

1 *Staple through the flange of the groove into the furring strip*

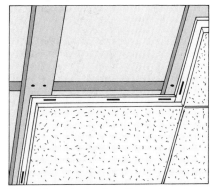

2 *Insert three staples down the leading edge and another in the back corner*

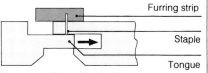

Furring strip
Staple
Tongue

The tongue fits neatly into the stapled groove

39
Tiling around an outlet box

You may have to cut a hole in at least one tile to accommodate a light fixture. To locate the cutting point, you will have to hold one edge against the outlet box and mark off its center point against the tile edge. You will then have to swivel the tile round to hold its adjacent edge against the box and again mark off the center point of the outlet box. If a line is extended from each mark, the two lines will intersect. This point marks the center of the fitting. A compass set to half the width of the box can then be used to trace a circular cutting line.

Finding the cutting line
Extend a line from the marks on both edges of the tile, indicating the halfway point of the box. Where they cross, put the point of a compass set to half the width of the box. Trace a circle and cut it out with a keyhole saw, then slide the tile over the fitting.

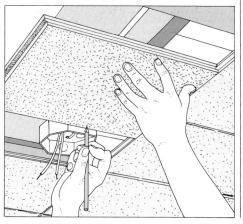

40
Replacing a damaged ceiling tile

Bad stains can be concealed by applying sealer and painting the entire ceiling with latex paint. Damaged tiles, on the other hand, will have to be replaced. These are cut free by working a knife through the staples on all four sides and pried out with a prybar. The cut tongues will still be in place in the grooves of adjacent tiles and will also have to be pried free. When all the remaining staples have been removed with a set of pliers or carpenter's pincers, a band of adhesive is spread on the furring strips. The new tile is then prepared for fitting. To ensure a neat fit, the tongue is cut from one of the edges and the tile is glued into place.

Removing and replacing a tile
*Use a sharp utility knife to sever through the tongues and staples, **1**, then pry the old tile out with a prybar. Remove the tongues lodged in the grooves of neighboring tiles and pull out any remaining staples with a pair of pliers. Cut off the tongue from the one of the edges of the new tile, and apply adhesive to the furring strips or joists, **2**. Then slide the tongue of the new tile into a groove and press the tile into position. Hold it until the adhesive has set.*

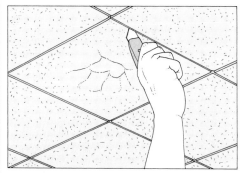

1 *Cut through the staples and tongues on each side*

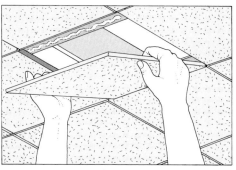

2 *Slot the tile into place and press it on to a band of adhesive on the furring strip*

41

Marking out a wall for tiling

It is unusual to be able to tile a wall without having to cut some tiles for the edges of the work. So, to ensure equal-sized border tiles, plan out the job carefully. The simplest way is to mark out your tile widths (of, for example 4in. or 12in.) on a piece of wood, say 6ft long. By holding the wood horizontally and vertically on a wall, you will quickly see how the tiles will end up from any given starting point.

Marking true horizontals and verticals
Since few rooms can claim to have perfectly true corners, window and door frames, these cannot be used as a guide for the first row of vertical tiles. Likewise, baseboards cannot be used as a horizontal base. Instead, you must establish a vertical pencil line, using a plumb line (see Job 17, p. 34), and set up a true horizontal, using a carpenter's level, by nailing a wooden batten to the foot of the wall. This will form a base for the first course of tiles.

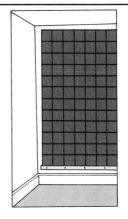

Outlining the area
Set up a true vertical and horizontal as a frame for the whole tiles. If a row of cut tiles is inevitable, these should fall along the baseboard, in the space left by the batten and in the corners. Try to avoid using cut tiles for the top course of tiles, unless the ceiling is crooked. If the walls are crooked, you will have to use some cut tiles to compensate.

Basic technique

How to apply ceramic wall tiles

Having established vertical and horizontal guide lines, the outlined area can be filled with whole tiles. The tiles are applied in horizontal rows from the bottom up, working in areas of 1yd². When the tiles have been in position for 24 hours, the horizontal batten can be removed and the borders filled with tiles cut to size. If plastic spacers have been used, they can also be removed at this stage and kept for re-use. After 24 hours, the joins between the tiles are grouted. Finally, the tiles are sponged clean and, when dry, are polished with a clean cloth.

Laying the first block of tiles
Beginning with the bottom left-hand corner, smooth a layer of adhesive over about 9ft² of wall, with a trowel. Then draw a notched spreader horizontally over the area so that its teeth touch the surface, 1. This will create uniform ridge lines through the adhesive. Place the first tile on the batten, 2, lined up against the vertical line and press it firmly into the adhesive with a slight twist. Continue laying the tiles in horizontal strips. If the tiles are self-spacing, butt them up closely so that the lugs are touching. If not, insert plastic spacers for uniform grouting lines, 3. When the first 9ft² is complete, check that the tiles are straight by holding a carpenter's level to the edges, 4, and make any necessary adjustments. Spread adhesive over the adjacent 9ft² of wall and continue to tile as before.

1 *Spread adhesive over the first 9ft²*

2 *Fix the first tile in the bottom corner*

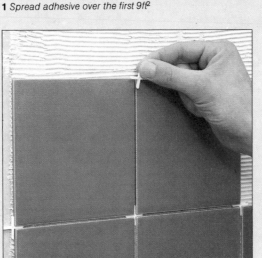
3 *Insert plastic spacers if the tiles have no lugs*

4 *Check the tile courses with a carpenter's level*

42

Cutting ceramic tiles

When all the whole tiles are in position, you may need to cut tiles for the borders. The tile to be cut is lined up on the wall, measured up against the gap, and marked with a pencil for cutting. There are various tile-cutting gadgets available, some incorporating a measuring and marking gauge. A regular tile cutter has a sharp, tungsten carbide tip, which scores on the glaze so that the tile can be snapped in half along the score line. Another type of tile cutter contains a small cutting wheel to score the glaze, and jaws to hold the tile. When the handles are squeezed, the jaws close and break the tile. If the cut edge is rough, it can be smoothed down with a tile file.

Using a tile cutter
If you are using a regular tile cutter, place the tile on a flat surface, decorative side up, and score a single line through the glaze, using a try square as a guide, 1. Exert even pressure on the tile to ensure a straight cut through the glaze. Place two kitchen matchsticks or pencils under the tile, one at each end and in line with the scored line. Press downward on either side of the tile until it breaks cleanly, 2. With the clamp-like cutter, place the tile in the jaws and squeeze.

1 Run the tile cutter across the glaze

2 Press each side to snap the tile

43

Shaping ceramic tiles

Where a specially shaped tile is needed, make a cardboard template of the shape you want and then transfer it to the tile. To cut out an L-shape (around a switch, for example), a pattern of the shape is traced on to the tile. The tile is then scored deeply and evenly along the cutting line. To break up the glaze, criss-cross shapes are scored through the waste portion of the tile. These can then be chipped away with tile clippers or ordinary pincers. If you have a lot of awkward-shaped tiles to cut, it would be worth buying a tile saw, which cuts the tile while it is held in a vice. A tile saw will almost certainly be needed if slivers of tile (less than $\frac{1}{2}$in.) have to be cut, although these should not be necessary if the job is well planned. To cut around pipes, the tile is split in two and an arc is nibbled from each half. Alternatively, use a tile saw.

Cutting an L-shape
To fit a tile round an obstacle, you may need to cut out an L-shaped tile. Either use a tile saw or make a template of the shape and trace the lines on to the tile. With a smooth motion, score deeply along the lines with a tile cutter, to pierce the glaze, 1. Then score criss-cross lines through the segment to be cut and clip it off in small pieces, 2. Trim to the deeply scored lines, then smooth the edges.

Cutting around a pipe
The easiest way to mark the position of a hole for a pipe is to make a paper template of the shape. Trace the outline on to the tile, then cut the tile in half. Chip or saw away an arc from each half, smooth the edge, then fit the tile.

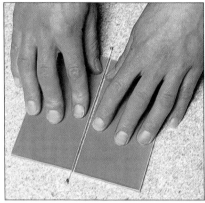

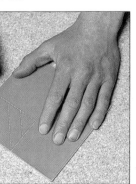

1 Score across the section to be cut

2 Chip away the waste section of the tile

44

Grouting ceramic tiles

When the tiles have been in place for about 48 hours, fill the joints with grouting cement. Grouting is sold ready-mixed, but it is more economical to use powdered grout to which you add water and mix until it forms a creamy consistency. Colored grout is also available – ready-mixed, as a dye to be added to the powder, or as a paint to be applied to the joints over old grouting.

Applying the grouting
Spread the grouting on to the surface of the tiles and, using a rubber squeegee-blade or a piece of damp sponge, 1, work it well into the cracks between the tiles. When the area is covered, draw a small rounded stick into each joint, 2, to press the grouting tightly home.

1 Work grouting well into the gaps with a sponge or rubber squeegee-blade

2 Run a rounded stick between the joints for a neat finish

45
Fixing mosaic tiles

Ceramic mosaic tiles are supplied as a sheet on a mesh backing and fixed to the wall with normal tile adhesive. Since the sheets may be as large as 13in. × 19½in., the main area of wall should be completed quickly, leaving borders and awkward shapes until last. As with normal tiles, meticulous planning and preparation are essential, and horizontal and vertical guide lines should be marked (*see Job 41, p. 50*). Having spread adhesive on the wall, press the sheets firmly into place, ensuring that any arrows on the back face the same way. To fit into corners and around obstacles, cut pieces to the required shape, and fix them to the gap. If protective paper covers the face of the tiling sheets, leave it on until they are securely fixed, then finish the job by grouting between the joints. Any small gaps may be filled with grouting.

Fitting border pieces
When the main area of the wall is covered by whole sheets, smaller pieces can be cut for the borders and to fit around obstacles. Measure the width and length of the area to be filled, then turn the sheet upside down and mark cutting lines on the back. Using a

sharp knife, slice through the mesh backing, **1,** *apply adhesive to the wall and fix the strip in place,* **2.** *Make sure the border piece is perfectly aligned with the adjacent sheet. If any small gaps remain at the edge, break off individual tiles from the sheet with a tile cutter and slot them into the space.*

1 *For border pieces, cut through the mesh backing*

2 *Align border strips with the main sheet*

46
Fixing ceramic tile accessories

Tile accessories, such as towel rings, soap dishes and tooth-brush holders, are either screw-fixed or glued to the wall. Those with a ceramic base the size of one or two tiles are fixed using standard tile adhesive.

Adhesive fixing
Fix one or two tiles (the size of the accessory base) lightly in position. After 48 hours, remove the tiles, "butter" adhesive on the back of the accessory and push it into place. Secure it in place for 48 hours, using adhesive tape. Finally remove the tape and fill the joint around the edges with grout.

Screw fixing
To fix a screw into ceramic tiles, you will need a masonry drill bit for use in an electric drill. Do not attempt to drill straight into a tile, since the bit may slide around erratically. Instead, stick adhesive tape over the hole position then drill

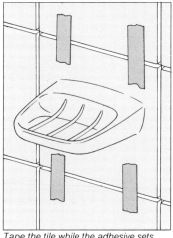
Tape the tile while the adhesive sets

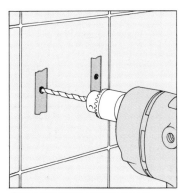
Drill a screw hole through tape to prevent the drill bit slipping

47
Finishing off

To prevent water seeping behind baths, basins and sinks, run a bead of silicone rubber sealant along the edges. This will remain flexible and so keep the gap permanently sealed despite any movement.

Smooth edging
At external corners, on a window sill, for example, a special plastic beading will form a neat, rounded finish to the edge tiles. The flat strip is bedded well down into the adhesive with the larger lip resting on the sill edge. The last course of tiles on the sill then butts up against the rounded lip. If cut tiles are inevitable on a window sill, these should lie at the back of the sill.

Over-tiling
If a wall has been half-tiled over existing tiles, the top rim needs to be smoothed off. The gap between wall and tiles can be filled with hardwood bead-ing – either plain or L-shaped – which will need varnish.

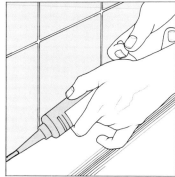
Use sealant around baths and basins to produce a waterproof seal

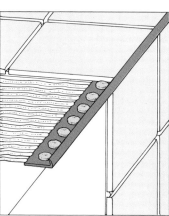
Add plastic beading to external corners for a neat finish

48
Fixing mirror tiles

Before applying these tiles, check that the surface is sound, dry and level. If it is of porous material, such as plaster or wood, seal it with a coat of oil-based paint, but do not use a high gloss. Leave it to dry for 72 hours. Remove any wallpaper from the area to be tiled and if the walls are cold, heat the room first, to ensure the tabs adhere firmly; newly plastered walls must be allowed to dry out. Tiles fixed to an un-even surface will produce a distorted reflection, so fix a sheet of concrete composition fiberglass-reinforced backer-board. The tiles must be perfectly aligned to achieve a good result, so mark guide lines (*see Job 41, p. 50*). If the sticky tabs used to fix the tiles are not already attached, they will have to be bought separately. Avoid other adhesives; they may cause discoloration. Mirror tiles are cut in the same way as glass and do not need grouting.

Applying the tiles to the wall
Remove the protective paper from the adhesive pads, 1, and, following the guide lines, as for ceramic tiles, place the tiles in horizontal rows, from the bottom of the wall up. Try to align the tiles accurately first time and leave a narrow gap between them, 2.

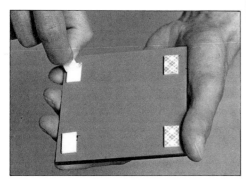

1 Peel off the protective paper

2 Leave a paper-thin gap between the tiles

49
Fixing cork wall tiles

Check that the wall is flat, smooth and dry before applying cork tiles. Fix a horizontal batten to the wall as a guide for the first row of tiles, draw a vertical guide, and proceed as for ceramic tiles (*see Basic technique, p. 50*). Using a special cork-tile adhesive, press the tiles firmly on to the wall, and butt joint them closely. If a tile has to be cut, place it on a flat surface and use a sharp knife held against a steel straight-edge. If the tiles are not pre-finished, apply a couple of coats of varnish sealer with a clean brush to leave an easy-clean surface. Allow the first coat to dry before adding the second. Where cork tiling is taken up to external corners, such as fireplaces, the exposed edges can be protected with wooden beading.

Cut cork tiles on a flat surface with a sharp knife held against a steel straight-edge

50
Fixing brick wall tiles

The secret of success with brick tiles lies in the careful planning of a realistic brick-bond pattern. The easiest way to plan the first few courses of brick is to draw them on to the wall. Butter the adhesive on the back of each tile, using a trowel or putty knife, and press the tile firmly on to the wall. As you lay each tile, insert spacers.

Cutting and pointing
To achieve an authentic look you will probably have to cut several bricks. Use either an electric grinder or circular power saw fitted with a masonry disc, or, though the method is slower, a tungsten-carbide rod saw fitted into a hacksaw frame.
   When the tiles have been in place for 24 hours, remove the spacers and fill the joints with mortar or pointing compound. Use a small pointing trowel or a filling knife and take care not to stain the bricks. If you prefer to avoid the labor of point-ing, paint the wall with gray latex paint before fixing the brick tiles.

Arranging the tiles
Lay out several rows of tiles on the floor to work out the most realistic brick-bond pattern and pencil the pattern on the wall as a guide. Stagger the joins to imitate a brick wall, 1, and where available, use L-shaped corner tiles for authen-ticity. To prevent the tiles slipping and to produce uniform joints, insert small pieces of wood, about ⅛ in. thick, between courses. Or saw up slabs of polystyrene packing material into small blocks.

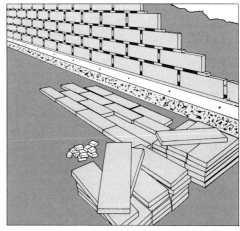

1 Keep a sample pattern on the floor as a guide while you fix the tiles

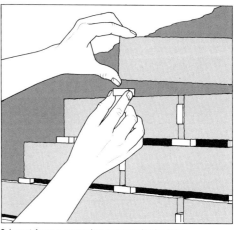

2 Insert foam or wooden spacers in the joints

51

Marking out a floor for tiling

When setting out and laying any type of tiled floor covering, always start in the middle of the room and work outward to the baseboards where tiles are cut to fit. Since few rooms are square, if you begin tiling against one baseboard, the tiles running along the adjacent wall will not run square. So mark the center point (*see Job 33, p. 46*), adjusting it to leave at least half-tile widths at each baseboard, then work outward. (*For Preparing the surface, see Job 32, p. 46.*)

Testing the tile height

Once you have planned out the job, test the height of the tiles against the door. If thick tiles are to be used, the door may bind against the new flooring. In this case, either remove the door and trim its lower edge, or fix rising butt hinges, to allow the door to rise as it opens.

52

Laying cork floor tiles

Cork-flooring adhesive is spread over an area of about 9ft² at a time and the tiles are laid in the same way as vinyl tiles. Some cork tiles are supplied ready sealed and waxed or coated with protective vinyl film and need no further treatment. Those sold without a protective, washable finish need to be sealed with wax or polyurethane before the room is used.

Use a template to trace the shape of architraves

53

Laying vinyl and plastic floor tiles

Most vinyl tiles are self-adhesive. The protective paper covering the adhesive on the backing should not be removed until the tile is ready to lay. If the tile is not self-adhesive, spread vinyl-tile adhesive over about 9ft² of the floor and cover it with tiles before applying adhesive to the next area. Always lay the tiles in the correct order (*see Job 34, p. 46*) and butt up the edges closely, taking care to press down each tile firmly all over, to ensure that it is well secured in the adhesive.

Cutting tiles to fit

At borders, mark and cut the tiles, taking care to match the design of any patterns. To cut edge tiles place the tile to be cut over the last full tile in the row, then put a marking tile on top, with its edge hard up against the baseboard. Using a marker, draw the opposite edge of the marking tile on the tile to be cut. Then cut along the line with scissors or a sharp knife held against a straight-edge.

For awkward shapes, such as around door architraves or pipes, make a cardboard template and transfer the shape on to the tile. When cutting a hole for a pipe, make a slit from the cut-out hole to the tile edge; it will then run from the back of the pipe to the baseboard, and be barely visible.

Removing the backing from self-adhesive tiles
Leave the protective paper intact when working out the starting point and cutting tiles. Just before laying, pull off the backing and stick down the tile. Try to align the tiles correctly first time. If the tiles need to be lifted and re-laid, the adhesive may weaken.

Cutting an L-shaped tile
One side of the L-shape will need to be the same width as adjacent border tiles. So use a marker tile to scribe the outline on to the tile to be cut, 1. Then move the tile round the corner and, in the same way, scribe the out-line of the gap to be filled on to the tile, 2. This line represents the second "leg" of the "L". Cut along the scribed lines, then fit the tile into place, so that it aligns accurately with neighboring tiles, 3. Alternatively, use a template.

1 *Use a marker tile to trace the gap between the baseboard and the last whole tile*

2 *Scribe the other side of the "L" on to the tile*

3 *Slide the tile into place*

Basic technique

How to lay ceramic floor tiles

The floor must be flat, dry, clean and stable before ceramic tiles are fitted. Timber floors should be well ventilated below and strong enough to support the tiling. The easiest way to provide a sound surface is to use either $\frac{1}{2}$in. exterior-grade particleboard or $\frac{1}{2}$in. plywood screwed to the floor at 12in. intervals. To ensure a good bond between the tiles and the floor, brush a primer over the whole floor and allow it to become "touch dry" before laying the tiles. (*For information on where to start, see Job 33, p. 46.*)

Applying floor adhesive
Ceramic floor-tile adhesive is supplied in large plastic buckets and should be prepared and applied according to the manufacturer's instructions. It is normal to stir the adhesive thoroughly and pour a thin layer over an area of about 1yd^2 at a time.

Fixing and grouting
Press and twist each tile into position so that it is well bedded down. When the first yd^2 is complete, clean away any surplus adhesive from the face of the tiles and clean out the joints, ready for grouting later. When the tiles have been in place for 24 hours, fill the joints with grouting. The tiles must not be walked on for at least 48 hours, however, so if grouting involves standing on the tiles, wait another 24 hours. It is best to tile a kitchen or bathroom in sections, so the room can be kept in use.

Fixing whole tiles
First ensure that the floor is clean and level, and, if it is wooden, apply a coat of primer, 1. Spread waterproof adhesive on the floor and, following your planned order of working (see Job 34, p. 46), bed each tile firmly into place, 2. Use chalked guide lines for positioning and work outward in both directions. Use spacer lugs if the tiles are not self-spacing.

Cutting and fixing border tiles
When all the whole tiles are in position and a narrow border remains to be covered, start cutting tiles to size. Lay the tile to be cut exactly over the last whole tile and half-cover them both with a marker tile, butted up against a spacer at the wall, 1. Trace its other (non-wall) edge on the tile, score along the line with a cutting knife, then snap the tile with heavy-duty

tile cutters, 2. Comb adhesive on to the back of the cut tile, 3, and carefully slot it into the gap, 4. Continue cutting and fitting until no gaps remain. After 24 hours, apply grouting flush with the tiles, and when the grout has set after a couple of hours, wipe the new floor with a damp cloth. Do not walk on the freshly laid tiles for 48 hours or you may dislodge them before the adhesive has solidified.

1 *Brush primer on to a wooden sub-floor*

1 *Mark the cutting line for an edge tile, allowing for a spacer lug*

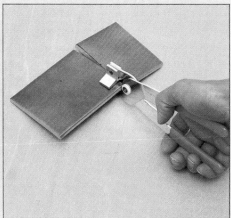

2 *Use tile cutters for a clean break*

2 *Press each whole tile firmly into the adhesive*

3 *Apply adhesive to the back of border tiles*

4 *Press the half-tile into the gap*

Carpeting

Estimating time and quantities
Preparing the floor ◇ Laying
padding ◇ How to lay and
stretch carpet ◇ Laying carpet
tiles ◇ Laying stair carpet
Carpet repairs

Carpets are available in a variety of materials and are constructed in one of three ways. Woven carpets such as Axminster and Wilton are made from tufts woven in with the backing; tufted types have the tufts inserted into a pre-woven backing; and non-woven carpets are bonded, not woven, on to the backing. The best indication of quality, however, is not the con- struction method, but how long the carpet is expected to last (*see Identifying carpet quality, p. 57*).

Manufacturers produce carpet in roll form (broadloom), in strips (body), in large squares or rect- angles (square) or as carpet tiles. The size and shape of the room will determine which type to choose. Carpet squares, for example, may have unbound edges if they are remnants from rolls and will be most suitable in a small room. Squares with bound edges, are intended for laying in the center of a room with a large area of floor visible around the edge. Carpet tiles are easy to lay and trim, and can be taken up easily to clean.

Points to remember

◇ Be sure to choose a suitable grade carpet for the room.
◇ Cure any damp problems first.
◇ Lay stair carpet with the pile running downward.

For more information on types of carpet, see Choosing materials, pp. 125-6.

Carpet types and widths

Broadloom carpet is the easiest type to lay in square or rectangular rooms. It is sold in roll widths ranging from 6ft to 18ft, but the most common widths are 9ft, 12ft and 15ft. Body carpet is useful for oddly-shaped rooms and for stairs and is sold in 3ft widths, although it can be professionally joined to form wider widths when necessary.

Padding
All carpets need a padding. Jute- or paper-backed rubber is the best type for most carpets, but where there is an under- floor heating system, use a heavy felt padding. Both are available in $4\frac{1}{2}$ft widths. Plastic foam padding may be suit- able in bedrooms, but it flattens easily and needs felt paper underneath to prevent the backing sticking to the floorboards. Felt paper, sold in 6ft and 3ft widths, is needed under foam-backed carpet and may also be used under rubber padding, if there are gaps between the floorboards that are not wide enough to warrant a layer of hardboard.

Estimating time

The time shown here give an idea of the comparative lengths of time needed to lay different types of carpet in a 13ft × 10ft room. In addition, time should be allowed for preparing the floor. On average, a solid floor will take $\frac{1}{4}$-$\frac{1}{2}$ hour to prepare, and a timber floor, a little longer. Likewise, straight stairs may take about $\frac{1}{2}$ hour and winding stairs perhaps $\frac{3}{4}$ hour. Carpet tiles take about 3-4 hours to lay.

Jute-backed carpet
Fixing tackless strip
(1)-(1½) hours

Laying padding
(¾)-(1¼) hours

Laying and stretching carpet
(1)-(2) hours

Trimming
(2)-(3) hours

Stair carpet
Carpeting straight stairs
(3)-(4) hours

Carpeting winding stairs
(3½)-(5) hours

Foam-backed carpet
Laying foam-backed carpet
(2½)-(3½) hours

Estimating quantities for floors

Some retailers will measure and estimate free. If this service is not available or if you wish to forecast and check the supplier's estimate, mark the measurements on a plan of the room. Then choose a suitable carpet width for the minimum of waste and calculate the length required. If your room is $15\frac{1}{2}$ft × $12\frac{1}{2}$ft and if a 13ft roll is not available, you would need a 12ft width with a 6in strip (if your supplier can match the pile direction). Or, you will have to use a 15ft width and waste a strip.

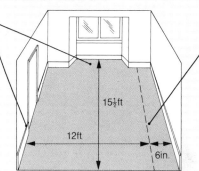

Drawing up a room plan
Sketch an outline of the room, including doors and windows. Measure the length and the width of the room, allowing for alcoves and doorways, then mark the maximum measurements on your plan. This will then act as a visual guide when you are calculating the most economic arrangement of lengths and joins.

15½ft

12ft

6in.

Where to position joins
If a standard carpet roll width will not fit con- veniently into your room, or if you are using carpet squares, you will have to make at least one join. Where possible, run the pile to face away from the light and position seams by a wall and at right angles to the main window. Do not lay strips in a doorway.

Estimating quantities for stairs

Either make an accurate plan for the supplier, or if you choose to estimate for yourself, follow these instructions. Assume that the landing carpet will overlap the top riser. Then, measure from the top tread over each tread and riser to the foot of the stairs. Add 1½in. to the total length of each tread to allow for the padding and for tucking into the tackless strips. Add a further 20in. to allow the carpet to be moved up or down occasionally to even out the wear. To establish the width of your carpet, measure the width of the treads, and if the treads have one open side, allow ¾in. for turning under at the edge.

Winding staircases

On winding stairs, measure along the outer edge for the longest length. Then allow 1½in. for tucking in the padding and an extra 20in. for moving the carpet, as with straight stair carpets.

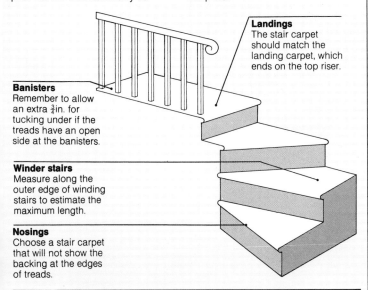

Banisters
Remember to allow an extra ¾in. for tucking under if the treads have an open side at the banisters.

Winder stairs
Measure along the outer edge of winding stairs to estimate the maximum length.

Nosings
Choose a stair carpet that will not show the backing at the edges of treads.

Landings
The stair carpet should match the landing carpet, which ends on the top riser.

Identifying carpet quality

Many woven and tufted carpets are classified into various "wear factor" categories, according to their quality. In addition most manufacturers and/or retailers have their own quality-grading system, which indicates how well the carpet will wear. Always choose the grade recommended for the purpose, or a better grade, because an inferior grade will prove a false economy, since it will not stand up well to the wear.

Grade	Type of carpet	Use
1	Light domestic	Bedrooms and secondary rooms with light traffic
2	Medium domestic Light contract	Secondary rooms
3	General domestic	Lightly used living rooms
4	Heavy domestic General contract	Heavily used areas, such as living rooms, halls, stairs
5	Heavy contract	Extremely heavily used areas
L	Luxury use	Long pile, better quality than Grade 3, but not for heavy traffic

Tools and equipment

The number of tools required depends on the type of carpet being laid. Foam-backed carpet simply demands cutting and fixing equipment, and carpet tiles may only need trimming. Jute-backed carpet, however, needs tools to ensure that it is stretched and securely attached.

Jute-backed carpet
A knee kicker, which ensures that the carpet is stretched taut, is the most important tool and is available for rent. Its head consists of forward-facing pins which pass through the pile and grip the backing of the carpet. These are adjustable to suit the thickness of the carpet pile. At the other end is a padded plate. The head is placed on the surface of the carpet so that the pins engage in the backing, and the pad is kicked with the muscle just above the knee cap, to smooth and tension the carpet.

Fixing equipment
Tackless strips hold the carpet taut after stretching, with an invisible fixing. The strips, which are nailed around the perimeter of the room or on to stairs, consist of plywood strips through which a series of angled nails protrude toward the skirting. The strips, about 1in. wide and ¼in. thick are usually available in 4ft and 5ft lengths and can be cut to length with a saw. They come with ordinary nails for fixing to wooden floors or with masonry nails for solid floors. Special angled strips are also obtainable for stair carpets. Carpet tacks, driven down into the pile, can be used instead of tackless strips and are needed to tack down the edge of a carpet along an open landing. Use ¾in. tacks where there is a double thickness and 1in. tacks at corners where there may be three thicknesses of carpet. Metal edging is a strip of aluminum, designed to give a neat and protective finish in doorways. Long lengths are available for finishing edges around stairwells, and double-sided edging can be used for the join between two carpets. Carpet tape, both self-adhesive and for use with adhesive, is used for joining carpet lengths.

Other essential tools
These include: a hammer and nail punch for fixing grippers; a utility knife, a straight-edge and cutting board; and a flat scraper, flat brick chisel or shim of wood for pressing carpet edges behind grippers.

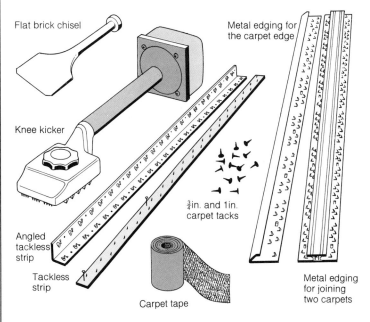

Flat brick chisel

Knee kicker

Metal edging for the carpet edge

Angled tackless strip

Tackless strip

¾in. and 1in. carpet tacks

Carpet tape

Metal edging for joining two carpets

Foam-backed carpet
For fixing down the edges, you will need double-sided adhesive tape or metal gripper strips with extra-large pins to penetrate the foam; also cutting tools and metal edging without pins.

Carpet tiles
In addition to cutting tools, you will need a chalkline for marking the room center, double-sided tape for fixing at doorways and in the room center; also metal edging.

Co-ordinating carpets

Choosing a carpet is an expensive decision, so it is tempting to "play safe" and settle for a plain carpet that will not "date" and will not need replacing with every redecoration. Nevertheless, a carpet can help to unify and bring life to a room; it can play visual tricks; it can suggest and reflect style; and it can bring interest to the flat expanse of the floor. But a carpet must be made to "work" with the decorating scheme. Its most important role is to co-ordinate with the walls, the furniture, furnishings and accessories. For good color balance, a room should be divided into three: 60 per cent covered in a basic color

Traditional designs
The rich color of oriental carpets create an appropriate, dignified backcloth for a traditional setting (right). Warm reds and golds breathe life into a subdued room and bring a luxurious, cozy feel to a study. Smaller oriental carpets and rugs laid in simple rooms often reflect Islamic or Far Eastern culture and lend an ethnic touch.

Modern designs
Geometrics are cool, clean and allow you to play games with shapes. A carpet with parallel stripes (right) for example, draws the eye from wall to wall and appears to elongate the room. A diagonal stripe on a winding stair (below), creates an intriguing network of angles with the lines of the banisters, and harmonizes with the conflicting shapes.

Achieving color balance
Traditionally, a carpet forms part of the basic color or the second color in a room, since it covers a large area. However, bright, accenting colors, introduced in the carpet can have an unusual and enlivening effect (right). The neutral charcoal gray background of the carpet co-ordinates with the gray furniture and furnishings, and offsets the plain white walls. This somber base forms a perfect canvas for splashes of stimulating color – vibrant, electric blue and pastels, bouncing between the carpet and the cushions. This focuses attention on the main living area of the room.

usually the walls and floor), 30 per cent in second color (often furnishings) and 0 per cent in a third, accenting color accessories). A fourth, neutral color woodwork) forms a useful link.

54
Preparing the floor

Before laying carpet you should check that the floor is smooth, dry, clean and firm. Repairs undertaken at this stage will save taking up the carpet later.

Hardwood floors
For information on replacing floorboards, see Basic Technique, pp. 68-9; for laying hardboard, see Job 75, p. 72; for laying particleboard, see Job 80, p. 74.

Solid floors
Concrete floors must be dry and smooth. Some slope toward a drain, others may be concealed beneath another surface. Undertake minor repairs but if the floor is uneven, apply leveling compound.

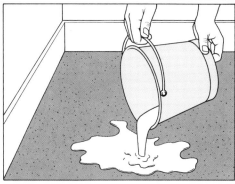

Applying leveling compound
Fill dents that are more than ¼ in. deep with mortar, remove grease and polish with steel wool soaked in alcohol. Apply a bonding and priming liquid to non-absorbent surfaces and dampen absorbent surfaces. Mix the compound with water until creamy, pour it on the floor, and spread it roughly with a trowel, working towards the door. The compound sets quickly and can be covered by carpet after 24 hours.

Minor repairs
To ensure that the surface is level, you may need to remove the existing floor covering. Take up vinyl sheeting, for example, and scrape away flaking or crumb-ling sections, 1. Vacuum the floor to remove dust and fill any indentations with cement mortar or filler. A coating of diluted pva bonding agent before filling will improve adhesion, 2.

1 Scrape off lumps and flaking pieces

2 Apply a coat of pva bonding agent before filling

55
Dealing with damp

If dampness is not detected and cured at an early stage, it will spread rapidly, and ruin any newly laid carpet. If you have noticed "tide marks" or if you suspect the room may be damp, test the area to see if the problem is caused by superficial condensation or water seepage. Before treatment for water seepage, ensure that the surface is clean and dust-free. (*For more information on the causes and treatment of damp and condensation, see pp. 204-7.*)

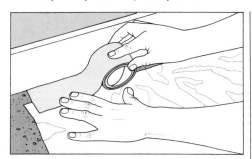

Testing for water seepage
Tape a square of plastic over the affected area of the floor, taking care to seal the edges. If moisture forms on the surface of the plastic, the cause is condensation, and the cure is better heating and ventilation. If droplets form on the underside, you have water seepage.

Curing water seepage
If the surface is dusty, vacuum the floor then apply a coat of diluted pva bonding agent and fill any indentations. Remove the baseboards and paint the floor with a waterproof sealing compound. Take the sealer up the wall a short way. Then replace the baseboards.

56

Fixing tackless strips

Before fitting padding, secure tackless strips around the edges of the room with the pins angled toward the wall. Leave a gap of about $\frac{1}{4}$in. between the strips and the wall to allow the edge of the carpet to be tucked down neatly against the baseboard. The strips should form a continuous line and shorter lengths can be butted together. On wooden floors, tackless strips can be nailed into position, but on concrete, use either hardened pins or an adhesive recommended by the manufacturer.

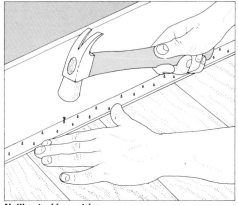

Nailing tackless strips
On wooden floors, nail strips around the edges of the room, using a hammer and nail punch. Position them $\frac{1}{4}$in. in from the baseboard, angled to the wall.

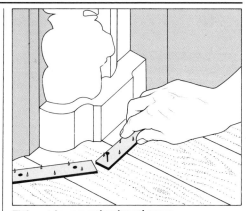

Fitting strips around awkward areas
Around curving places, such as door architraves, fireplaces and recesses, saw a strip into several short lengths and nail the pieces at each end.

57

Laying padding

A good-quality padding will improve a carpet's heat- and sound-insulating properties and will increase its life-expectancy. (*For information on padding, see Carpet types and widths, p. 56.*) The two chief types of padding are rubber and felt. They are fitted in slightly different ways because of their differing consistencies. and the fixing method is determined by the type of floor.

In most cases it is best to move the carpet into the room before fitting the padding. In this way, the padding is not disturbed when the carpet is dragged into the room. The carpet is then rolled back to allow the padding to be fitted.

If you are laying carpet over thermo-plastic tiles, always use felt instead of a rubber or plastic foam padding.

Securing rubber padding
Paper- or jute-backed padding must be laid rubber-side down. Cut the padding roughly to size and start fixing it in a corner of the room, with the carpet half rolled back. Then fasten it just inside the tackless strip running along an adjacent wall. On a wooden floor, secure the padding with rustproof staples or tacks, at 12in. intervals, 1. On a solid floor, anchor it with spots of adhesive. Next roll back the carpet on to the padding and fold back the other half. Then un-roll the rest of the pad-ding and fix it down at the far wall. When all sides are in position, trim the padding edges, so that they butt up against the tackless strip. If two pieces of padding need to be joined, overlap the edges of both pieces. Using a steel straight-edge and a sharp knife, 2, cut through both thicknesses then fix down the edges with adhesive, staples or tacks to form a neat seam.

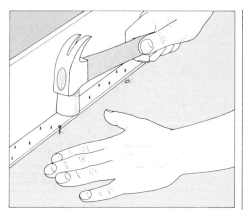

1 Tack or staple the padding on a timber floor

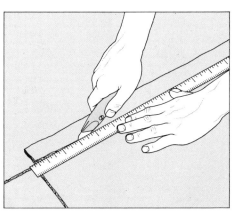

2 To make a join, cut through the overlapped edges

Securing felt-paper padding
A layer of felt-paper padding is essential under foam-backed carpet to prevent the foam backing sticking to the floor and for pro-tection if the backing begins to disintegrate. To form the padding first join strips of felt paper with heavy-duty adhesive tape, 1. Then secure it to the floor. On a wooden floor, fix down the paper with staples; on a solid floor, use adhesive, 2. In either case, the padding should stop 2in. from the baseboard so that double-sided adhesive tape can be used to secure the carpet edges. If felt paper is used under rubber or plastic foam padding to prevent dirt and dust rising from underneath the floor-boards, it should stop at the tackless strips. There is no need to allow an extra thickness of pad-ding in areas of heavy wear: this would produce a bump in the carpet and result in uneven wear.

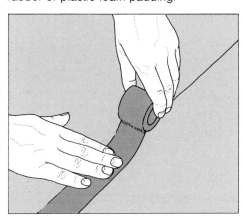

1 Use heavy tape to join felt-paper strips

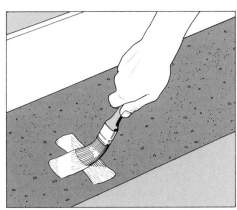

2 On a solid floor, fix the padding with adhesive

Basic technique

How to lay and stretch jute-back carpet

When the padding is down, the carpet can be rolled out on to the floor. It should be arranged so that the pile leans away from the light, to prevent uneven shading. It will save trimming the carpet along all four walls, if it is positioned so that only about ½in. of material turns up against two adjoining walls. The carpet is then fixed to the tackless strips or tacked on one side, stretched across the room and hooked on to the rest of the strips or tacked before trimming and finishing.

Fixing the carpet on to grippers

The first technique to master is how to secure the edge of the carpet on to the tackless strip. First bring the carpet to a corner and line it up so that it overlaps the tackless strips by ½in. on each wall. Push down the edge of the carpet with your fingers to hook its backing on to the tackless strip pins, 1, for about 12in. on each wall. Then rub along the tackless strip covered by carpet, with the side of a hammer or mallet, to ensure that the pins firmly engage into the carpet backing for a firm grip, 2.

Next, stretch the carpet across the room to an adjacent corner using the knee kicker and hook it on. Then complete the wall between the two corners.

Stretch the carpet across to the other corner and secure it on the tackless strip along the next wall. Finally, stretch and smooth the carpet right across the room, hook it into the corner and complete the last two walls, so that the surface of the carpet remains taut and wrinkle-free.

If you decide to use carpet tacks, insert temporary tacks about 6in. from the baseboard. When the carpet has been stretched in all directions, fold the edge under and drive tacks through the double thickness well down into the pile, at 6in. intervals, and remove the temporary tacks.

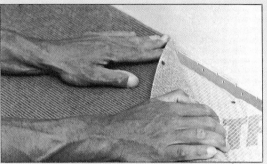

1 *Press the carpet edge on to the gripper pins*

2 *Run a mallet over the gripper to push the carpet home*

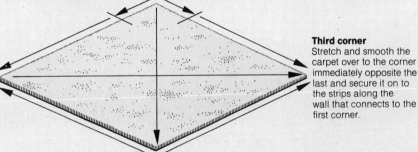

First corner
Hook the carpet on to the strips in one corner so that the carpet is secured for 12in. along the wall each side.

Second corner
Connect the carpet on to the strip at an adjacent corner. Then link the intervening wall. The carpet is now firmly held along the first wall.

Third corner
Stretch and smooth the carpet over to the corner immediately opposite the last and secure it on to the strips along the wall that connects to the first corner.

Fourth corner
Stretch the carpet over to the last corner and secure it, then hook it on to the gripper pins on the last two walls.

Stretching the carpet
Place the head of the knee kicker on the carpet, and adjust the pins so that they engage in the backing without tearing the pile. Then kick the pad with the muscle just above your knee cap (not the knee cap itself), while smoothing the carpet with your hands.

Trimming off excess carpet
Crease back the carpet at the baseboard and mark a cutting line along the back. Then fold the carpet right back and cut long the line, with a cutting board protecting the carpet beneath. Roll back the carpet to try the fit and re-trim, if necessary.

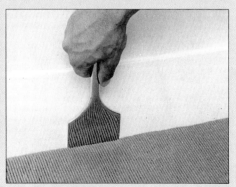

Finishing off edges
Once you have cut off excess carpet at the borders, trim it carefully against a straight-edge so that only ½in. rests against the wall. Press a paint scraper into the gully between the gripper and the wall, until the carpet is neatly tucked against the baseboard.

58
Laying foam-backed carpet

Foam-backed carpet needs no stretching. You simply lay it on the floor, butt up two adjacent edges against the baseboard and trim the other two edges to fit. Trim the carpet in position, or as for jute-backed carpet (see p. 61). Tackless strips with extra large pins are available for foam-backed carpet, but it may prove easier to fix down the edges with double-sided adhesive tape or tacks.

Trimming foam-backed carpet
Hold a sharp utility knife at an angle, with the handle pointing away from the wall to avoid over-trimming, and pull away the offcuts.

59
Fitting around problem areas

To allow the carpet to fit snugly in alcoves or around projections such as fireplaces, you must make vertical release cuts from the carpet edge to the floor. If the carpet has a tendency to fray, first coat the back with latex adhesive. To fit around pipes, cut a slit in the carpet from the front of the pipe to the edge of the carpet behind it. Ease the carpet around the pipe, making small release cuts where necessary, then trim to fit the wall. It will make the job easier if you cut off excess carpet first (see Basic technique, p. 61).

Door architraves
Make a series of release cuts in the carpet until it lies flat. Then trim the "tongues" as accurately as possible – with or without a template – until ½in. rests against the architrave. Push the carpet neatly behind the gripper pins.

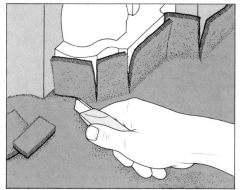

Fireplaces
Allow an overlap of 1in., then make a release cut at each internal and external corner. Press down the carpet until it lies flat and trim off the excess allowing ½in. to ride up against the fireplace. Then secure the edges behind the gripper pins or tack them down.

61
Joining carpet pieces

If seams are unavoidable, the options are to seal the edges with 2in. wide carpet tape and latex carpet adhesive, or, if the join falls in a doorway, to use an edging strip with twin grooves (see Tools and equipment, p. 57).

Using binder bars
These aluminum strips have angled grippers to hold the carpet taut and a protective edge to prevent the carpet from fraying. Trim the edge of the carpet, tuck it into the metal edging and press it down flat. Then, using a piece of softwood to protect the bar, hammer down the lip to meet the carpet surface.

Using carpet tape
Brush a 1in. band of adhesive along a half-width of the tape, **1**, and along the back of a carpet edge. When the adhesive is dry, press the glued carpet, leaving the other half of the tape free. Coat the remaining half-width of tape and the back of the other carpet. When the adhesive is nearly dry, join the glued surfaces, **2**, taking care to ensure a close joint without marks. On carpet squares, tape the entire border.

1 *Glue a half-width of tape and one carpet edge*

2 *Hold back the pile when securing the second edge*

60
Laying carpet tiles

The technique for planning out carpet tiles and the working sequence are the same as for floor tiles (see Job 33 and Job 34, p. 46, and Basic technique, p. 55). The first tile should be secured in place with double-sided adhesive tape, while subsequent tiles can be loose laid. If however, the tile manufacturer recommends securing the tiles at random intervals to prevent them moving and creating gaps, use a flooring adhesive or double-sided sticky tape. Working from the center, butt up the tiles tightly against each other and ensure that the arrows on the tile backs point in the same direction, unless you prefer to lay them in alternate directions for a checkerboard effect. Cut border tiles on a cutting board and secure them in doorways with a metal edging strip.

62

Preparing the stairs

Before laying carpet, it is wise to examine the stair surface and make any minor repairs. Loose nails should be pulled out or punched below the surface, and any suspect holes treated with insecticides. Any rotten treads or risers can be replaced by knocking out the glued wedges, removing the old board and sliding in a new one. A creaking stair will be silenced by gluing and screwing a wooden block into the angle between the front of the tread and the riser below, working from below the stairs. If the stairs are boarded in, screws through the front of the tread into the riser below should cure the squeak. Finally, the stairs should be vacuumed and, to avoid taking up the carpet later, the entire staircase should be given a fresh coat of paint.

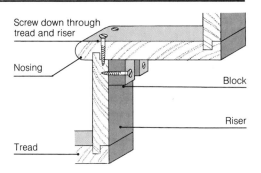

63

Fitting padding on stairs

There are two ways of fixing stair carpet: with tackless strips or with tacks. The method used will determine how the padding is to be fixed. If the carpet is to be tacked, the padding must also be tacked. If angled stair grippers are to be used to secure the carpet, a piece of padding is placed over each tread and half-way down the next riser, then tacked into place. Angled tackless strips are then fixed on top of the padding. If normal strips are to be used, these are nailed directly on to the stairs in pairs, with the pins pointing into the stair angle. The padding butts up to the edges of the grippers, leaving a gap between each pair for tucking in the carpet. Whichever method is used, guide lines must be marked for the position of both carpet and padding. However, if the carpet is to be fitted to the full width of the stairs, fit the tackless strips $\frac{3}{4}$in. from the banister edge and $\frac{1}{4}$in. from the wall.

Marking guide lines
On the first tread, mark with a pencil where the edges of the carpet will fall, **1**, *taking care to ensure that the borders are equal. Then make a second pencil line $\frac{3}{4}$in. inside each mark as a guide line for the padding. Repeat this procedure on the bottom tread. Then suspend two stringlines from the two inner points on the top tread, pull them taut, so that they form a straight line, and secure them to the two inner points on the bottom tread. You can then use the stringlines to make pencil guide lines for the position of both the carpet and the padding on each stair tread,* **2**.

1 *Mark the carpet position on the top tread*

2 *Use stringlines to mark the padding position of each tread*

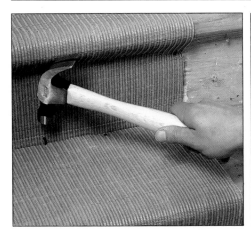

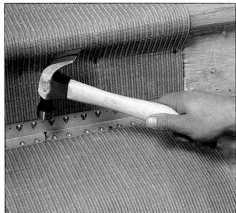

Using tacks
Position a piece of padding over the nose of each tread, so that it covers the entire tread, and half the riser below it. Check that it is centered then, using tacks or wire staples, secure the back edge of the padding on to the tread, $\frac{3}{4}$in. from the riser above, and fix the front edge on the face of the riser below. Tack or staple at 6in. intervals.

Using tackless strips
Fix one strip on the back of each tread, about $\frac{5}{8}$in. from the face of the riser. Fix a second on the riser below, $\frac{5}{8}$in. above the next tread. This will leave a gap between the two strips into which the carpet will be tucked. Then tack padding to the back of the tread, close to the strip, smooth it down over the nosing, and tack it down on the riser.

Using angled tackless strips
Single tackless strips with two rows of angled pins are available for stairs. These are fitted into the stair angle on top of the padding. First tack down the pads of underlay on to the stairs, positioned as for the tack-down method (see far left). Then press the strip down on to the padding and nail it to both the tread and the riser.

64

Carpeting a straight staircase

Once the padding is in position, the stair carpet can be fixed on top. The carpet *must* be securely held, or accidents may occur. The carpet can be fixed using either tacks or tackless strips, and this decision must be taken *before* fitting padding. If the padding is tacked, the carpet must also be tacked. If you have chosen to use plain tackless strips, the carpet is inserted into the gap between the strips, the "teeth" or pins hold the carpet backing. If angled tackless strips have been fixed, the carpet is inserted between the two rows of teeth on each strip. If the carpet is to be fitted to the full stair width, the strips are fixed $\frac{3}{4}$in. from the banister edge, to allow the cut edge to be turned and tacked. Although foam-backed carpet is not generally recommended for stairs, some types of foam-backed carpet are hard-wearing enough. Special tackless strips, without pins to tear the backing, are available, but tacks provide a firmer fixing.

Using tackless strips
Arrange the carpet with the pile running down the stairs and align the edges with the guide lines on the top tread, 1. Push it firmly on to the gripper teeth and tuck the edge into the stair angle. A tack at each side will ensure that the edge does not move while you fit the carpet. Draw the carpet tightly across the tread, down over the riser below and on to the next tread. Push the carpet securely on to the gripper pins by hammering a wooden shim or a thin, flat brick chisel, 2, into the gaps between tackless strips. Continue drawing the carpet over the stairs, 3, and fixing it on to the pins. If very thick carpet is being fitted, you may have to increase the gap slightly between the strips. From time to time, check the alignment of the carpet, by ensuring that a row of tufts runs across the nosing in a straight line and that the un-carpeted borders are equal in width. At the bottom, turn under a 3in.-4in. hem of carpet and neatly tack or staple it to the bottom riser, 4. Working from the center out, attach it at 2½in. intervals. This surplus will allow you to move up the carpet later.

1 *Hook the carpet on the first strip*

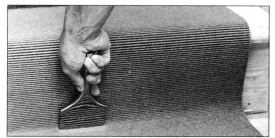

2 *Wedge the carpet firmly on the gripper pins*

3 *Smooth the material over each tread*

4 *Turn and back a hem on the bottom riser*

Using carpet tacks
With the top edge turned under by about 3in., align the carpet and tack it down on the top tread at 4in. intervals, 1. The riser above will be covered by the landing carpet. Check that the carpet is correctly aligned and that the pile runs downward, then begin fitting. Pull the carpet tightly over the first tread and down to the base of the riser below. Tack down one corner, into the base of the next tread down, stretch the carpet across the tread and tack the other corner. Insert tacks at the back of the tread, at 4in. intervals between the two holding tacks, 2. Repeat this process of securing, stretching and tacking down the carpet, until you reach the bottom stair. Pull the carpet taut over the last tread. Fold under a 3in.-4in. hem of surplus carpet, so that the crease lies in the angle between the bottom riser and the floor, 3, and fold the inner vertical edges under to give a neat single thickness. Tack or staple through both thicknesses on the bottom riser to encourage the hem to lie flat, 4.

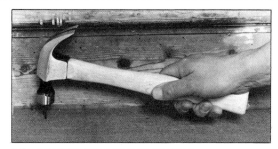

1 *Tack the folded top edge to the top tread*

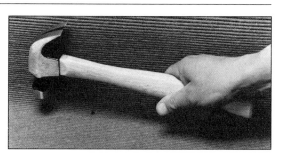

2 *Smooth the carpet over each stair and tack it down*

3 *Fold a hem at the base of the bottom riser*

4 *Tack through the double thickness*

65
Carpeting a winding staircase

The treads of corner stairs in a winding staircase are triangular, so it is best to use a separate piece of carpet for each tread with its riser. To ensure a good fit, it is wise to make a paper template of the stair shape. If tackless strips are to be used, two strips are fitted as for straight treads, to allow the carpet to be tucked down. But, in addition, a third is nailed along the wide, wall edge.

Ensuring a good fit
Fix two tackless strips in the stair angle and a third along the wide part of the step, ¼in. from the baseboard, 1. Then make a paper template for each tread and the riser below it, mark where the nosing of the tread falls on the template, 2, then lay the template on the carpet. Ensure that the noseline coincides with a row of tufts, then cut the carpet slightly oversize. Secure it on to pins, or tack it.

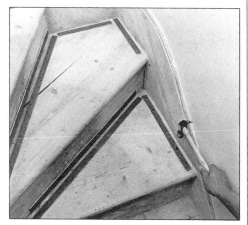
1 Use a third strip along each tread

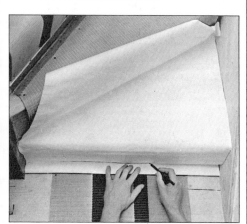

2 Make a template and mark the nosing line

66
Carpeting a landing

A landing carpet should be fitted in the same way as a floor carpet (*see Basic technique, p. 61*). On an open landing, the edge bordering the stairwell should be turned under and held with tacks or a metal edging strip. Take a flap of carpet over the first step to cover the top riser. Either fold under the edge and tack in to the base of the first riser, or hook the carpet on to the tackless strip on the first riser and tuck the edge into the angle.

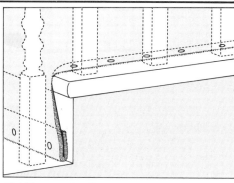
Finishing open landings
If the landing is not boxed in, fold and tack the edge at the banister. Take a flap of carpet over the first riser and secure it at the base.

67
Carpeting open-tread staircase

Since these stairs have no risers, each tread should be individually wrapped in carpet. When measuring, allow 1½in. for hemming. The padding is flapped over the tread and tacked or stapled to the underside, 2in. from the edge of the stair. The carpet is then laid on top so that the tufts line up with the nosing. The edges are then folded under by ¾in. and tacked at the center of the tread on the underside.

Securing the underside
Lay the carpet over the tread and tack down the folded edges under the tread, at the mid-point. Insert the fixing tacks 4in. apart.

68
Patching carpet

If the carpet has a woven (as opposed to foam) backing, the back of the damaged section must be coated with a band of latex carpet adhesive along the cutting line, to prevent fraying. When the adhesive is dry, the old patch is cut out from above. This is then used as a template for matching size, pattern and pile. The adhesive treatment is repeated before cutting the new piece, and carpet tape, fixed around the edge of the hole, on the back of the carpet, will hold the new patch in place.

Patching jute-backed carpet
Spread a band of adhesive on the back of the carpet, around the damaged area. Place a cutting board under the carpet and cut through the backing from above, 1. Place the old piece upside down on the back of a new piece and match the pattern and pile direction. Then apply the new piece and carefully cut out around the outline of the old one. Fix 2in. wide strips of carpet tape around the edge of the hole and press the new patch down into position, 2.

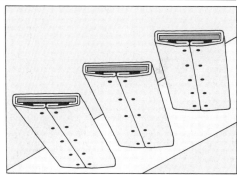
1 Cut around the damaged area from above and remove the old piece

2 Press the new patch on to the adhesive tape

Wooden flooring

Estimating time and quantities ◇ Tools and equipment ◇ How to remove and re-lay floorboards ◇ Filling gaps between boards Securing loose boards ◇ Replacing baseboards ◇ Laying hardboard ◇ Sanding a floor ◇ Laying particleboard ◇ Laying woodstrip flooring ◇ Laying woodblock flooring ◇ Laying parquet flooring

Wooden floors have a warmth, color, and subtlety of texture that cannot be matched by imitations. They look rich, are hardwearing, blend with both traditional and modern furnishings, and are comparable in price with other floorcoverings.

Wooden floors of all types are best for living rooms and areas where there is little dampness. Hardwood floors can be laid in kitchens and bathrooms, but there are more suitable types of floor for these rooms. Wooden floors are easy to maintain. Maintenance involves washing and occasional polishing with a paste floor wax. Rubbing the surface with a dry mop will improve the sheen. If the finish deteriorates, rub the floor surface in line with the grain with medium or fine steel wool soaked in alcohol to remove the old polish; then reseal the floor. Treat minor scratches with alcohol paste wax applied on a small cloth. You may be able to disguise large scratches using a wax repair crayon of the type used on furniture. Or you can sand the affected area and reseal it.

Points to remember

◇ Make sure the existing floorboards are level and that gaps are filled before fitting a new floor on top.
◇ Punch nails below the surface before sanding boards.
◇ If floorboards are loose for no apparent reason, check the joists underneath.
◇ Condition flooring materials by leaving them in the room where they are going to be fitted.
◇ Leave an expansion gap around the edges of woodstrip, woodblock, and parquet floors.
◇ If your room is not square, allow for the discrepancy at the edges.

For more information on types of wooden flooring, see Choosing materials, pp. 126-9.

Estimating time

The times shown here are for a floor area approximately 13ft × 10ft. The actual time taken will vary according to your own skill and experience. It will also depend on whether the room is exactly square (if it is not, you will have to allow extra time for dealing with irregular-shaped areas) and on how many obstructions there are. Remember that you may have to carry out floorboard repairs before laying woodstrip or woodblock flooring.

Floorboard repairs

Replacing a floorboard 13ft long

 hour

Re-laying a floor

 hours

Replacing baseboard

③-④ hours

Sub-floors

Laying hardboard

④-⑤ hours

Laying a particleboard floor

⑥-⑧ hours

Woodstrip and woodblock floors

Laying a woodstrip floor using nails

⑥-⑧ hours

Laying a woodstrip floor using glue

 hours

Laying a parquet floor

 hours

Laying a woodblock floor

⑤-⑦ hours

Finishing off a woodblock floor (one coat of sealer)

①-② hours

Estimating quantities

Hardwood flooring comes in packs, and manufacturers usually specify the floor area that each pack will cover. They also produce ready-reckoners that enable you to calculate easily how many packs you will need for a particular room size. With both woodstrip and woodblock types there is very little waste, even in odd-shaped rooms, because you can easily split up the panels into small units to work round obstructions and fill corners.

Types of wooden floors

To create an attractive wooden floor you may be able to renovate and seal the existing floorboards if they are not too badly patched, split, or uneven. Alternatively, you can lay a hardwood floor over any dry, level sub-floor. This can be made of lumber particleboard, hardboard, or concrete. The most hard-wearing of the woods commonly used for strip or block flooring is maple. This is followed by merbau, iroko, oak, teak, and mahogany. But with reputable brands, all the timbers are selected for their hardwearing qualities. So base your choice mainly on the color and grain pattern of the wood.

Decorative effects with sanded floorboards

Even the simplest of wooden floors can have a powerful influence on the character of a room. Floorboards that have been sanded, sealed, and polished can give a room an atmosphere of luxury, especially when combined with other polished wood surfaces and matching rugs and carpets. A natural-colored stain can bring out the richness of color in the wood.

But boards can also blend well with a simple decorative scheme, complementing a country-style interior. Because they wear well and are easy to clean and maintain, they are especially appropriate for living rooms, halls, passages and other areas of the home that have to stand up to heavy use.

Light, natural colors
Wooden flooring is particularly appropriate in this simple country interior. Its light color looks good with the white painted walls and the room does not look bare with even a minimum of furniture, because there is enough visual interest in the texture of the stone and the grain of the wood. An extra layer of wood seal lends added warmth to the color of a pale wood and enhances the pattern of the grain.

Rich warm tones
In this children's room the natural wood colors of the door, window frame, cornice, and floor harmonize to create a warm atmosphere. A wooden floor has other advantages for a children's room – it is both hardwearing and easy to clean. A good quality and well-maintained hardwood strip floor may also prove cheaper in the long run than other floor coverings, which may lose their quality finish.

Tools and equipment

For most jobs you will need a minimum of at least one hammer and one saw. In addition, a number of other items will be required, depending on the job you are doing. As well as the tools illustrated, a brick chisel is invaluable for levering up floorboards. For sanding wooden floorboards, you will need to rent specialized equipment (*see Sanding equipment and abrasives, p. 72*).

Saws
For cutting along the tongue before lifting floorboards you will need a circular power saw. A hand saw, designed specifically for floorboards is also available. It has a blade with a curved end to make it easier to start the cut. A circular saw with a tungsten-carbide blade should be used for cutting particleboard, which blunts normal blades quickly. A power saber saw is useful if you want to cut across floor-boards, but you can use a keyhole saw. You will need a drill to make starting holes before using these saws. Most need a hole about $\frac{3}{8}$in. in diameter. For intricate cuts – for example, when you are laying flooring round obstructions – use a coping saw, while you can use a back saw for trimming by hand.

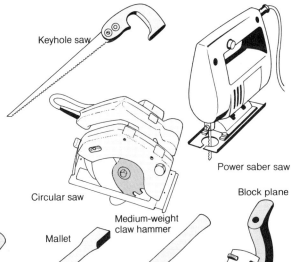

Keyhole saw

Power saber saw

Circular saw

Medium-weight claw hammer

Block plane

Pliers

Chisel

Mallet

Other equipment
A pair of pliers is useful for removing old carpet tacks and nails. You will need a medium- or light-weight hammer for most flooring work. For hammering down nails use a nail set. Some form of lever is needed for taking up floorboards. A broad-bladed chisel is good for this, and you may also find a strong length of steel useful. Use a block plane when filling gaps between floorboards with thin strips of wood. A mallet and chisel can be used to chip away wood from the underside of a new floorboard, so that it matches older surrounding boards, and for jobs like taking out damaged blocks in a wood block floor.

Floorboards can have either square or tongue-and-groove edges, which are harder to lift up. Before you begin to lift

Removing square-edged boards
*You can usually insert a broad chisel or a strong metal lever or prybar into the gaps between the boards, **1**. Use this to pry up each one, starting close to a convenient board end. Lift up the board until you can insert another chisel or lever on the opposite side, **2**. Then work both levers along the board until it is free.*
*To help loosen the board, try working part of the way along it with a chisel and then place a strong metal lever under the floorboard, resting it on the adjacent boards, **3**. When you press down on the free end it will be forced up farther along its length. Then move the lever along until you can lift the whole floorboard. If you cannot fit a brick chisel into any of the gaps, saw across one of the joins.*

1 *Insert a broad chisel into a gap between the boards*

69

Fitting new boards

You may have to cut new boards along their length to make them fit a long, narrow gap in a floor. A bench-mounted circular saw is useful for making these long, straight cuts.

The new boards may not be exactly the same thickness as those that make up the rest of the floor. If they are slightly too thin, use pieces of wood as packing between the boards and joists. If the new boards are too thick, use a chisel to make them thinner at the joist positions. You can fix most of the boards with $2\frac{1}{2}$in. cut floor brads or finishing nails. Screw down any boards that may have to be lifted in the future.

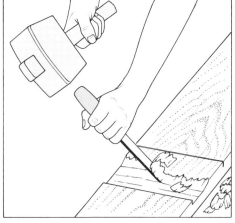

Chiseling away thick boards
Make two parallel saw cuts and chisel away the wood in between until the boards lie at the same height as the original ones.

70

Removing boards by cutting

If you want to lift only a short length of floorboard, or release a long board that is trapped under the baseboard, it may be necessary to cut across the boards before levering them up. This may also be a helpful method for taking up tongue-and-groove boards. The first thing to do is to locate the joists which support the floor-boards. Avoid cutting through the joists – cut alongside one of them. They will extend 1in. to 1½in. on each side of the nails. Mark a cutting line to one side of a joist, cut through the board with a saber saw, and lift it out.

Basic technique

How to remove and re-lay floorboards

either type, look for screwed-down boards. These are easy to lift and will tell you what type of boards make up your floor. Re-laying boards is straightforward. The main problem is getting them as close together as possible. To do this, use a pair of wooden shims to press together the floorboards before nailing them down permanently.

2 Use a seond chisel or lever to pry up the board

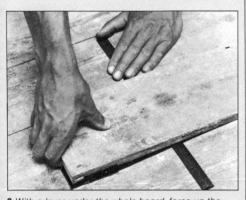

3 With a lever under the whole board, force up the board farther along its length

Removing tongue-and-groove boards

With tongue-and-groove floors the main difficulty is lifting the first board. When you have removed this, you can lever the others up fairly easily.

Start by cutting through the tongue by sawing along the length of the board. Use a circular saw, set to cut about $\frac{1}{2}$in. deep. Retract the guard, tilt the saw forward and lower the blade. This will leave a small gap which will need to be filled later. Alternatively, you can use a floorboard saw, which has a specially curved blade, so that you can start the cut easily.

Re-laying floorboards

If there are large damaged areas or many gaps between the boards it is best to lift the whole floor and re-lay it, putting in new boards where necessary and closing up all the gaps. To ensure that you press the boards tightly together, use a pair of shims made by cutting two pieces of board to a tapering shape. Lay four or five adjacent boards in position and nail a length of wood temporarily to the joists a short distance from the boards. Hammer the shims into place between the boards and the fixed length of wood. This will tighten the boards. You can then nail them in place before removing the shims and the temporary piece of wood. Repeat the process with further groups of boards until the floor is almost completed. At the end, you will probably be left with a narrow gap: cut a new floorboard to the right size to fill this space.

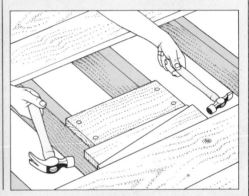

Cutting and lifting floorboards

With square-edged boards, insert a thin knife blade through the gap between the boards to help you find the joists. Drill a hole to take the saw blade at a position close to the joist edge. This hole should be about $\frac{3}{8}$in. in diameter. Then draw a line along the joist edge, **1**. Cut along the line with an electric saber saw, **2**, or a hand keyhole saw. As you do this, tilt the top of the blade slightly toward the center of the joist. This will create a chamfered edge, so that the board is supported when you replace it. Lift up the board, using a wide chisel, **3**, as a lever.

1 After drilling a hole, draw a line along the joist edge

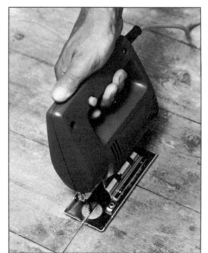

2 Cut along the line with the blade angled toward the center of the joist

3 Lift out the board, using a broad chisel or lever

71
Filling gaps between boards

If there are only a few gaps between the boards you can pack them using papier-mâché or wood putty. A better method is to use wood strips, planed along their length so that one side tapers. Apply pva glue to each side and tap the strip down so that it wedges into the gap. When the glue has dried, plane the wood level.

Filling with strips of wood
After you have allowed the adhesive to dry, plane each piece down to the existing floor level.

72
Dealing with gaps under baseboard

It is possible to use papier-mâché or wood putty to seal gaps between boards and baseboard, but they usually go on opening and closing as the room temperature varies. The best method is to nail molding around the baseboard to hide the gaps.

Fitting molding
Press the molding on to the floor and nail it to the baseboard only, so that the floor can still move.

73
Securing loose boards

Squeaking floors, caused by loose floor-boards can often be corrected from above by nailing or screwing through the board into the joist, so that the board cannot move. In other cases, loose boards are best corrected from below. If, for example, the board has parted from the sub-floor, it can be screwed down into position from beneath the floor. Or, if a board has shrunk from the joist, a wooden shim, driven into the gap will secure the board.

Securing from below
*You can gain access to the underside of first floor boards from the basement. If the board has parted from the sub-floor, insert wood screws with washers through the double thickness to draw the board back down. If the board has worked loose from a joist, knock a tapered wooden shim between the two surfaces, **2**.*

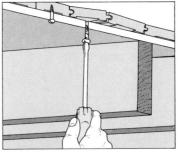

If the board has shrunk from the sub-floor, screw through both from below

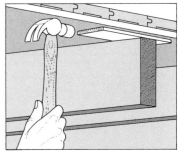

If it has parted from a joist, knock a tapered shim beneath the board

Nailing from above
Use 2½in. cut floor brads or finishing nails. Insert them slightly to one side of the original nail holes. Make sure that the nails go into the center of each joist and use two nails at each joist position to ensure a secure fit. If the boards are split, or may need lifting in the future, screw them down with 2in. gauge 10 countersunk-head woodscrews.

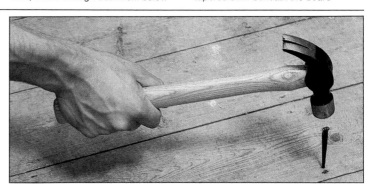

74
Replacing baseboard

If you need to replace baseboard, you should use the method that was employed when the original boards were fitted. If the wall is made of solid bricks, the baseboards may be attached directly to the wall with masonry brads or nailed to wood blocks fixed to the wall. Brads should be long enough to penetrate the wall by ¾in. With hollow partition walls, the baseboards should be fixed with nails into the studs that support the wall's internal frame.

Baseboard fixings
If the wall is a hollow type fix the baseboard with nails that pass through the plasterboard to the uprights of the frame. In older buildings the boards are often nailed to wood blocks. These may be set into the mortar joints between the bricks or simply nailed to the wall surface. With this type of construction, you should attach new blocks to the wall using screws and wallplugs. You can then nail the baseboards to the blocks.

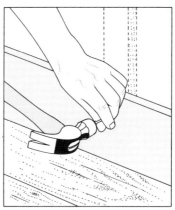

On a hollow partition wall, nail into the studs only

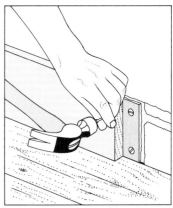

Attach wood blocks to masonry walls and nail into these

Effects with hardwood floors

Wooden floors can look effective in both traditional and modern homes. The most luxurious effects are usually obtained with hardwood floors, whether they are wood-strip or woodblock types. Narrow wood-strips can emphasize the length of a room, while parquet, laid in basket-weave form, provides an attractive yet unobtrusive pattern.

Another effect of this type of flooring is that it gives a room unity. Wooden floors set off a wide range of furnishings, from antique to ultra-modern, and help them look good together. An expanse of wooden flooring, for example, may echo the color and grain in wooden furniture while it offsets brighter fabrics. A selection of ethnic or oriental rugs help to add color, softness and comfort.

A modern interior
The large windows and empty central area of this modern room (left) would look stark and cold if it were not for the polished wood-strip floor. Its color adds warmth, and its lines guide the eye from the furniture at one end to the rug and chair at the other, making it seem less empty. This type of floor is available in many different woods, so it is possible to get a good natural match, as here, between the color of furniture and the floor.

A patterned effect
Parquet flooring creates a subtle pattern that does not dominate a room (above). Strongly patterned rugs can be placed on parquet without creating disharmony. The contents of this room encompass a wide variety of styles. Antique chairs, a modern table, and rugs of widely differing patterns are all included. But none of these items seems to clash because they all harmonize with the neutral wall color and the rich wood of the parquet floor.

75
Laying hardboard

Hardboard creates the ideal sub-floor for many floor coverings. Use standard hardboard, $\frac{1}{8}$in. thick, or $\frac{1}{4}$in. hardboard for very uneven floors. In kitchens and bathrooms, use tempered hardboard.

Before laying, condition the boards. Separate them and stand them on edge for 72 hours in the room where you are going to put them down. In kitchens and bathrooms they should be sprinkled with water. Fill any deep holes in the floor.

Fixing hardboard sheets
In new homes, kitchens, and bathrooms, sprinkle the rough sides with water, 1, and stack the boards flat, back to back. Leave standard board for 48 hours and tempered board for 72 hours. Cut each sheet in half to provide more expansion joints and cut some in half again. Use these pieces at the start of alternate rows, to give staggered joins, 2. Fix the boards smooth-side-down with ring-shank nails, hardboard pins, or flat staples. The fixings should be 4in. apart around the edges and 6in. apart over the rest of the board.

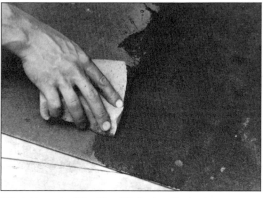

1 Sprinkle each of the 4ft × 8ft sheets with about 1 pint of water to condition them

2 Stagger the joins between the hardboard sheets

Sanding equipment and abrasives

The main item you need for sanding floorboards is an industrial drum floor sander. This will enable you to sand the main part of the floor. You will also need a smaller sander for the edges. You can rent both from tool rental shops, which will also supply abrasives. One day's rental should give you plenty of time to prepare a large room. You will also need a dust mask, a nail set and hammer, pliers for pulling out protruding tacks and nails, and a hand scraper for corners.

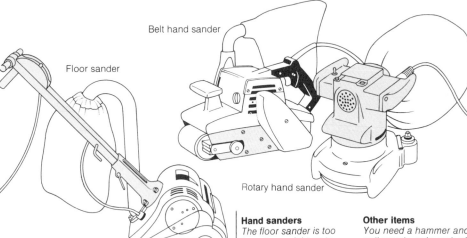

Belt hand sander

Floor sander

Rotary hand sander

Floor sander
This has a large revolving drum that takes the abrasive paper and is driven by a powerful electric motor. The machine has a vacuum action and a bag to remove most of the dust. The drum may be 8in. or 12in. wide. The smaller model is easier to handle and is suitable for all but the largest rooms. If the floor is in reasonable condition, you should start by using medium-grade abrasive and finish with fine grade. Coarse-grade paper is available for very uneven surfaces and extra-coarse may be needed if there is a build-up of wax polish on the floor.

Hand sanders
The floor sander is too large to go right up to the edges of the floor, so you also need a hand sanding machine. A hand belt sander is ideal, because it does not produce swirl marks on the wood surface. if you use a disk-type sander, take care not to score the surface. Both types of hand sanders should be fitted with a vacuum bag. A sanding attachment in an electric drill is not strong enough.

Other items
You need a hammer and nail punch and a pair of pliers for preparing the floor for sanding. A dust mask is also advisable, even with sanders that have a dust bag.

Dust mask

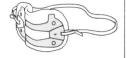

76
Preparing a floor for sanding

Make sure that all the boards are securely fixed. Look for split, damaged, or badly patched boards and replace them. (*For removing and re-laying floorboards, see Basic technique, p. 69.*) If the floor is badly damaged, it is best to lay new boards (*see Job 69, p. 68*). If there are a lot of gaps between the boards, take them up and re-lay them.

Pull out any protruding carpet tacks and nails using pliers. Then deal with the nails that fix the boards to the joists. If they protrude, they will tear the sanding belt, so drive them well below the surface using a nail set.

Punching down the nails
Drive all the nails well down into the floorboards with a nail set or another large nail that has had its tip filed off.

77
Sanding a floor

After you have prepared the floor, sand the main area with a large floor sander. Start with medium or coarse abrasive on the machine's drum, to strip away the surface, before changing to a finer grade to get a smoother finish. You will not be able to get right up to the edges of the room with the large sander, so use a hand sander for these areas. With both machines, work in a direction parallel to the boards. Even a hand sander cannot get right into the corners of a room, so you will have to finish off these small areas, together with places where there are other obstructions to the sander, using a simple hand scraper.

Although sanders have dust-collecting bags, these are not capable of picking up all the dust. So when you have finished sanding, vacuum the floor thoroughly. Then clean it carefully with a damp cloth and leave the surface to dry completely before sealing it.

Using sanding machines
Before you switch on a large belt sander, tilt it back so that the drum is raised off the floor, 1. Now switch it on and gradually lower the spinning drum on to the floor. The sander will tend to move forward and you will have to restrain it so that it travels slowly. But be careful not to restrain it too much, or it will continue to sand the same small area of floor and start to gouge out a depression. Work the machine forward and backward in the same direction as the floorboards, 2. Overlap each pass by about 3in. and make sure you keep the cable out of the way by running it over your shoulder. If the floor is very uneven, make the first few passes at 45° to the boards. You can start working parallel to the boards when you switch to finer paper. Never run a floor sander at right angles to the boards – it will not even out the bumps in the surface. When you have sanded the main floor area, tackle the edges with the hand sander, 3. Finally, finish off the corners and other confined areas with a hand scraper.

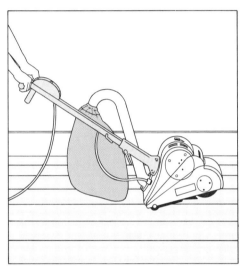

1 *Tilt the sander before switching it on and lowering it gently on to the floor surface*

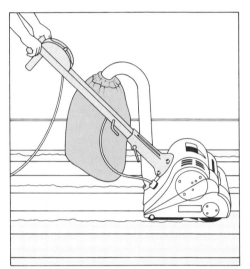

2 *Work parallel with the floorboards*

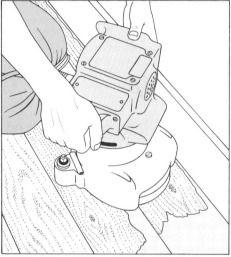

3 *Finish off the edges and corners of the floor with a smaller hand sander*

Tips for sanding

◇ Punch all nails well below the surface before you start.
◇ Use only sanders designed for floors – an electric drill with a sanding attachment is not sufficient.
◇ Let the drum sander move along the floor as soon as you lower it into position – if you do not let it move it will make an indentation in the floor.
◇ Work parallel with the floorboards, unless they are very rough.
◇ For floors in poor condition, start by sanding at 45° to the boards before sanding parallel with the boards.
◇ Do not sand at right angles to the boards – the sander will not even out the surface and serious scratching will result.
◇ Finish off the corners with a hand scraper.

78
Sealing floorboards

When you have sanded a floor, you need to protect its surface so that it will resist wear and can be kept clean easily. To do this, use a floorboard seal. These come in two types. Polyurethane-based seals form a clear, gloss or mat coat over the wood surface. Oleo-resinous types soak into the wood and give a scratch-resistant, luster surface. Both types usually have the effect of darkening the floor color slightly, but if you want to change the color of the boards more radically, you should apply a stain before sealing the floor.

When you are sure that the floor is perfectly clean and dry, apply the first coat of seal. Use a pad made from lint-free cloth, rubbing it well into the floor. As soon as the surface has dried (which will take about 12 hours) apply another coat. Do not spread it too thickly, and brush it well out. After another 12 hours apply a third coat, and, within a further 24-hour period, perhaps a fourth. Applying the seal at these intervals will ensure that each coat bonds closely with the previous one.

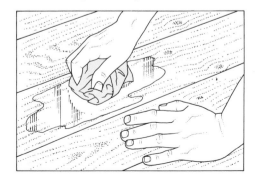

Applying the seal
Rub the first coat on to the floorboards using a pad of lint-free cloth.

79
Laying particleboard

Particleboard is a cheap and hardwearing material that is ideal for flooring. It is increasingly used as an alternative to other forms of floorboards, especially in new homes.

Particleboard comes with either straight or tongue-and-groove edges and in $\frac{3}{4}$in. and 1in. thicknesses. For most purposes, $\frac{3}{4}$in. is adequate, but use 1in. particleboard for joists spaced farther than 18in. apart. For a smooth, strong floor, tongue-and-groove edged sheets are best. These normally come in sheets measuring 2ft × 8ft.

If you use square-edged boards, nail and glue 2in. × 3in. wood between the joists so that all the edges are supported. This will cut down flexing. With tongue-and-groove particleboard there is no need for cross supports. The edges of each sheet should come half way across the supporting joists. Fix the sheets with $2\frac{1}{2}$in. finishing nails. Leave screwed-down access panels over cables and pipes. Particleboard blunts saw blades, so if you are going to cut many panels use a circular saw with a tungsten carbide tipped blade.

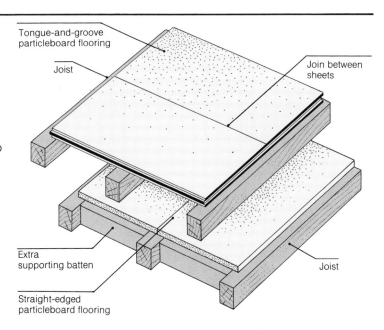

Tongue-and-groove particleboard flooring
Joist
Join between sheets
Extra supporting batten
Straight-edged particleboard flooring
Joist

80
Repairing particleboard

Particleboard floors require few repairs, but they can give problems when you have to lift a panel to gain access to cables, pipes, or joists beneath the floor. Sometimes a particleboard floor will flex as you walk across it, especially along the joints between adjacent sheets. The best solution to this problem is to rest all the unsupported edges on lengths of 2in. × 3in. wood, glued and nailed into position between the joists.

Particleboard is a strong material, but it is sometimes softened and weakened as a result of damp from a water leak. The only cure for this is to replace the affected section of the floor. Only in rare cases will a whole sheet of particleboard be affected, so the best method is to cut out the weakened area with a circular saw. It is then a simple matter to lever up the board. If you do need to take up a whole sheet, punch down the fixing nails and pry it up. You can repair the floor by fitting a new piece of particleboard, supporting it if necessary on cross supports placed between the joists and screwing it down with particleboard screws. You can fill gaps around a replacement sheet with wood filler.

Lifting a sheet
To stop the board crumbling, select the area you want to remove and make new cuts, rather than levering up an entire piece. First pencil cutting lines on the surface, 1. Run the lines alongside the nails, to avoid blunting the saw blade. Use a circular power saw and set the blade to cut $\frac{3}{4}$in. deep (or 1in. with thicker board) so that you do not saw through the joists. A blade with tungsten-carbide tips is best for particleboard. Hold the saw firmly and keep your feet clear as you cut, 2. To remove a whole sheet, saw round the join with adjacent sheets to free the board if it has tongues and grooves. Then, using a slim nail set, drive the fixing nails as deeply as possible below the surface and lever up the board.

Replacing a small sheet
A particleboard floor that has been damaged by water will swell and crumble, and you may need to replace a small sheet. After the water leak has been repaired, cut out the affected area of the particleboard (see left). If you used a circular saw for removing the board there will probably be a fairly wide saw cut round the edge of the sheet. You should therefore cut the replacement piece of particleboard slightly larger than the original. Fit cross supports between the joists so that all the edges are supported and then screw down the new small sheet using $1\frac{1}{2}$in. particleboard screws at intervals of about 12in. round the edge, 1. If you still end up with gaps in the floor, fill them with a wood filler, 2.

1 Mark lines for cutting alongside the nails to avoid blunting the saw

2 Keep a firm grip on the saw as you cut along the line

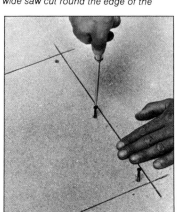
1 Use $1\frac{1}{2}$in. screws to secure replacement sheets

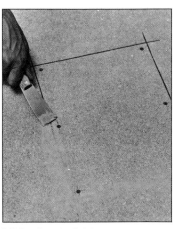
2 If the sheet is slightly too small, use wood filler in the gap

81
Preparing a floor for woodstrip or blocks

If your existing floor is made of wood, make sure that any loose boards are secured (*see Job 73, p. 70*). If necessary, lay hardboard sheets rough-side-up to give an even surface (*see Job 75, p. 72*).

If you want to insulate the floor at the same time, put rigid insulation board over the floor before laying the hardboard.

For better insulation, and to give a sound-deadening effect, lay rigid foam insulation under the hardboard. In kitchens and bathrooms, use a polyethylene vapor barrier. Fix down rigid insulation board using the same method as for hardboard. Use ring-shank nails or screw-nails (with a gradual spiral at the point end) long enough to penetrate the floorboards

by at least $\frac{1}{2}$in. Stick the hardboard to the insulation board with a contact, or pva adhesive. Make sure that the joints in the hardboard do not align with those in the insulation.

With solid floors you should also make sure that the surface is clean, smooth, and dry. If the floor is uneven, use a leveling compound, or smooth and insulate the surface using rigid foam insulation and hardboard. Always use a polyethylene vapor barrier with solid floors.

82
Laying woodstrip flooring

Woodstrip flooring consists of narrow pieces of tongue-and-groove edged wood which come in random lengths. The grain color can vary considerably, so it is a good idea to open the packs and check that the colors are consistent before you start to lay the floor.

Woodstrips often look best if laid in line with the doorway. But they can make long, narrow rooms seem wider if you lay them across the width of the room. It is best to put a few boards in position before you start, to see what looks best.

It is best to condition woodstrip flooring for at least 48 hours before laying it. Open the packs in the room where you are going to install the flooring and let the timber get acclimatized to the temperature and humidity levels of the room.

Laying woodstrip flooring involves preparing the existing floor so that it is clean, level, and dry. You can then lay insulating material to conserve heat and deaden noise. The woodstrips themselves are then attached using brads.

Underfloor heating can make woodstrip flooring shrink shortly after you have laid it. If you have this type of heating, you should consult the manufacturer of the flooring before laying the strips.

Fixing woodstrips
If the room is square, lay the first strip parallel to the wall and $\frac{3}{8}$in. away from it, to allow for expansion. The ends of the strips should also be $\frac{3}{8}$in. from the walls. If the room is not square, use a stringline to position the boards. Fit the first strip with the groove facing the wall, 1, at right angles to the floorboards. Attach it with brads 10in. part close to the wall. Punch the brad heads down and fill them later. Drive brads obliquely through the shoulders of the tongues using a nail set. To finish the row, butt join the strips. After nailing, add the next row by pushing the groove of the new strip over the tongue of the previous strip. Hammer the strip into place, protecting it with an offcut, 2. Nail the strip through the shoulder, 3. Stagger the joints between strips.

You may have to saw the last strip along its length so that it fits. Leave an expansion gap. If the strips are sealed, finish off by polishing, 4.

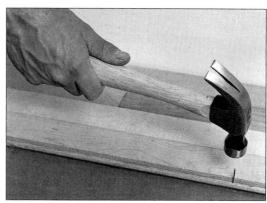

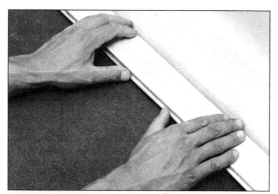

3 *Nail the strips in place using brads through the shoulder of the tongue*

1 *Leave an expansion gap of about $\frac{3}{8}$in. all the way around the room*

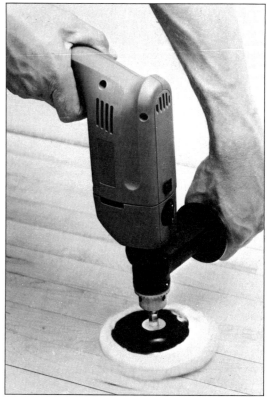

2 *Use an offcut to protect the strips as you hammer them into position*

4 *Finish off with an electric buffer*

83

Laying parquet flooring

Parquet panels consist of small pieces of hardwood shorter than those used in wood-strip flooring. They are glued to a wooden sub-floor or a vapor barrier over a concrete floor. The blocks are usually grouped together to make up a larger panel of basketweave pattern, although they can be separated so you can use individual blocks to fill small gaps and work round obstacles.

With parquet flooring the conditioning of the blocks before laying and the preparation of the floor itself are the same as for wood-strip flooring (*see Job 81, p. 75*).

Fixing parquet panels

Leave an expansion gap of ½ in. around the edge of the floor area. Use a cork strip to help maintain the gap.

Start by fitting the whole panels. Leave gaps where you have to trim and fit smaller pieces. Stick the panels down with flooring adhesive, applied to the floor using a notched spreader, 1. Once you have laid the first row of panels, spread the adhesive in blocks of about 5ft square and lay the next row. If the walls are not square, *use a stringline to help position them. 2. Cut some panels to fit the gap. To make them less obvious, put them at the side of the room farthest from the door, or where a large piece of furniture will stand.*

Tap the panels down firmly using a mallet, 3, and make sure that the edges butt tightly together.

For the small edge panels it is usually best to split up the large panels into sections to fill the gaps. To mark a panel for cutting, place it on top of the *last complete panel in a row. Place another panel on top of this with its edge ⅜ in. from the baseboard. Using the opposite edge of this panel as a guide, draw a cutting line on the lower panel, 4. Cut parquet panels with a back saw, a power saber saw, or a bench-mounted circular saw or handsaw. You can also use this method for cutting wood block panels. To go round pipes and similar obstacles, separate individual sections from panels and cut these into even smaller pieces if necessary.*

1 *Apply the adhesive directly to the floor using a notched spreader*

2 *Fit the parquet flooring in panels that are about 5ft square*

3 *Use a mallet to tap the panels down firmly, protecting the wood with an offcut*

4 *Mark the edge pieces for cutting by using the last complete panel as a guide*

84

Laying woodblock flooring

Wood blocks are assembled in a basketweave pattern and look rather like parquet blocks (*see Job 83, left*). But unlike parquet pieces they usually have tongue-and-groove edges so that they interlock and form a very flat, good-quality floor. Unlike parquet panels, wood-block does not require sanding.

Wood block flooring needs a good underlay. You should lay it over a hardboard sub-floor, with a layer of 15lb asphalt paper. The paper is laid between the sub-floor and finish floor and forms a good vapor barrier.

Wood blocks are usually loose laid. In other words, the panels simply "float" on the floor surface, and the inter-locking tongues and grooves hold them all tightly together. Wood block flooring normally comes ready-finished, so there is no extra work to do once you have laid the blocks.

85

Repairing a woodblock floor

To remove a damaged area, chisel out a central block. Once this is removed you can lift out any other affected pieces. The next stage is to scrape the floor surface clean. Then stick new matching blocks into place using flooring adhesive. The new blocks may be slightly thicker than the surrounding floor, especially if the original floor has become worn. Plane them down to the right level once the adhesive has dried.

Fixing wood blocks

First lay a hardboard sub-floor, **1**, smooth-side down (see Job 75, p. 72), leaving a ⅛ in. expansion gap around the perimeter and lay a sheet of asphalt paper. Cork expansion strips are available to prevent the blocks moving and to hold them tightly together. Join the small pieces together to form areas of basketweave pattern, **2**. Lay these on the floor and knock together more panels, protecting them with an offcut of wood, **3**.

Trim the edge blocks to fit the room in the same way as for parquet panels. At the edges plane off the tongues to leave the blocks straight. You then slip these final sections into the gap between the main area of flooring and the wall, **4**, and knock them into position. To do this you can use either a commercial knocking-up tool, which you may be able to rent for the purpose, or a hammer, protecting the edge from its blows with a scrap of flooring. Do not forget to leave an expansion gap. To fit the last corner block, you will have to cut off the tongue and the lower part of the grooves so that it simply drops into place. This will give you a good place to start if you ever have to dismantle the floor.

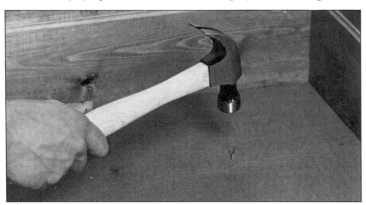

1 Fit a hardboard sub-floor before laying wood blocks

2 Join the small pieces of wood block loosely together to build up large panels

3 Protecting them with a wooden offcut, hammer the pieces firmly together

4 After you have cut off the protruding tongue, drop in the final corner piece

Chiseling out a block
To chip out a damaged wood block use a chisel and start at the center of the piece.

86
Finishing off a parquet or woodblock floor

To work round a door, saw horizontally through the base of the architrave at the height of the finished floor surface. Then push the flooring panels underneath. If you cannot do this, make a template and cut out the shape with a coping saw. Across the width of the doorway, finish off the edge with an aluminum metal edging or a hardwood strip that matches the wood of the floor.

Pre-sealed woodblock floors require no further treatment. Untreated types should be sanded smooth and sealed (see Job 78, p. 73). If there is a large area to sand, rent a floor sanding machine and use it with fine-grade abrasive paper. But usually only a light sanding is needed, and an electric belt sander, or even a smaller finishing sander, will be suitable unless the floor is very large.

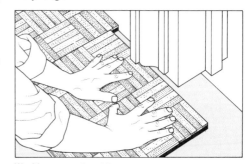

Working around architraves
Cut the architrave away at the base and slide the flooring underneath.

Sheet vinyl

Estimating time and quantities
Tools and equipment ◇ How to lay
and trim ◇ Joining and patching

Sheet vinyl is a durable, easy-to-clean and attractive floor covering, particularly suited to kitchens and bathrooms. Once laid, it needs little attention, except sweeping and occasional washing and polishing. Abrasive cleaner may damage the surface, so use mild detergent to remove any spills before they stain. If a glossy vinyl fades, it can be recoated with a wipe-over liquid coating.

Unlike its predecessor, linoleum, sheet vinyl is relatively easy to lay. And although it takes longer to put down than vinyl tiles, it involves fewer joins and has the added advantage of offering a wider choice of patterns. The name vinyl derives from polyvinyl chloride (pvc), the flexible plastic from which it is made. Other materials are added, but the best-quality vinyls contain a high proportion of pvc.

Points to remember

◇ Never remove old vinyl by sanding or grinding; harmful asbestos fibers may be released into the air.
◇ Roll widths vary according to the brand, but 6ft and 12ft are the most popular. The supplier will cut the length you require from the roll but check your measurements first.

For more information on types of sheet vinyl, see Choosing materials, pp. 130-3.

Types of vinyl

Sheet vinyl comes in a wide range of qualities, textures, patterns and colors The cheapest types are pressed on to a thin backing and have a clear, resilient coating. Most vinyls, however, have a cushioned backing, which makes them quieter, warmer and softer underfoot.

Lay-flat vinyl
The easiest type to put down is the "lay-flat" variety, which is stabilized with a glassfiber mesh backing to ensure that it remains flat throughout its life. This means that it needs no adhesive, except on doorway edges and seams. The reinforcement minimizes the risk of tearing and also allows the sheet to be folded without cracking, so that it can be taken home in the back of a car.

Choosing patterns
Each type of vinyl is available in a variety of colors and designs. If your room is irregular, a random pattern, such as a marble or stone effect, can help to disguise the shape. If the perimeters of the room are straight, then a pattern with distinct parallel lines, such as a tile effect, may look good.

Since vinyl is normally used in small rooms, a small pattern is usually best. This creates a feeling of space, makes pattern matching easy, and tends to conceal joins.

If the room already contains some geometric patterns – on the walls or curtains for example – any geometric design on the floor should be a similar shape and color scheme.

Avoiding seams
The latest vinyls come in roll widths of up to 13ft, and in virtually unlimited lengths, so that, by careful planning, all but the largest rooms can be covered with one sheet, thus avoiding time-consuming joins. Most vinyls, however, are available in an easy-match pattern, so that if smaller widths are used, the seams will not be too obvious.

Tools and equipment

For laying sheet vinyl, you simply need cutting, measuring and adhesive equipment and a ballpoint pen. Other useful items include a small block of wood for making trimming lines and some thick paper if you are going to make templates.

Care and storage
Remember to clean any dirty equipment after use and store rolls of vinyl on their side. Never stand unsupported rolls on end or the vinyl may distort and crack.

Cutting tools
You need a utility knife with some curved blades for roughly trimming the vinyl and a set of heavy-duty straight blades for accurate lines. A pair of large, sharp, unserrated scissors is also useful for cutting and trimming edges, and a large scraper for pushing the vinyl into corners.

Measuring tools
A steel rule, ideally 3ft long, is useful both for measuring and to provide a straight cutting edge when trimming.

Adhesive equipment
Use either vinyl flooring adhesive or double-sided adhesive tape for sticking down at doorways and along seams. Only use tape approved by a flooring manufacturer, since some types damage the vinyl in time. A plastic adhesive spreader may come with the can, but durable metal spreaders are available from tool stores for large jobs.

Extra equipment
A metal edging will make a neat finish in doorways.

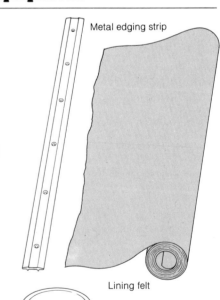

Metal edging strip

Lining felt

Strong adhesive tape

Vinyl flooring adhesive

Estimating quantities

Measure across the widest part of the room, from the base of the baseboard into the deepest part of door thresholds. Then measure the room length, allowing for any window bays and alcoves, and add 3in. for trimming in each direction. Draw up a room plan and decide how to lay the vinyl to look best from the main doorway into the room and without needing to butt join strips. The pattern should line up with the wall facing the door. Sheeting in the 13ft widths should be suitable for most rooms, but in a small room, it may prove more economical to use the 6½ft width (or 10ft where available) since there should be less wastage. When making your calculations, remember to allow for wastage caused by pattern matching.

A room plan
Draw up a plan of the room, including doors, windows and alcoves. Measure the maximum width and length, add 3in. on to each for trimming and note these on the plan. Then decide on the best direction to lay the vinyl, taking into account the roll widths available and the direction of the pattern. Aim to cover the main area of the room with one large piece of sheeting and try to position seams where they will be least noticeable.

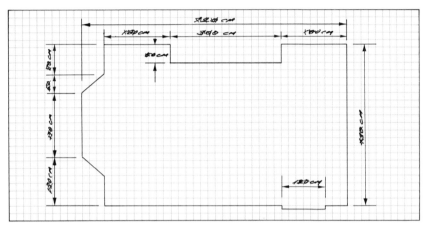

Estimating time

The most time-consuming element when laying sheet vinyl is the initial preparation of the floor. If this is minimal and there are few obstacles, a 13ft × 10ft room may be covered in under four hours.

Preparation
Sanding (with a floor sanding machine)
(4) **hours**

Laying hardboard
(4)–(5) **hours**

Making a template and cutting the vinyl
(1) **hour**

Laying
(¾)–(1¼) **hours**

Trimming
(2)–(3) **hours**

87

Preparing the floor and vinyl

Clear the room of all movable furniture and, to make the work easier, remove the doors. If you are fitting out a new bathroom, it may be a good idea to lay the vinyl before fitting baseboards or bathroom equipment. First screw down any loose floorboards (*see Job 73, p. 70*), and sand uneven areas (*see Job 77, p. 73*). If the floor is still distinctly colored by wood preservative or insecticide and smells strongly, it should be left for several months to dry out. If this is not practicable, or if the surface is uneven or unsound, cover the floor with building paper and tempered hardboard. (*See Job 75, p. 72.*) Finally, vacuum the surface.

Conditioning the vinyl
Leaving the vinyl to adjust to room temperature allows it to "relax" so it is more supple, easier to lay and stable before laying. Lay the vinyl on its side, loosely rolled with the pattern facing outward, and leave it for 24 hours in the room where it is to be fitted. In cold weather, heat the room to a comfortable working temperature.

88

Making a room template

A template cut to the dimensions of the floor will simplify fitting, particularly in small or irregularly shaped rooms. The best material to use is thick paper felt sold as carpet padding, which can be taped together to form the room shape. If replacement vinyl is being fitted, the old sheet can serve as the template. Outline the walls on the template, mark the position of any doorways and cut out holes to allow for awkward fittings. Lay out the template on the vinyl in a larger room or outdoors and centralize the pattern, then stick the template to the vinyl with adhesive tape. Transfer the outline of any obstacles from the template to the vinyl and cut a hole within the outline to allow for trimming. Then cut the vinyl about 2in. larger than the template.

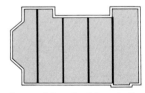

Join strips of paper felt and cut them to the outline of the room, allowing for irregular shapes

Tracing obstacles on to the template
*Cut a line from the edge of the template to the back of the pedestal and rough cut a hole around it. Then, using a 1in. wooden block to trace the contour, pencil a line, 1in. larger than the object, **1**. When transferring the shape to the vinyl, use the block to make the hole 1in. smaller than on the template, **2**.*

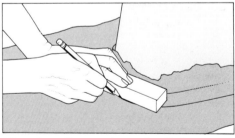

1 *Trace the outline on to the template 1in. larger than the object and make release cuts if needed*

2 *On the vinyl, trace your cutting line 1in. within the template outline*

Basic technique

How to lay and trim sheet vinyl

If you have used the template method described on the previous page, lay the cut-out vinyl sheet on the floor, taking care to align the pattern with the walls. Smooth out the main area, eliminate any bubbles, and allow the surplus to rest against the walls. Fit the pre-cut holes around the fixed obstructions by making release cuts to the edge of the vinyl — if possible, follow the natural lines in the pattern to disguise the cut marks. When the sheeting is in position, first trim and fit the internal corners, then the external corners, and finally, the borders of the room. Pull back the vinyl at doorways and seams, spread a band of adhesive on the floor and smooth the vinyl back down into position.

If the room is too large to be completed with a single sheet, cut several lengths and join them (*see Job 89, opposite*).

Fitting internal corners
*The corners of the room should always be fitted first. Gently push the vinyl into the corner with 2in. surplus riding up the wall. Fold it back and mark the position of the corner on the back of the material in a series of dots. Then join up the dots against a steel rule. Make a release cut down to the mark on the backing at the point of the corner, **1**. Then cut away small pieces to remove the surplus until the vinyl lies flat along one wall, **2**, but work carefully to avoid overcutting. The vinyl will then need to be trimmed against the other wall.*

Fitting external corners
Make slanting release cuts from the edge of the vinyl to the point where it touches the floor at each protruding corner. Press the vinyl against the baseboard, cut off the excess material and trim neatly to fit against one wall. Then trim the other side.

1 *Make a release cut to the point of the corner*

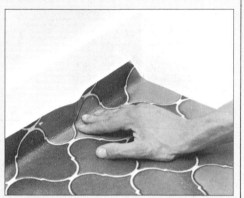

2 *Continue trimming the surplus until the vinyl fits against one wall*

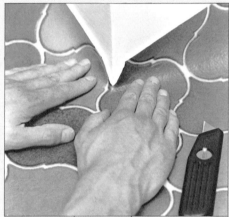

Trimming with scissors
*Having fitted the corners, the remaining edges need to be trimmed around the baseboards. The easiest way is to use scissors. Press the vinyl into the baseboard with a large scraper, fold back the surplus material and mark dots along the fold line, **1**. Pull the vinyl right back until it lays flat, join up the dots with a rule, and cut along the line with scissors, **2**. If the vinyl buckles slightly at the wall when it is replaced, re-trim the edges until it lays flat. Always cut off less than you think necessary, or you may be left with a gap at the baseboard. Take particular care with the last two edges; there will be no surplus.*

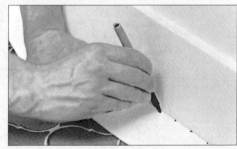

1 *Mark a series of dots along the fold*

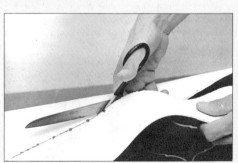

2 *Trim along the dotted line*

Trimming with a knife
The fastest way to trim the edges is to cut free-hand, but this may need some practice to ensure a good fit. Press the vinyl firmly into the angle between the floor and the baseboard with a broad paint scraper and cut to fit with a sharp trimming knife, held at an angle. Continue working around the room and cut off the remnant strips.

Marking trimming lines with a scriber
Another method is to use a block of wood and pencil to mark a cutting line. Pull the vinyl slightly away from the wall, keeping the line of the material straight. Lodge the block against the wall and trace the room's contours on the vinyl. Cut and fit, then repeat the sequence along the remaining walls.

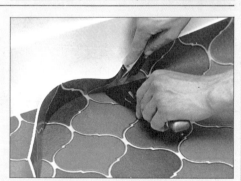

89
Joining sheets

Where more than one sheet is to be used, and joins are inevitable, add 3in. to each sheet for trimming on the overlap. You should mark a chalked guide line across the floor for the first length and try not to position seams in heavy-traffic areas.

Matching up the edges
The sheets are first fitted to the perimeter of the room, ensuring that the pattern matches and aligns exactly at the overlap. The edges are then trimmed. At this stage, if the vinyl is not the "lay-flat" variety, it can be secured to the floor with an overall coating of adhesive. Where the two sheets meet in the main area of the room, a cut is made through both sheets, along a suitable pattern line. When the offcuts are removed from above and below, the two edges are pressed down on to a band of adhesive on the floor, so that they form a neat seam. Any subsequent sheets are joined in the same way, and when the last sheet is in place, any loose edges can be secured with adhesive. Wipe surplus adhesive off the surface with a damp cloth.

Making the first join
When the first sheet is fitted in place, overlap the edge of the second sheet on top. Hold a steel straight-edge against a suitable pattern line, and, using a sharp utility knife held vertically, cut through the double thickness of vinyl, **1**. Remove the top offcut strip, then fold back the edges of both sheets and remove the other, **2**. Spread a 8in. band of vinyl adhesive on the floor along the join line. Replace the edges and press down firmly, **3**, if necessary using a wallpaper seam roller to ensure a firm bond, **4**. Finally, wipe surplus adhesive off the surface with a damp cloth before it begins to set.

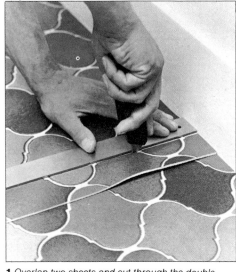
1 Overlap two sheets and cut through the double thickness

2 Remove the offcut from beneath the overlap

3 Spread a band of adhesive on the floor and press down the edges to form a seam

4 Finish with a seam roller for a firm join

90
Using metal strips

A threshold strip fastened on to the edge of vinyl in a doorway will protect the material from scuffing and will neatly cover the join between carpet and vinyl. It will also help to hide a bad join between two sheets of vinyl. Metal edging strips have evenly spaced, pre-drilled holes and are fixed in position with screws. They are available in aluminum, but a strip of hardwood could be used instead.

Screwing down the strip
Cut the metal edging strip to size, taking a little off each end to ensure the fixing points remain evenly spaced. Then screw it in the door threshold over the join between the two materials.

91
Patching tears

Any large areas of damage should be patched with an offcut. The new patch will need to be cut larger than the tear and adjusted to match the pattern. Having chosen a suitable line of pattern for the edge of the patch, you cut through both pieces of vinyl, using a sharp knife. The old piece is removed and the new patch coated with adhesive and pressed into place.

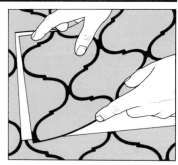
Fitting a new patch
Check the new patch for fit and pattern match, before gluing it into the gap left by the old piece. Use vinyl repair adhesive to "weld" the edges of the tear at the surface.

Paneling

Planning ◇ Estimating time and quantities ◇ Tools and equipment ◇ Preparing a wall for paneling ◇ How to put up board and sheet paneling
Paneling around corners and obstructions
Cladding ceilings

Paneling can form an attractive feature in a room. It provides a simple way of leveling an irregular wall surface and creates a permanent form of decoration that will require little attention in the future. You can also conceal insulating material and new wiring behind the panels. Paneling can be made of individual boards or of sheet material designed to imitate boards. Individual boards are easy to transport. But using sheet materials involves less work.

Two basic board types are available: tongue-and-groove, where the boards interlock, and shiplap, where each board rests over a lip on the previous one.

Sheet paneling varies greatly in cost and quality. Cheap boards often consist of a photographic reproduction of wooden paneling printed on to a thin vinyl sheet.

Points to remember

◇ Allow for overlaps when estimating quantities of paneling.
◇ Use battens or board offcuts to support the baseboard.
◇ Start paneling at one corner of the room for the neatest result.
◇ Make sure all boards or sheets are exactly vertical.

For more information on types of paneling, see Choosing materials, pp. 126-9.

Planning

Apart from the paneling itself, you will probably need to attach supporting furring strips to the wall. These should be 2in. × 1in. and can be unplaned as they will be concealed under the paneling. If the furring strips are for an exterior wall, it is worth getting the wood treated with preservative so that it will not rot. If the paneling is intended to increase insulation, you should consider putting glassfiber, mineral wool, or rigid board insulation between the boards and the wall.

For the paneling itself, a selection of colors is available. If you are choosing paneling for a small room, remember that dark paneling can produce a claustrophobic effect and make the room seem smaller and darker. Natural wood veneers normally come pre-sealed, so there is no finishing to do.

Estimating time

The figures give an estimate of the time it will take to panel a 13ft × 7½ft wall with either individual boards or sheet material. The time for preparing the wall surface includes time for putting up furring strips. The total time for putting up the paneling will vary according to your own skill and many obstructions there are in the wall, and whether you have to panel around corners and into window reveals. But you can use these figures as a guide, converting them for your own wall sizes.

The other factor that will affect the time the job will take is whether you use boards or a sheet paneling material. Of course, individual boards usually take longer to put up than large sheets. But working round obstructions can be more time-consuming with sheet paneling since it is necessary to cut holes in the middle of sheets.

Ceilings usually take longer because you are working in an awkward position. The time shown here is for a ceiling 13ft × 10ft.

Preparing a wall

Basic preparation

④ - ⑧ **hours**

Fixing furring strips around a window

(¼) - (½) **hour**

Putting up board paneling

Paneling a wall

⑥ - ⑧ **hours**

Paneling around a window

① - (1¾) **hours**

Fitting paneling around a door

(½) - (¾) **hour**

Fitting paneling around a receptacle

(¼) - (¾) **hour**

Putting up sheet paneling

Paneling a wall

③ - ⑤ **hours**

Paneling around a window

① - ② **hours**

Fitting paneling around a door ·

(¾) - ① **hour**

Fitting paneling around a receptacle

(¼) - ① **hour**

Cladding a ceiling

⑧ - ⑫ **hours**

Estimating quantities

Measure the room width and height. Both tongue-and-groove and shiplap paneling are made up of individual boards that overlap (see right). So when you are using individual boards, take this into account when measuring. For vertical paneling divide the exact width of one board into the total room width. Then multiply the result by the room height. Add 10 per cent for wastage and joins.

For sheet materials you need pieces that are long enough to reach from floor to ceiling. So measure the room width to find out how many sheets you will require and allow for wastage. Most sheets measure 4ft × 8ft.

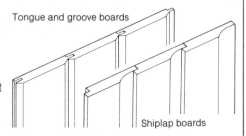

Tongue and groove boards

Shiplap boards

Tools and equipment

For sheet materials, use a circular saw with a fine blade or a cross-cut hand saw. One with eight teeth to 1in. is best. For cutting individual boards and furring strips, use a back saw. You will also need a key-hole saw or a saber saw for cutting holes. Other equipment includes a claw and pin hammers, a nail set, a drill, a steel tape measure, a carpenter's level, and a square. For panel adhesive, you will need a caulking gun and adhesive cartridges. For boards, panel clips are very useful.

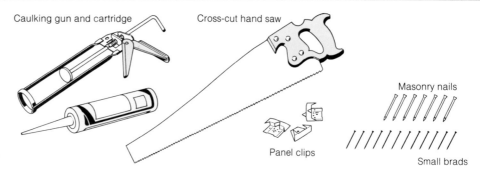

Caulking gun and cartridge

Cross-cut hand saw

Masonry nails

Panel clips

Small brads

92

Preparing a wall for paneling

Adding paneling will hide the wall completely, so you should make sure it is well prepared and free of problems such as dampness. Internal walls usually give no dampness problems, but external walls must be perfectly dry. Do not worry if there is condensation on the wall.

You should also examine porous walls for damage to the pointing. Rake out and replace all loose and crumbling mortar and brickwork. Finally, treat the whole wall with a silicone water repellent. This will prevent water getting in, yet still allow the wall to "breathe". It is a good idea to fix a poly-ethylene vapor barrier over the wall surface before attaching the furring strips. This will stop condensation forming.

To allow for the supporting furring strips, you will also need to remove the base-board and any picture rail. If you are going to use insulation material under the panel-ing, this should be inserted after the furring strips are in position.

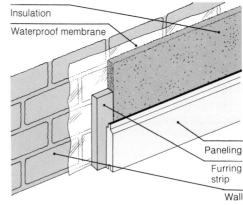

Insulation

Waterproof membrane

Paneling

Furring strip

Wall

Removing baseboards

If you want to replace the baseboards in front of your paneling, be careful not to damage them. Loosen a section of the baseboard with an old chisel, and then slip the claw of a hammer under the board to lever it away. Pull out any nails in the baseboard from the back – if you take them out from the front you will damage the face of the board.

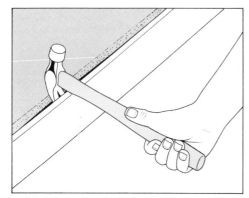

Removing picture rails

You need only take these away if they stand proud of the furring strips and obstruct the paneling. Make a cut in the rail close to one of the nails and break the rail away. It will be easier if you use a length of steel pushed under the rail to lever it up. By using this method you will avoid doing too much damage to the surrounding plaster.

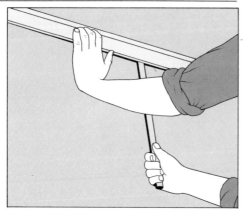

Fixing furring strips for vertical boards

For vertical boards, you should fix hori-zontal furring strips at intervals of approximately 15in. Use a carpenter's level to get them exactly straight. Put hardboard packing pieces behind the strips if you need to level them. Secure the strips to the wall with masonry nails, or with wallplugs and screws, depending on the condition of the wall. At base-board level fit short lengths of furring strip vertically, to support the baseboard when you put it back in place. It is im-portant to put these pieces at carefully set distances so that you can locate them easily under the paneling when you come to refit the baseboard.

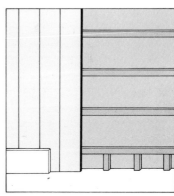

Fixing furring strips for horizontal boards

For horizontal paneling, the strips should be vertical and placed about the same distance apart as for vertical boards. The lowest board should go behind the baseboard, but it need not go right down to the floor. If this is the case, support the baseboard on short lengths of paneling attached between the furring strips and the baseboard itself.

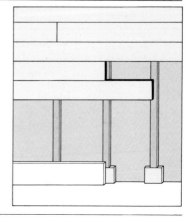

Basic technique

How to put up sheet paneling

For sheet paneling you need horizontal furring strips with additional vertical strips placed so that their center lines correspond to the edges of the sheets. If, however, you are fitting this type of paneling on to a hollow wall, the simplest method is to remove any wallpaper and stick the sheets directly on to the wall. If you prefer to use furring strips, you should find wooden studs in the wall and nail the furring strips to these. The plasterboard itself cannot give adequate support for the furring strips.

If the walls are square, you can stick the panels on to them using panel adhesive and a caulking gun. Alternatively, fix horizontal furring strips at 15in. intervals. You will also need one vertical strip for each joint in the paneling. It is difficult to butt the sheets perfectly together. A good solution is to make a feature of the joint, either by hiding it with beading, or by leaving a slight decorative gap. If you do this, allow for the width of the gap.

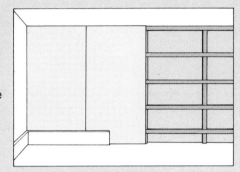

Battening for sheet paneling
For the large sheets that make up this type of paneling, you need horizontal and vertical battens.

Fixing sheet paneling using pins
When you have removed the base-board, start paneling from one corner. Make sure that your first sheet is vertical. If the walls are not square, leave a small gap in the corner. You can conceal this with quarter-round molding later. You should leave a gap – of about $\frac{1}{4}$in. – at the bottom to allow for expansion. This will be covered by the baseboard. If your panels are grooved, drive brads through the grooves and sink them slightly below the surface. If your sheet paneling does not have grooves, you will have to pin through the board. You should sink the nails with a punch and later fill the holes.

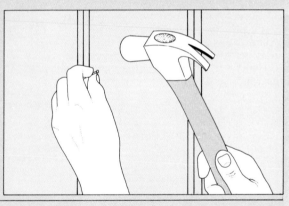

Fixing sheet paneling using adhesive
Panel adhesive can be used to glue sheets to furring strips or directly to the wall. It has slight gap-filling properties, so it will take up any small variations in the wall surface. If you are sticking the panels straight on to the wall, apply ribbons of adhesive on the back of the sheet at about 15in. intervals. Press the sheet on to the wall, working from the bottom to the top. It is important to work quickly. If the adhesive is losing its effect by the time you put the board up to the wall, try cutting up the boards so you are dealing with a smaller area at a time.

If the wall is very uneven, it is best to use furring strips. Pack the strips with shims of hard-board to allow for the unevenness in the wall. Apply the adhesive liberally to the relevant strips and, working quickly, press the sheet on to it, making sure that all the strips are in contact.

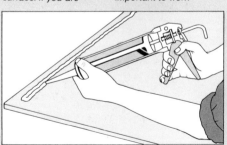

When not using furring strips, apply the adhesive to the boards themselves

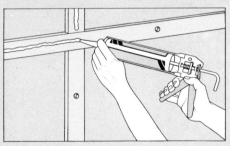

If you are using furring strips, apply a generous layer of adhesive directly to them

---

Fitting sheet paneling around corners

There are two basic problems when you are paneling up to a corner with sheet material – measuring (*see opposite*) and finishing off the corner (*see below*). With external corners you have to overlap slightly and sand one sheet back.

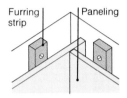 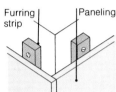

Internal corners
Take one piece right into the corner and butt the next piece over it at right angles.

External corners
Overlap slightly with one piece and then sand it back with fine-grade sandpaper.

Fitting sheet paneling around obstructions

The greatest problem with sheet materials is cutting holes of the right shape to fit around obstructions such as electrical fixtures. The safest way is to make an accurate template in thin cardboard. Transfer the pattern to your sheet when you are sure it is accurate. If you are in any doubt, cut the holes on the small side – you can always enlarge them later.

To cut around doors and windows you should use the same method as for individual boards (*see Job 98, p. 87*).

Finishing off sheet paneling

If you have left small gaps between each sheet, you can either cover these with a wood or plastic strip, or leave them as they are. As an alternative to creating exact butt joints at the corners (*see Job 93, above*), you can leave a narrow gap to allow for variations in the width of the wall and finish off the corners with beading. You can also put beading at the top for a neat join with the ceiling.

Cutting sheet paneling to fit a corner
If your walls are perfectly square, you can measure the distance between your last sheet and the corner and draw a cutting line on the paneling with a set square and ruler. But if your walls are not square, you will probably have to mark the final panel for cutting, using a simple scribing block. This technique allows you to draw a line for cutting that corresponds exactly to the contour of the wall.

Cut a sheet about 4in. wider than you require, raise it to the corner, and check with a carpenter's level that it is perfectly vertical, **1**.

Next, with a simple scribing block in contact with the wall, draw a pencil line on the sheet that will correspond to the contour of the wall, **2**. *Use a fine-toothed keyhole saw to cut along this line. When you have done this, put the sheet up to the corner to check that it fits. You should then mark on the other edge of the sheet the exact position of the adjoining sheet,* **3**, *and join the marks with a straight edge. When you have cut to this line the piece should fit exactly in the corner space.*

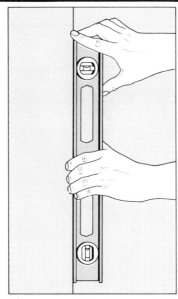

1 Use a carpenter's level to ensure that the corner panel is vertical

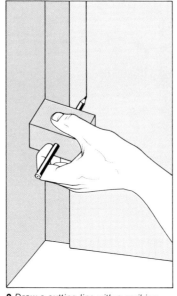

2 Draw a cutting line with a scribing block held against the wall

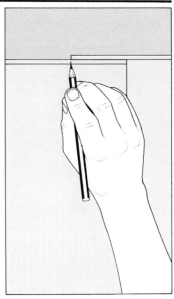

3 Mark the edge position of the adjoining sheet

96
Paneling ceilings

Paneled ceilings can look very attractive, and paneling is useful to disguise ceilings in poor condition. All ceiling panels – whether sheet or board – will need to be attached to furring strips; do not glue paneling to ceilings.

Drill and countersink your furring strips to take wood screws and fix the strips to the joists at 2in. intervals. Run them at right angles to the ceiling joists, so that you have regular fixing points.

If you are going to make use of an existing light fixture, lower it to the same level as the new paneling. If you are not going to use it, you may have to replace it with a junction box from which you can take lengths of cable for new light fixtures. Put in extra lengths of furring strip to take the light fixtures.

Decorate the panels before putting them up. If you are putting up the paneling in a bathroom or kitchen, seal both sides of the wood so that it does not absorb moisture.

Start working from one wall and use the same techniques as for wall paneling. Clips offer the easiest method of securing the boards because you can put them in position before raising the panels up to them. If you use pins, make start holes in the wood first. If you are using cut pieces of board, arrange the joins over the centers of the furring strips.

Getting an exact fit around the perimeter of a ceiling is not easy, but any gaps can be concealed with a narrow decorative beading or molding to finish off.

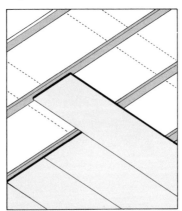

Supporting ceiling paneling
For ceiling paneling, attach supporting furring strips to the ceiling joists

The effects of paneling in a room

Wooden paneling can transform a room. The wood's natural appearance and the strong lines created by the gaps between boards are the most important elements.

Using paneling in a bathroom
Paneling with boards can emphasize the length of a small room. In a bathroom, paneling the bath and other fixtures, and building in a mirror, can add to this effect. The other advantage of the boards is that they conceal pipes.

Basic technique

How to put up board paneling

At least a week before you start, take the paneling into the room where you are going to fit it. This will allow the wood's moisture content to adjust to the room. It is particularly important if there is a big difference between the storage and room conditions. If the wood has been stored outdoors and is then brought into a centrally heated room, it will shrink considerably, and if you put up the paneling too soon, unsightly gaps can open up between the boards.

There are two main ways of fixing boards. The traditional method is to drive small brads through the boards into the furring strips. But clip systems are now available that provide invisible fixings for tongue-and-groove boards.

Fixing shiplap paneling
Position the first board in one corner of the room and make sure that it is exactly vertical. Then hammer the brads through the face of the board into the furring strips, just to one side of the rabbeted section, 1. Sink the brads with a nail set and take care not to let the hammer slip and bruise the wood.

Then go on to the rest of the boards. It is best to tap each board when you position it, to get it as near the previous one as possible. When you do this, protect the wood with a scrap of paneling to prevent the hammer bruising the wood. You should also check each individual board with a carpenter's level, to make sure that it is vertical. If you do not do this, you will repeat any error in every board. Pin each board to the strips at the same position as with the first board, 2. The overlap will help secure the board. When you have finished, fill the nail holes with a matching putty.

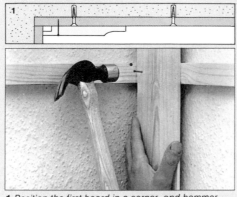

1 *Position the first board in a corner, and hammer brads through its face into the furring strip*

2 *Tap each subsequent board into place and pin it in the same way*

Fixing tongue-and-groove paneling using brads
Fit the first board with its groove pointing into a corner. Make sure the board is vertical, then pin it to each furring strip. Do not worry if there is a slight gap between the board and the wall – you can cover this with beading when you finish off the paneling. The brads should be about $\frac{1}{2}$ in. from the groove edge, 1. Drive each brad below the surface with a nail set. Then hammer brads through the shoulder of the tongue, angling them into the wood. The board is now held by two brads in each furring strip. Nailing in this way means that when you place the next board over the tongue, its groove should hide the brads.

When you add the second and subsequent boards, you only need to put one pin into each furring strip. This is because the interlocking tongues and grooves themselves help to secure the paneling. So for these boards you only need to hammer brads into the shoulder of the tongue, 2. If your wood is slightly brittle, it is worth making start holes for the brads using a fine twist drill in a wheel brace. If you do split the tongues you will find it very difficult to slot it into the next groove, and will probably have to remove and replace the board.

When you have finished, go back and fill the holes made by the nail set in the first board, using a matching wood putty.

Fixing tongue-and-groove paneling using clips
Different clip systems are available to fit particular board profiles. Some systems offer two types of clips – starter plates and standard clips. With systems that provide starter plates, begin paneling in one corner and, using the galvanized brads supplied, fix a starter plate to each furring strip. This should be level with the edge position of the first board. If the wall is not square, make sure the first board is vertical. You can conceal any slight gap with beading later. After stripping off the tongue from the first board, press the cut edge on to the starter plates, 1. You may have to tap it into position. If so, protect the wood from damage with a piece of scrap wood held between the hammer and panel.

If you are using a system without starter clips, you should pin the tongue edge of the first board directly to the furring strips, hammering down the brads with a nail set so that you can fill the holes later.

With the first board in place, you fit standard clips in the groove of this board and pin these clips to the furring strips so that the board is secure. Next place the tongue of the second board in the groove of the first, 2, and press it home. Then fit another set of standard clips in the groove of the second board. You can cover the whole wall surface in this way.

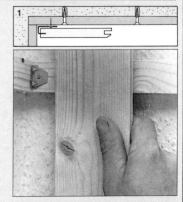

1 *Fit the first board with a starter plate*

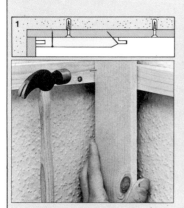

1 *On the first board, insert clips $\frac{1}{2}$in. from the groove edge*

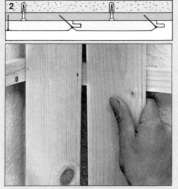

2 *Pin all subsequent boards through the shoulder of the tongue*

2 *Fit clips into each groove and press in the next tongue*

97
Fitting board paneling around corners

At an internal wall corner with tongue-and-groove boards, make a neat joint of two grooves. Tuck one tightly into the corner, and butt the next one up to it. Use clips only if they leave no gap between boards.

Work away from external corners for a neat result. If you are using clips, remove the tongues from the corner boards, secure them so that they just touch and fill the gap with beading. If you are using brads, bring two grooves together at the corner. Fill the gap with beading. With shiplap, you will get the neatest result with the squared ends in the corners.

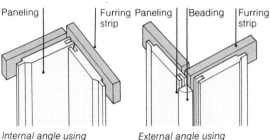
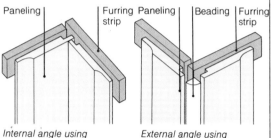

Internal angle using tongue-and-groove boards

External angle using tongue-and groove boards

Internal angle using shiplap boards

External angle using shiplap boards

98
Fitting board paneling around obstacles

The main problems with paneling come when you have to work round obstructions such as doors, windows, and electrical fixtures. Where possible, it is best to bring switches and receptacles to the surface of the paneling by building them up from behind.

With windows, you can use beading to produce neat edges where the paneling meets the window reveal. With doors, you can also use beading to finish off, but you should remove the architrave and replace it over the paneling.

When you are paneling round electrical fixtures you should cut a cardboard template to fit around the obstruction. Then transfer the pattern to the boards and use a keyhole saw to cut away the waste material. Remember that you will have to raise flush-mounted units above the wall surface. If you put new wiring behind the boards, put it in conduit.

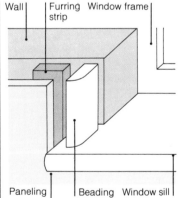
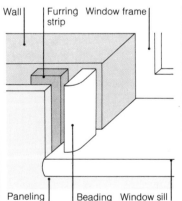
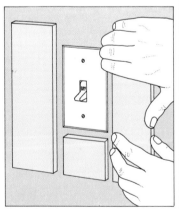

Doors
Carefully pry up the architrave that surrounds the door opening, letting the nails pull through the back so that the front is not damaged. Attach a vertical furring strip to the wall to support the edge of the paneling. When you have secured the paneling, choose a beading that will conceal both the batten and the join with the paneling. Then pin back the original architrave.

Windows
With windows, the main problem is turning the paneling into the reveals. This requires neat external angles (see Job 97, above). For most window reveals, it is easiest to stick the paneling to the wall, because there is no room to fit furring strips. Alternatively, you can stop the paneling about $\frac{1}{4}$in. from the turn and finish it off with strips of beading.

Receptacles
After cutting the paneling to fit around the switch or socket, surround the unit with short pieces of furring strip, putting them as close to the fitting as possible and securing them with panel adhesive. With flush-mounted receptacles and switches, raise the boxes behind, so that the top edges are flush with the panel surface.

99
Joining boards

If necessary, short lengths of board can be butt-joined, provided that the join is positioned over a batten. For a neat finish, cut the ends of butt-joined boards to a perfect right angle. Mark them with a set square, then use a miter box for cutting a true angle.

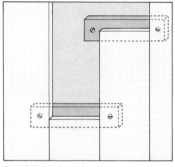

Butt joining boards
Where there is no batten on the wall, insert extra, short lengths at the join.

100
Finishing off board paneling

Cut your final board so that a gap of about $\frac{1}{4}$in. is left between it and the wall. This is to allow for expansion. If you do not leave a gap, the paneling may bow if it expands. You can hide the gap later by fitting a length of beading or a piece of decorative molding.

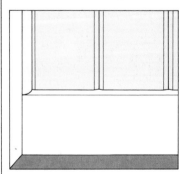

Using beading or molding
These will hide the expansion gap and conceal any irregularity in the wall.

Dry walling

Estimating time and quantities ◇ Tools and equipment ◇ Preparing the wall ◇ How to apply wallboard to walls and ceilings Dealing with obstructions ◇ Repairing plaster and wallboard

Gypsum wallboard can be used to dry-line a solid wall, to cover a previously plastered wall, or to create a non-load bearing partition wall. It provides a good base for decorating with paint, wallpaper or lightweight tiles and paneling, and for a more perfect surface can be given a skim coat of plaster before decorating.

Wallboard also improves the insulation and sound-proofing of a room. Special thermal and fire-resistant boards are available for added protection. Alternatively, a double layer of ordinary wallboard can be fitted to increase the heat, sound and fire-insulating properties of the wall or ceiling.

While plastering demands a level of skill, applying wallboard is a relatively quick and easy job for the non-professional. There is little wastage, and unlike plaster, wallboard requires no drying time. Small plaster repairs, however, such as filling cracks and holes in an otherwise sound plaster wall, are well within the scope of the amateur.

Large sheets of wallboard should be handled with care. Less stress is imposed on the board if it is carried vertically, and the boards are also less likely to crack if they are stored on a dry, flat surface. In many cases, small cracks, holes and dents can be repaired.

Points to remember

◇ Avoid cutting panels slightly too large or the edges will crumble when the board is fitted.
◇ A metal corner bead will protect corners from damage.
◇ Check your building codes before you buy wallboard to be sure you choose the right thickness and quality.
◇ When nailing boards into place, start in a corner.

Estimating time

Fitting a wallboard may not take as long as you think. The most time-consuming element is removing old plaster. If you are applying wallboard to a smooth, medium-sized wall or to a stud partition, it may take only five hours to complete.

But if old plaster is to be removed, it could take 12 hours. The times given below give an approximate idea how long it would take to apply wallboard to a 12 × 7ft area. Remember to allow a little time for planning and for cutting boards.

Preparing the surface and repairing damaged plaster
($\frac{1}{2}$)-(1) hours

Fixing furring strips
(4)-(8) hours

Nailing boards to ceilings
($1\frac{1}{2}$)-($2\frac{1}{2}$) hours

Nailing boards to walls
(2)-(3) hours

Cutting round obstructions
(1) hour

Finishing joints
($\frac{3}{4}$)-($1\frac{1}{2}$) hours

Finishing corners
(1) hour

Estimating quantities

Standard wallboards are sold as 4 × 8ft sheets. Larger 4 × 10ft and 4 × 12ft sizes are also available but are heavier. Boards are usually hung horizontally, since this involves 25 percent fewer joins if your ceiling is under 8ft. But if you are working alone, if your ceiling is higher than 8ft or if the position of a window or door dictates a different arrangement, it may be better to fit them vertically. If, for example,

your wall is 12 × 7ft, you would need two 4 × 8ft boards, installed horizontally, one above the other, with one cut to 3 × 8ft, and two more boards cut to 4 × 4ft (or a vertically fitted board cut to 4 × 7ft). But if the wall was 12 × 8ft 2in. with a central window, you would need two 4 × 8ft boards installed vertically either side of the window and a third, cut to accommodate the window.

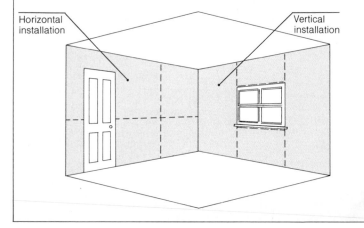

Horizontal installation

Vertical installation

Types of plasterboard

Plasterboard is a layer of chalklike gypsum plaster sandwiched between two sheets of heavy paper. The paper extends over the long (8ft) edges of the boards, but not over the short ends (4ft).

Standard wallboard
Standard wallboard is $\frac{1}{2}$in. thick and has one smooth, ivory-coloured face for painting or papering and one coarser, gray paper face, which can be plastered. Other thicknesses are available, such as $\frac{3}{8}$in. boards, often used as a sound-deadening backer panel if two layers of wallboard are installed, and $\frac{5}{8}$in. boards.

Specialist wallboards
Other types of wallboard are manufactured for specific requirements. Type X has a special fire-resistant core and is specified in some local building codes for areas of high fire risk, such as garages. Vapor-check wallboard, identified by a green finish, is highly water-resistant and so designed for bath and shower rooms. Thermal board is also made, for increased insulating properties. Always consult your local building codes for the type, thickness and finishing method required.

Finishes
Some wallboards have decorative surfaces, such as imitation wood grain, textures or patterns. These are designed to be painted over and will need a coat of primer or base paint before painting. Boards are also sold with a variety of edge profiles.

Types of edge profile
The most basic wallboards have squared edges, but tapered, beveled, rounded and tongue-and-groove edges are also manufactured for neat joins. Square edges are joined with tape and jointing finish, but tapered edges form a shallow trough and so allow the joints to be reinforced unobtrusively. Beveled edges allow two boards to slide together and form a decorative V-joint. Tongue-and-groove wallboards like tiles and wooden panels have a protruding tongue at one edge and a grooved indentation at the other. The tongue of each panel thus slots into the groove of its neighbor.

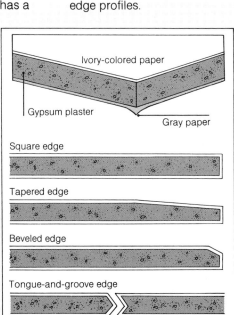

Ivory-colored paper

Gypsum plaster

Gray paper

Square edge

Tapered edge

Beveled edge

Tongue-and-groove edge

Thermal wallboard
This type of board is bonded to a thick backing layer of insulating foam and is widely used for lining cold exterior walls. Some types also incorporate a vapor-check plastic membrane.

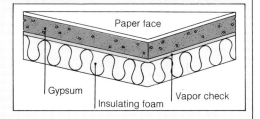

Paper face

Gypsum

Insulating foam

Vapor check

Tools and equipment

The only specialist equipment needed for dry walling are jointing compound and tape and a corner angle and tool. For patching plaster a trowel and a float are the essentials. For preparing the surface, you may also need a broad-bladed chisel and a baby sledge hammer to remove old plaster.

Plasterboard tools
You will need a sharp knife and a keyhole saw to cut the boards and coated nails to secure them. Use $1\frac{5}{8}$in. nails on $\frac{1}{2}$in. and $\frac{3}{8}$in. boards and $1\frac{7}{8}$in. nails on $\frac{5}{8}$in. boards. Allow $5\frac{1}{4}$lbs for every 1000 square feet of board. For finishing, you will need a putty knife and two 60ft rolls of tape and a 5 gal. pail of jointing compound for the same area. Metal corner beads are for finishing external corners, and a taping tool for internal corners.

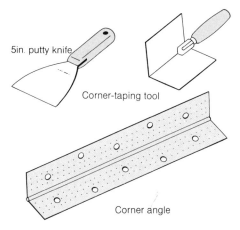

5in. putty knife

Corner-taping tool

Corner angle

Plastering tools
The most important tool for applying plaster to cracks and holes is a rectangular steel trowel, roughly 10 × 5in. Use a wooden float with three or four nails driven in to it, for devilling the surface and use screed beads to reinforce vulnerable areas and bridge gaps.

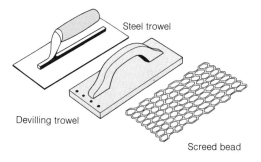

Steel trowel

Devilling trowel

Screed bead

101
Preparing the surface

Before you begin any wallboarding job, it is important to prepare the background thoroughly. On an old masonry wall, hack off the old plaster with a brick chisel and baby sledge hammer, rake out the loose plaster and dust it off, then repoint any crumbling pointing with mortar (*see Job 195, p. 202*). Smooth surfaces, such as timber and concrete should be completely dry. Before fitting boards check that there is enough insulation at external walls, and, if necessary, fit insulating batts.

Removing old plaster
If the wall is covered with a layer of old plaster, you should take it right back to the brick. Knock off the old plaster using a baby sledge hammer and brick chisel. If the pointing is crumbling, clean it and fill the holes with mortar.

Basic technique

How to apply wallboard

Wallboard should be nailed to the wooden stud framework on a partition wall, or to wooden furring strips to dry-line a solid wall, so that the boards can be nailed into solid wood. When you have planned out the position of the boards, and whether to fit the boards vertically or horizontally (*see Estimating quantities, p. 88*) you will have to cut some of the boards to size. If the boards are to be applied horizontally, it is best to install the top boards first to fit snugly against the ceiling. It is usually easiest to get a helper to hold the boards in position, while you insert temporary nails into the wooden framework. Permanent nails can then be added about 7in. apart on all the studs. If you are positioning the boards vertically, the long edge of the board is aligned with a vertical section of the framework, the top edge is pushed against the ceiling and any gap at the foot can be covered later with the baseboard. To ensure a close fit at ceiling level, and to leave both hands free for nailing, vertical boards can be raised off the ground with a "foot lever." Again the board is lightly nailed to the studs. For a firmer fixing, you can use a combined adhesive and nail-on fixing. In this case, adhesive is applied to the studs and the board is only nailed to the studs around its perimeter, instead of to all the studs.

Installing furring strips
If the existing wall does not have a stud framework, you will have to erect a wooden framework of furring strips. First remove the moldings and trim and work out a layout to suit the positioning of the boards. A typical arrangement is to install vertical furring strips at 16in. intervals, then add horizontal strips, again at 16in. intervals, to form a grid of 16in. squares. Mark guide lines on the wall, using a plumb bob or carpenters level to ensure that all verticals and horizontals are true. Secure the 1 × 2in. strips into position, using adhesive or masonry nails or a combination of the two. If the surface is uneven, you may need to insert wooden shims behind some strips.

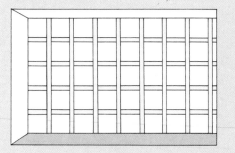

Cutting boards to size
Unless you are fortunate enough to find boards to fit exactly into the dimensions of your walls, you will have to use cut pieces. First mark a cutting line, using a pencil and straight-edge and score along the line with a sharp knife to cut through the paper layer. Stand the board on edge, with the cut line vertical, and grip the top end of the waste piece. Then slap this section with your other hand, while pulling it back slightly with your first hand. This should break the core and leave the paper intact the other side. Fold the board to 90°, then run a knife down the fold to cut the paper and free the waste piece, **1**. To fit around obstacles, however, use a keyhole saw, **2**. If the hole is the middle of a board, push the point of the saw blade firmly through the board and try to make a clean-edged cut. At external corners, when cutting boards to width, where possible, arrange for a paper-covered board edge to overlap a cut one.

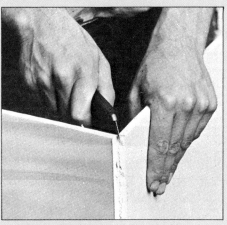

1 *Break the core of the board, then bend it and slice through the paper*

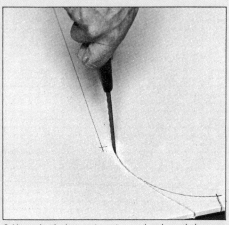

2 *Use a keyhole saw to cut round awkward shapes*

Securing the boards in place
*Maneuver the cut-to-size board into position against the wall. All boards need to fit tightly up against the ceiling and vertical boards should finish just below the top of the baseboard, so use a "foot lever", made from scraps of wood, to pry it up and leave both hands free to drive in the fixing nails, **1**. Use coated 1¼in. wallboard nails and insert them into the wooden studs or furring strips at 6in. intervals and no closer than ½in. from the board* edge, **2**. Hammer them in until the head just grips the surface of the paper, then tap lightly until the hammer head just dimples the board surface without bursting it. You can fill the dimple with plaster later, for an invisible fixing. Fit subsequent boards in the same way, and push each one closely against its neighbor to form neat butt joints. Apply horizontal boards in the same way, but if possible, get a helper to hold the board against the ceiling while you nail it into position.

1 *Use a foot lever with vertical boards to ensure a close fit at ceiling level*

2 *Insert plasterboard nails at least ½in. from the board edge*

102

Applying plasterboard to a ceiling

If you are installing wallboard to both the walls and the ceilings, it is usually easier to fit the ceilings first so that the boards on the walls butt up against the ceiling boards. The ceiling boards can be positioned parallel to the joists or perpendicular to them, so your first task will be to work out the most economical plan, with the fewest joins to fall at a joist for a convenient fixing point. You should then set up

a safe working platform (see Job 14, p. 32). The most secure fixing is with both adhesive and nails. The adhesive is applied to the joists, the boards are held in position and securing nails are inserted through the boards into the joists at regular intervals. For ease of working, it is best to ask a helper to hold one end of the board in position, while you install a supporting T-brace at the other end. Ceiling boards are cut in the same way as for wallboards (see left) and it is usually best to cut boards slightly smaller rather than larger than required. If a board is too big, the edges may crumble, but if it is too small, the gap can be filled later with a filler strip.

Gluing and nailing the boards
The easiest way to apply adhesive to the joists is to insert a tube of wallboard adhesive into a large caulking gun and squeeze a line of adhesive down the center of each joist, **1**. Leave a 6in. gap at either end to prevent adhesive leaking out when the board is pressed into place. Then position the first board and get a helper to hold it firmly against the joists, while you insert a T-bar, **2**, under the board. This bar needs to be slightly taller than

the height of the ceiling. Keeping the board level, push the T-section against the ceiling, and kick the foot of the bar until it is firmly wedged beneath the board. Then begin nailing the board to the joists, **3**, at 6in. intervals, but no closer than 1in. to the edge of

the board. Tap the nails lightly until they dimple the surface. If you need to fill gaps by the wall, cut a strip from the tapered edge of a board, and nail it into the joists, so that the tapered edge makes a smooth joint with the adjoining board, **4**.

1 Apply a strip of adhesive down the center of each joist

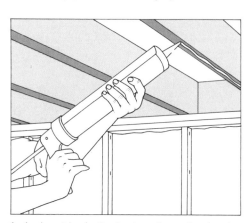

3 Insert nails at 6in. intervals along the joists

2 Hold the board in place and insert a T-bar as a support

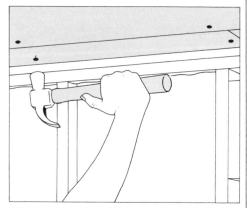

4 Fill any gaps with a strip of wallboard, cut to fit

103

Cutting wallboard around light fittings

In most rooms, you will need to accommodate an outlet box, a switch or a light fitting. This means cutting a hole of the right size in the correct position on the board. Your measurements will need to be precise, so the best method is to use a steel measuring tape to measure both the dimensions of the obstruction and its distance from both edges of the board. These measurements can then be transferred on to the board, so that the hole can be cut before the board is applied. Alternatively, if you are planning to hang a vertical wallboard, you could get a helper to hold the board in position while you trace the outline of the fitting on to the back of the board.

Marking and cutting
Measure from the point where the long edge of the board will fall, to the near side of the obstruction, then to the far side. Then measure from the nearest short

edge of the board to the near and far side of the fitting. Then transfer these lengths on to the board and mark the outline of the fitting, **1**. Cut around the lines with a keyhole saw, **2**.

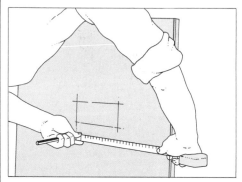

1 Trace the outline of the obstacle on to the board

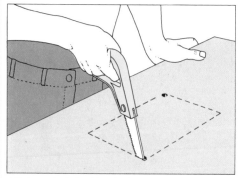

2 Cut out the hole with a keyhole saw

104

Finishing joints between boards

When all the boards have been nailed into position, the joints need to be concealed and reinforced. The cracks between the boards are first filled with a layer of good grade pre-mixed jointing compound. A band of special perforated tape is then embedded into the compound to secure the join. When the first layer of compound is dry, two more coats of jointing compound are applied for a neat finish. Each band of compound should be slightly wider than the last and should be allowed to dry thoroughly before another is added. The final coat is usually diluted with water for a smooth finish. This top layer is finally sanded gently with a fine-grit sandpaper, but care must be taken not to abrade the surface of the board. Tapered boards are designed to allow for the joints to be filled with compound, but if you are using square-edged boards, you will have to take care not to build up a thick ridge of compound.

The small indentations left by the nail heads will also have to be filled with jointing compound. Three layers are usually applied and care must be taken not to apply too much pressure or the compound will not stick.

The anatomy of the layers
The first layer of jointing compound should be spread to a width of about 3in. This forms a bed for a length of reinforcing tape which forces the compound to spread. The second layer of compound is spread to a width of about 6 to 8in. The third and final coat is usually a 10in. wide strip. With square-edged boards, the combined thickness of the tape and compound should not exceed $\frac{1}{8}$in.

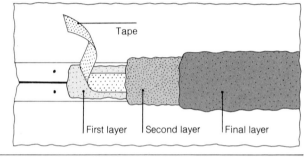

Tape

First layer | Second layer | Final layer

Taping the joins
Dip a 4in. putty knife into the jointing compound and cover half the width of the blade. Then draw the blade down the center of the seam, applying even pressure and spreading the compound into a 3in. band, **1**. *Reload the knife when necessary. Then cut off a strip of tape to the length of the join, press it into the compound and draw a clean knife down the strip to bed it in,* **2**. *At the end of the board, tear off any excess tape against the edge of the blade. Then pass the knife over the tape and scrape off any extra compound. Leave to dry for 2-3 hours, then apply a second layer of compound, spreading it smoothly to cover the tape each side,* **3**. *After a further 2-3 hours, spread on a third coat to a 10in. width and carefully feather the edges. When this final coat is dry, sand it smooth, to ensure the edges do not leave ridges,* **4**.

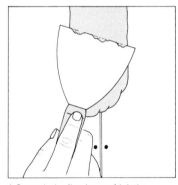

1 *Smooth the first layer of jointing compound with a 4in. putty knife*

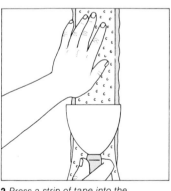

2 *Press a strip of tape into the compound so that it covers the join*

3 *Apply a second wider layer of compound and allow to dry*

4 *Sand down the third layer with a fine-grade sandpaper when dry*

105

Finishing board at corners

Joints at inside corners can be finished with tape and jointing compound. The tape is cut to run along the extent of the corner and is folded along its length to span both sides of the corner. It is pressed into a layer of jointing compound with a tool shaped specifically for the purpose. External corners need protection against accidental knocks and are best finished with metal corner beads. These are angled strips of metal with perforations to allow the compound to ooze through. They are first nailed into position on the boards and compound is then applied on top for a smooth finish.

Covering internal corners
Spread filler along both sides of the corner joint, leaving a slightly thicker layer at the joint itself. Cut the tape to length, fold and crease it in half, then press it into place with a corner taping tool. Apply a second layer, leave to dry, then add a third.

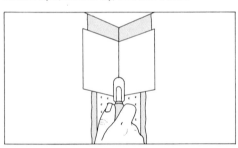

Covering external corners
Nail angled corner beads over the edges of the corner boards, then apply compound first to one side of the corner, then the other and scrape off any excess. Apply a second and third layer, taking care to feather the edges and finally sand the finish smooth.

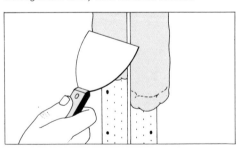

106

Patching plasterboard

Since a cavity lies behind each piece of plasterboard, holes have to be patched rather than filled. A piece of plasterboard is cut to fill the gap and is secured in place with plaster or nails. The plastered area is then finished with plaster.

Patching small holes
Cut a piece of plaster-board slightly wider than the hole in both directions. Make a hole in the middle of the piece, feed in a short length of string and tie a nail to one end. Dab some freshly mixed plaster on the face opposite the nail. Holding the string in one hand, guide the

piece into the hole, with the plastered side facing you, 1. Pull the string to wedge it back against the inner face of the board. Hold the string and press more plaster into the hole, 2, until it lies ⅛in. below the surface and leave it to harden. Cut the string, dampen the patch and fill the hole flush.

Patching large holes
Holes larger than 3in. across are best patched from the outside. Cut out a rectangle of plaster-board back to the studs on each side. Then cut a new piece to match the cut-out and nail it to the studs on each side with

plasterboard nails. To support the top and bottom edges of the patch, apply tape to the joins. Or use a plasterer's trowel to force some finishing plaster into the gaps before smoothing a top coat over the patch.

1 *Insert the patch into the hole*

2 *Hold the string and fill the hole with plaster*

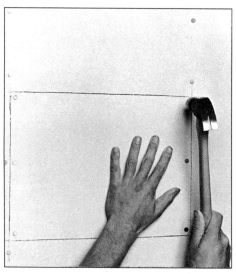

107

Filling holes in plaster

Plastered walls which are basically sound, but damaged in patches, can be repaired

without plastering. Interior filler or finishing plaster can be used, but a plaster that dries in two stages leaves the best finish and will remain workable for up to two hours. Before filling holes, consider the extent of the repair. If a solid wall sounds hollow when tapped, the plaster needs to be entirely replaced.

Repairing holes in solid walls
Score around the edges of the hole with an old nail. Brush out the dust and moisten the surface with a small brush. If you are using dry filler or plaster, mix it up to a stiff consistency. Then push it into the hole and allow it to harden. Add a second layer, and when this has set, sand the repair flush with the surface, or use a broad-bladed scraper to remove the excess. (For small holes and cracks, see Basic technique, p. 17.)

Repairing holes in lath and plaster
Cut away the loose plaster to expose the laths, and brush out the dust. If the laths are damaged, bridge the gap with a small piece of expanded metal mesh wedged into the base of the hole. Then fill to just below the surface. Cross-hatch the plaster with your knife-edge and leave it to harden for 30 minutes. Mix more plaster, wet the patch and fill it completely. Add a finishing coat and sand when dry.

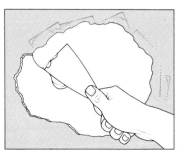

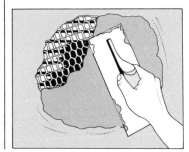

108

Repairing chipped plaster at corners

Plastered corners are particularly prone to damage. To ensure a straight line and a true angle at the corner, it is

best to fit a batten first to one side of the corner, then to the other, while you fill the damaged area with plaster. If, however, the corner already has a metal corner bead, simply patch the hole between the edges of the damaged area and the nosing of the beading on each face of the corner, and level off against the angle.

Using a batten
Pin a batten to one side of the corner, its edge flush with the other side. Fill the hole on one side, with a trowel or putty knife, so that the plaster lies flush with the batten. When this has set, remove the batten and fix it over the filled patch. Repeat the process on the other side and finally sand the corner.

Patching a reinforced corner
If a metal corner bead was inserted when the wall was plastered, patch the hole by filling over the damaged area. Draw the trowel or knife upward and smooth off against each face of the screed bead. When the filler is dry, sand the corner.

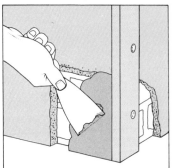

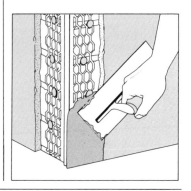

Windows

Estimating time◇ Types of window and glass◇Tools and equipment◇Removing broken glass◇Cutting glass◇How to replace a window pane ◇Glazing doors◇Fitting a new window frame◇Easing a sticking window Preventing window rattle ◇ Replacing a double-hung window ◇ Double glazing

Windows perform three important functions: they let in light, they enable you to look out, and they provide ventilation. To fulfil these functions, not all the panes need to be openable, and many windows are made up of a combination of fixed panes (or "lights"), which you cannot open, and opening panes. These opening panes are usually either sashes, which slide up and down or from side to side, or casements, which are hinged on both sides.

For improved insulation, there are double-glazed equivalents of most types of window. You can fit some designs yourself, while others are installed by the manufacturer.

The type of glass used also varies. Standard (single or double strength) glass is the most common type, but there are also various kinds of toughened glass, as well as patterned and tinted glass.

Points to remember

◇ Always wear stout gloves when handling pieces of glass.
◇ When measuring a window for a new pane, take measurements at several points along the frame.
◇ The larger the size of the pane, the thicker the glass you should use.
◇ When glazing a window, leave the putty for about two weeks before attempting to paint over it.
◇ Measure carefully for replacement frames – fit frames that are no more than ⅛in. smaller than the existing opening in the wall.
◇ If one sash cord in a window has broken, replace the others too.

Double-hung windows are the most common type. They consist of two sliding sashes, one in front of the other. The upper sash is opened to release hot air and the lower sash is opened to admit cool air. Each sash is counter-balanced by a hidden weight or a spring lift system.

Casement windows swing outward on hinges at the top and the bottom, like doors. Modern versions are operated by a crank-type handle, while older models are opened and closed by hand. The panes may be joined together in a curved shape to create a bow window, or in a rectangular or angled shape to make a bay.

Pivoting windows are usually made from wood and have a single pane that pivots about a central point on the frame. Their main advantage is that you can clean both sides of the glass from the inside.

Traditional French windows consist of a pair of full-length glazed and hinged wooden doors opening outwards. The edges of the windows that meet in the middle are rabbeted so that one closes on to the other.

Replacement windows

If you have to replace a window there are two alternatives: an exact copy of the original window, or a double-glazed replacement window. Many double-glazing makers will provide only made-to-measure windows which they install for you. But replacement windows that you fit yourself are also available. These come in four different materials: wood; aluminum; unplasticized polyvinyl chloride (upvc), which is usually white; and steel – either galvanized or in a white finish.

Estimating time

The times shown here are based on a window measuring 3ft × 5 ft. Most of the jobs will take longer if the window is larger, and times will also vary according to your own skill and experience. With large windows and those reached from a step ladder, you may need help, particularly when removing sashes and replacing large panes of glass.

Removing broken glass
(½)-(1) **hour**

Cutting glass
(¼) **hour**

Replacing a window pane
(½)-(1) **hour**

Replacing a leaded light
(½)-(1) **hour**

Glazing a door
(1½)-(2½) **hours**

Replacing a double-hung window
(1½)-(2½) **hours**

Fitting a window frame
(1½)-(2) **hours**

Freeing a sticking window
(½)-(1) **hour**

Preventing window rattle
(½)-(1) **hour**

Replacing sash cords
(1½)-(2½) **hours**

Adjusting a spring lift
(½)-(1) **hour**

Types of window

Casement windows
Most widely available with wooden frames, these windows come in a large number of standard sizes. There are also casement windows that have steel frames within an overall wooden surround. These have a thinner section, and therefore provide poorer thermal insulation than window frames that are made completely of wood.

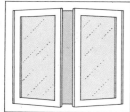

Double-hung windows
These windows are elegant, easy to clean, and allow good control over ventilation. Their main disadvantages are that the sash cords can break and the windows can rattle and stick. Modern sash windows use spring lifts rather than weights and are therefore more reliable. They also often have double-glazed panes.

Jalousie windows
These windows consist of thin horizontal slats of glass that are usually set in a metal frame. They are connected to a crank mechanism that enables you to open a group of louvers with each turn of the crank. When closed, jalousie windows may allow drafts so should only be fitted in un-heated areas.

Pivoting windows
Because they are easy to clean from the inside, pivoting windows are very convenient, especially on upper floors. But they have one safety drawback. They are very easy to push open, and therefore should not be fitted where a small child could open them and crawl through.

Sliding windows
Some modern windows slide horizontally. This is a design that is particularly popular for full-length patio windows, which are available in a wide range of materials including wood, aluminum, and upvc. Modern sliding windows usually have double-glazed panes.

French windows
Glazed double doors are often known as French windows. They are normally fastened by top and bottom bolts, with one door's inner edge overlapping the other, to give a good fit.

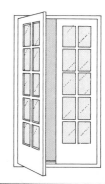

Types of glass

Most glass sold today is "float" glass, so-called because the method of manufacture involves floating the glass out of the furnace on molten tin. This gives a good surface finish and a distortion-free appearance. In addition, there are various types of safety glass.

When choosing which type of glass to use, first decide whether the area you are going to glaze is a "high-risk" one. Glazing within $2\frac{1}{2}$ft of the floor, doors or windows that might be mistaken for holes in the wall, and large expanses of glass that could get broken accidentally, all constitute a high risk.

Choosing the right thickness
Another important factor is the likely wind loading on the glass. The greater the exposure to wind, the thicker the glass required. In areas where the risk is not high, avoid $\frac{1}{8}$in. glass except for very small panes. Use $\frac{1}{6}$in. glass for windows up to 3ft wide. For anything larger use 1/5in. or $\frac{1}{4}$in. glass.

In a high-risk area you should not glaze an area larger than 2ft² with $\frac{1}{8}$in. glass; with 1/5in. glass the largest area is 9ft²; with $\frac{1}{4}$in. glass the largest area is 19ft²; and with $\frac{1}{2}$in. glass you can glaze an area up to 36ft². For larger panes than this, use toughened or laminated glass.

Patterned glass
This type of glass can provide privacy as well as decoration. There is a wide choice of designs and some patterned glass is also tinted.

Wired glass
The wire grid does not make the glass stronger, but it holds the pieces together if it is broken. It also makes the glass more visible. It is available in both clear and opaque forms.

Tempered glass
This type of glass undergoes a special heat treatment that makes it four to five times stronger than standard glass. The treatment also makes it impossible to cut once it has hardened.

Laminated glass
This consists of a thin layer of plastic sandwiched between two layers of glass. This strengthens it and also means that if it does break, the fragments of glass are held by the plastic.

Solar-control glass
To prevent rooms getting too hot in the summer, use plain or tinted solar-control glass. A self-adhesive reflective film, stuck on to an existing glass pane, will give a similar effect.

Glass bullions
In Georgian panes, glass bullions give an old-fashioned appearance. Other decorative effects can be achieved with stained and engraved glass.

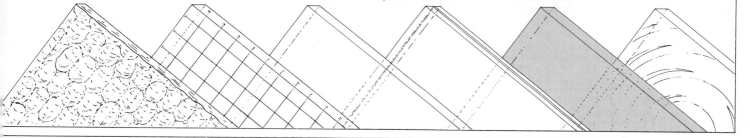

Tools and equipment

There are only a few specialized tools for glazing. If you intend to cut glass yourself, you will need a glass cutter and possibly some glass pliers.

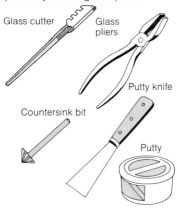

Glass cutter
Glass pliers
Putty knife
Countersink bit
Putty

Equipment for working with glass
Use glass pliers to snap off small pieces of glass from the edge of a pane, or to remove a long, narrow strip of glass after you have scored it with a glass cutter. The chisel is useful for removing broken glass and old putty from a window frame. When replacing a window frame, use a countersink drill bit, so that you can conceal the screw heads.

Removing broken glass

Before starting to remove any glass, lay newspaper on the floor and, if possible, on the ground outside, to catch any falling pieces of glass. Wear thick gardening gloves to protect your hands and stout shoes to protect your feet. A pair of goggles is also useful – it will prevent flying fragments of glass getting in your eyes.

If possible, start by removing the large pieces of glass. Take care, because they may break up as you handle them. Then gently pull or knock out the smaller pieces.

If you have to break the glass in the frame in order to remove it, put strips of adhesive tape over it to hold the fragments together, and cover the glass with a cloth. The remaining pieces, together with the old putty, can be removed with an old chisel. Pull out any glazing points or clips that were used to hold the glass in place. Keep the clips from a metal window frame and mark their positions, but discard the points.

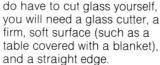

Removing putty
Use a chisel to remove small pieces of glass and old putty.

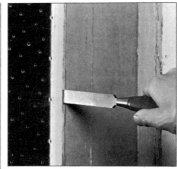

Taking off beading
To pry off beading, begin in the middle of the length.

For most types of window, you will need putty. $2\frac{1}{4}$lb of putty will be enough for about $11\frac{1}{2}$ft of frame. There are different types of putty for aluminum and wooden windows, while solar control glass needs a special non-setting compound. You will also need glazing points (for wooden windows) or clips (for aluminum frames) to hold the glass in place. Some windows use different fixing methods. Modern double-glazed windows have gaskets to hold the glass in position. Replacing panels in louvered windows is simply a matter of sliding in a piece of glass of the correct size. To cut down the security risk with this type of window, you can glue the pieces into place.

After you have removed the old pane, prepare the frame. Clean out the rabbet that holds the glass. If the frame is wooden, next apply the appropriate primer If you have a steel frame, remove any rust.

109
Cutting glass

Hardware stores will normally cut glass to size for you and this is always best, especially with irregular shapes. But if you do have to cut glass yourself, you will need a glass cutter, a firm, soft surface (such as a table covered with a blanket), and a straight edge.

If you are cutting glass for a replacement window pane, check the width and the height of the window at several places.

The size of the glass should be $\frac{1}{8}$in. *less* than the smallest measurement. If the window is so badly out of true that you need an irregular-shaped piece of glass, either remove the window and take it to the store or make a paper template of the shape.

Making a straight cut
Make sure the glass is clean. Put it on a firm, soft surface and, using a straight-edge and a glass cutter score a straight line on the glass, 1. Pull the cutter towards you, using firm, consistent pressure. To help make a clean cut, apply alcohol. Tapping lightly with the cutter will also help keep the cut clean. Break the glass over a wooden rule, a batten or a dowel placed under the scored line, 2.

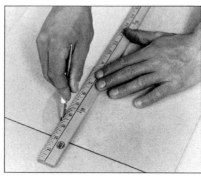

1 Pull the glass cutter towards you along the straight edge and keep the pressure even

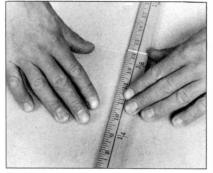

2 Place the glass over a long dowel to break it

110
Replacing a leaded light

The glass in leaded-light windows is held in by strips of lead which are bent over the glass and then soldered at the corners. If the shape of the pane you want to replace is irregular, it is best to make a cardboard template and take this to the hardware store, rather than trying to cut out the shape yourself. To remove a pane, first break these joints and bend back the lead. When you have cleaned out the strips of lead and inserted a new piece of glass, the lead should be bent back and the joints soldered back into place.

Basic technique

How to replace a window pane

Glazing a door

Applying putty and fitting the glass
After preparing the frame, apply about an $\frac{1}{8}$in. layer of putty to the rabbet. The best way to apply putty is to hold a ball of it in your hand and squeeze it out between the thumb and forefinger, 1. When you have done this, push the glass in gently on top of the putty. Press the glass only at the edges, not in the middle and, to get the correct clearance all round, support it on toothpicks at the bottom, 2. Next put in the glazing points or clips and remove the toothpicks. Put in points every 6in. using a small hammer or chisel and sliding it along the surface of the glass, 3. If you are using metal clips, put them back into their original holes. Finally, apply a second layer of putty to the outside and smooth it off to the correct angle (about 45°) using a putty knife, 4. When smoothing putty always use firm pressure and smooth strokes. If the knife sticks, moisten it with water. Finish it off with a paint-brush moistened in water. Remove any excess putty with a knife, and clean any finger marks from the glass with plain or denatured alcohol. Leave the putty for about two weeks before painting it. When you do paint it, make sure that the edges are sealed by overlapping the paint on to the glass. If you do not do this the putty will dry out and crack.

1 Push the putty into the rabbet with your thumb and forefinger

2 Support the glass on toothpicks to keep it in the right position

3 Use a chisel to tap in the glazing points

4 Smooth off the external layer of putty to give an angle of about 45°

Fitting wooden glazing beading or quarter round molding is a good idea if you are glazing a hardwood door. It is also a useful method for a window that you want to finish with a clear preservative woodstain. Glazing beading comes in long strips, which you can cut into mitered lengths. Check all the measurements carefully if you are glazing an old door or window – it may not be exactly squared. A miter box will help you get the corner angles exactly right.

Interior doors can be glazed in this way without any putty. Exterior doors should have a thin layer of putty on both sides of the glass to keep out the dampness. Use colored putty if your door is made of hardwood.

Fixing the beading
Attach the glazing beading with nails. To avoid splitting the beading, blunt the nails before putting them in. And, to reduce the risk of damaging the glass, hammer the nails part of the way into the beading before putting it in place. To get a neat finish, punch the nails below the surface. Clean any excess putty off the pane and protect the beading with paint or varnish.

Fitting the pane
Using a sharp knife or an old chisel, break the bottom two joints and ease back the lead, 1. Next remove the broken glass and clean out the old putty from the lead strips. Use an old chisel and a steel brush, 2. The new piece of glass should be a fraction shorter than the opening.

You will need a small amount of putty – either the type made specially for leaded lights, or metal casement putty. Put a thin layer of putty inside the lead strip and insert the new piece of glass from the bottom, gently pressing it into position and squeezing out the putty, 3. Fold the lead strips over the glass and clean the lead with fine sandpaper. Resolder the joints, 4, using a soldering iron with a fine point.

 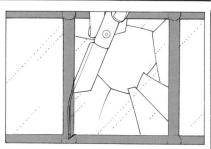

1 Gently pry away the lead at the bottom of the pane you want to replace

2 Carefully clean out the surround

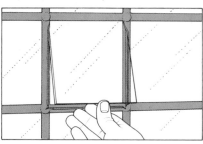 

3 Surplus putty will squeeze out as you put in the piece of glass

4 Solder back the joints to keep the new pane in place

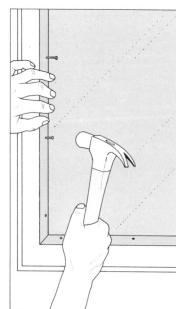

The anatomy of a double-hung window

A double-hung window is made up of two sashes, which are operated by a weight and pulley system. Aluminum or vinyl windows are unlikely to need repairs, but wooden windows may warp or swell; and the sill, the sash cord or the entire window may need replacing. Before buying a new window, you will have to measure the old one and buy a pre-assembled replacement of the same size. The old sashes are removed from the inside by prying off the inside trim and the parting strip. The outside casing, the sill and the jambs are removed from the outside and the new unit is slotted into place and secured with nails. A pre-assembled unit will come complete with a parting strip and jamb and some include a new outside casing.

How the window works
The stops provide a channel in which the two sashes slide. The lower sash falls behind a stool which connects to the sloping sill. The trim and outer casing cover the gap between the wall and the jambs.

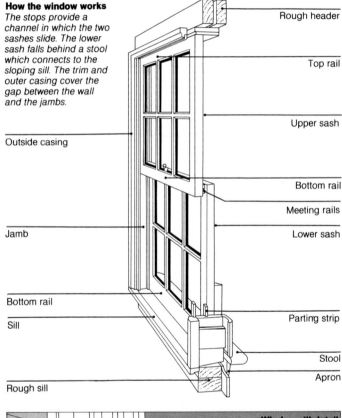

- Rough header
- Top rail
- Upper sash
- Bottom rail
- Meeting rails
- Lower sash
- Parting strip
- Stool
- Apron

- Outside casing
- Jamb
- Bottom rail
- Sill
- Rough sill

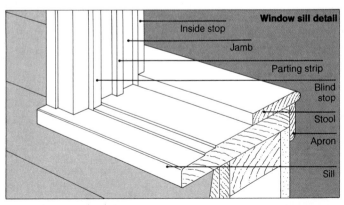

Window sill detail
- Inside stop
- Jamb
- Parting strip
- Blind stop
- Stool
- Apron
- Sill

112

Replacing a window sill

Window sills are constantly exposed to rain, snow and sun. Although they are sloped to deflect the worst of the weather, over time they are likely to split, warp and rot. Minor problems can be solved by filling cracks and holes and a good layer of paint will help to protect the surface. But a badly worn sill will have to be replaced. You will have to pry off the outside casing and the inside stops to remove the sash, and then pry out the old apron. Extract the nails from the stool and try to remove it in one piece. Before removing the sill, measure the length between the jambs for the new piece. It is usually easiest to remove the old sill by cutting it into three pieces, so that you can remove the center piece and pull or cut the end pieces free. The new sill can then be nailed in place. You should use rust-resistant nails, countersink them and caulk the nail heads.

Fitting the new sill
First cut out the old sill, 1. For the new sill, choose a wood that has been treated with a preservative compatible with the paint you plan to use. Mark it up for cutting, allowing for grooves in the jambs, and saw along the cutting lines. Then bevel the edges and paint a coat of primer on to the sides and edges. When dry, slot the new sill into place, gently tapping with a hammer against a protective wood block, 2. If it does not slot in easily, remove it and sand the edges until it fits. If it is slightly loose, add shims at the sides or underneath. Next nail through the sill and shim from above, 3, and countersink the nails. Finally caulk the nailheads and the edges of the sill and reassemble the stool, apron, sash and casings, 4.

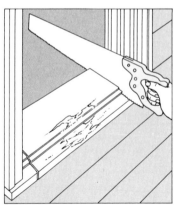

1 *For easy removal, cut the old sill into three pieces*

2 *Protect the new sill with a wooden block as you tap it into place*

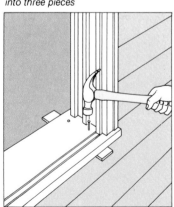

3 *Add shims to ensure a good fit and nail the sill in place*

4 *Use a caulking gun to seal the edges of the sill and the nail heads*

113
Freeing a sticking window

Windows can stick because of an excessive build-up of paint or because dampness has made them swell. Stripping or planing is the best cure for this. Loose joints are another common cause. Re-gluing the

Stripping and planing
If the problem is too much paint, remove the paint using stripper or a hot-air gun (see Job 6, pp. 18-19). Do not use a blowlamp as this can damage the glass. Then rub down the frame with coarse sandpaper. If this does not give enough clearance, or if there is swelling, plane down the

window. Use a primer on the bare wood before repainting (see Job 5, p. 18). If it is not obvious where the window is sticking, insert a piece of carbon paper between the window and the frame. The area where the paintwork is marked will indicate the place where the wood should be removed.

joints and clamping them together can solve this problem. Loose hinges can make casement windows stick. Curing loose hinges may simply be a matter of tightening the fixing screws. If they continue to work loose, drill out the holes, glue in pieces of dowel and make new holes for larger screws. Sticking double-hung windows can be caused by loose sash cords (*see Job 115, p. 100*).

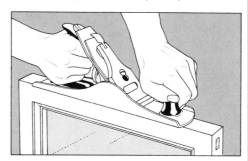

Tips for repairing gaps and leaks

◇ Foam weather stripping can stop leaks and is easy to apply.
◇ For uneven gaps, try silicone weather stripping, which comes in a tube.
◇ When there are gaps between the window and brickwork, seal them with caulk, applied with a special applicator.
◇ When using a caulking gun, apply firm and steady pressure to the trigger as you move along the gap, and try to keep

the resulting strip of caulk straight.
◇ An alternative method is to use the type of silicone sealant normally used around baths and kitchen worktops.
◇ Fill internal gaps with crack filler after you have applied the caulk.
◇ Check that the drip grooves on the undersides of window sills are clear.
◇ Replace flashing around roof windows with self-adhesive flashing.

114
Preventing window rattle

Casement windows rattle if the catch does not hold them tightly. The solution is to fit weather stripping around the window frame. If the window is distorted, straighten it by closing it on to a thin sliver of wood which forces it in the opposite direction to the way it is twisted. Repeat the process, gradually increasing the thickness of the wood until the frame has been reshaped.

Rattling double-hung windows are caused by wear creating too much space around each sash. Fit the type of weather stripping with a nylon pile, so that the sash slides along it.

Fitting weather stripping
The simplest type to fit is self-adhesive foam strip, though this needs replacing regularly. The strip comes in different

thicknesses to cope with different sizes of gap. If the gap is uneven, put one layer on top of another where the gap is at its largest.

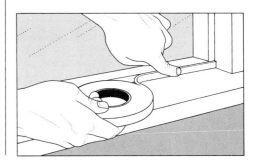

Types of window fastening

Most double-hung windows are secured by a simple butterfly thumb catch. This is easy to fit – you simply screw the hook section to the bottom rail of the top sash, and the thumb catch section to the top rail of the bottom sash. An improved version of this, the Griptite lock, is fitted in the same way. It pulls the two sashes closer together and so eliminates the crack.

Casement windows are usually operated by a crank handle, which either fits through a slot in the window frame or is surface-mounted on the bottom rail of the frame. In either case the handle is secured with wood screws. Casements that are pushed open instead of cranked are secured with a latch.

French doors are secured with a vertical bolt which stretches the height of the door.

Butterfly thumb catch
Rotate the thumb lever clockwise to hold the sashes closed.

Casement crank
Whether surface-mounted, right, or through-fitted, far right, the handle which links to a gear and slide arm, turns counter-clockwise to open the window.

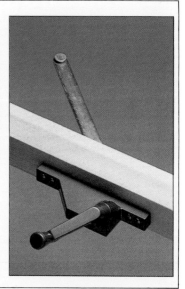

115

Removing a sash cord

Fitting a new sash cord involves removing the window from its frame – a fairly big job and one which damages the paintwork. So it is sensible to replace all the sash cords at the same time – if one cord has broken, the others will probably soon need renewing. Use rot-proof man-made sash cord rather than the traditional waxed hemp. If the window is a large one, you may need someone to help you when it comes to taking it out of the frame.

The job involves removing both sashes, cutting new cords to exactly the right length, and re-assembling the window with the new cords. When both sashes are replaced, you will probably have to paint the window frame.

Removing and refitting the cord
Carefully pry off the beading around the edge of the window with a screw-driver or old chisel, 1. Cut any unbroken cords in the sash nearest to you and let the weights fall down into their boxes. Then remove the inner sash. To take out the other sash, first pry out the parting strips that separate the two sashes. To give access to the sash weights there is a small panel, usually held in place by a screw. Remove the panel and pull out the weights and the remaining lengths of cord, 2. Untie the weights from the old cords and remove the cord from the sides of the sashes, where it will be nailed in place. It is important to get the

length of the new cords exactly right. Judge the length either by using an undamaged cord from the same sash, or by ensuring that the weight is just clear of the bottom of the box when the window is fully up. Do this by marking the position of the end of the sash cord on the frame and cutting the cord to size once it is in place.

When replacing the cords and windows, start with the outer sash. To get the new sash cord over the pulley, tie a thin piece of string to the cord and attach a small lead weight or screw to this. When you pass the weight over the pulley, it will fall, taking the string and cord with it. After removing the string, tie the sash cord to the weight, cut it

to the right length, and temporarily knot the free end to stop it going over the pulley. When you have repeated the process for the other cord, hold the sash up to the frame and nail the free ends of the cords on to the window with galvanized clout nails, 3. Keep these 1in. from the top of the frame. Make sure that the cords lie properly in their grooves and that the position of the weight is correct. Replace the parting strip and ensure that the window slides up and down as it should. Put back the inner sash in the same way and refit the stop molding. Nail them in position with finishing nails and drive these beneath the surface of the wood with a nail set.

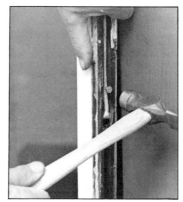

1 *Start by taking off the vertical stop moldings, working from the middle*

2 *Take off the panel and remove the sash weights*

3 *Nail the sash cord to the window*

116

Adjusting a spring lift

Modern double-hung windows are balanced by a mechanism that consists of a spiral rod inside a metal or plastic tube secured to the inside of the frame. Spring lift mechanisms are usually more reliable than sash cords, although the spring can lose its tension, which means that the mechanism needs adjusting. This is done by twisting the tube.

Spring lift repairs
Pull the sash down and unscrew the tube from the frame. Then twist the tube clockwise to tighten the spring. After a few turns, re-secure the tube. If this does not solve the problem, replace the whole mechanism. This involves taking out the sash (see Job 115, above) and the spring lift. To fit the new mecha-nism, you first attach it to the sash and then lift it up to the window frame. With the sash in its middle position, ten-sion the spring by turn-ing the tube then secure the tube to the frame and replace the beading.

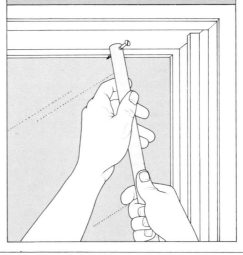

Windows are responsible for about 10 per cent of the heat loss from houses, while another 15 per cent is lost through gaps around windows and doors. As well as making a room uncom-fortable, cold windows can cause condensation, which is produced when the warm, moist air inside the house meets the colder inner surface of the glass or the metal frame. Condensation looks unsightly and can lead to paint damage and rot.

Double glazing offers a solution to these problems. Double glazing is simply a way of fitting two panes of glass into a window instead of one. The second pane adds some-thing to the heat saving, but it is mainly the air gap between the panes that gives the benefits. To be effective, this air gap should be at least $\frac{1}{2}$in. wide. A gap of $\frac{2}{3}$in. or $\frac{3}{4}$in. is better still, but a larger gap will not give any further im-provement. If you want your double glazing to act as a sound-proofing measure, the gap between the panes should be much larger – between 4in. and 8in.

Types of storm windows
There are three main types of double glazing, sealed units, secondary panes, and second-ary sashes and casements. Sealed units consist of pairs of glass panes that are hermetic-ally sealed together in the factory and which simply replace the conventional glass panes. Secondary panes are fixed sheets of glass or plastic fitted to the inside of the win-dows. Secondary sashes are, in effect, framed windows fitted in front of the existing ones.

Most double-glazing systems are designed for use with $\frac{1}{8}$in. glass. Tempered glass should be used for double glazing very large panes. As a cheaper alternative, use clear plastic sheets over the panes.

Types of double glazing

Sealed units

Sealed units have two big advantages: they are unobtrusive and, unlike other types of double glazing, they do not cause condensation. They are usually fitted into the window with gaskets made of rubber or synthetic material. Some units are gas-filled and have heat-reflecting qualities, and manufacturers make additional heat-saving claims for these. Some sealed units have a small unobtrusive air gap.

You can fit complete replacement windows with sealed units, which are available in standard sizes. A more economical method is to replace the existing panes with sealed units. The units are available in a range of different glass types in standard sizes or they can be made to measure. Units with a stepped profile are available if the depth of the window rabbet will not take a normal unit.

Sealed inner frame
On this type, the inner metal frame is sealed to the outer frame of wood.

Outer pane

Inner pane

Sill

Drip groove

Gasket
Ensures a good seal, so that the sealed unit fits tight inside the outer frame.

Air gap
On sealed units, the air gap is usually very narrow. The result is an unobtrusive design with efficient heat insulation, but a narrow air gap is not very effective for sound insulation.

Wooden window frame

Secondary panes

The simplest form of secondary pane is a thin plastic sheet stretched over the window frame. Next in terms of simplicity is the type that is kept in place by a self-adhesive magnetic strip stuck to the edges of a sheet of rigid plastic. The magnet fits on to a strip of steel attached to the window frame. Finally, there is a variety of designs in which the secondary pane is surrounded by a plastic frame and attach-ed to the window with clips, plastic strips, or other fasteners.

None of these panes can be opened easily for normal ventilation, although they can all be removed for cleaning or summer storage. But if the system allows you to fit the pane to an opening casement, both the original window and the secondary pane will open at the same time. You will need room for the casement crank when the panes are fitted.

Air gap
This type of double glazing allows for a generous air gap between the two panes.

Sill

Drip groove

Wooden window frame

Outer pane and frame
These are the pane and frame of the original window, which you can still open when the inner pane is not in place.

Inner pane
This can be made of glass or plastic. On this design, the metal frame surrounding the glass is held magnetically to metal plates attached to the wooden frame.

Secondary sashes and casements

These are more substantial double-glazing systems, which usually consist of sheets of glass or plastic with aluminum or plastic frames. They can either be fixed in position, or hinged or sliding so that they open independently of the main windows. Sliding panes are usually fitted in tracks attached to the reveal. They generally slide horizontally, but you can also get vertical sliding systems which are particularly useful for sash windows.

If your window sizes are not standard, you can get secondary casement or sash systems made to measure. You take the measurements and fit the system, but the manufacturer carries out the job of constructing the frame and fitting the glass.

Outer pane and frame
These are the pane and frame of the original window. They can easily be opened.

Sill

Drip groove

Wooden window frame

Inner pane and frame
This fits neatly to the original window frame and is opened by sliding the pane to one side.

Air gap
A large air gap for sound insulation can be obtained by fitting the outer panes to the inner edge of the original window frame.

Curing condensation

Condensation on the inside of the outer pane can be a problem on double-glazed windows. It can be alleviated by placing a moisture-absorbing substance (such as silica gel) in the gap. The crystals need replacing regularly. Weatherproofing the inner window may provide a permanent solution to this problem. If this does not work, try ventilating the air gap between the panes by drilling downward-sloping holes in the outer frame and filling them with glass fiber.

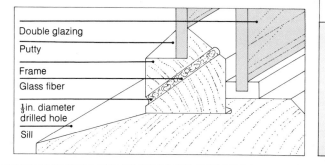

Double glazing

Putty

Frame

Glass fiber

$\frac{1}{8}$ in. diameter drilled hole

Sill

Safety tips

◇ When fitting double glazing or strengthened safety glass, remember that windows offer important escape routes in case of fire.
◇ Provide opening windows at escape points.
◇ Leave keys for window locks where they are easy to find from inside in an emergency.

Curtains, blinds and shutters

Estimating time and quantities ◇ Tools and equipment ◇ Putting up curtain tracks Types of curtain fitting ◇ Making a roller shade ◇ Types of shutters

By day, window hangings and shutters are simply decorative, but at night they afford privacy, conserve heat, and muffle outside noise. Even if your windows are not overlooked, the glass at night becomes a cold, black, reflective surface, and drawing curtains or pulling down a blind will make the room seem much more hospitable.

When choosing curtains, blinds, or shutters, remember to check what they will look like from the outside as well as from within. Try to unify the decorative scheme from the outside, so that different windows on the same side of the house get a consistent treatment.

Points to remember

◇ When measuring for curtains, always allow extra material for hems, headings, and pattern repeats.
◇ Make sure that any curtain tracks or poles you want to use are available in sufficient lengths – joins are not usually possible, unless you use an overlap arm.
◇ If you are using a batten to support curtain track brackets, fix it securely to the wall using screws and, if necessary, adhesive.
◇ Buy roller shades slightly larger than you need, so you can cut them down to the exact length required.
◇ Always use a carpenter's level to check that curtain tracks and shade fixings are horizontal.

Estimating time

The time taken for putting up curtains will vary according to whether or not you have to put up a batten. Fitting hooks and sprung wire for sheer curtains is much quicker.

Curtains

Fitting a curtain track

 hour

Shades

Making a roller shade

 hours

Estimating quantities

When measuring for curtains and blinds, use a wooden rule or a steel tape measure, and hold it at eye level.

Measuring for curtains
Two dimensions are required: the width of the track and the length of the finished curtains measured from the point where the hooks are suspended. For floor-length curtains, measure down to 1in. above the floor; for sill-length curtains, measure to $\frac{1}{8}$in. below the sill.

The heading tape will allow you to control the fullness of the finished curtain, so multiply the track width by $1\frac{1}{2}$ or 2 to give the fullness required. Divide this total width by the width of the fabric, to find the number of drops needed. Each drop should be the length of one curtain, plus a heading and hemming allowance of 10in. Multiply the number of drops by the length of each drop. Add any extra you will need for matching tie-backs or cornices, and round up the total to the nearest 10in. Add extra for pattern matching.

Measuring for blinds
First decide whether you want your shade to hang inside or outside the window recess. If you are going to fit it inside, measure the width of the recess and then subtract an amount to allow for the shade fixings on either side. If you are installing the shade outside the recess, allow for an overlap of at least 2in. on each side. Measure the length from where you want to fix the shade to the bottom when fully lowered. To turn these measurements into fabric estimates, add 10in. to the length. The amount you add to the width depends on the type of shade. For a roller shade, you should not add anything to the width. With a gathered shade, add 2in. to give a 1in. seam allowance on either side. For a festoon blind multiply the width by the fullness required and add 2in. to give a 1in. seam allowance on either side.

Tools and equipment

For curtains, you will need rings, hooks, or clips to suit your track or rod. Heading tape for the curtains will also be required. Equipment for making a roller shade usually comes in kit form with roller, fittings, pull cord, and fabric.

For more information on types of curtain fabric, see Choosing materials, pp. 134-6.

Effects with curtains

For a dramatic effect, or if paired curtains would overpower a narrow window, a single, asymmetrical curtain can be very effective. A flat curtain suspended from hooks through eyelet holes in the fabric can be attractive, and tie-backs can create interesting shapes.

Other interesting effects can be created with sheer curtains. While their main purpose is to prevent people seeing in, you can use them more imaginatively by draping them elaborately or gathering them on the type of headings used on conventional window curtains.

Matching fittings
Curtains, tie-backs, cornices, and cushions (top left) made of the same fabric create a harmonious effect in this bay window.

Combining curtains and blinds
This combination (bottom left) gives great flexibility – the shade lets in some light, while the curtains act as light shields.

Using sheer curtains to diffuse light
If you have a large window that lets in a lot of bright sunlight, you can diffuse it with full-length sheer curtains. In this room (above) the striped and textured effect of the full sheer curtains is picked up by the reflective glass surface of the coffee table.

Types of curtain tracks, cornices and headings

As well as the fabric that you choose, there are a number of other factors that will influence the way your curtains look. Particularly important are the type of curtain heading you use, the track or rod on which you hang the curtains, and whether or not you fit a cornice. Different degrees of fullness and types of pleating are possible with different headings. Some rods and track are highly ornate, while others are invisible when you close the curtains. Cornices can act as a simple way of concealing the curtain track, as a means of unifying two windows in the same wall, or they can have a much stronger decora-

Types of curtain rail and rod
Whichever type you choose, make sure it is available in long enough lengths for your windows; joins are impractical. It must also be strong enough for the type of curtain you want. If you have curved or bay windows, choose a track that can be bent around corners. Check also whether a cording set can be fitted to your track. Most types of straight track accept pull cords, so that you can close and open the curtains from one side. But some types of curved track will not take pull cords. The traditional brass curtain track has been largely superseded by nylon, plastic, and aluminum tracks, together with wooden rods.

As well as the traditional brass tracks, those intended for use with a cornice include aluminum and plastic types with nylon runners. These are strong and easy to bend round corners, which makes them ideal for bay windows. Most can also be fitted with cords for drawing the curtains.

Tracks designed for use without a cornice are usually made from aluminum or plastic. Most use large hooks, so that the curtains cover the track when they are drawn.

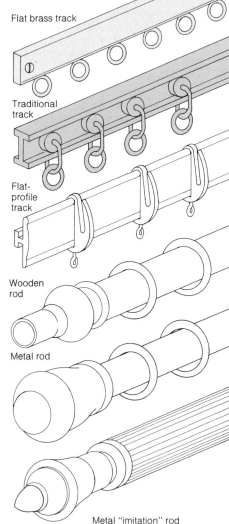

Flat brass track

Traditional track

Flat-profile track

Wooden rod

Metal rod

Metal "imitation" rod

Types of cornice
To hide the heading and give interest to the top of the curtain, you can use a cornice. Cornices allow you to fit the curtain track in two pieces with an overlap at the centre. They are also useful to give two adjacent windows a unified look.

There are two basic types of cornice – those made of wood and those made of cloth. Hardboard is a common material and is particularly suitable for bay and bow windows because it can be bent round corners. Cornices can also be constructed out of plywood or softwood, while hardwood cornices

look attractive with windows that are made of hardwood or that are set in a hardwood subframe.

There is a variety of fabric cornice designs. They can either take the form of a gathered valance or be treated with a stiffener. Valance cornices can be hung from a shelf above the window or suspended from a second curtain track in front of the main one.

Another type of cornice, sometimes known as a draped cornice, is made up of swags draped across the top of the window and tails decorating the edge. This type of cornice looks

very effective on large windows, but takes up a lot of fabric. So before you commit yourself by buying material, it is best to experiment with a sheet to find out approximately how much you will need to get the effect you require.

It is also possible to combine the strength of a wooden cornice construction with the elegance of a fabric design to produce a fabric-covered wooden cornice. This can either have a simple rectangular shape or have curved edges to give an effect similar to a valanced cornice. The fabric can either match or contrast with the curtain material.

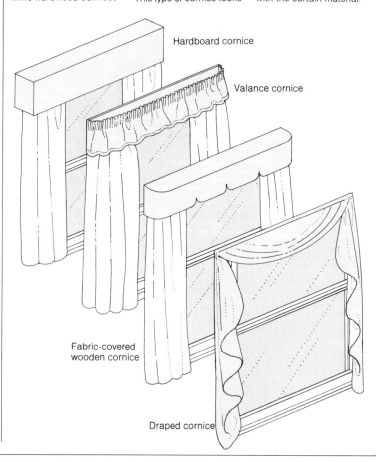

Hardboard cornice

Valance cornice

Fabric-covered wooden cornice

Draped cornice

Accessories for tracks and rods
In addition to normal brackets for tracks and rods, other types are available. Extension brackets hold the rail away from the wall, overlap arms allow one curtain to pass in front of the other where they meet, and return brackets enable the ends of the rail to turn in toward the wall and some allow for a dual track.

Extension bracket

Overlapping tracks

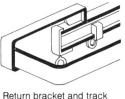

Return bracket and track

tive role, making use of gathered fabric, and swags and tails of material. You can also improve your curtains by fitting accessories such as overlap arms and return brackets.

Types of curtain heading

By using different heading tapes you can change the way your curtains hang. But different heading tapes also require varying widths of fabric. Standard tape gives a simple gathered heading. It makes the curtains look quite full and takes fabric that is about twice the total width of the track.

Pencil pleating creates a crisp, regularly pleated heading, but it takes more fabric – often 2¼ to 2½ times the width of the track.

Pinch pleating is more economical than this, requiring fabric about twice the width of the track. There are two types of pinch pleating tape. With one, the pleats are made by drawing up a cord; with the other, you insert a pronged hook into the tape. The cord type is much easier to use.

Cartridge pleating gives a cylindrical pleat. To improve the roundness of the cylinder, the heading pleats are stuffed with tissue paper. This draws back tightly when the curtains are open.

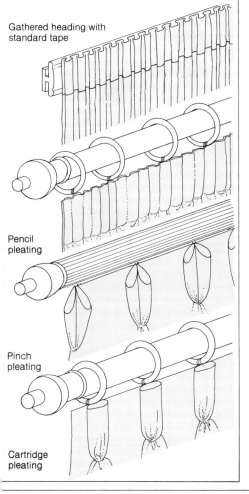

Gathered heading with standard tape

Pencil pleating

Pinch pleating

Cartridge pleating

117

Fixing curtain tracks to a wall

Most curtain tracks are sold with the brackets you need to put them up, sometimes with the screws and wallplugs as well. Putting up rods involves the same techniques as putting up curtain tracks. True rods only require brackets at either end. So they may not be the best choice for long windows, unless they are strong enough to take the curtains without sagging. Imitation rods allow you to put brackets at intervals along their length.

Curtain tracks can be fitted to the window frame itself, but it is unlikely that there will be enough space in the reveal for anything except lightweight sheer curtains. So the most popular choice is to fit the track to the wall above the window. Drilling the wall and inserting wall plugs should be simple with a hammer drill and a masonry bit unless there is a concrete lintel above the window that is too hard to drill into. In this case, the best solution is to fit a batten above the window.

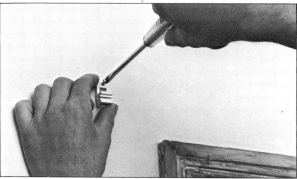

Fitting brackets to the wall
Drill holes in the wall at regular intervals to take the screws and wallplugs. When you mark the positions for the holes, use a carpenter's level to make sure that they are level. Use a screwdriver to ensure a tight fixing.

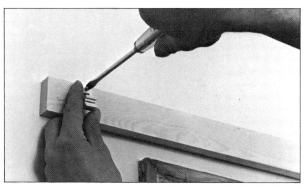

Fitting brackets to a batten
If the lintel above the window is too tough for a hammer drill, fit a batten of 2in. × 1in. wood to the wall and screw the brackets to that. The batten should be longer than the lintel so that you can drill into the brickwork at either end. Remove any paper from the area of the wall the batten will cover. Then attach it at either end with screws and wallplugs and secure the central part with contact adhesive. Paint or paper over the batten.

118

Fixing curtain tracks to a ceiling

If the top of the window is very close to the ceiling, it may be easier to fix the brackets to the ceiling. Hollow wallplugs in the ceiling itself will not be strong enough. Find the positions of the joists above the ceiling and screw into these. They are usually about 16in. apart. On lower floors, the easiest way to pinpoint joists is to lift a floorboard in the room above (*see Job 70, p. 68*) and make a tiny marking hole through the ceiling next to the joists. On top floors, it is easy to find the joists by going into the attic.

Attaching brackets to the joists
If the joists run at right-angles to the wall, fix a bracket to each one. Use screws that are long enough to go through the full thickness of the ceiling plaster and into the joists themselves. If the joists run the other way, you will have to fit short lengths of batten between the joist and the wall to take the screws.

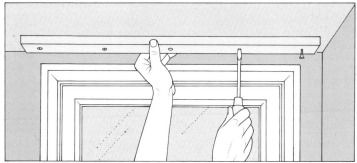

119

Making a roller shade

A roller-shade kit consists of a spring-loaded roller, a wooden lath or plastic bar for the bottom of the shade, a pull cord, and the necessary fixings and screws. The roller can be made either of aluminum or wood. The fabric for the shade is often bought separately. Kits are sold in a range of sizes – buy one slightly larger than you need so that you can cut it down to the required dimensions. Roller shades can be fitted either inside the window recess or to the wall outside the recess.

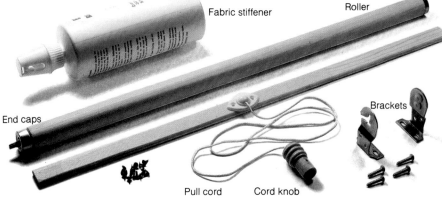

Fabric stiffener   Roller

End caps

Brackets

Pull cord   Cord knob

Assembling and fitting the blind
First check the roller length that you will need. Take into account the projecting brads that fit on to the ends of the roller – they usually take up about 1in. at each end. Depending on the design of the brackets, you may also need a little space to allow for the fixing screws. Cut the roller to the correct length at the non-spring end. Make sure you cut it square by measuring the length in several places, marking it all the way round, and using a fine-toothed saw, such as a back saw, for wood, or a hacksaw for

aluminum. Smooth off the cut end with sandpaper and attach the fixing to the roller. On an aluminum roller this means simply pushing on the end caps. On a wooden roller, drill a pilot hole for fixing brad to help keep it straight, push on the end caps, and tap the brad home, 1.

Mark the bracket positions on the window frame using a carpenter's level to ensure that the blind will be level, 2. When you attach the brackets to the frame, the one with the round hole should go on the right, the one with the slot on the left.

To prepare the material, cut it to the right size, iron it flat, and stiffen it. The easiest and quickest way to do this is to use a spray can stiffener. With other types of stiffener, you have to make a solution with water and soak the fabric in order to stiffen it.

Fitting the bar at the bottom of the fabric is usually simple. Cut it about ½in. shorter than the shade and either glue it to the fabric or fit it into a pocket sewn along the bottom edge, 3. Screw the holder for the pull cord to the center of the bar.

With aluminum rollers, the material

either fits into a slot in the roller or is secured with screw clips. With wooden rollers, the best method is first to glue the fabric to the roller to keep it in the right position and then to fix it permanently with tacks or staples, 4.

When the material is attached, all you have to do is roll it up tightly, put the roller on the brackets, 5, and tension the spring so that the blind rolls and unrolls properly. If the tension is wrong, unhook the non-spring end, turn the roller by hand to increase or decrease the tension, 6, and refit it to the bracket.

1 *Push the end pieces into place on either end of the metal or wooden roller*

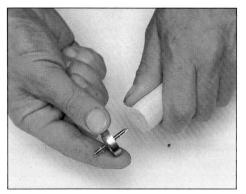

2 *Mark the bracket positions and check them with a carpenter's level*

3 *Attach the bar to the bottom edge of the blind*

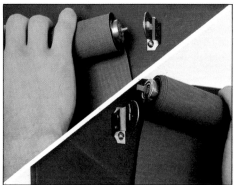

4 *Staple the fabric to the roller after gluing it in place*

5 *Put the shade up and check the tension*

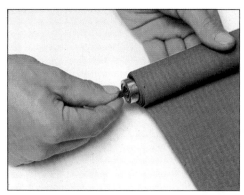

6 *Adjust the tension by turning the roller around*

Effects with blinds

The simple roller is not the only type of blind you can use. A number of other designs, such as vertical louver blinds, festoon, and Venetian blinds, are available. They all have different decorative effects.

Vertical louver blinds offer a good alternative to louvered doors and can be used as a room partition. They can be adjusted to admit filtered light from a window or neighboring room or to form a complete light screen.

Venetian blinds work on the same principle, except that the slats are angled upwards not sideways. Both types will fit into a variety of decorative schemes and offer versatile adjustments. The shape of your room may dictate your choice.

Festoon blinds are gathered on a curtain heading and controlled by cords. The result is a pretty blind that falls in gentle swags.

Venetian blinds
The horizontal blades of Venetian blinds (below) can form a strong design element in a room. In this room, the blinds have been continued all over the wall, on either side of the window, to make the horizontal lines even stronger. Slats designed to mimic the blinds below the window continue the effect.

Festoon blind
Combined with curtains of the same material, a large festoon blind can look striking (left). The ornate folds of the blind contrast with the other plain, flat surfaces in the room and add a rich quality to the otherwise simple furnishings.

Picture blinds
Matching picture blinds can provide an element of humor (above). Here, the picture shows a view through a window. The effect is enhanced by the "mirror-images" of the two blinds. The simplicity of this design is very effective in an uncluttered room.

Types of shutters

Shutters keep in more heat than curtains or blinds and if they fit well they can also help keep out window drafts. In addition, well-made shutters can help make the home more secure.

There are several different designs suitable for interior use. Folding types range from English Georgian and Victorian shutters that tuck into the window reveal when not in use, to plantation shutters,

which are louvered and first appeared in the southern United States. There are also sliding interior shutters and both hinged and sliding exterior shutters.

Folding shutters
In Georgian and Victorian homes window shutters were common on the inside of the house. By day, they folded back into storage recesses at the side of the window. At night, or when the house was unoccupied, the shutters were unfolded and secured by strong iron bars. If you have a home with shutters like this, they are well worth restoring. To free shutters that have been painted shut use paint stripper and a knife. If the shutters have been removed, you may be able to find genuine old shutters that will fit your windows, from an architectural salvage firm. But it is more likely that you will have to make a set, or get

them made by a local carpenter.

Georgian and Victorian shutters are usually paneled and fold back accordion-fashion. This is an idea that you can copy for any windows that are set in deep recesses. Although the shutters will probably not fold back fully clear of the window, they can be fitted so that curtains either side will hide them from the inside when they are not in use.

Plantation-style shutters, which also fold, can be bought ready-made. They are intended to filter light rather than to contain heat, and the slats are adjustable to let in more or less sunshine as you wish. They are usually made of pine.

Sliding shutters
These come in two forms. One type slides within the window recess, guided by runners like those used for secondary double-glazing. With this arrangement, one shutter will slide behind the other and, when they are in place, only part of the window can be unshuttered at any one time. But it is easy to remove the shutters completely by lifting them out of their runners. The other type slides on runners fitted outside the window recess and can be pulled aside.

Sliding shutters can also be fitted from floor to ceiling using the type of track intended for use with sliding doors. The shutters can either run in a single groove or one behind the other.

Exterior shutters
On the ground floor, external shutters can be closed and opened from the outside and secured with a hasp and padlock. On the upper floors, external shutters are difficult to use unless the windows open inwards. One compromise is to fit working shutters downstairs and matching, decorative fixed shutters on the floors above.

Exterior shutters are available pre-fabricated, but the choice is limited and, as it is important that the shutters match the style of the house, it is better to make your own. Tongue-and-groove board is a good material to use. You can make it up into panels and strengthen it behind with horizontal tracks and diagonal braces.

   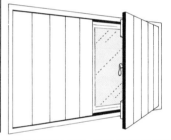

Effects with shutters

Louvered interior shutters form an effective alternative to curtains or blinds. They can have a natural wood finish, or be painted to match the windows and other woodwork.

The most versatile types are plantation-style shutters, which allow you to control the louvers to let in more or less light. Throwing them fully open gives you natural light from the whole window, while opening them partially, or opening some of the louvers, can provide a variety of lighting effects.

To get the best use of interior shutters, you need space on either side of the window and, ideally, a deep reveal. But shutters can work well in more confined spaces.

Plantation-style shutters
Opening the louvers in some panels and leaving others closed diffuses bright light and gives an interesting variety of surface patterns on the shutters.

Folding shutters
These fixed-louver shutters fold neatly into the reveal when they are open. In combination with curtains, they make a simple window look more decorative.

Doors

Estimating time ◇ Types of door ◇ Measuring and cutting a door ◇ Fitting hinges ◇ How to hang a door ◇ Fitting a door handle ◇ Repairing faults in doors

Doors come in different materials (wood, metal, glass, and plastic), and in a range of styles (hinged, sliding, and folding). They are designed for a variety of uses – for example, internal and external doors are made to different specifications.

Most doors are made from wood and hung on hinges. The two most common wooden types are paneled and flush doors. Paneled doors have a framework of solid wood with the space between filled with solid wood, plywood, or glass. Flush doors have a much lighter framework which is covered on both sides with facing sheets of hardboard or plywood.

Points to remember

◇ Measure a door carefully before cutting it to size – check your measurements by holding the door in place.
◇ Strong hardwood and aluminum doors are best for exterior use.
◇ When planing a door, work with the grain and keep checking that the edge is straight.
◇ Use three hinges on heavy doors and bathroom doors.
◇ When hanging a door make sure that the hinge side of the frame is vertical.

For more information on types of door fitting, see Choosing materials, pp. 137-9.

Estimating time

The time shown here for hanging a door is for a conventional hinged door. You will need more time for double doors (add 2 to 3 hours) or for sliding and folding doors (add up to 2 hours). If your doors fit exactly, you should be able to hang them more quickly. Remember, you will have to allow extra time if you plan to paint or varnish the door.

Measuring and cutting a door
(½)-(1½) **hours**

Fitting hinges
(½)-(1) **hour**

Hanging a door
(4)-(5) **hours**

Fitting a door handle
(¼)-(1) **hour**

Curing a sticking door
(½)-(1) **hour**

Curing a sagging door
(¼)-(½) **hour**

Repairing a warped door
(½)-(1½) **hour**

Tightening a door or frame
(½)-(1) **hour**

Types of door

For exterior use, strong, hardwood paneled doors are best on older houses, while aluminum glazed doors blend in well with modern homes. Indoors, many homes have flush doors, although paneled doors often look more attractive. Fire-check doors are often required in apartments and tall buildings.

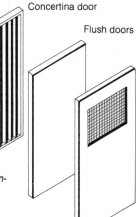

Paneled door

Paneled doors
These are available in a wide range of designs. Outdoors, where strength and security are important, choose a door with a hardwood frame. The wood should be protected with a preservative stain. Safety glass should be used if the panels are glazed with single, large panes. If the panes are smaller, glaze them with beveled-edge glass, to give a more attractive effect. Indoors, paneled doors with softwood frames are adequate. These can be made of redwood or fir.

Paneled door

Louvered door

Stable door

Aluminum door

Sliding door

Bi-folding door

Concertina door

Flush doors

Flush doors
*These are much lighter than paneled doors. They vary greatly in cost, depending on the quality of the facing material and the internal core. Those with hardboard facing are suitable only for indoors, while plywood flush doors can be used either inside or outside.
Some flush doors have a molded facing, to make them look like paneled doors. Others have an opening to take a pane of glass. Fire-check doors are usually flush doors in which the core is made up of fireproof material.*

Louvered doors
Available in a wide range of sizes, these doors are especially popular for closets. They can be painted or sealed for a natural wood effect.

Stable doors
These doors are split horizontally into two halves. By sliding a bolt, the top half can be opened independently of the bottom, providing light and ventilation.

Aluminum doors
Hinged doors made from aluminum are widely available. They usually have two glass panels and come ready-glazed with frosted safety glass.

Sliding doors
Any door can be made into a space-saving sliding door if it is combined with the appropriate sliding door gear. This is usually made up of rollers and tracks.

Bi-folding doors
These are made up of two parts connected by a hinge. As you open it, the door folds, and only half of it projects.

Concertina doors
This type of door consists of a number of vertical plastic or timber slats that fold against each other when the door is open.

120

Measuring and cutting doors

Before buying a door, measure the width of the door frame and check it at several points. Then measure the height. The door should be ¼in. less than the width of the frame, with a ⅛in. gap at the top and sufficient space at the bottom to clear the floor covering when the door opens.

If you cannot get a standard door of exactly the right size, remove some wood from a larger door to make it fit. Start by using a set square to check that the frame is square at the corners. The hinge side of the frame should be vertical. If it is not, the door frame should be removed and refixed, or replaced if necessary before you attempt to hang the door.

Do not rely on measurements alone when marking a door for cutting. Check them by positioning the door in the frame with supporting shims underneath to raise it up and keep the hinge side vertical. Then mark the outline of the frame on the door. Flush doors are more difficult to cut to size than paneled doors because they often have only a very thin wooden frame. The best solution is to cut equal amounts from either side of the door.

Planing a door
If you need to remove only a small amount of wood from a door, use a plane. If you are going the full length of the door, use the biggest plane you have and work with the grain. On the top and bottom, plane inward from the edges, so you do not split the wood. Check constantly that the edge of the door is square, except on the opening edge, where the outside of the door should be a fraction narrower than the inside to allow for opening.

Sawing a door
If there is a lot of material to remove, use a saw. A circular saw is less tiring to use than a hand saw, and has a base plate, which helps you cut accurately. Cut just inside the line, so that you can finish off with a plane. You can cut up to ¾in. from a panel door, but only half of this from a flush door. If you have to take a lot of wood off a door, try to remove equal amounts from both sides or from the top and the bottom of the door.

121

Fitting hinges

With a new door and frame, the hinge positions should be about 6in. from the top and about 8in. from the bottom. For heavy doors, a third hinge is required, which you should place centrally, equidistant from the other two hinges. When rehanging an existing door or using a frame that is already fitted, it may be simpler to use the existing hinge positions. For light internal doors use 3in. hinges. Use two 4in. hinges for other internal doors, and three 4in. hinges for heavy external and bathroom doors.

Cutting hinge mortises
First mark the hinge positions. Use a hinge itself to trace the dimensions and hole positions, 1, and a try square to draw the lines. Next cut mortises in the door and frame. These should be long enough for the inside face of the hinge to be flush with the door. The width of the mortise should allow the hinge pin to be just clear of the door. To make the mortises, first cut along the lines with a sharp knife, then use a sharp chisel and mallet to remove the wood, 2. Hold the chisel with the beveled face down so that it produces a flat-bottomed recess. Take off small amounts of wood *at a time. Unless you are using the existing frame positions, fit the hinges to the door. Drill small pilot holes and fit the hinges using countersunk screws of the same material as the hinges, 3. Finally, holding the door in place, mark the hinge positions on the door frame.*

1 *Score round the hinge and mark the positions of the screw holes*

2 *Chisel out the wood a little at a time*

3 *Use countersunk wood screws to secure the hinges*

The most common type, the hinged door, is easy to hang provided that you can find a satisfactory method of holding it in the frame while you are inserting the screws in the hinges. A number of shims and a lever that you can work with your foot provide the best solution to this problem.

Sliding doors are usually lighter and easier to lift into position. There are various types of sliding mechanism, and exact instructions for fitting are generally supplied with the door gear. But the basic principle usually involves fitting a wooden batten to the wall and attaching the track from which the door is suspended.

Folding doors
Bi-folding doors normally come with fitting instructions. Once you have trimmed them to the right size, fitting is straightforward. They have a track that fits along the inside of the door frame at the top. Pivot pins are inserted into holes drilled into the top two corners of the doors. One rotates, the other slides along the track.

A concertina door has a track that fits all the way around the frame. The width of the door frame is not as important for this type as it is for other types of door. If the door is already assembled, fitting is very easy. You simply fix the door into the track. With some designs, the door has to be assembled first and, to finish off, a cornice is fitted to hide the working parts at the top. This has to be cut to the right length.

Basic technique

How to hang a door

Hanging a hinged door
After you have fitted the hinges to the door (see Job 121, opposite) and drilled pilot holes in the door frame, lift the door into place in the frame to check that it hangs properly. It is useful to have some assistance when doing this, but if you are hanging a heavy door on your own, you will need a way of moving it by small amounts without lifting it bodily. Wooden shims under the door will help, 1, but it is also useful to put some sort of lever under the door and over a block of wood. Applying pressure with your foot will then lift the door until the hinges are in the right position. Insert one screw in each hinge, 2, to check that the door fits.

At this stage, if the door does not fit properly, you may have to deepen or enlarge the recesses, 3. Be careful not to deepen the recesses too much – or the door will bind. If you do cut them too deep, pack the recesses with card-board.

When the door fits, insert the remaining screws, 4. Use wood filler for any gaps that you have chiseled out un-intentionally. On external doors, fit a sweep along the bottom edge to throw off rainwater.

When you are hanging double doors or French doors, both sides of the frame must be vertical. Most double doors come in standard sizes, so it is best to use doors and frames that match in size. Otherwise, the method for hanging double doors is the same as that for hanging single doors. It is easier if you glaze the doors after you have hung them.

1 *Shims under the door will help you get it into position*

2 *Put one screw into each hinge to check that the door fits*

3 *If necessary, deepen the mortise on the door frame*

4 *When the door hangs properly, put in the remaining screws*

Hanging a sliding door
First prepare the door opening. The door stop – the piece of wood against which the door opens – can be removed by levering it up with a chisel. This may damage the paint and reveal nails underneath which hold the door frame in place. Punch these below the wood surface and use filler to give a smooth finish before repainting. Next fill the hinge mortises. Use thin pieces of wood glued into place and finish off with filler. The architrave should also be removed from the side on which the door is to be fitted.

If you are using the existing door, you will have to reduce the size of the original opening so that the sliding door overlaps slightly when it is fitted. Fix thin lengths of wood to the frame, cut to the right width.

Fix a batten to the wall to support the track from which the door is suspended, 1. With hollow partition walls, the batten must be fixed to the studs. Find these by tapping the wall – once you have found one, the next should be about 16in. away. The batten should be at least as long as the track, and

longer if this is necessary to fix it to the studs in the wall. If you are going to fit a cornice, you should also allow space to attach this to the ends of the batten. The thickness of the batten should allow the door to clear the frame at both sides.

The instructions will tell you at what height to fit the track – there should

be enough space at the bottom to keep the door well clear of the floor. Make sure the track is perfectly horizontal, then fix the plates and bolts to the top of the door, secure the guide to the floor and hang the door on the track, 2. If weather stripping has not been supplied with the door gear, fit a brush type to prevent heat loss.

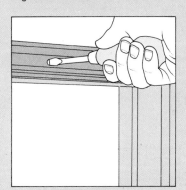
1 *Fix the track to a batten so that the door clears the frame*

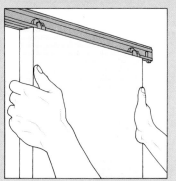
2 *Hang the door on the track at the top of the frame*

Fitting a door handle

There are two types of handle that can be fitted to doors where a mortise lock has been installed. One sort, usually called a knob set, is secured by small setscrews to a square spindle that passes through the center of the lock.

The other type of door handle is screwed to the door itself and fits over the spindle. The only problem with this type is that some doors are too thin to give a proper fixing for the screw and accommodate the mortise lock. With doors that are too thin, the solution is to fit a piece of wood to each side of the door, to which you can attach the handle. You can either glue it in place or screw it to the door beyond the line of the lock.

Fitting a knob set
Little extra work is required to fit the handles once the mortise lock has been installed (see Job 203, p. 212). The spindle must be cut to the right length to leave the handle in the correct position. It is then simple to slide the knob on to the spindle, 1, and insert the setscrews to secure it, 2.

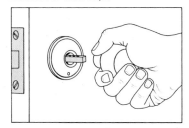
1 *Check the length of the spindle by sliding on the knob*

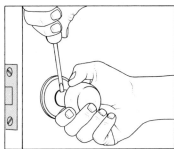
2 *Attach the knob to the spindle with setscrews*

123
Curing squeaking and sticking doors

Squeaking doors have two main causes. The hinges may need oiling, or part of the door may be catching on the frame as it opens. If neither of these things seems to be happening, the door may be warped (*see Job 126, below*). Squeaky hinges can usually be cured with a little household oil. But if they are very dry and stiff, it is worth removing them, applying a more penetrating oil, and working them free

before replacing them. Stiff hinges put a strain on the fixing screws.

If part of a door is catching on the frame, it may be that the hinges are recessed too far into either the door or the frame. If this is the case, remove the door and pack the recesses with cardboard.

Squeaks are often caused by protrusions on the hinge side of a door. Sand down any small high spots in the woodwork.

A door that sticks probably either has too much paint or has swollen because of moisture in the atmosphere (this is particularly likely if it is an outside or kitchen or bathroom door). In either case the solution is to plane off the swollen area.

Finding where a door is sticking
If you are not sure exactly which part of a door is sticking, close it on to a strip of carbon paper. This will rub on the door or frame where the door is sticking, and will leave a mark to show you which area to plane down.

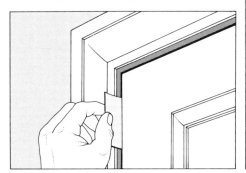

Refitting door hinges
If the hinges are recessed too far into the mortises, pack them out to the correct position. Use thin pieces of cardboard and build these up until the door hangs straight. It should then open and close easily without squeaking or sticking in the frame.

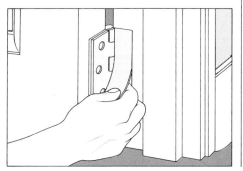

124
Repairing loose doors and frames

Door frames, especially internal ones, are often only loosely attached to the wall. If a door frame is loose, drill new holes and refix it to the wall. Doors rattle when they have shrunk and become too small for the frame. There are two solutions. Fitting foam weather stripping round the frame will probably cure the problem and keep out drafts. If this does not work, move the striking plate of the catch or lock.

Refixing a loose door frame
Remove the frame and drill new, deeper holes into the masonry with a masonry drill bit. Insert wallplugs of the correct size and put back the frame, attaching it with long screws that pass deep into the masonry to give a firm fixing.

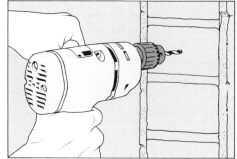

125
Curing a sagging door

A door will sag either because its hinges have got loose or because the joints of the door itself have worked loose. If the hinges are loose, you may be able to solve the problem by simply tightening the screws or fitting larger ones. If this does not work, the old screw holes may need plugging. In some cases the original hinges are too small, and they can become distorted. Replace them with larger hinges, or add a third hinge between the original two. Doors with loose joints should be strengthened using glue and dowels.

Refitting hinges
Tightening the screws of the hinges on a sagging door may only be a temporary solution to the problem. If the door starts to sag again, remove the old screws, drill larger holes, and fill these with glued dowels. When the glue has dried, fix larger screws.

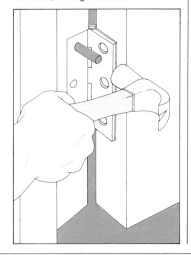

126
Dealing with a warped door

If the door has warped on the hinge side, you may be able to cure it by fitting a third hinge. But warping is more common on the other side, preventing the door from closing properly. Where this has happened and the top or bottom of the door will not fit inside the frame, push the door closed by inserting thin slivers of wood to force it into place. When it is the middle of the door that is preventing it from closing, fit temporary bolts to the top and bottom of the door and force it closed with a sliver of wood at the center.

Bending back a warped door
Inserting thin strips of wood between the door and the frame will force a warped door back at the top or bottom. If you leave the door like this or repeat the process often enough, it will eventually be pulled back permanently into its original shape.

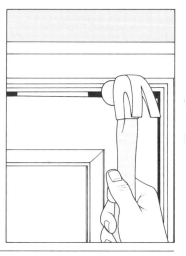

Choosing materials

Paints, stains and varnishes ◇ Wallcoverings
Tiles ◇ Wooden surfaces ◇ Floor coverings
Furnishing fabrics ◇ Door hardware

In all do-it-yourself work, successful and long-lasting results depend on using the right materials. One of the first considerations in making your choice is the room itself: is it subjected to damp, dirt, splashes and spillages (kitchen, bathroom) or heavy wear and tear? Are the surfaces in good or poor condition? Another point to bear in mind is your skill; if you are tackling a job for the first time, you may want to choose a material that is easy to handle. Finally, you will need to compare prices and select a suitable color, pattern and texture for your own home. This section is a photographic "buyer's guide" to decorating materials. It mirrors the topics in the previous chapter, illustrating the range of paints, fabrics, wallpapers, woods, tiles and so on, and compares the particular qualities and design features of different types. Each color "glossary" is backed up with detailed comparisons and practical advice on choosing the right materials and accessories for the individual job in hand.

Paints, stains and varnishes

Paint serves a dual purpose – to decorate and to protect a surface. Paints are available for both interior and exterior use, but it is outside where protection is of paramount importance. Paints can be divided into three categories: preparatory paints, such as primers; top coats, including alkyd and latex; and special purpose paints, such as masonry and floor paints. Most paints are made up of three ingredients: pigment, which provides color; a binder, usually a resin, which causes the pigment to stick to the surface; and a liquid, either oil or water, which combines the two. Thus top coats are divided into oil-based paints, which are available in gloss, semigloss and flat finishes, for use on wood and metal; and water-based paints or latex paints, which come in flat or semigloss finishes, for use on plaster, paper and brick.

Stains and varnishes also decorate and protect a surface, but provide a transparent covering. So, unlike paint, these natural finishes are used solely on bare wood; they can change its color, while allowing the pattern of the wood grain to show through. There are three basic kinds of stain: water-based, oil-based and alcohol-based.

For information on applying paints, see pp. 12-27.

Paints

Surface treatments

Knotting
A shellac-based liquid, applied to knots in wood before applying primer. It prevents resin oozing through and staining new paint.

Filler
For cracks and holes in wood and plaster, the best fillers are resin-based. These are sold as powder, and are mixed with water to form a paste.

Wood-colored putty
A paste that dries to a natural wood color and is designed to fill holes in wood that is to be given a clear finish. It is sold as paste with a separate hardener to be mixed in.

Preparatory paints

Primer
A thick liquid designed to clog the pores of wood and so reduce absorbency. It also forms a uniform surface on wood, metal and masonry before painting. A multi-purpose primer is manufactured, but specific types are available for various surfaces, such as wood and metal.

Aluminum primer-sealer
Not to be confused with aluminum paint, this preparation is made from fine aluminum scales and seals off stains, such as water-damage marks.

Undercoat
Used under alkyd, this paint is designed to obliterate other colors, and provide a good surface, prior to using a top coat. It does not weather well on its own.

Top coats

Latex
A water-thinned paint, based mainly on vinyl resins, and widely used for walls and ceilings. It is quick drying and is available in a flat or silk finish. It is available in liquid, jellified or solid form.

Alkyd
A solvent-based paint, based mainly on alkyd resins, and used on wood and metalwork. It is available either as a thin decorative coating, or as a jellified "non-drip" (thixotropic) paint.

Eggshell
Although similar in make-up to alkyd paint, eggshell produces a sheen instead of a gloss finish and helps to conceal surface faults.

New paints
A new family of decorative paints is now on the market. They have no generic name, but provide a complete system, needing no undercoat and no primer on wood. They also allow the surface to "breathe", and are now available in white as well as a variety of colors.

Special paints

Enamel paint
A solvent-based paint that needs no primer and gives a very high gloss finish, but is considerably more expensive than alkyd.

Anti-condensation paint
Provides an insulating film between a cold surface and a humid atmosphere, and so reduces condensation.

Textured paint
More a coating than a paint, this is widely used on ceilings to create a pattern or texture. The design is added after the paint has been applied, although some types automatically form a stipple pattern during application.

Masonry paint
A durable latex for external use. It contains mica, nylon fiber, sand or other materials to add bulk for filling gaps and hiding cracks and to prevent erosion.

Floor paint
Tough epoxy resin paint often strengthened with rubber to withstand heavy foot traffic.

Spray paint
A solvent-based paint thinned down so that it can be dispensed through a fine nozzle. Several coats are needed to give good coverage.

Eggshell paint on lining paper

Primer, undercoat and alkyd on

Polyurethane satin seal on parquet flooring

Decorative stain on shiplap

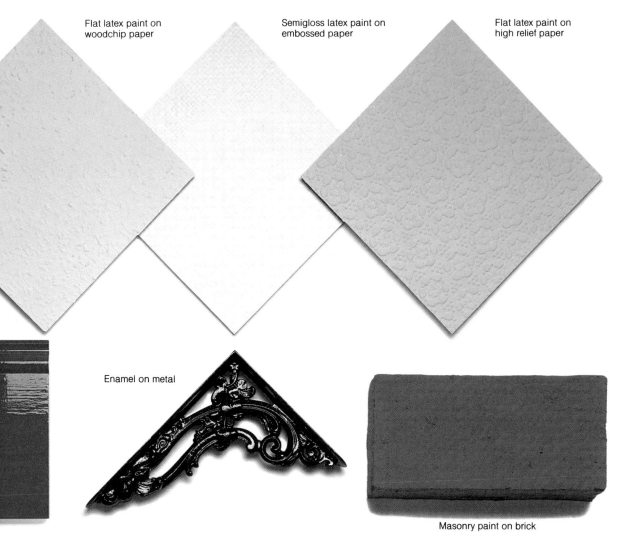

Flat latex paint on woodchip paper

Semigloss latex paint on embossed paper

Flat latex paint on high relief paper

Enamel on metal

Masonry paint on brick

Teak oil on balustrade

Wood preservative (light oak) on trellis

Polyurethane varnish (teak) on wall paneling

Polyurethane varnish (teak) on wall paneling

Stains and varnishes

Oil-based stains

Linseed oil
Still available in many stores in both plain and boiled form. However, it tends to become gummy and attract dirt and dust. It is also hard to remove.
Teak oil
Gives an attractive, protective coating to wooden furniture.
Oil-stain preservative
This new family of decorative finishes offers the protection of paint with the transparent appeal of varnish.

Seals

Polyurethane varnish seal
Widely used for wood finishing, and available in flat or gloss. The flat type gives a more mellow, natural finish than the gloss.
Seal and stain combined
Many varnish seals are available in a range of wood colors, so you can decorate and seal at the same time. Each new coat darkens the wood.

Varnishes and lacquers

Varnishes
A range of tough finishes, sold as yacht varnish in hardware stores are suitable for exterior decorative wood, such as hardwood front doors and garden furniture.
Cellulose lacquer
Tough and resistant to abrasion. It is fast drying and available in clear and colored finishes.
Two-part cold cure lacquer
Produces a tough, glossy finish, but is not easy to apply and can make timber look artificial.
Exterior preservatives
Available for use on exterior timber, such as garden fencing, these include creosote and a range of decorative preservatives in a limited range of colors.

Paints, stains and varnishes

Choosing the right paint

Price is not necessarily the best guide to quality of paint, largely because competition between brands and trading groups have distorted price categories. The best advice is to buy a well-known make, or an "own brand" in one of the homecenters or trading groups. Unknown, cheap paints, particularly latex paints, usually give an inferior result with little durability. Try to buy primer, undercoat and top coat from the same manufacturer, since they will have been formulated to be compatible.

It is best to estimate the quantities you will need and to buy the full amount in one batch to be sure of a good color match. This is particularly important if you are having the paint custom-mixed by the supplier. Paints of the same type can be mixed, provided they come from the same manufacturer. If you are mixing your own paint, make a note of the quantity and names of pigments used.

Color strengths

The small area of color on a manufacturer's color chart rarely gives a clear idea of how the paint will look in a room. The combined effect of the color on the walls and the ceiling may intensify the shade as much as 50 per cent above the paint color chart. If you have a piece of fabric in a similar shade, try holding it up to the wall to gauge the color strength. Alternatively, buy a small quantity and test it on a hidden area of wall.

Tips on buying paint

◇ Be sure to buy enough to finish a job with one batch. Pigments can vary slightly from batch to batch. Remember to allow for enough coats.
◇ It is cheaper to buy one large container than several smaller cans.
◇ Avoid mixing paints made by different manufacturers.
◇ Do not buy cheap paint with an unknown brand name.
◇ Consider the color of the paint in relation to the rest of the decoration.

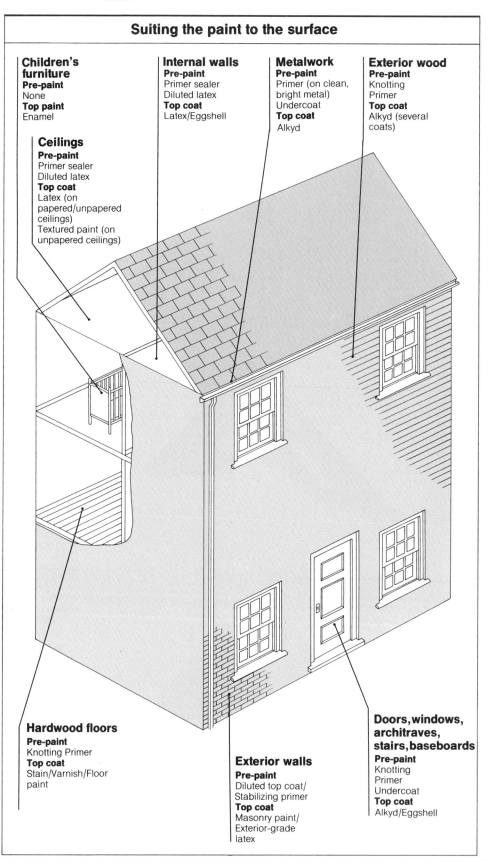

Suiting the paint to the surface

Children's furniture
Pre-paint
None
Top paint
Enamel

Ceilings
Pre-paint
Primer sealer
Diluted latex
Top coat
Latex (on papered/unpapered ceilings)
Textured paint (on unpapered ceilings)

Internal walls
Pre-paint
Primer sealer
Diluted latex
Top coat
Latex/Eggshell

Metalwork
Pre-paint
Primer (on clean, bright metal)
Undercoat
Top coat
Alkyd

Exterior wood
Pre-paint
Knotting
Primer
Top coat
Alkyd (several coats)

Hardwood floors
Pre-paint
Knotting Primer
Top coat
Stain/Varnish/Floor paint

Exterior walls
Pre-paint
Diluted top coat/
Stabilizing primer
Top coat
Masonry paint/
Exterior-grade latex

Doors, windows, architraves, stairs, baseboards
Pre-paint
Knotting
Primer
Undercoat
Top coat
Alkyd/Eggshell

When to use latex paint

Of all the top coats, latex is the easiest to apply. It spreads well and dries quickly to a smooth, even finish. On new plaster surfaces, it is usual to use a thinned paint and water coating as a primer. On previously painted or papered surfaces, it is advisable to apply the paint sparingly, recoating, if necessary, to ensure that paint covers well and seeps into any crevices. Latex is not ideal on bare wood, since the water content raises the grain, producing a rough finish.

When to use oil-based paint

Alkyd needs to be more thoroughly brushed out than latex and should be applied in thin coats to avoid runs. Nondrip (thixotropic) alkyd paint, however, is laid on in a thick layer, without much brushing. The alkyd is simply a protective finishing coat, so previous colors must be obliterated by layers of undercoat. Generally alkyd paints do not need to be thinned, unless for use in a spray gun.

Enamel needs to be brushed on extremely carefully, since the high gloss finish will show up irregularities. Like latex, it needs to be built up coat by coat, allowing each layer to dry. For small items, dipping is very effective.

Suiting the stains/varnish to the surface

Surface	Treatment
Woodblock Woodstrip	Polyurethane seal
Floorboards	Polyurethane or yacht varnish
Wall/ceiling/paneling	Polyurethane seal
Interior joinery	Polyurethane seal and stain
Exterior joinery	Oil stain preservative Yacht varnish
Sheds Fencing	Decorative preservatives
Garden furniture	Oil stain preservatives
Timber cladding	Oil stain preservatives

Choosing the right stain and varnish

As with paints, it is best to choose a well-known brand to be sure of a quality finish. If you are treating exterior wood, it is particularly important to choose a protective, exterior-quality stain or varnish.

Color strengths
It is not always easy to choose the right colored wood stain for the effect you have in mind, because the final color will be influenced by the initial color of the wood and its rate of absorption. So, where possible, make a test on a small piece of the wood, remembering that additional coats will intensify the color and that most stains will darken as they dry. To lighten the shade, water-based stains can

be thinned with water and oil, and solvent-based stains thinned with alcohol. Wood stains of the same brand can also be mixed to produce various colors.

Application techniques
Oil-based stains are the easiest to use, because their slow drying time produces a more even color. Alcohol-based stains need an expert hand as they dry very quickly. Water-based stains tend to raise the wood

grain, so need rubbing down after staining. This can be an advantage, however, if you wish to reduce the color slightly.

Polyurethanes are best built up in a number of coats, the first rubbed into the wood with a lint-free cloth to act as a seal to the wood surface. It is lightly sanded when dry before subsequent coats are brushed on. If used outdoors, these stains will be affected by bright sunlight and the edges must be sealed against dampness.

Tips on buying stain and varnish

◇ If using stains for the first time, choose an oil-based type.
◇ If you find your chosen stain is too pale, add extra coats to darken the wood. To lighten a stain, sand the surface of the wood and dilute the stain.

◇ Varnish will last longer on mahogany-type woods, than on coarser woods, such as oak and Western red cedar.
◇ If you plan to add a coat of varnish over a stain, check that they have a compatible chemical base.

Wall coverings

Modern wall coverings fall into three main categories: paper, plastic and fabric. Yet, within these three groups, the range of decorative styles and practical properties can be overwhelming, so, to limit the choice, it is usually best to consider the practical details first.

The most resilient materials are usually plastic – they will withstand wear and tear, scrubbing and scuffing. Some also have insulating and water-resistant properties. Wallpapers, whether designed to be painted after hanging or not, are less hard-wearing; however, they can help to disguise an imperfect surface. Some papers and fabrics such as silk are purely decorative.

Color, pattern and design influence the style and proportions of a room (see *Color and pattern for effect, p. 31*), so it is important to choose with great care.

Price may also influence your decision. The range is wide – from the cheapest printed paper to expensive silks, and it is worth "shopping around" for the best prices. It may not be possible to cover an entire room in an expensive fabric, so consider using one or two rolls as a panel against a less expensive, but harmonizing backcloth.

Most wall coverings are supplied in rolls, 33ft long by 21in. wide, but wider rolls are sometimes available. You will usually find details of the sizes specified in the manufacturer's pattern book.

For information on applying wall coverings, see pp. 28-43.

Lining papers

White lining paper
A pure white paper specially made to provide a smooth surface for painting.

Off-white lining paper
Used as a base for wallpaper, the lining comes in three weights: lightweight, for use over non-absorbent surfaces, such as alkyd paint, when a standard wall covering is to be used; medium-weight, for normal surfaces; and heavyweight, when a thick wall covering or a vinyl is being used. Brown lining paper is used under extra heavy coverings, such as flock wallpaper.

Reinforced linen-backed lining paper
A heavy white lining paper backed with fine linen scrim, used for very uneven surfaces and those subject to movement, such as tongue-and-groove boards.

Wallpapers

Standard wallpaper
A roll of smooth paper with pattern and color printed on it. Although inexpensive, this is the least resilient of the wall coverings.

Pre-pasted paper
A convenience paper: the backing is pre-coated with water-active adhesive and is dipped in water before hanging. This avoids the time-consuming job of pasting the paper and ensures an even covering of adhesive. Washable vinyl and woodchip papers come pre-pasted.

High relief paper
A variety of wall coverings with a pronounced relief pattern, imitating stone, stucco, tiles, plaster daub or random relief patterns. Good for concealing a lumpy surface, high relief paper is also designed to be painted.

Hand-printed paper
Printed by hand (by block or screen methods) instead of machine, and available from specialist suppliers. Roll widths and lengths are not always standard.

Flock paper
A fine pile is added to selected areas of the paper to produce a flocked pattern. It needs careful handling to prevent paste staining the surface. Flocks with a vinyl base are more durable, easier to clean and some are pre-pasted. Flock papers are most suitable in a formal room.

Borders and friezes
Thin ribbons of printed wallpaper, usually supplied in rolls and often in designs that co-ordinate with wallpaper ranges. Friezes are usually hung just below ceiling level, and borders are positioned around walls or doorways, to separate two wall coverings or to finish the edge of a papered wall.

Plastic wall coverings

Washable paper
A thin transparent vinyl coating makes this paper easy to clean and resistant to stains but difficult to remove once hung. It may not adhere well in areas of high humidity. Some types are available pre-pasted.

Vinyl paper
Not to be confused with washable paper, this consists of a thick layer of vinyl bonded on to a paper backing. Cloth-backed vinyls, however, are also available. Vinyls may be hand- or machine-printed. Machine-printed types come pre-trimmed; hand-printed types have to be trimmed before hanging. The printing has improved immensely in recent years and light-reflective surfaces and wet-look finishes can be incorporated into the design for use in areas that may need frequent cleaning, such as kitchens and bathrooms.

Foamed vinyl
The pattern is raised or embossed by a heat process after printing. This provides a relief effect while retaining a smooth backing. Designed to be painted, it is tougher than embossed paper and cannot be spoiled by pressing out.

Relief vinyl
Using photographic techniques, these produce a realistic imitation of all kinds of tile, and are an inexpensive substitute for the real thing.

Metallic foils
A metallized plastic film, finely embossed with colored patterns to reflect the light. It is especially useful in kitchens and bathrooms, since it is easy to wipe clean. A smooth wall is essential since the shine tends to highlight any defects.

Fabric coverings

Burlap
Normally sold in 3ft-wide rolls and usually hung by pasting the wall. It is available unbacked, but the paper-backed version is easier to cut and hang. Like other fabrics, it should only be hung in clean, dry rooms with light traffic.

Grasscloth
A fragile fabric consisting of natural grasses woven into a fine cotton weft and bonded on to a paper backing. It must be hung carefully and with a special adhesive.

Silk
Plain or patterned silk stuck to a paper backing. It is important not to contaminate the face of the material with paste, since it stains easily.

Woven fabrics
A variety of fabrics are sold purpose-made with a paper backing. Alternatively, furnishing fabric can be cut into lengths and applied to a pre-pasted wall. Some fabrics are hung with special adhesives.

Cork
A thin veneer of cork mounted on to a painted paper backing to give a two-tone effect. Careful hanging is essential and lining paper and a special, pre-mixed adhesive should be used. It is best to restrict it to areas of light traffic.

From the outer strip inward:
Off-white lining paper
Expanded polystyrene
Pre-pasted paper
Foamed polyethylene
Relief vinyl

From the outer strip inward:
Grasscloth
Woven fabric
Silk
Burlap

From the outer strip inward:
Metallic foil
High relief paper
Hand-printed paper

From the outer strip inward:
Standard wallpaper
Woodchip paper
Plain embossed paper
Flock paper

Wall coverings

Comparing types of wall covering

The durability of wall coverings varies. Vinyls and some of the thicker fabrics stand up well to wear and tear, while thin papers and delicate fabrics are more vulnerable.

Ease of cleaning
Some materials are also easier to clean than others. Papers divide into three sorts: spongeable types (which can be gently sponged clean); washable types (which can be washed with a wet, soapy cloth); and scrubbable types (which withstand washing with a mild abrasive). Fabrics are more prone to staining than papers, and vinyl less so.

Ease of hanging
The thicker and washable materials are the easiest to handle. Foamed vinyls, for example, hold their shape well when pasted and as the backings are smooth, they use far less paste than the traditional embosses. When pressure is applied to the pattern (when securing the edges with a seam roller, for example) the foam will flatten but recover, whereas an emboss will remain flat.

Pre-pasted papers are also easy to hang, since they save the labor of pasting and booking each length. They also save the expense of buying adhesive.

The most luxurious finishes are usually the most expensive, and often demand a slightly different hanging technique (*see Textured wall coverings, pp. 42-3*). Greater care is needed to keep paste off the surface, and to avoid expensive cutting mistakes. However, once hung, they usually have a long life.

Tips on buying wall coverings

◇ Check that you receive the exact design you ordered from the supplier and that all rolls display the same lot number.
◇ Generally rolls on display are cheaper than paper ordered from a pattern book, so shop around.
◇ Avoid thin, cheap papers; they will tear easily after pasting.

Comparing types of wall covering

Wall covering		Durable	Easy to clean	Easy to hang	Inexpensive
		In each case, a score of 5 indicates the highest score from an average sample.			
Standard paper		3	3	5	5
Pre-pasted		5	5	4	3
High relief		4	4	5	5
Hand printed		3	3	2	2
Flock		2	2	2	3
Plastics					
Vinyl		5	5	5	3
Washable		5	5	5	3
Cloth-backed vinyl		5	5	3	2
Wet-look vinyl		5	5	4	4
Vinyl flock		3	4	3	2
Relief vinyl		4	5	4	2
Metallic foil		3	4	4	2
Wallcovering fabrics					
Burlap (paper-backed)		3	2	4	2
Grasscloth (paper-backed)		2	1	1	1
Silk (paper-backed)		1	1	1	1
Woven fabrics (paper-backed)		2	2	2	1
Cork (paper-backed)		3	2	4	3

Suiting the wall covering to the room

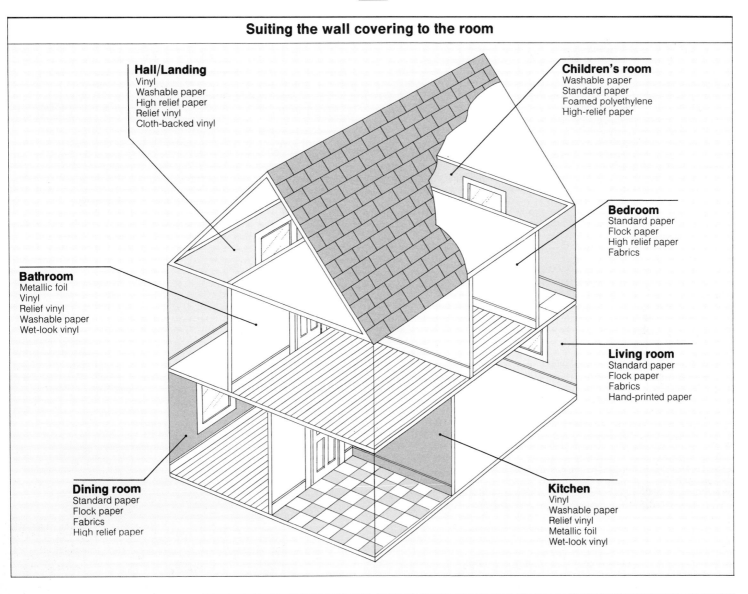

Hall/Landing
Vinyl
Washable paper
High relief paper
Relief vinyl
Cloth-backed vinyl

Children's room
Washable paper
Standard paper
Foamed polyethylene
High-relief paper

Bedroom
Standard paper
Flock paper
High relief paper
Fabrics

Bathroom
Metallic foil
Vinyl
Relief vinyl
Washable paper
Wet-look vinyl

Living room
Standard paper
Flock paper
Fabrics
Hand-printed paper

Dining room
Standard paper
Flock paper
Fabrics
High relief paper

Kitchen
Vinyl
Washable paper
Relief vinyl
Metallic foil
Wet-look vinyl

Choosing the right adhesive

Pre-applied pastes
Many wallcoverings are available pre-pasted, and the adhesive has to be activated by immersing the wall covering in a water trough. A compromise has to be made by the manufacturers as to how much paste is applied, and on some impervious surfaces, there may be a surplus of paste which will have to be wiped away.

Ordinary pastes
If you are not using a pre-pasted paper, you will have to buy adhesive. It is vitally important to choose an adhesive compatible with your wall covering, or it may ruin your decoration. So, it makes sense to

choose your wall covering before buying adhesive. If in doubt, consult the store staff. For wallpapers, there is a choice of powder adhesives designed to be mixed with cold water. As a general rule, the heavier the paper, the thicker the paste should be.

Using glue size
It is still good practice to "size" walls prior to decorating (see Job 15, p. 33). This improves adhesion and makes positioning easier, allowing the wall covering to slip into place. Many pastes can be used as size, and instructions about quantities are usually given on the packet.

Specialist pastes
For vinyl and heavyweight papers, there are, in addition to powders, a number of pre-mixed pastes used straight from the container. For vinyls and other impervious materials, it is essential to use a paste which contains fungicide, on both the top covering and the lining, to prevent mould growing under the surface. Fungicides are poisonous, so always wash your hands after using these pastes. Some materials, such as burlap and grasscloth, demand a special heavy-weight paste.

Most paper-backed wall coverings expand when pasted. It is therefore important to allow the paper to "soak".

Tiles

Ceramic wall tiles, available from hardware stores, homecenters and special tile shops, come in a wide range of colors, patterns, textures and shapes. The range of ceramic floor tiles is less extensive. Plain tiles are often colored to match standard bathroom fittings, and can be combined with complementary patterned tiles. Some patterned tiles carry an individual pattern and can be used as random cameos within plain tiling, while others, such as tile murals, are designed to be used in groups to complete a motif. Both smooth and textured finishes are available – also hand-painted tiles which are very expensive but can be used sparingly in strategic places. Heat-resistant and frost-proof tiles can also be used where required. Other materials, such as cork, metal, glass and vinyl, offer an additional range of design effects and practical properties.

Most tiles are sold by the square foot, which makes it easy to calculate quantities. Take care, however, to measure and estimate accurately (see Estimating quantities, p. 45) and allow a few extra tiles for breakages, and for future repairs.

Tiled surfaces are easy to maintain and many modern tiles – adhesive-backed tiles and sheets of mosaic tiling with pre-grouted joints for example – are easy to install.

For information on applying tiles see pp. 44-5.

Ceiling tiles

Fiberboard tiles
Made from compressed wood or mineral fibers, and thicker than polystyrene tiles. Some have tongue-and-groove edges which allow them to interlock together and to be stapled invisibly to the ceiling joists. Others have straight edges and are fixed with adhesive. Both types come with either a plain or an embossed surface. Most are fire-resistant and some are accoustically quieting.

Polystyrene tiles
The least expensive ceiling covering after paint, these tiles are available plain for over-painting or with a design embossed on to the surface. Avoid using polystyrene above cookers, since it may constitute a fire risk. Only use water-based latex paints for over-painting polystyrene tiles.

Wall tiles

Ceramic tiles
Modern ceramic wall tiles consist of slabs of clay, decorated on one side with a colored glaze. They are fired to produce a durable, stain- and water-resistant surface.

Cork tiles
Manufactured from pressed layers of tree bark, and available either sealed or un-sealed, these come in a variety of natural colors, sometimes with a slight grain direction. Cork is warm to the touch and a good heat and sound insulator, but the surface must be sealed with a polyurethane varnish if it is to be cleaned easily. Some are also treated with a washable and steam-proof finish.

Mosaic tiles
These consist of tiny ceramic tiles – square shaped or interlocking –
mounted on a mesh backing sheet. They are laid and grouted in the same way as ceramic tiles and have the same qualities, but are more expensive.

Mirror tiles
Square or rectangular pieces of clear or tinted mirrored glass. They are easier to work with than mirror sheets, but the wall surface must be perfectly smooth before the tiles are laid or the reflection will be distorted.

Brick tiles
Thin slices of real brick or artificial brick con-

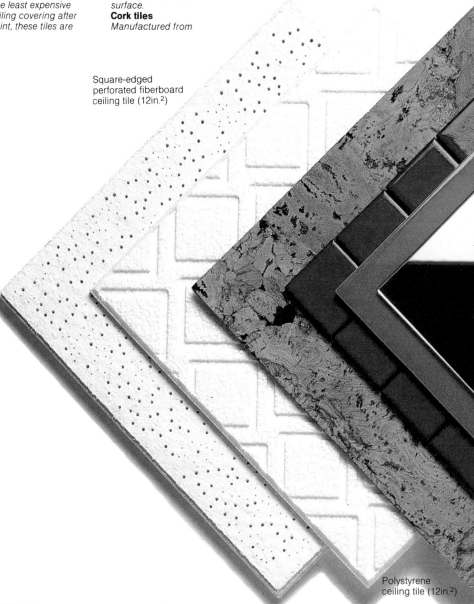

Square-edged perforated fiberboard ceiling tile (12in.²)

Polystyrene ceiling tile (12in.²)

struction, available in several colors and cut to the same size as real bricks to give the wall an authentic appearance.

Metallic tiles
Usually colored gold, silver or copper in a flat or shiny finish, these provide a heat-proof surface. They are washable, but any splash marks must be cleaned off immediately. They have hollow backs, can be cut to shape with scissors, or bent around corners, and are fixed with self-adhesive pads. Since metal conducts

electricity, these tiles should be trimmed around light switches.

Vinyl and plastic tiles
Made from thin plastic or vinyl sheet, these are warm to the touch and help reduce noise. Like metallic tiles, they have hollow backs, can be cut with scissors, and are fixed with self-adhesive pads.

Floor tiles

Ceramic floor tiles
Slightly thicker than

ceramic wall tiles and fired at a higher temperature, so that the particles fuse, making the tile almost unbreakable when laid. They may be bought glazed or unglazed in a variety of earth colors. Glazed tiles may be cold and noisy underfoot but the slip-resistant types are less dangerous when wet. Unglazed tiles should be sealed before use.

Quarry tiles
These are unglazed and therefore rougher in finish and cheaper than ceramic tiles but they

have the same properties. They are laid in a mortar bed, then sealed and polished. Colors are normally restricted to earth reds and browns.

Vinyl tiles
Solid vinyl, latex-backed tiles are durable and comfortable, but can be slippery when wet. They are easier to lay than sheet flooring and less wasteful, especially in awkward-shaped rooms. A choice of plain colors and patterns is available, some imitating other materials, such as stone and wood.

Vinyl-coated tiles
Smooth and easy to clean, these tiles are much cheaper, but less comfortable and durable than vinyl tiles.

Rubber tiles
Quiet and comfortable, rubber tiles are expensive but hard-wearing. The color range is limited, but studs and other embosses can create a "high tech" style.

Marble tiles
Durable and luxurious, marble tiles come in slabs of the natural marble colors – pink, green, gray and black,

and are laid on a bed of mortar.

Stone tiles
Like marble, stone tiles are enduring and expensive floor coverings. Slate is available in gray, green and blue squares or rectangles and is laid on a cement bed.

Cork tiles
Cork is comfortable to walk on but not very durable. Some types are supplied with a polyurethane or thin vinyl finish, others have to be sanded and sealed after laying to prevent water penetrating between the tiles.

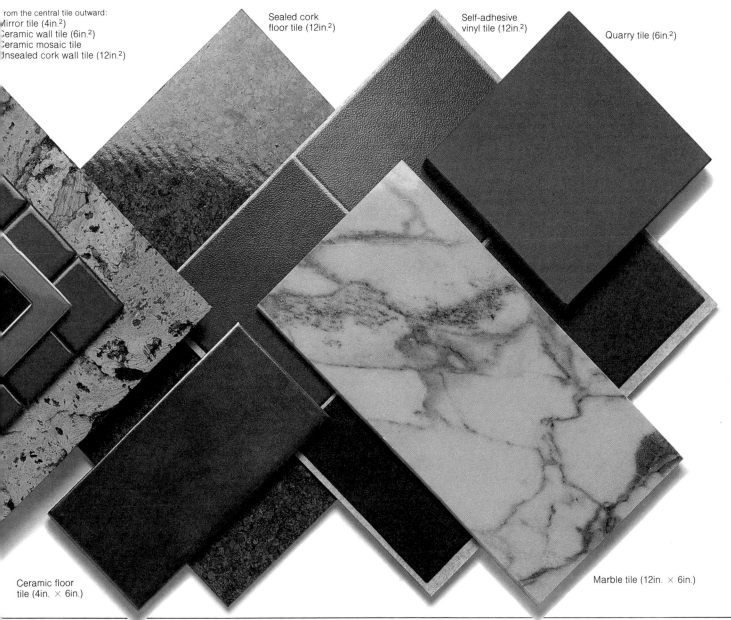

rom the central tile outward:
Mirror tile (4in.²)
Ceramic wall tile (6in.²)
Ceramic mosaic tile
Unsealed cork wall tile (12in.²)

Sealed cork floor tile (12in.²)

Self-adhesive vinyl tile (12in.²)

Quarry tile (6in.²)

Ceramic floor tile (4in. × 6in.)

Marble tile (12in. × 6in.)

Tiles

The range of tile shapes

Most ceramic tiles are either square or oblong, but a range of interlocking circular, hexagonal and Provençale-shaped tiles are also to be found. Square and rectangular shapes, however, are generally less expensive and easier to lay. The most common type of tile, known as a "field" tile, has square edges, sometimes with spacer lugs to allow space between the tiles for grouting. Some manufacturers also produce "universal" tiles which have one or two glazed edges for finishing exposed edges. Quadrant tiles are round-edged slivers for use as border tiles on corners, such as window sills. Other types of tile, such as cork, vinyl, mirror and plastic, come as squares or rectangles, and brick tiles are the same shape and size as natural bricks. Ceramic wall tiles usually come in 4in.^{2} or 6in.^{2} sizes, ceramic floor tiles come in 4in. $\times$ 6in. sizes, whereas most other tiles are 12in.^{2}

Choosing the right adhesive

As with wallpapers, it is crucial to choose the correct adhesive for the type of tile, the conditions and the area in which it is to be used. Ceramic tiles should be fixed with ceramic tile adhesive, which is sold pre-mixed or in powder form.

Waterproof types are available for shower cubicles and tub surrounds; frost-proof types for use on patios or balconies; and heat-resistant ones for kitchens and fireplaces. There is also a flexible adhesive for tiling over a surface which is prone to movement, such as hardboard and particleboard; it often comes in two parts to be mixed before use. A thick-bed adhesive should be used on uneven surfaces.

Cork tiles should be fixed with either non-flammable cork wall or floor adhesive, or a water-based contact adhesive, depending on the instructions supplied. A specific adhesive is also available for brick tiles. Mirror, plastic and metallic tiles are secured in place with sticky tabs. For each square yard of tiling, you will need about 1 quart of adhesive.

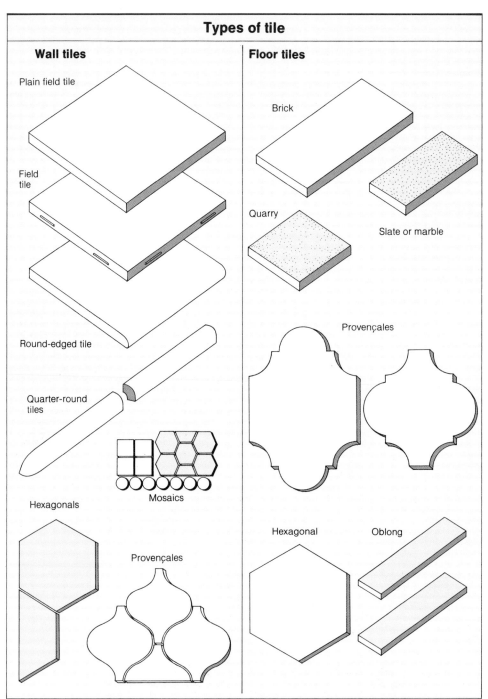

Types of tile

Wall tiles

Plain field tile

Field tile

Round-edged tile

Quarter-round tiles

Hexagonals

Mosaics

Provençales

Floor tiles

Brick

Quarry

Slate or marble

Provençales

Hexagonal

Oblong

Tips on buying tiles

◇ Estimate the quantity of whole tiles and trim you need before buying.
◇ Count part tiles as whole tiles for estimating purposes, but remember that with large cork or vinyl tiles, one tile can be cut into several border pieces.
◇ Always check tiles for chips and color differences when you get them home.
◇ Allow a few extra tiles (about five per cent) for breakages and for future repairs.
◇ When cutting tiles, always exert even pressure and keep the tile supported, to be sure of a clean break.

Suiting the wall tile to the room

Type	Qualities	Room	Adhesive
Ceramic	Hard-wearing, waterproof, stain-resistant	Kitchens and bathrooms	Ceramic wall tile adhesive – waterproof adhesive in areas likely to be splashed by water
Mosaics	Hard-wearing, waterproof, stain-resistant	Kitchens and bathrooms	As for ceramic tiles
Cork	Warm, reasonably hard-wearing and stain-resistant	Anywhere except excessively wet areas, e.g. showers	Cork wall tile adhesive. Non-flammable latex types are safest. Contact adhesive is an alternative
Mirror	Hard-wearing, stain-resistant Ideal for small feature areas Gives a feeling of space	Anywhere except wet areas	Adhesive tabs
Brick	Hard-wearing, ideal for complete walls or feature areas	Any room but avoid areas where bricks could be affected by grease, excessive steam or water splashes	Brick wall tile adhesive
Plastic and metallic	Fairly easy to clean but some can be damaged by abrasive cleaners. Reasonably hard-wearing	Kitchens and bathrooms but avoid using plastics near heat, and metallics near steam	Adhesive tabs or contact adhesive

Suiting the floor tile to the room

Type	Qualities	Room	Adhesive
Ceramic	Hard-wearing, waterproof, stain-resistant but cold and noisy	Kitchens, bathrooms and halls	Ceramic floor tile adhesive
Quarry	As above	Kitchens, bathrooms and halls	Ceramic floor tile adhesive or (for thicker types) mortar cement
Cork	Very comfortable, warm and quiet. Not very durable. Reasonably able to withstand water	Any room	Cork floor tile adhesive as recommended by tile manu-facturers
Vinyl	Very comfortable, warm and quiet. Durable on well-laid sub-floor. Reasonably able to withstand water.	Any room but mostly kitchens and bathrooms	Some are self-adhesive. Others are laid with vinyl floor adhesive
Marble	Hard-wearing and waterproof	Kitchens, bathrooms and halls	Mortar cement

Wooden surfaces

Wood forms a warm, smooth and attractive surface. It is extremely durable, has acoustic and insulating properties and, thanks to modern wood finishes, is easy to maintain. It therefore forms an ideal covering for walls and ceilings in any room and for floors in all but kitchens and bathrooms.

Wooden paneling for walls and ceilings is available as boards or as sheets. Tongue-and-groove boards are made from planed planks which are designed to interlock together to form a broad, gap-free area of paneling. Most have chamfered edges to form a decorative "V" joint. Man-made sheet wallboards, designed to simulate boards, are usually sheets of thin plywood with a real wood veneer or a printed plastic or paper surface, simulating various types of decorative wood. Embossed panels, printed with deeply textured wood effects, are also available.

Most wooden flooring is solid hardwood laid over an ordinary sub-floor, such as particleboard, plywood or hardboard. Some types, however, consist of a hardwood layer bonded to a plywood backing. Flooring comes as either long strips of wood (wood strip) or blocks arranged into patterns (wood block or mosaic panels). Wood blocks can be arranged into a variety of patterns and basketweave parquet panels can be laid square or diagonally across the room.

For information on fitting wooden paneling and flooring, see pp. 66-77 and 82-87.

Paneling

Sheet paneling

Wallboards
These thin plywood or hardboard sheets come with a variety of surfaces. The best quality sheets have a veneer of real wood, which may also be grooved to simulate tongue-and-groove boards. Cheaper varieties have a photographic image of a wooden surface printed on paper or plastic and bonded on to the plywood backing. Both types come in sheets measuring 4ft × 8ft and $\frac{1}{8}$in. or $\frac{1}{4}$in. thick. This height is usually sufficient to cover a wall from floor to ceiling in one sheet without horizontal joins.

Board paneling

Tongue-and-groove boards
These are usually available in softwoods, such as redwood, oak, spruce, pine, cedar, cypress and hemlock and often in a good range of more unusual decorative hardwoods (see chart overleaf). They usually come with chamfered edges, to form a decorative "V" joint and with either a flat or a decorative face – channeled or scalloped, for example. The standard thickness is $\frac{1}{2}$in., although $\frac{3}{4}$in. and $\frac{3}{8}$in. thick boards are readily available. The nominal width is generally 4in. (the actual covering width is $3\frac{1}{2}$in.), but 6in. tongue-and-groove boards are not uncommon. The most usual length is 8ft, although some suppliers stock longer random lengths.

Shiplap boards
These are similar to tongue-and-groove, except that the top edge of each board fits under a rabbet in the edge of the previous board. When fixed horizontally, the water will run down the face of the boards without penetrating the surface. Shiplap boards are usually available only in two sizes: $\frac{3}{4}$in. × $4\frac{1}{4}$in. and 1in. × 6in.

Flooring

Wooden sub-floors

Particleboard
This man-made material consists of resin-coated wood chips compressed under heat and pressure into a board. Standard particleboard is usually used as a self-contained sub-floor, but an extra-strong type has tongue-

Tongue and groove board (Pine)

Pine veneered wallboard

Walnut veneered wallboard

Shiplap board (Pine)

From the central piece out Particleboard ($\frac{3}{4}$in.)
3-ply plywood ($\frac{1}{2}$in.)
Hardboard ($\frac{1}{8}$in.)

and-groove edges and a hardboard veneer.

Plywood

Plywood is composed of thin sheets (veneers) of wood glued together. The grain runs alternately along and across the wood, giving the composite sheet greater uniformity of strength than wood. There are two basic types of plywood: timber ply, which is made from a single type of wood and is used as a sub-floor; and veneered ply, which is made from a variety of woods and can be used as a substitute for wooden flooring. Tongue-and-groove plywood is available for this purpose and the wood is graded

according to the quality of the surface veneer and the glue. There are also special surface finishes, such as plastic, metal and varnish. For exterior use, choose boards made with moisture- and weather-proof glue. Softwood plywood comes as interior-grade, or exterior-grade. Choose an exterior-grade for areas of high humidity, such as bathrooms.

Hardboard

This is made from pulped wood fiber, hot-pressed into thin sheets, and since it bends easily, it is generally used as a sub-floor over timber boards. There are a variety of types and finishes, but standard

and water-resistant tempered hardboard are usual floor coverings. Standard hardboard has one smooth face and a textured back. Medium hardboard has a softer surface for lining walls and ceilings. Double-faced and plastic-coated hardboards are also available.

Woodstrip flooring

Hardwood woodstrip

Solid tongue-and-groove boards about $2\frac{1}{4}$in. wide and in random lengths slot together to form narrow floorboards. They are laid at right angles to the sub-floor and come in a range of

solid woods to form a luxury floor.

Plywood woodstrip

Some woodstrip floors are made from plywood strips overlaid with hardwood. The strips are either slotted together with tongues and grooves, allowing them to "float" on the sub-floor as one piece; or, the plywood has interlocking "ears" which are pinned to the floor. The floor thickness can vary from $\frac{1}{4}$ to $\frac{1}{2}$in. overall.

Woodblock flooring

Parquet panels

Each panel is made up of five or seven hardwood "fingers" in four

parts (20 or 28 pieces overall), which are glued together. The panels are usually either 12in. or 18in. square and the individual "fingers" in each panel are arranged to build up a basket-weave pattern. This type of floor usually requires sanding and sealing after laying. Some hardwood parquet floors are supplied tongued-and-grooved, pre-sealed and finished in rigid panels, which are strengthened with soft aluminum pins or a plywood backing.

Woodblock

A woodblock floor consists of shallow blocks, about 8in. × $2\frac{1}{2}$in. and $\frac{3}{4}$in. thick, which are interlocked

with tongues and grooves into panels, to create a flat, solid surface. They are available in a range of hardwoods. Traditional blocks can be laid in a variety of patterns – usually basket-weave, but also traditional herringbone, brick-pattern and others. Unlike parquet panels, woodblocks are prefinished and simply float on a sub-floor. Traditional parquet blocks, however, are not tongue-and-groove, and must be both sanded and sealed after laying.

Woodblock (Merbau)

Hardwood woodstrip (Light oak)

Straight-edged parquet panel (teak)

Tongue and groove parquet panel (Red oak)

Wooden surfaces

Comparing types of wooden paneling

Types of wood vary dramatically in graining, color and properties, so take time to choose a wood that is suitable for both the purpose and the style of the room. Remember that stains and varnishes can be used to modify the color and the gloss of the surface, although nothing can be done to change the grain. Hardwoods are generally more durable and decorative, although more expensive than softwoods. However, the quality is more variable and they are not always as readily available.

Price differences
Spruce paneling is about one-third the price of hardwood, redwood and cedar, and Douglas fir. Pine is slightly more expensive than spruce – almost exactly half the price of hemlock and Douglas fir. Wood veneer wallboards allow luxurious hardwood finishes to be used at reasonable prices. The prices are roughly equivalent to paneling in traditional pine, although rosewood is about twice the price of other types. Flame-retardant treated panels are also available at about twice the price of conventional veneered boards. Embossed hardboard wall panels are in the same price bracket as real wood veneer panels, while printed face wallboards are about half the price. Some wood merchants charge on a sliding scale for cutting, so it may work out cheaper to buy a full-size board.

Choosing between sheet and board paneling

Individual tongue-and-groove boards offer the widest choice of pattern. They are also more versatile than sheet paneling, since they comprise smaller units. Wallboards, on the other hand, are usually large enough to stretch from floor to ceiling and will cover a wall in a few sheets butted side by side, and so involve less work. For a large area, tongue-and-groove boards are usually best, because the end joins can be neatly staggered and so form part of the overall pattern.

The range of lumbers for wooden paneling			
Wood type	**Description**	**Comments**	**Price** A = High B = Medium C = Moderate
Solid boards			
Cedar	Pronounced straight grain	Will withstand high temperature	Ⓐ
Pine	Pale yellow/cream, pronounced knots	Quality of finish varies	Ⓒ
Spruce	Creamy-white to light golden yellow	Tools must be sharp	Ⓓ
Douglas fir	Gold, reddish-brown, pronounced wavy grain	Tools must be sharp	Ⓑ
Hardwood	Reddish brown, open grain	Some timbers may need sanding	Ⓐ
Veneered sheets			
Cherry	Medium, wavy grain		Ⓒ
Sapele	Reddish-brown, straight open grain		Ⓒ
Rosewood	Dark brown, wavy black grain		Ⓐ
Teak	Reddish-brown attractive graining	Resists acid, fire and rot	Ⓒ
Elm	Light brown, close grain		Ⓒ
Cedar	Golden reddish-brown, wavy grain		Ⓒ
Oak	Beige/brown, long straight grain	Durable, needs sharp tools	Ⓒ
Ash	Creamy-brown, wavy grain	Bends well	Ⓒ

Tips on buying lumber

◇ Many homecenters and hardware stores sell wooden panels, strips, blocks and sheets, pre-cut in packs, complete with a coverage guide. Always check that there is a good mixture of light and dark grains.

◇ Wood merchants sell wood planed and pre-cut to standard sizes, and most will cut hardwood to a special size if given a few days notice.

◇ Lumber yards are often cheaper than homecenters, especially for larger quantities, and will usually give good advice.

◇ Before buying, check boards for defects and avoid those that are bowed, cupped, twisted or heavily knotted. It will be impossible to straighten a distorted board. A few knots can look attractive, but always check that they are sound and show no sign of loosening.

◇ Prices vary according to the outlet and the availability of wood, so shop around.

Choosing between strip and block flooring

Woodstrip flooring is a glorified form of floorboard, but with the range of attractive grains and colors afforded by natural lumbers and wood stains, it can become a high-quality floor. Woodstrip is quicker and easier to lay than woodblock. However, it may shrink when underfloor heating is used, so always check with the supplier first. Woodblock flooring is the most popular wooden floor. It is more versatile than woodstrip, giving more opportunity for pattern and texture, and produces a smoother, more luxurious finish. Both parquet and woodblock floors need to be sealed and sanded after laying, unless they have been pre-sealed.

Woodstrip flooring is at the top of the price range, followed by woodblock, then parquet panels. Solid and pre-finished woodstrip is more expensive than plywood overlaid with hardwood and unfinished woodstrip, that needs to be sanded and sealed after laying.

Some man-made softwood boards, such as particleboard and plywood, can be used as a top floor covering, provided they have a special veneer or finish, although the result can never compete with solid wood.

The range of lumbers for wooden flooring

Wood type	Description	Woodblock	Woodstrip	Parquet	Price A = High B = Medium C = Moderate
Teak	Dark brown Good for heavy traffic	◇	◇	◇	Ⓐ
Walnut	Mid brown Hard-wearing	◇		◇	Ⓐ
Mahogany	Reddish-brown Hard-wearing			◇	Ⓑ
Tasmanian oak (Eucalyptus)	Cream, straight grain Fairly hard-wearing			◇	Ⓒ
Light oak	Light straw color Hard-wearing	◇		◇	Ⓒ
Dark oak	Rich brown Hard-wearing			◇	Ⓒ
Maple	Cream. Exceptionally hard-wearing	◇	◇	◇	Ⓑ
Ash	Pale cream. Hard-wearing		◇		Ⓒ
Birch	Creamy brown, light grain. Hard-wearing		◇		Ⓑ

Comparing types of wooden flooring

Wooden flooring receives more wear than paneling, and the wood needs to be more durable. The availability of lumber for different floor types varies. Mahogany and oak, for example, are usually only available for mosaic panels, while ash and beech are generally only found as woodstrip flooring.

Price differences

Prices of wood vary, and teak, the most hard-wearing, costs a little more than maple and birch. Oak and ash are less expensive. In woodblock flooring, all woods cost the same, but ordinary woodblock costs a third of the price of pre-finished woodblock. In the parquet panel range, teak again is the most costly, followed by mahogany; maple is about three-quarters of the price of teak. Thus, one of the most expensive floors is teak woodstrip, and one of the cheapest, oak parquet.

Comparing types of man-made boards

Man-made boards, such as plywood and hardboard, are cheap, hard-wearing and form excellent sub-floors over old boards. Plywood is the strongest of the three types and is not prone to splitting or warping.

Hardboard is more brittle and needs to be cut and fitted carefully to avoid damaging the edges. Particle board is coarser and even less expensive and can be fixed directly to the floor joists.

Particleboard
Standard particleboard for sub-floors is supplied with sanded faces, but sealed particleboard is available for finishing off with gloss and wood-veneered types for a top floor covering.

Plywood
The thinnest types of plywood are 3-ply, but multi-ply boards are also available with up to 11 layers. Plywood strips with a surface veneer of a decorative hardwood are available for a quality finish.

Hardboard
Standard hardboard has one smooth face and a coarse, mesh back face. Tempered hardboard is impregnated with oils for extra strength and water-resistance and medium hardboard is less coarse.

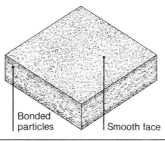

Bonded particles | Smooth face

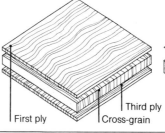

First ply | Third ply | Cross-grain

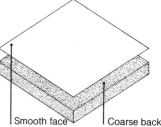

Smooth face | Coarse back

Floor coverings

Any new floor covering represents a major furnishing buy, and the choice can be bewildering, so it is important to know what to expect for your money.

Each type of covering performs a slightly different function. Carpeting provides luxury underfoot – it is warm, comfortable, sound-proofing and comes in a wide range of colors, patterns and qualities to suit most rooms in the house. For kitchens and bathrooms, sheet vinyl makes an excellent waterproof barrier, and is softer, quieter, cheaper and less slippery than tiles. Matting is a budget-priced alternative to carpets – useful for rented apartments and if you are planning to move house soon. Rugs which include pieces of carpet under 43ft square hide worn carpet and form a soft and decorative accessory over carpet, tiles or wooden flooring.

Carpets can be broadly divided into the following categories. There are tufted, woven and bonded types, which refer to the construction method; there are cut, looped cord and twisted types, which refer to the pile; and there are jute-backed and foam-backed which refer to the backing material.

For information on laying floor coverings, see pp. 56-65 and 78-81.

Padding

Felt
This traditional type of padding has been largely replaced by jute-backed rubber underlay, but it absorbs underfloor dust more efficiently.

Rubber
Jute-backed or paper-backed rubber are the best quality paddings for most carpets and are essential for stairs.

Foam rubber
Only suitable for use in areas of light wear, it should have a layer of felt paper beneath.

Felt paper
Used under foam-backed carpet and foam rubber padding to prevent them sticking to the floor.

Other types
Other materials include hard-wearing jute, waterproof pvc, and felt-substitutes.

Foam rubber

Felt paper

Rubber

Latex

Felt

Carpets

Standard short pile
A standard pile carpet is available in either a woven form (such as Axminster and Wilton carpets, named after the looms on which they are woven) or in a cheaper tufted form. The pile is cut short.

Loop pile
In this case, fine or coarse yarn is woven into the carpet, but left uncut to make a series of loops.

Sculptured pile
A woven or tufted carpet that is a mixture of cut and looped pile. Some loops are cut and some left looped, to produce a three dimensional effect, which, though attractive can be difficult to clean.

Hair and woolcord
The yarn is woven into the backing, pulled tight and left uncut, to give a hard-wearing surface.

Twist
Before the carpet is woven, the yarn is twisted to give the carpet a textured, springy and very hard-wearing surface.

Velvet
The pile is extremely dense, deep and smooth and is cut to produce a luxurious finish, with a definite right and wrong way. It will shade and track when walked on.

Shag
A luxurious carpet with a long cut pile of 1 in. The pile treads down easily and needs to be raked and cleaned regularly.

Berber
These carpets have a dense, looped pile and are made from undyed sheep wool.

Foam-backed carpet
Usually a tufted carpet with a foam backing. It is easier to lay than jute-backed types, but normally it does not wear so well.

Carpet tiles
Available in woven, tufted, cord and bonded carpets in a variety of fibers. Most are loose laid.

Standard short pile

Foam-backed

Carpet tile

Berber

Twist pile

Velvet pile

Woolcord

Loop pile

Shag pile

Rugs and matting

Ethnic rugs
Available in cotton and wool, ethnic Indian, African, European and American rugs are generally flat weave. The price varies according to the fiber content and the intricacy of the design. Cotton rugs may "bleed" if laid over a pale carpet, so it is best to line them with fabric or paper and dry-clean.

Fleece rugs
Some cultures have used different weaving techniques to produce unusual rugs. Greek fleece rugs, which have a luxurious, deep pile, are made from woven wool fleece. They are machine washable.

Rush matting
Usually woven in 12in. squares, rush matting can be sewn together to form larger pieces. It is available in a variety of designs, can be loose laid directly on to wood or concrete without an underlay and is easily rolled up to take with you when you move. However, it collects dirt, and should be regularly lifted to sweep away the dust. It can be gently scrubbed with a soap-less detergent.

Coconut matting
This is the coarse matting found at front and back doors, and is available in a variety of sizes for use in areas of heavy and dirty traffic.

Coir matting
A more refined form of coconut matting, coir comes in a variety of thicknesses, colors, textures and weaves, from simple crossweave to a heavier, tighter loop with a non-slip backing.

Split cane matting
Similar to rush matting, but more rigid, split cane is likewise inexpensive and hard-wearing, but attracts the dust.

Sisal matting
This tough, naturally white fiber makes a good floor covering in halls and passageways.

Plastic matting
Useful in kitchens and bathrooms, plastic matting is cheap, easy to clean and comes in a range of bright colors.

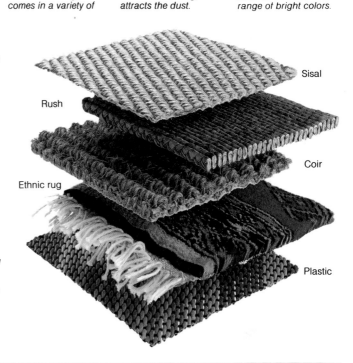

Sisal

Rush

Coir

Ethnic rug

Plastic

Sheet flooring

Sheet vinyl
Some types, known as "lay flat vinyl", can be loose laid, others need to be stuck around the edges to the sub-floor with double-sided tape. The better qualities, known as cushioned vinyl, have a layer of foam between the vinyl and the backings, making them soft, quiet and very comfortable to walk on. Vinyls come in a wide variety of colors, designs and textures, including imitation tiles. Vinyl is impervious to water, oil, fat and most household chemicals, but most grades are not immune to burns.

Rubber flooring
Usually made from a mixture of natural and synthetic rubber, this type of flooring is hard-wearing, quiet and water-proof; but is not as easy to lay as vinyl and marks more easily. Modern designs feature ribs, studs and squares to give a smart, non-slip surface. Rubber floors can be cleaned with soapy water, but must be rinsed well.

Linoleum
Made from a mixture of wood, linseed oil, ground cork, flour and resins, linoleum comes in various thicknesses. It is hard-wearing, but is inclined to rot if water gets underneath. In recent years, it has lost in popularity to vinyl but modern designs are now appearing in tile form.

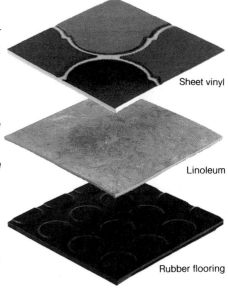

Sheet vinyl

Linoleum

Rubber flooring

Floor coverings

Comparing types of carpet fiber

Carpet fibers are divided into three basic types: pure wool, synthetics and mixtures of the two: the fiber content should be clearly labeled together with other details on every carpet.

Wool, the traditional carpet fiber, is expensive and it does need moth-proofing but it is warm, hard-wearing, dirt-resistant, naturally fire-resistant and easy to clean. Synthetics include the following materials: acrylic, which is closest to wool in feel and appearance; nylon, which is cheap and hard-wearing, but attracts dirt and dust; polyester, which is soft and reasonably water-resistant for bathrooms, but less hard-wearing; and polypropylene, which is used for indoor/outdoor carpeting. Mixtures are a blend of two fibers to combine the best properties of each. The most popular combination is 80 per cent wool, 20 per cent synthetic, since it reduces the price of the carpet, but looks, feels and wears like wool.

Suiting the padding to the carpet

Padding plays an important part in the life of your carpet, increases its heat- and sound-insulating properties and gives it a softer tread, so be sure to choose the right one. Carpets with a woven backing need to be laid over a good quality rubber padding with a paper or jute backing or over felt padding. Foam rubber paddings are also available, but are only advisable in areas of light wear. They need a layer of paper underneath to prevent them sticking to the floor. Most cheaper carpets have a built-in foam backing and should be laid over felt paper padding.

Jute-backed carpet
You will need paper-backed or jute-backed rubber padding for most rooms. Alternatively, use felt, especially in rooms with underfloor heating. For rarely used rooms, a foam-rubber padding will be adequate.

Foam-backed carpet
The only padding appropriate to a foam-backed carpet is a felt paper one.

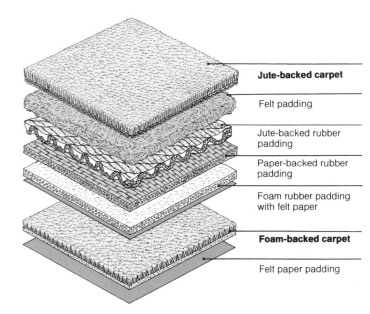

- Jute-backed carpet
- Felt padding
- Jute-backed rubber padding
- Paper-backed rubber padding
- Foam rubber padding with felt paper
- Foam-backed carpet
- Felt paper padding

Comparing types of carpet construction

There are three different ways of connecting the carpet fiber to its backing: by close interweaving; by stitching and gluing; and by simple glue bonding. Woven, tufted and bonded carpets are all available in a variety of fibers, pile lengths and roll widths. When you are looking at carpet samples, bend them back to see how dense the pile is, and how it has been connected to the backing. Then tug at a few tufts to check that the fiber is securely fixed to the backing.

Woven carpet
All woven carpets are made by either the Wilton or the Axminster method. These are two different weaving techniques, not brand names. Axminster carpets are woven one row of tufts at a time, so that the loom anchors the U-shaped tufts into the backing material as it weaves each row. Wilton carpets are woven in one continuous length, and the pile and backing are closely interwoven for extra strength and thickness. Wilton backings are usually flatter than Axminster, and denser, with 10 or more rows of pile to the inch.

Tufted carpet
These are not woven at all. The yarn is stitched into a pre-woven "primary" backing to give a looped or cut pile. The backing is then coated with latex to secure the tufts and a second backing is added for strength and easy handling.

Bonded carpet
This is a relatively new manufacturing process in which the pile fiber is bonded on to a pre-woven backing. Bonded carpets will not fray when cut, but are available in plain colors only.

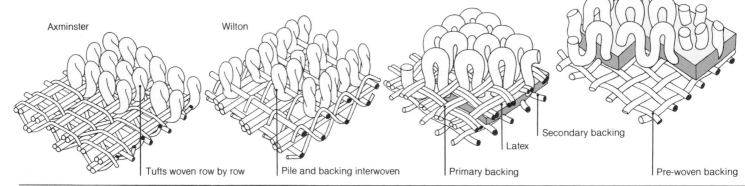

Axminster — Tufts woven row by row
Wilton — Pile and backing interwoven
Primary backing | Latex | Secondary backing
Pre-woven backing

Suiting the floor covering to the room

Before choosing a floor covering, it is important to consider the demands that will be put on it – whether it will be subject to splashing, scratching, spillages or heavy traffic. The first decision is the type of floor covering – carpet, vinyl or matting; the next is the quality. Price will naturally be a controlling factor, but when selecting carpet, it is essential to choose a grade that will withstand the wear and not to make false economies. (*For carpet grades, see p. 57.*) Once you have chosen the most appropriate type of flooring, it is worth buying the best quality you can afford: it will last longer.

Room	Carpet	Sheet flooring	Rugs and matting
Kitchen	Short pile nylon or synthetic for easy cleaning or loose-lay carpet tiles	Perfect	Rush mats give a country feel; plastic fits a modern style.
Bathroom	Only if recommended since it must have a waterproof backing. Preferably a polyester	Perfect. Sheet vinyl is water-resistant	Plastic mats or loose-lay washable cotton rugs
Living room	Choose a hard-wearing grade	Not the best choice	To brighten a large expanse of carpet or to hide worn areas
Dining room	Choose a medium grade	Not unless the dining area runs into the kitchen	Add a rug or mat over a vinyl floor for comfort
Bedrooms	The lightest and cheapest grades make economic sense	Practical in a young child's room, but too hard for adults	Add rugs beside the bed for comfort
Hall	Needs to be very hard-wearing to stand up to heavy traffic	Practical if you have children, dogs – or both	Coir is hard-wearing. Dhurries make a bright and cheap covering over tiles, vinyl or plain carpet

Comparing types of sheet flooring construction

The quality of sheet flooring is determined by its construction. Sheet vinyl consists of an outer "wear" layer, a filling and a backing. The most comfortable vinyl has a "cushioned" filling layer; the cheaper types have a pattern layer instead of foam cushion; while in the more durable solid vinyl the design is integrated in the material. Rubber flooring consists of layers of natural and synthetic rubber, compressed under high pressure and temperatures into a strong sheet.

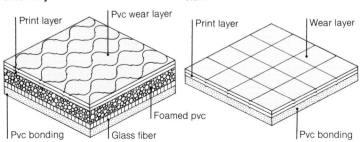

Sheet vinyl — Print layer, Pvc wear layer, Pvc bonding, Glass fiber, Foamed pvc

Rubber — Print layer, Wear layer, Pvc bonding

Tips on buying floor coverings

◇ A new floor covering should see you through several changes of decoration, so choose colors with care.

◇ Remember that dark colors show up dust and dirt more quickly than muted tones.

◇ Small homes can be made to appear larger by using the same color carpet throughout the ground floor and up the stairs; and sheet vinyl with a small pattern in the kitchen.

◇ "Lay flat" vinyl is easier to lay and transport than other types.

◇ All carpets should carry a label indicating the widths available, the construction method, the fiber content and any special laying and cleaning instructions.

◇ Buy the correct carpet quality grade for the room in which it is to be used (*see Identifying carpet quality, p. 57*).

◇ If one supplier does not stock the roll width of carpet or sheet flooring you require, shop around to avoid unnecessary joins and wastage.

◇ For stair carpets, choose a strong padding and a resilient carpet that will not reveal the backing on the treads.

◇ Vinyl and plastic sheeting is widely available from hardware stores but carpets and matting are best bought from carpet stores, who will measure and estimate free.

Furnishing fabrics

When choosing fabrics for curtains, shades and upholstery, it is important to select color, pattern and texture to suit the style of the room and choose practical properties that suit the area to be covered. Some designs are available in a wide range of fabrics, so that furnishings can be co-ordinated. The price, of course, will also be a significant consideration, and it is always better to buy a slightly less expensive fabric, and use it lavishly, than to skimp on more expensive material. Curtains, for example, need to be about 2-2½ times the width of the window, and will never look good if they are not full enough. Moreover, if you run out of furnishing fabric before you finish a job, you may have difficulty matching it exactly, so always measure and estimate carefully, and allow for wastage.

For information on curtains and shades, see pp. 102-7; for care and repair of fabrics, see pp. 140-3; and for making curtains and upholstery, see pp. 150-7.

Velvet cushion

Chair border

Tassel

Curtain and upholstery fabrics

Cotton
This natural fiber is made into a number of fabrics and can be blended with synthetic fibers. Cotton and cotton mixtures come with a variety of finishes, such as crêpe, chintz and seersucker, or with a pattern woven into the fabric – herringbone or gingham, for instance. Cotton takes printed patterns well, and is easy to work with and to launder, although it may shrink when washed and fade in harsh sunlight.
Wool
This hard-wearing, natural fabric is usually made up into worsted or crêpe fabrics. Most are too heavy for curtains and are better used for upholstery. Wool tends to attract the dirt and stain easily, and may shrink.
Silk
Luxurious, soft, smooth and easily dyed, pure

silk is extremely expensive. Silk blended with other fibers is more reasonable, and 100 per cent synthetic silk substitutes cost a fraction of the price, while offering a comparable look.
Moiré
This finish gives a wavy, watermark effect to silk, triacetate and acetate fabrics at the printing stage. It looks shiny and luxurious and lends itself to generously gathered, full-length curtains or festoon blinds, although synthetic types tend to fray and are slippery to work with. Moiré must be dry-cleaned, or the pattern will disappear.
Velvet
Any cloth with a pile shorter than ⅛in. is known as velvet. It is available in cotton, silk, and synthetic fibres in a broad range of prices. All velvets dye well and

can be used for formal curtains and upholstery.
Canvas
This heavy, tough fabric is usually made from cotton or linen yarns and comes in plain colors or simple stripes. It can be used to make straight, simple curtains, but is usually used for loose covers or for upholstery.
Synthetics
Unlike natural fibers, synthetics are all made entirely from chemicals. Different chemical combinations produce acetate, viscose, acrylic and polyester, each of which has its own properties. They can be blended with more expensive natural fibers, to reduce their price.
Corduroy
A hard-wearing cotton, woven with extra weft threads to produce cut-pile ribs of varying widths. Suitable for upholstery.

Fringing

Braid

Gimp

Moiré

Cotton/polyester

Cotton

Silk

Quilted cushion cover

Acrylic

Corduroy

Wool

Sheer fabrics

Lace
*Lace used to be hand-made, but is now almost exclusively made by machine. Available in nylon, cotton or viscose in a range of elaborate designs, lace is expensive and its crisp texture is best suited to gently gathered curtains. Lace should be given a lining – a net backing will accentuate the design. Lace and other sheer fabrics can be difficult to sew and may slip on a sew-*ing machine so put tissue paper under it.*

Net
The fibers are knotted instead of woven or knitted together, to form a mesh. Usually made from synthetics, such as nylon or polyester, net is not expensive and comes plain, patterned or with a patterned border. Like loose weaves, net will diffuse the light coming through the window and colored net will soften the effect.

Loose weaves
These will add texture to lined curtains and filter harsh sunlight through a window. They are made from most natural fibers and come plain or with a simple design woven in.

Cheesecloth
A soft cotton or cotton/polyester blend, this gauzy fabric is loosely woven to give a sheer texture. Naturally cream colored, it can be dyed and is cheap enough to be used generously.

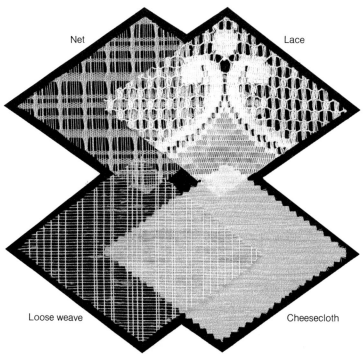

Net

Lace

Loose weave

Cheesecloth

Quilted fabrics

Quilted fabrics consist of light polyester stuffing, sandwiched between a top layer and backing of layer and backing of fabric – usually cotton, silk, and linen. Double-sided quilts are also available to make a reversible quilt fabric. Quilts are too rigid for curtains, but are good upholstery, curtain and bedcover fabrics.

Upholstery accessories

There is a wide range of braids, bobbles, fringing and piping to trim the edges of upholstery or curtains in co-ordinating colors. The trim should be colorfast and non-shrink, unless it is to be hand stitched, so that it can be unpicked when the fabric is cleaned. Piping cord usually shrinks, so it is best to wash it before making it up. Cord should be covered with bias strips in a similar weight fabric to that of the main upholstery. Buttons should also be covered in fabric. Narrow braid, known as "gimp", is available for covering tacks and raw edges of newly upholstered furniture. It is more expensive than normal braid, since it is designed to fit smoothly round corners. When buying fringed curtain pulls, check that the stitching is strong – inferior qualities tend to unravel.

Furnishing fabrics

Choosing the right curtain fabric

Fabrics vary widely in their natural properties and decorative effects, so the choice of curtain material for each room must be considered individually.

Practical properties

Curtains act as both insulators and light shields, so the first consideration is the weight of the fabric. A heavy, textured fabric, such as velvet or brocade, is suitable for winter curtains. It will form a barrier against drafts and will also act as a sound-proofing agent. A light, sheer fabric is a good summer fabric. It will let in the light and give a fresh, airy feel. In north-facing rooms, exposed to bright sunlight, however, you should choose a fabric that will not fade. For kitchens, a flame-proof finish is an advantage.

Lining fabrics

A lining protects curtains against dirt and fading, makes them hang more elegantly and increases their warmth. The most usual lining material is cotton sateen, but there are more expensive types, such as aluminum-backed insulating lining.

Choosing the right upholstery fabric

Not all upholstery receives the same amount of wear, and you should take this into account when making your choice of fabric. Everyday dining chairs, for example, need a tougher fabric than a bedroom chair, and those exposed to spills, stains and pets every day will need to be easily cleaned. If the fabric is chosen to be durable, the pattern should likewise blend easily with other furnishings and be adaptable to a change in decoration. If you are using a pattern, you should aim to center it on the back and the seat.

Suiting the fabric to the furnishing

Situation	Fabric	Design
Curtains		
Formal, full length curtains	Heavy fabrics: silk, brocades, velvet	Richly patterned, textured or with a large, dominant pattern
Sill length curtains	Light fabrics: sheer, silk or synthetic	Plain or textured with a small design
Blinds		
Shades	Firm fabrics: cotton twill, cotton/linen blend	Plain or lightly patterned
Festoon blinds	Soft light fabrics: light cottons, moiré, silk, synthetics	Plain or lightly patterned
Roller blinds	Tightly woven fabrics: firm cotton, cotton blend, canvas	Plain or lightly patterned
Upholstery		
Loose covers	Colorfast, non-shrink, washable fabric: cotton, synthetic, canvas	Any. Small prints are easiest to match
Upholstery	Heavy, tough fabrics: heavy cotton, wool, corduroy, canvas, leather	Any. Plain or muted pattern
Cushions	Soft, smooth fabrics: silk, acetate, velvet polyester	Use a small design on small cushions

Tips on buying fabric

◇ When buying fabric to co-ordinate with an existing color scheme, bring offcuts of wallpaper, furnishing fabrics and paint cards to compare shades.

◇ Take material to the daylight to see its true color, and ask to see the fabric unrolled to check that the color is even, and that there are no flaws. Check that the grain is straight – the horizontal and vertical threads should lie at a true right angle. Also check that the pattern lines up with the grain, or the final result will be crooked.

◇ When choosing curtain fabric, it is worth buying lining at the same time; it will extend the life of the fabric.

◇ Before buying, check whether the fabric is washable or must be dry cleaned; if it will fade, bleed, shrink or stretch; and if it can be ironed. Always buy a little more than you need for wastage and future repairs.

◇ When home sewing for the first time, a medium- or lightweight cotton in a plain or easy-match pattern is the easiest to handle.

◇ When buying patterned fabric, allow a little extra for pattern-matching, and when buying linen and cotton, allow extra for shrinkage.

◇ Choose a thread in a slightly darker shade than the fabric.

◇ A layer of inter-lining between the curtain and the lining increases insulation.

Door hardware

Door fittings including handles, hinges, knobs, knockers and catches allow a door to fulfil its function as a means of entry and exit. If it is to work properly, it needs the correct accessories. They are available from hardware, furnishing and specialist stores, where the range is usually on display. Alternatively, you may prefer to consult several manufacturers' catalogs to make your choice. Always check that your measurements are correct and that both the size and material of all the fittings are compatible with each other. Remember that the door fittings should be fixed into place after the door surface has been painted, stained or varnished. It is wise to lubricate metal catches and hinges with a drop of oil from time to time. If nylon fittings squeak, loosen the screw heads a fraction. (*For more information on the range of materials, see overleaf.*)

The range of door handles

There are two basic types of door handle: a turning handle that forms an integral part of a catch; and a static handle, which is used for pulling and pushing a door with a lock or an independent catch. Turning door handles come in two forms – as levers or as knobs. Both operate by rotating a square metal spindle, which passes through the door and the catch. If the door is very thin, you may need to cut the spindle. (*For fitting a door handle, see Job 123, p. 111.*)

A knob set
One one side of a knob set sits a knob attached to an escutcheon, which is screwed to the face of the door. A long, square-shaped spindle fits into the knob through an escutcheon, and passes through a hole in the door and the catch. On the other side of the door, a knob, attached to an escutcheon, slides over the spindle and is secured to the door face.

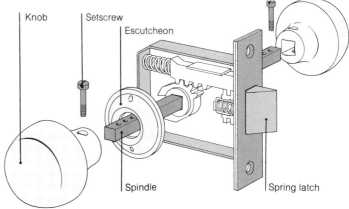

Knob   Setscrew   Escutcheon   Spindle   Spring latch

The range of door hinges

Hinges must be strong enough to support the weight of the door and must allow it to open wide enough. The best qualities are metal, but plastic types are adequate for small doors. A variety of hinges are designed for specific types of door and it is important to choose a suitable type in the correct size. You will generally need a 3in. size for internal flush doors, and a 4in. size for paneled and external doors, and smaller sizes for closets and cabinets. You will have to decide how wide you would like the door to open. The standard hinge opens to 95°, but 110° types are available for wider opening, and 170° hinges will allow the door to lie flat against the adjoining surface. If you want your door to remain shut without a catch, you will need a "sprung" hinge. Finally, you should check that the hinge will allow the door to open the way you intend. If you wish the door to open toward you with the hinge on the right, you should ask for a right-hand hinge; if you wish the door to open toward you with the hinge on the left, ask for a left-hand hinge. Most internal room and furniture doors need two hinges; heavy doors benefit from a third fitted half-way up the door. (*For fitting door hinges, see Job 122, p. 110.*)

Butt hinges
The standard hinge for most doors, the butt hinge is fixed first to the door, then to the door frame. The hinge is either recessed into the door, or into both the door and the frame. The pins on both hinges must be perfectly aligned with each other and with the door edge, for the hinge to work efficiently. The rising butt hinge, which allows the door to rise over a carpet as it opens, is fitted in the same way.
Loose joint hinge
For use on cabinets, this hinge allows the door to be removed easily for cleaning or painting. It is available in a butt or cranked shape and comes as either a left-handed or a right-handed hinge.

Flap hinge
For lightweight doors, a flap hinge is simply screwed on to the surface of the door edge and frame without cutting a mortise. This is possible, since one flap closes within the other.

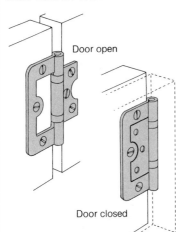

Door open

Door closed

Spring hinge
To encourage a door to swing closed of its own accord, a spring hinge can be fitted. A single hinge allows for one-way opening, and a double hinge allows a door to swing both ways.

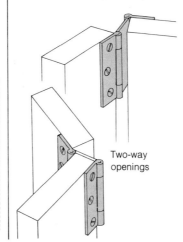

Two-way openings

Concealed hinge
Useful for cabinets, when room space is short, this hinge allows the door edge to remain flush with the frame when opened. It is only visible on the inside face of the door and may be recessed or fixed to the surface and the door can be adjusted after fitting to ensure accurate alignment.

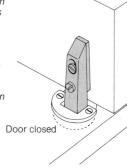

Door closed

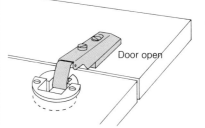

Door open

Door hardware

The range of door and furniture fittings is huge. Your choice of materials for knobs, knockers, handles, and other fittings, is largely an aesthetic decision, although the size and type will be determined by the door's function. Newly painted or varnished doors may show up scratches and wear on old door hardware, so to set off new decoration to advantage it may be worth the relatively small expense of a new set of door hardware. Shiny brass or gold-plated fittings usually look best on alkyd-painted or varnished doors, particularly front doors, while wood, china or plastic lend themselves to interior and closet doors. Try to use clean-cut, modern-style fittings in a new home and more traditional styles in an older house. If choice is governed by price, you may find that many synthetic and plated materials now provide good imitations. However, brass, gold-plate, zinc and aluminum hinges supply stronger support for heavy doors.

For information on fitting doors, see pp. 118-21. For more information on types of door hardware, see previous page.

Brass door knob

Large brass door knocker

Surround for cylinder door lock

Cylinder lock cover

Porcelain handle and escutcheon

Glass handle

Brass handle

Chromium-plated pull handle

Chromium-plated pull handle

Stainless steel pull handle

Plastic pull han[...]

Plastic pull handles

Wooden knob

Porcelain knobs

Brass knob

Knobs, knockers and handles

Front door hardware

Door knobs
Knobs, knockers, letterboxes, key plates and key covers fixed on to front doors are primarily decorative, but retain a practical function. The range of designs and materials is huge and coordinating sets are available. Front door knobs are usually made of solid brass, gold plate, bronze or steel. Some are lacquered for a protective finish and these should not be polished with metal cleaner, which will abrade the surface. If, however, the metal begins to weather, you will need to strip off the surface and apply a new coat of lacquer.

Door knockers
Door knockers are also made of metal, to create a resonant sound on wood. Brass and bronze look particularly effective against a natural wood

finish. Black ironware is designed for an antique look and is best restricted to old and rural houses.

Keyhole plates
Keyhole plates (escutcheons) for front doors are usually brass or bronze and some come with a ledge for pulling the door closed. For added decoration, keyhole covers, bell pulls and house numbers can be chosen to coordinate with the rest of the fittings. Prices vary according to the metal used.

Internal door handles

Turning handles
Turning, or bolt-through handles, which operate a spring latch, come as knob or lever handles. The choice of shapes and sizes is wide, and most come in a range of metals, including brass,

chrome, gold-plate and stainless steel, but wood, glass, porcelain and plastic will also stand up well to wear. Some turning handles are made with matching escutcheons. When replacing door handles, it is often advisable to take the old one with you, to check the size.

Pull handles
Used in conjunction with an independent catch, pull handles may be round or long, and come in the same range of metals as turning handles.

Furniture and drawer handles

Smaller knobs and handles, used for wardrobe, closet and cabinet doors and drawers are also made in a variety of decorative shapes and sizes, in wood, metal, glass and plastic.

Antique ironwork
door knocker

astic lever handle
d escutcheon

Brass lever
latch handle

Stainless steel knob

Plastic knob

Brass cabinet handles

Hinges

Door hinges

Butt hinge
Widely used for room doors and windows, this hinge is especially suitable for solid wooden doors. Available in 1¼in.-4in. sizes.

Rising butt hinge
Designed for doors that need to rise over carpets, the rising butt hinge is open-ended. Available in 1¼in.-4in. sizes.

Flap hinge
Used for lightweight doors, the flap hinge is designed to act like a butt hinge, but does not need to be recessed. Available in 1½in.-4in. sizes.

Furniture hinges

Piano hinge
Originally for piano lids, this hinge is used where a continuous hinge is
needed along a door or lid. It is made in plastic or aluminum, in standard cut lengths of 33in., and can be cut to size.

Concealed hinge
Popular for cabinets, this hinge is only visible on the inside face of the door and may be recessed.

Brass cylinder hinge
Even less obtrusive than the concealed cabinet hinge, the two halves of this hinge fit into holes drilled in the edge of the door and the frame.

Catches

Door catches

Ball or roller catch
Suitable for a light internal or closet door, this catch consists of a spring-loaded ball or roller inside a cylinder. When the door is closed, the ball or roller fits into a recess in the strike plate fixed to the door frame.

French window catch
This vertical bolt consists of two long
sliding bolts, which slot into recesses at the head and sill of the door frame. The bolts, which extend the full length of the door, are operated by a central handle.

Furniture catches

Magnetic catch
There are various types and shapes available, but all consist of a nickel-coated plate, which is fixed to the door, and a cased magnet, which is fixed to the closet or cabinet.

Block joints

Block joints
Used to form an accurate right angled butt joint when joining two particle-board panels, this fitting is supplied as two square or rectangular blocks of plastic, a washer head, screw and retaining nut. Cam fittings, consisting of a cam and bolt section, may be used for the same purpose.

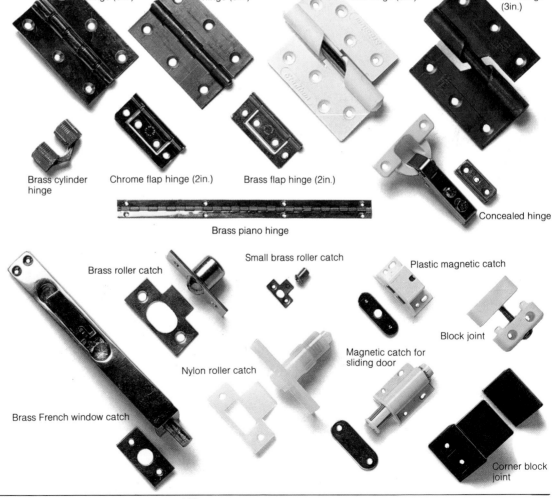

Brass butt hinge (3in.)

Steel butt hinge (3in.)

Plastic rising butt hinge (3in.)

Steel rising butt hinge (3in.)

Brass cylinder hinge

Chrome flap hinge (2in.)

Brass flap hinge (2in.)

Concealed hinge

Brass piano hinge

Brass roller catch

Small brass roller catch

Plastic magnetic catch

Block joint

Nylon roller catch

Magnetic catch for sliding door

Brass French window catch

Corner block joint

Room-by-room guide

Before choosing color schemes, decorative styles and textures, you will have to consider the practical requirements of individual rooms. Your choice of wall, floor, ceiling and window materials should be largely governed by the purpose of the room. There are a number of questions you will have to ask yourself, and the chart below divides these into categories, to aid the decision-making process, and offers some practical suggestions for choices you might make.

Hall/landing

	Easy to apply	Easy to clean	Inexpensive	Durable	To cover an imperfect surface	To cover a good surface	Luxurious
Walls	paint, washable paper, vinyl paper	paint, washable paper, relief vinyl, vinyl paper, sealed cork	paint, standard paper	washable paper, vinyl paper	relief vinyl, paneling	fabric, flock paper, hand-printed paper	fabric, flock paper, hand-printed paper, paneling
Ceiling	paint, standard paper	paint, standard paper	paint, standard paper	ceiling tiles, paneling	textured paint, ceiling tiles, relief paper, paneling	latex paint, standard paper	paneling
Floor	carpet tiles, rugs, matting	ceramic/quarry tiles, cushioned vinyl, rugs, matting	carpet tiles, matting, vinyl tiles	grade 4/5 carpet tiles, wooden flooring, vinyl/rubber flooring	hardboard, particleboard	rugs	thick pile, high-grade carpet, rugs, wooden flooring

Living/dining room

	Easy to apply	Easy to clean	Inexpensive	Durable	To cover an imperfect surface	To cover a good surface	Luxurious
Walls	standard paper, vinyl paper	paint, vinyl paper, sealed cork	paint, standard paper, washable paper, murals	gloss paint, cork, burlap, vinyl paper, paneling	textured paint,	fabric, flock paper, hand-printed paper	fabric, flock paper, hand-printed paper paneling
Ceiling	paint, standard paper	paint, standard paper	paint, standard paper	ceiling tiles, paneling	textured paint, relief paper, paneling, ceiling tiles	paint, standard paper	paneling, fibrous plasterwork
Floor	carpet tiles, rugs, woodstrip flooring	carpet, wooden flooring	cord carpet	grade 4 carpet, wooden flooring	hardboard, particleboard	carpet, rugs	thick pile carpet, oriental rugs, woodstrip flooring, with rugs.

Bedroom

	Easy to apply	Easy to clean	Inexpensive	Durable	To cover an imperfect surface	To cover a good surface	Luxurious
Walls	paint, standard paper, vinyl paper, foamed vinyl	paint, vinyl paper, foamed vinyl, washable paper	paint, standard paper	burlap, vinyl paper	smooth textured paint, high relief paper	flock paper, fabrics, cork	flock paper, fabrics, cork
Ceiling	paint	paint	paint	relief paper, textured paper, ceiling tiles	textured paint, relief paper, ceiling tiles	paint, standard	mural
Floor	carpet tiles, rugs, matting	carpet, rugs, matting, cork	grade 1 carpet matting	grade 2+ carpet	hardboard, particleboard	rugs, carpet	high-grade carpet

Kitchen/bathroom

	Easy to apply	Easy to clean	Inexpensive	Durable	To cover an imperfect surface	To cover a good surface	Luxurious
Walls	paint, vinyl paper, washable paper,	vinyl paper, washable paper, condensation paint	paint, washable paper, vinyl, metallic tiles	ceramic tiles, vinyl vinyl paper, relief paper, paneling	textured paint, ceramic tiles, paneling	metallic foil, mirror tiles	ceramic tiles, cork mosaic tiles, paneling
Ceiling	paint, standard paper	washable paper, vinyl paper, anti-condensation tiles	paint, standard paper	textured paint, paneling, ceiling tiles	textured paint, relief paper, ceiling tiles, suspended ceiling	paint, standard paper	paneling
Floor	vinyl tiles, rush plastic matting	sheet vinyl linoleum, vinyl tiles, ceramic tiles	rush matting, vinyl tiles, sheet vinyl	quarry tiles, ceramic tiles, sheet vinyl	hardboard, particleboard	vinyl flooring, rubber flooring, sheet vinyl	ceramic tiles, (polyester carpet in bathroom)

Home contents

Cleaning, care and repair ◇ Renovating wooden
furniture ◇ Renovating upholstery ◇ Lighting
Pictures and mirrors ◇ Storage and shelving
Appliance fault-finding

However well you decorate and maintain your home, it will
only look good and run efficiently if you care for the contents.
Stains on a carpet, a broken chair leg, or a marked dining
table, for example, detract from an otherwise attractive
interior, yet the solution is often quite simple, and the investment of time and effort minimal. This chapter is concerned
with the care, repair and cleaning of furniture, furnishings and
general household items, and with the arrangement of lighting, shelving and pictures. It ranges from soft furnishings and
glassware, through wooden furniture and electrical appliances, to storage space and lighting effects. You will find
step-by-step instructions on re-caning, re-rushing and re-
upholstering a chair, on framing and hanging a picture and
putting up shelves. The emphasis is on essential jobs that
require no specialist skills but demand a little know-how and
the correct tools and equipment.

Cleaning, care and repair

Cleaning and mending china, glass, metalwork and fabrics
Sharpening blades ◇ Caring for plastics and leather
Removing stains

Regular care, cleaning and repair extends the life and efficiency of the contents of any home. Having invested in your furniture and furnishings and perhaps a re-decoration, it makes good sense to spend a little time ensuring that it continues to look and feel good. When buying anything for the home, you should find out how it should be cleaned. Modern products, including cleaning agents, polishes and glues, are designed for ease of use and for specific materials, so it is important to choose the right one. Valuable antiques and precious glass should be given to an expert for repair, but most small repairs of less valuable objects can be completed simply and quickly with the correct tools.

Points to remember

◇ Heat may weaken a repair, so wash any glued items carefully by hand, not in a dishwasher.
◇ It is often cheaper to replace than repair everyday items, particularly if you need an expensive adhesive.
◇ Always test dry-cleaning agents on an inconspicuous part of a fabric before use.
◇ Remove excess adhesive immediately after a repair.

Tools and equipment

For cleaning household equipment, you will need the usual range of brushes, mops, cloths, buckets and a vacuum cleaner; also dishwashing liquid for china, metal and glass and detergents for fabrics. More specialist cleaning equipment includes dry-cleaning fluid, carpet shampoos and applicators, and upholstery shampoo. For removing stains you may need plain or denatured alcohol, ammonia, borax and peroxide. A variety of polishes, all applied with a soft cloth, is available for wood, metal, glass, plastics and leather. Whiting, a powdered white chalk, is used for polishing metal. To sharpen knife blades, use either an oil-stone, a steel or a hand or electric sharpener. Use a slipstone for scissor blades.

Repairing equipment
It is important to choose the right adhesive for repairs. Epoxy resins, used for china, metal and glass repairs, are strong, and heat and water-resistant. They usually come in two separate tubes to be mixed together. Clear contact adhesive sets almost immediately, so there is no need to hold the pieces in place. Latex adhesive is used for patching fabrics and carpets. The glue required for mending plastics depends on the type of plastic (see Caring for plastics, p. 145). Masking tape and gummed paper strips are also useful for china and glass repairs. For darning upholstery fabrics, you will need a sturdy needle, thread and thimble, and a pair of needlework scissors.

Cleaning china and glass

Everyday crockery and glass, such as cups, mugs, plates and bowls, should be washed up soon after use and dried before storing.

Washing china
If you are leaving crockery to soak, use cold, soapy water. Hot water tends to "bake" some food, such as egg yolks, on to the china. If you have a dishwasher, load the crockery as you use it and pre-rinse if the machine has that facility. To remove tea or coffee stains, leave to soak overnight in a detergent solution. Modern china, even delicate porcelain, may be dishwasher-proof, but always check before loading.

Handling ornaments
China and pottery ornaments should be dusted regularly with a light feather duster. If a layer of dirt has built up, soak in a bowl of warm, soapy water, then rinse and dry thoroughly. Bad stains can be removed with a damp cloth dipped in bicarbonate of soda or borax. Hard-water marks usually respond to vinegar and water, and hard rubbing.

Washing glass
If you cannot wash drinking glasses immediately, leave them to soak on their sides in warm, soapy water. Each glass should be washed individually with a long-handled, soft-headed brush in a large bowl of clean, soapy water. To clean the crevices of cut crystal, use an old, soft toothbrush. Rinse glasses well in clean, hot (not boiling) water for a sparkling finish and stand them upside down on a rack or a clean, folded cloth. When they have drained, dry thoroughly with a linen cloth. Glass tables and shelves can be cleaned with a cloth soaked in denatured alcohol.

Removing stains from glass
Glass which is cloudy or stained should be filled with water and two teaspoons of ammonia, left overnight, then rinsed and washed. A badly stained glass may respond to soaking in a solution of one cup caustic soda to 2 quarts of warm water, but be sure to rinse the glass thoroughly afterwards. To remove water marks from vases, soak in distilled water or a vinegar and water solution. To remove liquor stains from the inside of a decanter half fill with vinegar and cooking salt, then add half a cup of uncooked rice or sand and swill around. Rinse it well in clean water and leave to drain. Tables and shelves can be cleaned with denatured alcohol on a cloth.

Storing glass
It is best to store glasses the right way up, to avoid damaging the rim, and away from strong smells. Lavender bags, camphor balls and other distinct aromas will contaminate the glass and taint your drinks. Polish glasses with a clean linen cloth before you use them, rather than when you put them away.

Basic techique

Mending broken china and glass

Modern adhesives have greatly improved the results achieved by gluing broken china and glass. Epoxy resins, which are strong and heat-resistant, do not set immediately and therefore allow time for accurate positioning. Setting times vary, but will be quicker in a warm room and can be accelerated by placing the article near a radiator. Contact adhesives, which are less expensive, set almost immediately, so are more difficult to use, although the thixotropic type allows more time for repositioning. Special adhesives are available for clear glass. It is worth repairing cracks and chips in valuable items or to prolong the life of a favorite item; others are best thrown away in a newspaper wrapping and replaced.

Mending simple breaks
Clean, simple breaks in glass and china can be repaired more successfully than fractures and multiple breaks. Repairs in stems and bases will also be less noticeable than, for example, in the rim of a glass or mug. Before mending china or glass, ensure all pieces are clean. Wipe the pieces with a solvent, such as denatured alcohol or mineral spirits, ensuring that any old adhesive and grease is removed. Then rinse and allow to dry. Work out how the pieces fit together and use masking tape or gummed paper strips to hold them in position. Never use clear, adhesive tape, since it will be difficult to remove without dislodging the pieces. Then remove the pieces and roughen the broken edges with sandpaper before applying adhesive. Mix the adhesive according to the pack instructions and carefully glue the pieces together, removing any excess with denatured alcohol. While the glue is drying, support the pieces in position. Use modeling clay to hold glass stems, 1, spouts or small pieces in place. With larger breaks, support the item with crumpled kitchen foil or a box of sand, 2. If the item is broken in more than two pieces, glue them one at a time, allowing the adhesive to set between the individual repairs.

1 *Use two strands of modeling clay to support a glued stem*

2 *Support larger items in a bowl of sand*

Mending multiple breaks
It is usually only worth mending multiple breaks on large or decorative pieces, such as vases and ornaments. Following the same technique as for simple breaks, use a solvent to clean each individual piece. Work out how the pieces fit together, using masking tape or gummed paper strips (never clear tape) across the breaks. Then number the pieces with a felt pen. Remove the tape, disassemble the pieces and smear a little epoxy resin along the side of the main item and along the side of the first piece to be attached, 1, and press together. Working from the inside piece out, secure each piece in place with masking tape, 2, and wipe away excess glue with denatured alcohol. Use modeling clay, crumpled kitchen foil or a bowl of sand to support the item. When the first piece is dry, glue on the next, apply masking tape, allow to dry and so on until the broken object is complete. If you wish to speed up the drying process, use a hair dryer, or leave the item near a heater. When the adhesive has set, scrape off any ridges with a scalpel or razor blade until the repair lies flush with the surface and wipe away the dust. If a handle or stem also has multiple breaks, repair it as a whole, before sticking it on to the main item.

1 *Smear epoxy resin along the broken edge of each piece*

2 *Hold the pieces together with masking tape, while the glue sets*

Mending small holes and chips
Chips are difficult to disguise in clear glass, but you could take a favorite or valuable piece to a professional glass and china repairer to re-grind a chipped rim. It can be difficult to make cracks invisible, but a special epoxy adhesive is available for this purpose and is less noticeable than normal types. Chips in china can be concealed by filling out the surface and painting over the repair to match the rest of the piece. First clean the chip or hole with denatured alcohol or mineral spirits. Then make up a mixture of epoxy resin adhesive and titanium dioxide, a white powder available from artists' suppliers, 1. *Press the filler firmly into the crevice with a smooth, rounded stick, eliminating air pockets as you work,* 2. *When the cavity is well packed and the filler lies proud of the surface, remove any smears with denatured alcohol. When the filler has set, rub it down with sandpaper, until it lies flush. If the chip is deep, apply the filler in several layers, allowing each to dry before applying the next. Then paint over the repair. To match a color, mix in artists' powder color until you reach the right shade and test it on spare filler. If the chip is large, support the piece until the mixture has set. Finish with a coat of varnish to match the glaze of the china.*

1 *Make a filler from epoxy adhesive and titanium dioxide*

2 *Apply the filler to the crevice with a smooth, rounded stick*

Cleaning metalwork

Everyday silverware should be washed in warm, soapy water, as soon as possible after use, since food remains and even soaking in water will cause stains and pitting. A spoonful of mustard added to the rinsing water will remove fishy smells on silverware. Pots and pans should be soaked thoroughly to remove burnt food deposits, then washed (not scoured) in hot, soapy water. Leave to drain, then dry carefully, especially untreated cast-iron cookware, which tends to rust.

Dealing with corrosion
Regular cleaning and polishing will prevent rust forming on metalware.

However, if it does develop, use a proprietary cleaner to remove most of the corrosion, taking care to follow the instructions carefully. If iron or steel have rusted badly, scrape off the worst and use a rust remover. Badly corroded bronze should be scraped carefully with a knife or special brush or wiped with a 10 per cent solution of acetic acid in water. Never use a steel brush or steel wool, however, or you will damage the surface. Corrosion on brass may be removed by soaking for an hour in a strong, warm solution of washing soda. Wash off and repeat if one application is not successful. Corrosion on pewter can

be loosened by scraping gently or rubbing with steel wool or crocus powder (available from hardware stores) and finishing with whiting and polish.

Protective finishes
Most proprietary metal cleaners will protect against tarnishing to some extent, but an extra finish will provide greater protection. Brassware can be given a coat of varnish or lacquer; chrome will be protected by a layer of Vaseline; untreated iron or steel should be greased or primed and painted with a special paint; silver can be kept in tarnish-retardant bags or in a drawer with a soft lining.

Metal	Cleaning method
Anodized aluminum (Trays, trolleys, light fittings)	Wipe off marks and stains with a damp cloth, then polish with a soft, dry one.
Brass (Saucepans, kettles, ornaments, door furniture)	Wash in hot water with a cupful of ammonia. Dry and polish with a cleaner recommended for brass. Lacquered or varnished brass tarnishes less quickly, but if marked, remove tarnish with acetone. Clean off the marks, polish and repaint or spray with lacquer or varnish. Finally buff with a soft, clean cloth.
Bronze (Door hardware, ornaments)	Wash in a hot detergent solution or rub with a cloth soaked in turpentine or kerosene.
Chrome (Electrical appliances, door furniture)	Clean with a dry cloth and a little bicarbonate of soda, or wipe with a damp, soapy cloth then buff with a soft cloth when dry.

Metal	Cleaning method
Copper (Saucepans, kettles, ornaments)	Rub with a piece of lemon, dipped in salt and vinegar, then rinse in hot, soapy water. Dry well, then buff it until it shines.
Gold	Wash in warm detergent solution with a cupful of ammonia. Then rinse and polish with a dry cloth. varnish. Finally buff with a soft, clean cloth.
Pewter	Clean regularly to prevent corrosion. Wash in warm, soapy water and dry with a soft cloth.
Silver	Clean regularly to prevent corrosion. Clean with a proprietary dip or cleaner, then polish with a chamois leather. You can make your own silver dip by immersing a small piece of aluminum foil in boiling water with two tablespoons of washing soda. Rinse well in clean water, dry and polish.

127

Mending damaged metalwork

Most metal cleaners and protective finishes are designed to minimize the effects of minor scratches and knocks; and regular polishing should provide a good, sheeny finish and remove rust. Dents in pewter, copper and hollow brass can be removed, but dented gold or silverware will have to be taken to a professional repair shop. Broken metal will normally have to be soldered by an expert, but small holes and cracks can be fixed with acrylic or epoxy resin adhesive. Acrylic resin can be mixed with metal (such as brass) filings for a good color match.

Removing scratches
On some metals, such as copper, scratches are impossible to remove. However, on most metals, a layer of the appropriate polish will help to disguise them (below). On brassware, try polishing with a paste from powdered whiting, available from hardware stores. To remove silver scratches, apply denatured alcohol, mixed with jeweler's rouge, available from jewelry makers' suppliers.

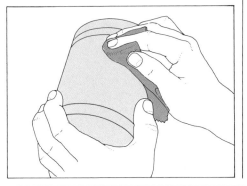

Removing dents
Take a short length of wood and use a rasp and spokeshave to shape the end to fit the curve of the damaged item. Hold the wood in a vise and gently press and rub the metal (pewter, copper or brass) against the shaped end until the dent is pushed out (below). Never try hammering – it usually increases the damage. Finally rub down with crocus powder, then with whiting, and polish.

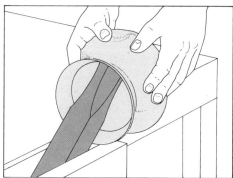

Basic technique

How to sharpen knives and scissors

Kitchen knives should be sharpened regularly, especially those with carbon steel blades, which blunt more quickly than stainless steel. Five types of sharpener are available from hardware stores – an oilstone, a sharpening steel, a hand sharpener, an electric sharpener and a fine slipstone. On each type of sharpener, the blade is sharpened gradually, at an angle of 30 degrees, working first one side, then the other. Saw-edged tools, however, need to be sharpened with specialist tools. Blunt scissors may be caused by a loose screw joint between the blades. To cure this, place the scissors with the head of the screw on a metal surface and hit the other end with a hammer. If the scissors are still blunt, you will have to use a slipstone. Never sharpen table cutlery or scissors with rounded ends designed for children's use.

Using an oilstone
Place the stone on a flat surface at hand level and cover it with a light oil. Draw one side of the blade away from you along the stone, then turn the blade and pull it back along the stone toward you. Repeat several times.

Using a sharpening steel
Hold the blade edge away from you and cross the knife and steel at right angles near the handles. Holding the blade at 30 degrees to the steel, draw it across, first on one side, then on the other and repeat about 10 times.

Using an electric sharpener
Follow the manufacturer's instructions and take care not to over-sharpen the knife. You can see if the blade is sharp by tracing a line of light reflected in the blade – dull patches or a broken line of light will show up blunt areas.

Using a slipstone
Draw the slipstone along the face of the blunt scissor blade, working at right angles to the blade. If the edge of the blade is damaged, run the slip-stone, lightly oiled, over the inner face of the blade.

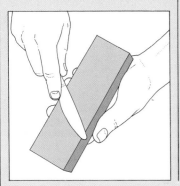
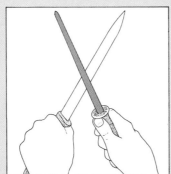
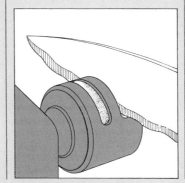
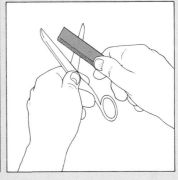

Caring for plastics

Plastic furniture and surfaces should be cleaned carefully with a damp cloth to prevent particles of grit scratching the finish. Use undiluted dishwashing liquid to remove any stubborn patches, then rinse off and dry carefully. Plastic laminates can be wiped down in the same way, but should be rinsed well to avoid streaking. Cream cleansers are best on plastic baths to avoid scratching and plastic lampshades can be washed in a warm water and detergent solution. To remove stains in tableware, use denture cleaner or a bicarbonate of soda paste.

Mending broken plastic
Cracked and broken plastic tableware will attract germs, so they should be thrown away, never mended. Plastic furniture and toys, however, can be repaired successfully with the appropriate adhesive. Contact adhesive is ideal for ABS plastic (utensils, tool handles), rigid pvc (shower units, furniture) or decorative laminates (table tops). It is applied to both surfaces, left to dry, then pressed together. Clear adhesive is suitable for polystyrene (bathroom units, furniture) and flexible pvc (blinds, shower curtains). Epoxy adhesives are the most expensive and provide the strongest bond. They should be used for thermo-setting plastics (handles, switches), nylon (curtain rails) and acetal (taps).

Caring for leather

Leather needs regular care and attention, or it soon becomes hard and powdery. Before cleaning leather upholstery, test for color fastness by rubbing a small hidden area with soap and a damp cloth. If the color comes off on your cloth, the leather is untreated and needs to be cleaned carefully. The best way to protect treated leather is to rub in hide food regularly, or to polish it with a wax or cream.

Cleaning treated leather
Wash with warm water and pure soap, taking care not to make the leather too wet. To remove stubborn stains, rub gently with a soft nail brush. If the mark persists, use a mixture of three parts castor oil, two parts rubbing alcohol and leave for 24 hours, then wipe off with castor oil.

Cleaning untreated leather
Sponge off grease marks with a little alcohol on a soft cloth, then use soap and a slightly damp cloth. To remove bad stains, squeeze on a little rubber solution and leave to dry for 24 hours. The solution should absorb the stain and remove it.

Renovating leather
Restore faded leather by touching it up with a leather stain or colored lacquer. Work saddle soap into stiff, dry leather until it regains its suppleness.

Cleaning furnishing fabrics

Regular care and cleaning of soft furnishings will help to prolong their life and keep them looking fresh. Dirt and dust can permanently damage the fabric, so it is worth vacuuming, brushing and shaking out the dust every week. Spills and stains should be treated immediately and fabrics should be washed before dirt becomes ingrained.

Protective treatments
Use a dirt-repellent spray on new fabric and re-apply regularly after cleaning. Slip covers will help to protect the arms and backs of upholstery and linings help to prolong the life of curtains.

Upholstery
Upholstery should be cleaned two or three times a year, with upholstery shampoo. Always test for color fastness first by wetting a small area and pressing with a warm iron between two pieces of plain white cotton. If no color comes off on the cotton, the fabric is color-fast; if the color smudges, the fabric will have to be dry cleaned.

Washable loose covers
Any tears should be mended before the fabric is shampooed. If it is not recommended for machine washing, you will need to launder it gently by hand in warm water and mild detergent. Iron while still damp, on the wrong side for mat finishes and on the right side for shiny ones. Fabrics with special finishes are best drip-dried; stretch covers can usually be machine washed and do not need ironing.

Curtains
All curtains should be washed or cleaned regularly to prevent the fabric wearing out quickly. Lined, interlined and heavy fabrics will probably have to be dry cleaned. Before washing or cleaning, remove hooks, ease out the gathers, and shake out any loose dirt. If washing, soak in cold water with liquid detergent for 10 minutes, then rinse, wash, drip-dry and iron while damp.

Fabric lampshades
Turn off the electricity, remove the shade and take off the trimmings if they are not color-fast. Clean washable fabrics in warm, soapy water, rinse in clear, lukewarm water and allow to dry naturally. Non-washable fabrics should be dry cleaned.

Carpets
Regular vacuuming to remove dirt and lint will prolong the life of a carpet. For the first few weeks after laying a new carpet, however, use a hand brush or carpet sweeper instead of a vacuum cleaner to allow the pile to settle. After a while the carpet will need to be cleaned with carpet shampoo, using a hand-operated shampoo applicator or an electric carpet shampooer. Heavily soiled carpet should be cleaned with a professional carpet shampoo machine.

It is best to deal with spills and stains as quickly as possible. Blot or scrape a spill, immediately, working

For solvent-soluble stains (Dry cleaning)
Use a dry-cleaning agent, but test it first on an inconspicuous part of the fabric. Follow the instructions carefully and leave for 15 minutes to check that it does not discolor the fabric. To treat a stain, place a wad of white tissues or cotton batting under the fabric, then apply the cleaner to the right side of the fabric with another pad. Take care not to soak the fabric too much, and work from the outer edge of the stain inward to prevent it spreading. Change the pads frequently, and blot the stain dry after each application. When the stain has disappeared, wash or dry clean the fabric as normal.

For solvent soluble stains (Shampooing)
Washable fabrics, except for wool, silk and non-colorfast materials, should be soaked immediately in a solution of the suggested cleaner (see right). To remove fresh stains on colorfast linens, stretch the fabric over the basin, sprinkle on some powdered detergent or stain remover, pour boiling water through, then rinse. If the stain remains, rub cleaner gently into it, rinse then wash.

With non-washable fabrics, stretch the fabric over a jar and pour cold water through the stain. If the stain remains, put an absorbent pad under it and work in the cleaning solution with a pad, then sponge with clear water and blot dry. Repeat if necessary.

128

Repairing torn upholstery

Small tears and holes in upholstery should be repaired as soon as possible to prevent them fraying. Burnt, worn and torn areas can be darned or patched with a small piece of matching fabric from inside a seam or hem. If the damage is bad, however, you will have to disguise it. Worn arms on chairs can be covered with a pair of simple arm caps, made from remnants. Bad stains can sometimes be disguised by appliqué motifs provided the fabric is the same weight.

Repairing small tears
Remove the damaged fabric from the chair and press it flat. Then cut a piece of "iron-on interfacing" ⅜ in. larger than the tear. Place it centrally over the tear on the wrong side of the fabric and fix it in position with a hot iron. Then, using a length of thread to match the thickness of the original weave and small, neat stitches, darn across the line of the tear.

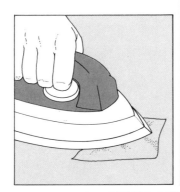

Patching large tears or holes
Snip off any loose threads and cut a small piece of matching fabric from inside the seam, hem or other unobtrusive area, matching the design closely. Slide the patch under the tear and stick it into position with a latex adhesive. When it is nearly dry, press the edges firmly for a few minutes to ensure a strong bond. Alternatively, sew on the patch.

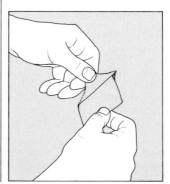

Removing stains from soft furnishings

from the edge to avoid spreading it. If the stain is greasy, sprinkle on an absorbent, such as talcum powder, leave for 30 minutes, then brush or shake and vacuum. Then dry clean. If it is water-based, rinse immediately in cold water. Then wash or shampoo. To make up an ammonia or borax solution, mix one tablespoon of ammonia or borax in $1\frac{1}{2}$ pints of warm water. For a peroxide solution, add one part of 20 vol peroxide to four parts cold water, and add a drop of ammonia.

Stain	Method of removal
Adhesive	**Clear and contact adhesive** Use acetone, banana oil or non-oily nail polish remover. Then dry clean. **Latex and model maker's cement** Remove the worst with a spatula then use dry cleaner. **Epoxy resin** Cannot remove once hardened. Try acetone, amyl acetate or lighter fuel before the stain dries.
Ballpoint and felt pen marks	Use denatured alcohol and a dry cleaner.
Candle wax	Scrape off as much as you can with a blunt blade. Place slightly damp blotting paper or tissues over (and if possible under) the fabric and press quickly with a warm iron. Repeat until the wax is absorbed. On furniture, chill with an ice cube then scrape off. Alternatively, use dry cleaner.
Chewing gum	Chill with an ice cube to harden then scrape off before using dry cleaner.
Cream, ice cream	Use dry cleaner. For washable fabrics, try biological detergent or borax solution first.
Beer	Use detergent or shampoo. For dried stains, add one egg cup of white vinegar to 600ml of water.
Blood	Soak fresh stains in cold water – never boil, this sets the stain. For dried stains, sponge with salt water (1 tsp salt to 1 litre water) or use biological detergent or carpet shampoo.
Coffee, tea and chocolate	Use borax or peroxide solution or carpet shampoo. With dried stains, loosen with glycerine first.
Fruit juice and jelly	On white table linen, pour salt on the fresh stain to stop it spreading, then rinse with boiling water. Otherwise, use peroxide, borax solution or carpet shampoo.
Brown sauce	Use biological detergent.
Ink	Rinse in cold water and wash.
Lemon juice	Use borax solution then wash.
Mildew	Brush off excess then use upholstery shampoo.
Milk	Rinse fresh stains in lukewarm water. For dried stains, use borax solution or carpet shampoo.

Stain	Method of removal
Gravy	If it contains grease use dry cleaner.
Grease	Remove as much as possible with an absorbent, then use a dry cleaner. On wallpaper, dab lightly with mild talcum powder on cotton batting or try holding blotting paper over the stain and press quickly with a warm iron but take care not to scorch the paper.
Mustard	For non-washable fabrics, use denatured alcohol or dry cleaner. Soften old stains with glycerine, then rinse with lukewarm water and dry before using dry cleaner.
Nail varnish	Use acetone, amyl acetate or non-oil nail-polish remover.
Nicotine	Use eucalyptus oil or denatured alcohol.
Oil and paraffin	Soak up as much as possible with absorbent then use dry cleaner. For bicycle or motor oil, try eucalyptus oil.
Paint and varnish	For enamel and oil paints use paint remover or turpentine. For cellulose paint, use an acetone or amyl acetate. Fresh latex paint can be rinsed off with cold water. Dried stains cannot usually be removed, but try denatured alcohol.
Mustard	For washable fabrics, try detergent.
Nicotine	As an alternative to the dry-cleaning method, try detergent or peroxide solution.
Soft drinks	Rinse with boiling water then wash.
Soot	On washables and carpets, vacuum the excess then try detergent or shampoo before dry cleaner.
Urine	Use biological detergent or carpet shampoo, adding one egg cup of white vinegar to $1\frac{1}{2}$ pints of water to the shampoo solution.
Vomit and faeces	If necessary, use an absorbent first, then biological detergent, borax solution or carpet shampoo.
Water	Rainspots on felt, velvet and taffeta can be removed by holding in the steam from a boiling kettle, not too near the spout. Remove alkaline drinking water marks by sponging one teaspoon of white vinegar to $1\frac{1}{2}$ pints warm water solution.
Wine	Use an absorbent to prevent the stain spreading, sponge with clean warm water then use upholstery shampoo on non-washables. For washables, soak in a solution of borax for about half an hour before washing.

Renovating wooden furniture

How to finish wood
Repairing chairs and tables
Repairing table tops and
drawers ◇ Re-caning and
re-rushing chairs

However well you care for your home, sooner or later most pieces of furniture will need renovating, repairing or replacing. Replacing some items, particularly large pieces of furniture, can be very expensive, so it is always worth considering renovating articles you are fond of. A fresh coat of varnish on a fading table or a freshly caned seat on an old chair, for example, can make it feel like new.

A number of basic furniture repairs can be effected without specialist skills or equipment and prove cheaper and more satisfying than buying a replacement. Any valuable antiques, however, should be taken to a professional restorer.

Points to remember

◇ When attaching wooden sections together, remove traces of old glue.
◇ Keep wooden furniture away from heat sources, or the joints may shrink.
◇ Polish wood regularly and treat it with an extra coat at the beginning and end of winter.
◇ To identify a wood finish, rub on a drop of turpentine: if it reveals bare wood, the surface is coated with oil or wax; if the sheen persists, a stain, varnish or polish has been applied.

Tools and equipment

For everyday care of wooden furniture and simple repairs, you do not need a full set of woodworking tools. You will, however, need a few specific tools for some repair jobs, and special equipment for rushing and caning chairs. Use a sharp saw to shorten chair legs or a rail, to cut a new drawer base and to remove dowel ends. To repair a joint, you will need a vise, a hand drill and dowel bit to make holes, and dowels to insert in them. You may also need a plane if you are fitting a new drawer base to size or building up a short chair leg. You will need pva woodworking adhesive for a variety of furniture repairs. To clean wood, keep a plentiful supply of soft cloths and use burnishing cream or metal polish for removing stains. A small paint brush will be useful for applying wood finishes.

Caning equipment
You will need one bundle of "fine fine" split cane for the chair seat and a bundle of No. 6 split cane for edging, one bundle of $\frac{1}{8}$in. plugging cane; also some pva woodworking adhesive to hold the pegs in place. Caning tools include a large bodkin to help thread the cane, and about 20 small wooden pegs (or golf tees). You will also need a sharp trimming knife, a drill or twist bit to

clear holes in the seat frame, a small hand-sprayer to keep the cane moist and a hammer to insert the pegs.

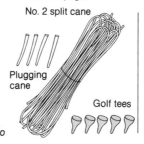

No. 2 split cane

Plugging cane

Golf tees

Rushing equipment
Seagrass, a twisted, rush-like material, is normally used, since genuine rushes are difficult to obtain. Real rushes produce a more attractive color and texture but you will have to twist them while you weave. For an average chair seat, you will need a large bundle of rushes. Use a sharp knife or secateurs for cutting the seagrass and a hard-board or cardboard

winder for holding the lengths of seagrass. A mallet and a scrap of wood are used to keep the seat tightly packed.

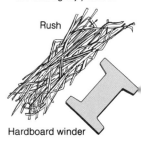

Rush

Hardboard winder

Caring for wood

Polish wood regularly to give it a protective coat. Cover the surface of dining tables with mats and cloths and try to remove spills before a stain develops.

Removing water stains
Dark rings and spots, which are most obvious on French polished or cellulose finishes, are usually water stains. Lay some blotting paper over the area and briefly press a warm iron over it once or twice, to dry out the wood. Alternatively, wipe burnishing cream or metal polish over the stain with a soft cloth.

Removing other stains
White rings and spots are usually caused by spilt coffee or alcohol or a scalding cup. Apply some burnishing cream or metal polish to a soft cloth and work it over the stain, in the direction of the grain, until the stain disappears. If you do not have either product in the house, try a mixture of lubricating oil and a sprinkling of salt. These stains are usually superficial, but if the mark has penetrated through the surface, the finish will have to be stripped off and a new finish applied.

129

Dealing with cigarette burns

A superficial burn can be treated like a heat or water mark, but if it penetrates the surface, strip off the surrounding finish and start again. You may, however, be able to treat the localized area of the burn.

Treating the burnt area
First scrape away the charred edges with a very sharp blade and rub the mark gently with fine-grade sandpaper. Then fill the damage with the appropriate finish. If the wood was treated with a

clear coating, apply several coats of poly-urethane varnish or French polish. Then use fine-grade wet or dry sandpaper to smooth the repair, then apply metal polish with a soft cloth to restore the shine.

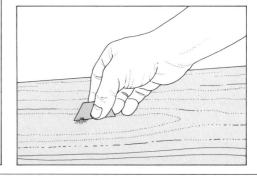

Basic technique

How to apply a wood finish

Wood can be given a variety of protective finishes – including stain, varnish, wax, polish and oil – to prevent moisture, heat, scratches and insects penetrating the surface. In each case the wood should be prepared carefully: stripped of old paint or varnish, filled with wood filler or putty, sealed with knotting and smoothed ready for finishing (see Jobs 4, 5 and 6, pp. 17-19). Before applying a clear finish, you will need to smooth and seal the surface with a grain filler (a runny cream), which comes in different colors. You will need a natural wood color for light and bleached woods, and the appropriate wood shade for darker woods. The grain filler is applied across the grain, with a piece of burlap or a coarse rag and left to harden overnight. If the wood is to be stained, the grain filler and stain can be mixed and applied in one operation. (For more information, see pp. 114-7.)

Applying French polish
French polish includes many different types of polish, all based on shellac and mixed with industrial alcohol. It leaves a good shine, but is not heat- or water-proof. First make a special pad. Spread out a clean, white linen handkerchief and put a lump of cotton batting in the center. Pour some polish on to the cotton batting until it is soaked, then wrap over the linen to form a smooth, wrinkle-free, pear-shaped pad. Gently press the pad on to a spare piece of wood to remove excess polish,

and so prevent runs forming. Use a few drops of linseed oil to keep the pad lubricated and sweep the pad in figures-of-eight over the surface, taking in the edges. As the polish begins to fade, increase the hand pressure and when it is dry, open the pad and re-load it with polish. Apply several coats, allowing each to dry, and store the pad in an air-tight jar between coats. After six hours, make another pad with a double thickness of linen, dampen it with denatured alcohol and work it gently along the grain to finish off.

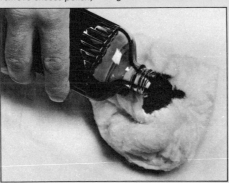

Applying a seal or varnish
Seals and varnishes leave a tough surface. Apply with a good quality, clean paint brush, using a flowing action, and leave to dry for at least 6-12 hours in a dust-free atmosphere. When dry, lightly sand the surface, remove the dust with a clean rag moistened with alcohol. For the best results, thin the first coat with 10 per cent alcohol and apply at least four coats.

Applying stains, oils and waxes
Using a soft, clean, lint-free rag, spread a first coat sparingly over the surface, working with the grain. Allow to dry and, if necessary, add a second coat. With a stain, if the color is too light, add extra layers. If it is too dark, lightly sand the surface. With wax, apply two coats for a good finish. With teak oil apply a second thinner coat, leave it to dry for 24 hours, then rub with steel wool and polish.

130

Treating scratches in wood

A minor scratch should be gently rubbed away with fine-grade wet or dry sandpaper. Metal polish or burnishing cream applied with a soft cloth will bring back the finish. Alternatively, try rubbing in some colored wax or shoe polish of a matching color. A severe scratch which has penetrated below the surface finish and into the wood can only be repaired by stripping and refinishing. A medium-depth scratch, however, can be disguised with a varnish stain.

Disguising a scratch
Thin the varnish slightly with denatured alcohol and apply it with a small paint brush, working with the grain. Paint on several coats, allowing each to dry, until the repair lies above the surface. Finally, use fine-grade wet or dry abrasive paper to rub the varnish flush with the surface, wipe away the dust, and finally, to restore the shine, apply a thin coat of metal polish with a soft cloth.

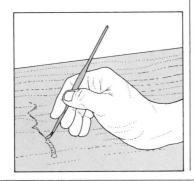

131

Treating bruises and dents in wood

A dent can be disguised by treating it with a clear or stained finish, although if it is deep, you will have to use wood filler or stopping of the appropriate color first, to build up the surface. Bruises and small dents can be removed by using water to swell the wood. The finish is removed with alcohol, then water and heat is applied. After the wood has swelled, it must be allowed to dry before sanding, re-coloring, if necessary, with a matching stain, and re-polishing.

Using water to raise a dent
Place a damp cloth on the damaged area, and run a hot iron over the top, keeping the iron on the move to avoid scorching. Eventually the wood will swell to fill the dent. Alternatively, wrap a wad of cotton batting in clean linen and soak it in boiling water before applying it. Repeat several times. In either case, allow a few hours for the wood fibers to rise, sand and color if necessary, then finish with wax or varnish.

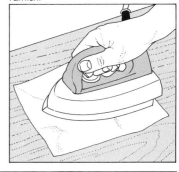

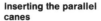

132

Preparing a chair for caning

Pre-woven panels of split cane for seats and chair backs are available, but are difficult to fix to an adequate tension, so it is best to use the traditional method, which will take about 6-8 hours for an average-sized chair. You will first need to cut out the old cane with a sharp trimming knife, keeping a small sample of the caning as a pattern guide. If necessary, drill out the old bits of cane from the holes in the seat frame. Check that the chair is sound and carry out any repairs. Meanwhile, leave the new cane to soak in water for about 15 minutes, then remove it, shake off the water and keep it in a plastic bag until the job is finished. Re-caning a chair involves fitting strands through peg holes, first lengthwise, then crosswise and building up criss-cross layers before finishing off with a series of woven diagonals. To be sure of a straight weave first mark out the chair seat with pegs. (See *Tools and equipment, p. 148*.)

Pegging out the chair
First insert wooden pegs or tees into the center holes in the front and back rails of the seat frame. Put another tee in the back right-hand corner hole of the frame and count the number of holes between the tees in the back rail. Count the same number in the front rail and insert another tee. There will be more holes in the front rail than in the back if the chair seat tapers.

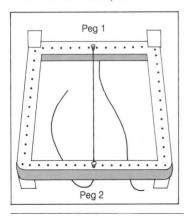

133

Fixing the first layer of cane

The first layer of cane consists of a series of parallel strands, running from front to back and from side to side. The canes slot into the peg holes.

Inserting the parallel canes
Push one end of the cane through the central hole in the back rail, until about ½in. protrudes underneath. Peg the cane in place with the flat, glossy side uppermost, then draw it forward to the central hole in the front rail. Check that the cane is neither twisted nor too tight and peg it in place.

Then bring the first strand up through the next hole to the right and pull it back to the corresponding hole in the back rail, so that the strands are parallel. Continue in this way, until the right-hand side of the seat is filled with parallel canes, **1**. Fill the left-hand side in the same way. Next take canes across the seat at right angles to the first line of canes, **2**. If the seat tapers, take the cane from extra holes in the front rail to holes in the side rails. Peg a cane into the back left-hand corner of the seat, keeping the corner holes free if possible, and take it across to the back right-hand corner then back across to the left-hand side and so on until the seat is filled with parallel canes running from side to side.

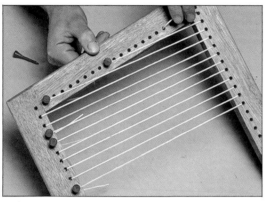

1 Working from the center, insert canes between the front and back rails

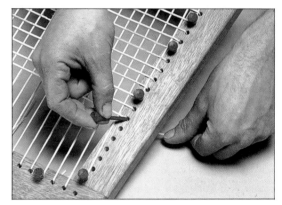

2 Add a layer of cross canes between the two side rails

134

Adding the second layer of cane

The second layer is built up in the same way as the first, so that the cross canes of the first layer are sandwiched between two rows of canes running from front to back.

Threading in the second set of canes
*Now take a second set of canes from front to back on top of the previous layer, using the existing strands as a guide, **1**. At this stage, the strands need to be slightly slack to allow for weaving in the second layer of cross-canes. As each length of cane runs out, instead of plugging in a new strand, you will be able to wind it around*

the loops that have formed on the underside. Where possible, remove the pegs holding in previous strands and tidy up the loose ends. When the second row of front-to-back canes is complete, the weaving can begin with the second row of cross canes. First moisten the canes by spraying with a mist of water, to prevent them cracking while you weave. Secure the first

cane in the back left-hand corner and weave it under and over both sets of canes running from front to back until you reach the back right-hand corner. Insert it into a hole, back through the next, and weave back from right to left. Continue weaving until the layer is complete, then use your thumbnail or toothpick to push the canes into neat double strands.

1 Thread a second layer of cane through the holes in the front and back rails

2 Weave the second layer of cross canes through the strands running from front to back

135
Weaving the diagonal layer

The top layer of cane consists of two rows of cane running diagonally across the seat – one from back left to front right, the other from back right to front left. They are woven through the intersecting canes to form an intricate pattern. Any weaving errors will be noticeable and can only be corrected by unthreading and reweaving, so work carefully.

Building up the pattern
Start at the back left-hand corner, this time using the extreme corner hole, and take the cane to the opposite corner, weaving it under each pair of cross canes and over each pair of front-to-back canes, 1. At the front corner, take the cane down into the extreme corner hole and up through the next hole to the left. Weave this strand diagonally back across the seat, keeping it parallel with the first.

As the holes become more crowded, you may need to use a bodkin. When the left-hand side of the seat is filled with diagonals, return to the back left-hand corner and continue as before, but working to the right to complete the seat. Working from the back right-hand corner to the front left-hand corner, weave a second set of diagonals, 2. This time take the canes over the cross canes and under the front-to-back canes.

1 *Weave a diagonal layer under the cross canes and over the front-to-back canes*

2 *Weave a second set of diagonals in the opposite direction*

136
Finishing off

The neatest way to finish off a cane chair seat is to plug alternate holes to lodge the canes in position, and fix a strand of beading over the peg holes.

Plugging
To prevent the cane slipping out of place, plug the holes. Cut the ⅛in. wide basket cane into ¾in. lengths, and smear each with a little pva woodworking glue. Using a hammer, drive the plugs into alternate holes all round the edge of the seat, until they lie just below the surface, but keeping the corner holes clear. If the plugs will not fit easily into the holes, taper the ends with a sharp knife. If you find a hole is plugged with a temporary peg, remove it, but hold the loose end of cane taut, while you insert the permanent peg. If you find that a hole you do not plan to peg has a loose end of cane, push the end into an adjacent hole and plug that instead.

Beading
Cut four pieces of "common" edging bead 2in. longer than each seat rail and cut one end of each strand into a taper. Take one strand and peg it into a corner of the frame. Then take a strand of ordinary, "fine fine" cane, pass it up through the next unplugged hole, loop it over the beading cane and take it down the same hole to hold the beading flat against the seat. Take the securing cane along to the next unplugged hole and again up and over the beading cane, and so on until the front, back and each side of the seat have been separately beaded. Before tightening the last loop, tuck the end of the beading into a corner hole.

Finishing off
Finally, hammer cane plugs into each corner of the seat to secure the ends of the beading. Turn the chair upside down, apply glue to the remaining pieces of plugging cane and hammer them into the unplugged holes. Once the adhesive has set, trim off the loose ends on the underside, and for a glossy finish, varnish the new cane seat. If the chair has a rounded seat, apply the beading in a single strip and when you reach the hole where you started, remove the peg and drive in the end of the beading strip. If the chair was dismantled to extract the seat frame before starting work, reassemble it, using pva woodworking adhesive for a firm bond (see Job 137, p. 152).

You will need "common" beading cane and "fine fine" cane to secure it in position. If, however, the holes are very narrow or close together, use "narrow medium" cane for both. Alternatively, the canes can be fixed in place by plugging each hole with a permanent peg. Finally, the beading needs to be plugged into the corner holes.

Insert glued plugs into the holes to secure the canes

Secure the edging bead with loops of cane

Use a sharp knife to trim off the untidy ends on the underside

137

Repairing loose chair joints

Chair joints are often heavily stressed, causing them to work loose. If the joint is covered in upholstery, you will have to remove it and take note of how it should be replaced. In this case, because the repair is to be concealed, joints can be repaired by screwing an L-shaped metal bracket to the inside of the frame. However, remaking the joint will produce a stronger repair – even though doing so will involve taking several joints apart and if the joint links the seat to a leg, removing a triangular reinforcing block. If the joint is visible, you will also need to take it apart to make a neat repair.

Remaking the joint
Unscrew the reinforcing block, then tap it sharply with a hammer or mallet to break the glue bond, 1. Separate the two pieces of wood and if the dowels have sheared off, use a drill to bore through and remove them taking care to stop short of the decorative side. Buy hardwood dowels to suit the diameter of the holes, measure the hole depth and cut a dowel $\frac{1}{4}$in. shorter than the combined depth of the matching holes. Cut a groove down the length of each dowel, fill it with adhesive, then tap each into position with a hammer, 2. Tap the joint together with a mallet, refit the corner blocks, 3, and leave until the adhesive is dry.

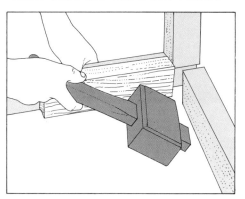

1 *Knock out the unscrewed joint block with a mallet*

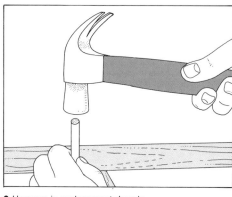

2 *Hammer in replacement dowels*

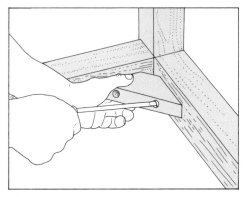

3 *Screw in the new reinforcing joint blocks*

138

Mending broken chair rails

If a rail used to reinforce chair legs dislodges where the rail enters the hole, you can usually fix a hardwood dowel through the leg and the rail end to secure it back in place. A clean break in the middle of a rail may be re-glued. However, in most cases you will either have to search for a matching rail or ask a carpenter to make up a new one.

Replacing a rail
Remove the old rail with a back saw, drill out the remaining stubs and clean the holes with a small file. Cut the new rail to length, allowing for the ends which enter the legs. Measure the diameter of the holes in the legs, 1, and draw a circle of the same diameter on the new rail, using a compass, then file the ends of the rail until they fit snugly in the holes. Apply pva woodworking adhesive to the holes and the rail ends. Then pull apart the chair legs slightly, to allow the rail to fit into position, 2, but try not to dislodge the other joints. Finally, wipe off excess glue and wind a string or fabric tourniquet around the chair legs to hold the rail in place until the adhesive has firmly set. To prevent marks forming on the legs, however, insert cotton batting pads under the tourniquet at the points of highest pressure. Finally, if necessary, stain the rail to match the color of the rest of the chair.

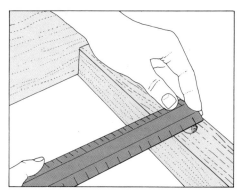

1 *Measure the width of the holes in the chair leg*

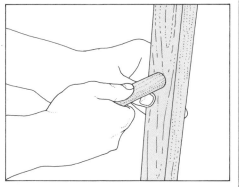

2 *Insert the glued end of the new rail into the chair leg*

139

Repairing uneven chair and table legs

A chair or table becomes unsteady when one leg is too short. The solution is either to trim the three longer legs or to add a sliver of wood to the shorter leg. To trim the legs, measure from the short leg to the floor and cut the excess off the other legs.

Building up a short leg
Stand the chair on a flat surface, making sure that the three longer legs are in contact with the surface. Then, by trial and error, plane down a scrap of wood until it fits snugly under the short leg. Glue and screw the packing block in place and allow it to dry.

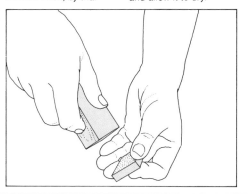

140

Repairing drawers

Drawers are often mis-handled. If they are used frequently and roughly, worn runners may cause them to stick; if they have been stored in damp or hot conditions, the sides may swell or warp, also causing them to stick. If they are over-loaded, the bottom panel may bow, making the drawer impossible to open or the panel may break away completely. Instead of runners, some older drawers have grooves cut in the side to allow it to run over rails. If the groove has worn, you will have to recut it with a circular saw, set to the correct depth, and chisel out the excess wood. If the rail is worn, it will have to be replaced.

Curing a sticking drawer
If the runners are worn, simply remove the old ones and replace them. If the sides are swollen, allow to dry out in warm conditions for a couple of weeks. Or, sandpaper the sides and runners and lubricate them with candle wax (below).

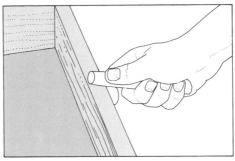

Rub candle wax along the runners to stop the drawer sticking

Curing a bowed drawer
Lever out the bottom panel with a knife or steel ruler and apply fresh adhesive to the grooves before re-assembling. If the bottom panel is broken, cut a new piece of plywood of the same thickness and fix into the grooves. Or, weigh down the old panel.

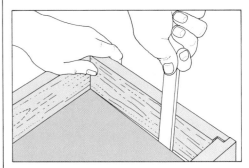

Insert a steel ruler into the joints to lever out the bottom panel of the drawer

---

141

Mending casters

If the casters have become stiff, lightly oil them. If the screws holding the caster to the legs have worked loose, fill the worn screw holes with slivers of wood and replace the screws. If the wheel starts to buckle under the chair, tighten the shaft by tapping it lightly with a hammer and punch. In cases where the caster has simply snapped off, it must be replaced. Casters are fixed to the leg by a central screw or via a cup socket.

Replacing a caster
If the caster has a cup fitting, first remove the brass screws at the side of the cup and lightly tap round the base of the leg to release the caster. If it has a screw fitting, remove the wood screws and unscrew the caster by hand. Then check the new caster for fit. If the leg is too wide, trim it with a chisel or file; if it is too thin, pack it out with slivers of wood (below). If the fixing holes do not line up, plug the old ones and drill new holes, then insert new screws.

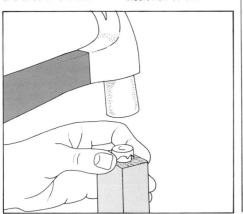

142

Repairing table tops

If the top has become warped, it can be straightened by screwing thick lengths of wood to the underside and tightening the screws connecting the top to the carcass. With a veneer, ensure that the top is well screwed down on to the carcass. A cracked top can be fixed by simply filling the opened joints with the appropriate shade of plastic wood filler or stopping. However, if the joints of a leafed table begin to open, it is best to remove the top and separate the pieces.

Closing the cracks
Remove the top and separate the pieces, then plane the edges absolutely flat. Check both edges with a carpenter's level or straight-edge. When the two pieces are identical, drill several matching holes in each edge, clean them out and fill them with glued dowels. Glue the two pieces together, clamp them firmly and leave until the adhesive sets. Finally replace the top on the table legs.

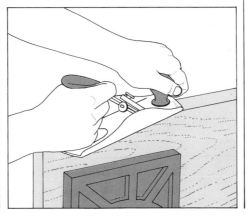

143

Treating veneer blisters

You may be able to remove a blister by covering it with a damp cloth and pressing it lightly with a warm iron, to extract moisture in the wood. This will soften the adhesive, so that if a heavy weight is left on the blister for a couple of days, the blister should deflate. If it returns, try injecting some pva adhesive behind the blister with a hypodermic syringe and weigh down the blister. If this does not work, you will have to make a slit in line with the grain, through the blister, to apply adhesive beneath the two flaps.

Slitting the blister
Use a very sharp knife to make a clean cut through the blister in the direction of the grain. If the blister is very small, make an elongated cross. Raise the flaps and clean out any old adhesive. Apply fresh pva adhesive to both surfaces, then weigh down the blister for 24 hours.

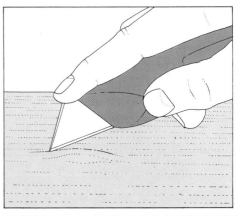

144

Preparing a seat for re-rushing

Genuine rushes are difficult to find, so you may have to use seagrass, a twisted, rush-like material of a slightly different color (*see Tools and equipment, p. 148*). Rush or seagrass is normally quite flexible, but if it seems brittle, soak it in water for about 15 minutes, remove it and shake off the excess water before starting work. For a strong seat, it is best to have the minimum of joins, so wind as much as you can handle on to the hardboard winder. As a rough guide, allow 2-3 hours for re-rushing an average-sized chair seat.

To remove the old seat, you will have to cut through the old rushes with a sharp knife. This produces a lot of dust and rush splinters, so, if possible, work outside, or lay down a drop cloth.

145

Working out the sequence for rushing

The job involves winding the rushes around the frame from corner to corner. If, however, the seat is wider at the front than at the back, you will need extra turns around the front rail to keep the line of the weave running in a straight line from front to back. Likewise, with a rectangular seat, when the left and right segments are full, you will have to take extra turns over the front and back rails to fill the gaps.

Filling a square frame
A pattern automatically forms as a strand of rush is woven around the frame, and looped over

each corner. This gives the impression that diagonal seams divide the chair into four segments.

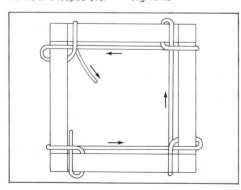

146

Weaving in the rushes

The first strand is fixed to the frame with a knot and is then wrapped around each corner in succession until it runs out. The second strand is then wrapped around the hardboard winder and tied to the end of the previous strand, on the underside of the seat. This process continues until the entire seat is covered. When you have used up all the rush on the hardboard winder, you will have to tie a new length to the old one with a simple knot on the underside of the seat.

Building up the pattern
Start in the front left-hand corner and tie the rush on to the frame, so that it exits from under a rail. Work around the seat in a counter-clockwise direction, taking the rush over the rail in the front right-hand corner of the seat. The strand is taken around this corner so that it exits from under the front rail and on to

the back right-hand corner. From here it is taken over the back rail, around this corner, and out from under the rail, 1. Continue winding counter-clockwise in the same sequence, building up the seat from the corners and working toward the center of the seat, 2. As you pass strands over a rail, twist them, to ensure a neat finish and leave lower strands untwisted.

1 *Pass the rush under and over the rail at the corners*

2 *Continue working counter-clockwise so that a pattern builds up*

147

Tightening and packing the rushes

To ensure that the frame is well covered, and that the diagonals lie straight, the strands need to be pushed tightly and evenly together, after about eight rows have been woven in each corner. At this stage, you should also pack the cavity between the top and bottom layers with broken pieces of rush, to give the seat greater comfort and strength, and to prevent it sagging. This process should be repeated after every eight strands.

Filling up the gaps
To tighten the strands, use a scrap of wood and a mallet to drive them together, until the chair frame is not visible underneath. Insert the wood between the strands and tap firmly with the mallet. Alternatively, use your fingers to pull the strands firmly toward the frame. Take a few strands at a time,

lodge your knee against the frame and ease the strands together, 1. To pack out the seat, fold offcuts of rush in half and push them between the two layers of woven rush at the corners, using a blunt knife or scissors to ensure a tight fit, 2. Continue pushing in the offcuts until you can push no more in. Then continue weaving.

1 *Pull the strands toward the frame to tighten the weave*

2 *Push offcuts of rush into the space between the two layers.*

148
Finishing off

When the seat is filled, the woven rows will have to be eased apart with a blunt knife, to leave room for the last few strands. The last piece of rush is wound over the rail to the underside, or pushed through the central hole and secured with a knot. If the chair was dismantled before work started, reassemble it, using pva adhesive to ensure strong joints (see *Job 137, p. 152*). Finally, add a coat of wax or polish to give the rush a rich and protective finish and a lustrous sheen.

Securing the last strand
Wrap the last strand over the rail to the underside of the seat. Pull it to the center, and gently ease down a woven strand far enough to allow the final strand to be slipped underneath. Finally, tie a stopper knot in it, to prevent it slipping out of place and trim off any free ends. Alternatively, for a more secure finish, push the last two strands

through the hole in the center of the seat to the underside, 1, and tie them both together with a firm knot, 2. Then tidy up the loose ends, and, if you have removed the chair seat from its legs and back, glue the joints back together again.

1 Push the last strands through to the underside

2 Tie the strands tightly together with a secure knot on the underside

Rush and cane furniture

Rush, cane, wicker and bamboo bring warm, natural colors and textures. Natural products are versatile and will blend well into a modern or traditional setting or may constitute the entire decor of a room, with furniture, blinds, matting, picture frames, flower pots all in rush, cane or wicker. The materials are hard-wearing, but attract dust, so should be washed regularly. A scrub-down with warm salt water will remove stains and bleach cane, and a coat of French polish will add a tinge of color or a slight sheen to the surface.

A formal setting
Bamboo or cane blinds can be used to soften a cold, harsh light from the windows (right). Elegantly shaped cane furniture in an expansive setting gives a clean, sophisti-cated air in an otherwise cold and dark room

A domestic setting
Golden cane and wicker give a warm, sunny feel in daylight and blend naturally with house-plants (below). The slatted and latticed patterns in cane can also be used to good effect in artificial light, and cast delicate shadows.

Renewing upholstery

Construction of an upholstered chair ◇ Renewing webbing, burlap and padding
Replacing springs
Re-covering a fixed seat

There are two basic types of upholstered seat: a fixed seat, which forms an integral part of the chair, and a loose seat, which contains no springs and simply drops into the chair frame.

If a chair seat is sagging or lumpy, it needs to be stripped, and the old webbing, padding and springs replaced. In many cases, however, the outer fabric wears before the inner padding. Nevertheless, when re-covering the seat, it is wise to renew the padding.

Although the same basic technique is used for all types of chair, a drop-in seat is easier to work on than a fixed seat, because it can be detached and turned to any angle, and because it contains no springs.

Points to remember

◇ Always use a strong cover fabric that is recommended for upholstery.
◇ Make sure the springs are sewn upright on the webbing, that they are not distorted, and that the new springs are the right size.
◇ When upholstering for the first time, avoid striped fabrics, since the stripes are difficult to align.

For information on types of upholstery fabrics, see Choosing materials, pp. 134-5.

Estimating time

The length of time needed to re-upholster a chair will depend on your experience and the complexity of the job. However, as a rough guide, an average chair will take about 6 hours to re-upholster completely. Allow 1 hour to replace the webbing, a total of $1\frac{3}{4}$ hours to replace the burlap, padding and muslin, 5-10 minutes per spring, and $\frac{3}{4}$ hour for finishing off with braid and "bottoming". If you are only replacing the top fabric, however, allow about $1\frac{1}{2}$ to 2 hours to re-cover a fixed seat and 1 hour to re-cover a loose seat.

Tools and equipment

Specialist upholstery tools and materials, available from needlework and hardware stores and upholsterers, are essential. Woven webbing, which comes in jute, linen or cotton mixtures, is used for traditional upholstery. Rubber webbing, used with foam rubber padding, is for modern furniture. The burlap should be the 16oz "tarpaulin" type. For traditional upholstery, horsehair and sheep's wool are best, but those mixed with other animal hairs are less expensive and more readily available. You will need a tack lifter to remove old tacks, and a sharp knife to cut the springs free from the webbing. Webbing is secured with $\frac{1}{2}$in.-$\frac{5}{8}$in. tin tacks, burlap and muslin with $\frac{5}{8}$in. tacks and the covering material with $\frac{3}{8}$in. fine-headed tacks.

Fixing equipment
Tacks are driven in with a small tacking hammer. The springs are attached with No. 1 upholsterer's twine and a 4in.-6in. spring needle, and the padding with light-weight upholsterer's twine and a 10in. stitching needle. Scissors are useful for cutting all materials and latex adhesive is needed for gluing the gimp over the tacks.

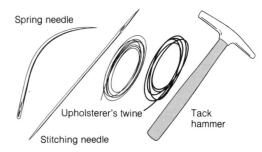

Spring needle
Upholsterer's twine
Tack hammer
Stitching needle

The construction of an upholstered chair

A traditional upholstered chair consists of a network of webbing at the bottom, which supports the springs; these are covered with a layer of burlap, which supports padding. This in turn is held in place with a covering of muslin. The covering fabric forms the top layer and the bottom of the seat is sealed with black linen.

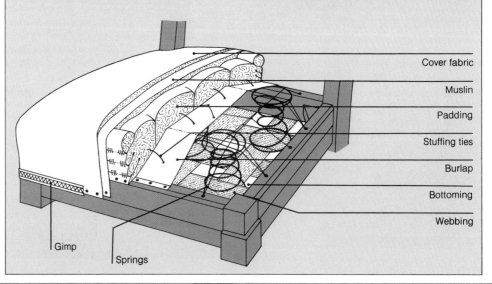

Cover fabric
Muslin
Padding
Stuffing ties
Burlap
Bottoming
Webbing
Gimp
Springs

149

Renewing webbing

Before you start, you will have to turn the chair upside down and use the tack lifter to remove the tacks holding the layer of "bottoming" and the old webbing. You should also cut through the twine holding the springs to the old webbing. At this stage you should replace any broken or distorted springs. On a traditional chair, you will need woven webbing, which is fixed in a series of strips, first from front to back, then from left to right, until it forms a criss-cross network. It is best to keep the webbing in one long strip and to cut as you go, to be sure of the correct measurements. On a modern chair, you will need rubber webbing, which stretches when pulled, or sat upon, so it is important that each strip is fixed under the same tension. For dining and other smaller chairs, you only need to fix rubber webbing in one direction, but for larger chairs, you should interweave a second row for extra strength. With both types, you will finally have to attach the springs to the new webbing (see Job 150, below).

Using woven webbing
Fold under ⅜in. of webbing, position the folded edge halfway across the back rail of the seat and tack it just to one side of the old tack holes. Hammer in three tacks across the webbing ¼in. from the fold, then add two more, evenly spaced below the first row. Pull the webbing straight across the chair frame, using a block of wood (16in. × 3in. × 1in.) to hold it taut. Then fasten it to the front rail, using three tacks as before. Cut off the excess webbing ⅜in. beyond the tacks, fold it back over the tacks and hammer in two more tacks to secure it, 1. Fix more strips in the same way, again just to the side of the old tack holes until you have a series of parallel strips running from the back to the front of the frame. Then fix more webbing in the same way, this time working from left to right and weaving in and out of the previous layer, 2, to form a network.

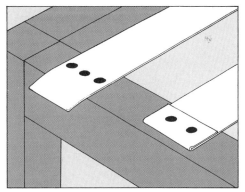

1 Attach the webbing to the rail with three tacks, then turn and tack the surplus

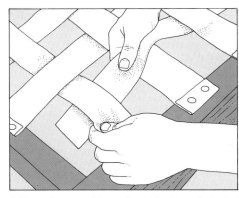

2 Weave the second layer of webbing through the first

Using rubber webbing
Measure the distance from the center of the back rail to the center of the front rail. To transfer this on to the webbing, first draw a line ⅜in. from one end of the webbing, then measure off the chair span from this line and draw a second line. Next mark a third line ¾in. inside the second. Position the webbing on the chair with the first line lying half-way across the back rail and hammer in four tacks across it at equal distances, 1. Lay the webbing straight across the frame so that the third line lies halfway across the front rail. Then fix it in position as before and cut off the surplus, 2. To ensure that each strip has the same tension, measure and fix each in the same way until equally spaced strips span the frame. On a large chair, add a second row in the same way, and stretched evenly but running from left to right and interweaving the first layer.

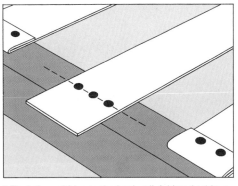

1 Tack the webbing to the back rail, fold and add two more tacks

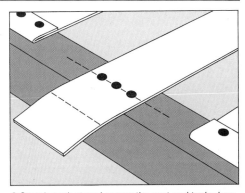

2 Stretch each strand across the seat and tack along the tacking line

150

Replacing springs

If you have just renewed the webbing, you will need to re-attach the springs. If you are not re-upholstering, but need to secure a loose spring or insert a new one, you will first need to remove the "bottoming", and release the webbing by prying off the securing tacks. To fix the springs to the webbing, cut a length of 1-cord upholsterer's twine and thread it to a spring needle. When you have secured the springs in position on the webbing, it is wise to lace the springs together and to the seat frame with a piece of string.

Sewing the springs to the webbing
Arrange the springs so that they are evenly supported by the webbing, and their ends face the center of the chair Then push the threaded needle through the webbing and make a stitch over the base of the spring, using a half-hitch knot to fasten it beneath the webbing, 1 Make two more stitches, at equal intervals around the spring base and repeat the process for the other springs. Then connect the springs together and to the sides of the frame with cord.

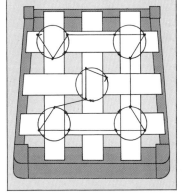

1 Sew each spring to the webbing with three stitches

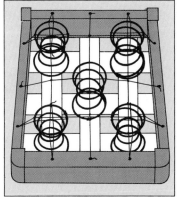

2 Lace the springs to the sides of the frame

151
Fitting new burlap

The springs need to be covered with a layer of strong burlap to support the padding and prevent it falling through the seat. You will need to mark position guide lines on the seat frame before tacking the new piece of burlap in place.

Positioning the burlap
Draw a line all round the top edge of the seat frame, 1in. in from the outer edge. Then mark the center point of each rail. Measure the size of the seat frame and cut a piece of burlap to size, adding on ¾in. all round. Center the burlap over the frame and partially drive in tacks at the center of each rail. On the back rail, fold the edge of the burlap to align with the line on the frame and tack in at the center mark. Then stretch the folded edge to the corners of the back rail and tack the burlap in place, inserting more tacks along the folded edge at 1in. intervals, 1. Next pull the burlap to the front, fold the fabric and tack it in place then repeat on the side edges. Then sew the burlap to the springs, 2.

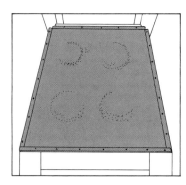

1 *Center the burlap over the seat, fold the edges and tack them to the frame*

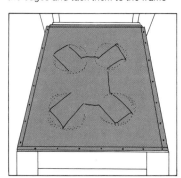

2 *Make three stitches through the burlap around each spring*

152
Replacing the padding

On traditional chairs, horse-hair, wool or vegetable fiber padding is positioned on top of the burlap and is anchored with stuffing ties sewn across the burlap, then covered with

Replacing traditional padding
Thread a spring needle with stitching twine and make a small securing stitch in the hem of the burlap at the front. Take the needle halfway to the back of the seat and make a 2in. back stitch through the burlap. Then take the needle to the back of the chair and make a small stitch in the hem of the burlap, leaving both loops of

thread across the seat slightly loose. Take the thread over to the adjacent side and again make a back stitch halfway, so that the loops lie about 3in. from the edge of the seat. Continue around the seat until each side contains two loops, 1. To shape the filling, tease out the padding to make sure there are no lumps and tuck handfuls of it under all eight loops.

a layer of muslin. Modern chairs, however, are usually padded with foam rubber, which is fitted directly over rubber webbing. Foam rubber can be used on traditionally shaped chairs, provided the woven webbing is replaced with rubber for extra resilience. The foam rubber is cut to size with ¾in. extra added all round and is secured to the frame with muslin surround.

Most chairs take more padding than you would expect, so keep pressing it down firmly until the space is filled. When the loops are tightly packed with padding, fill in the center. Tease out the filling with your fingers to spread it into a dome about 2in. high in the center, 2 and taper it toward the back. Make sure the filling forms an even shape, then cover with a layer of muslin.

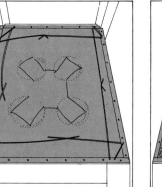

1 *Stitch twine to the burlap to create eight large stuffing ties*

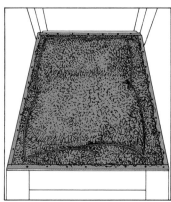

2 *Pack the padding under the ties and fill out the center into a dome*

Replacing foam-rubber padding
Foam-rubber padding is secured on to the frame with a band of muslin fixed around its edges. Measure the depth of the foam cushion, double it and add 1in. Cut out four pieces of muslin to this width and the length of one side of the chair seat. Fold each piece of muslin in half lengthwise and spread fabric glue along one side of the fold line. Then stick one along the top edge of each side of the foam. Position the foam in the frame. Then pull the muslin down tightly and tack to the frame at the center of each rail. Insert more tacks at 1in. intervals, to within 2in. of the front corners, and drive home the center tacks. Pull the fabric around the corners, cut off the excess and tack it firmly in place.

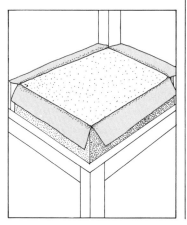

153
Making a muslin undercover

Traditional padding, held in place with stuffing ties, needs to be completely covered with a layer of muslin to preserve its shape before the final fabric is added. Foam padding is simply secured with a muslin border (*see Job 152, left*).

Tacking on the muslin
Cut the muslin to the size of the seat, allowing 3in. extra all round. Center it over the padding, pull it down at the sides and temporarily tack it at the center of each side of the frame, 1. Stretch the muslin at the corners, and insert temporary tacks, making sure that the padding is smooth. Then tack the muslin to the frame along the back rail at 1in. intervals and drive the temporary tacks home. Repeat along the front rail then the sides. At the back corners, make diagonal release cuts, trim away the excess fabric to reduce the bulk, then neatly fold in the edge and retack. At the front corners, neatly fold the muslin into a pleat and tack. Finally, trim the muslin close to the tacks all round, with a sharp knife, 2.

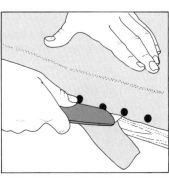

1 *Center the muslin and insert four temporary tacks*

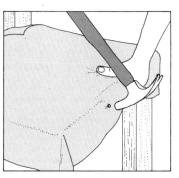

2 *Trim off the excess muslin close to the tacks*

Basic technique

How to re-cover chairs

When replacing the cover of a fixed, or a drop-in seat, the covering fabric will need to be resilient upholstery-weight material. It is cut to the size of the chair, allowing 2¾in. extra all round for turning and trimming. A piece of cotton stuffing, cut to the exact size of the seat, is inserted underneath for extra strength and comfort. On a fixed seat, the cover is tacked on to the side of the chair frame, and a piece of black linen "bottoming" is fitted to the underside of the seat, then a length of braid or gimp is cut to fit the perimeter of the seat.

1 Secure the cover to the frame with temporary tacks at 1in. intervals.

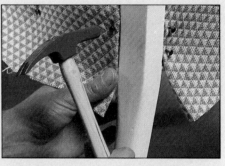

2 Fold in the fabric each side of the back uprights and tack

Re-covering a fixed seat
Place the stuffing centrally on the chair seat, then lay the new cover on top of it. Using fine-headed tacks, temporarily tack the cover to the frame, first at the center of each side edge of the chair frame, then at 1in. intervals to within 2in. of the corners, keeping the fabric smooth and taut, **1**. Fold the corners back on to the seat, diagonally, then make a diagonal release cut from the corner of the fabric to the line of the fold. Take the resulting triangles down, either side of the upright, folding them in vertically to fit neatly against the upright. Trim away the extra fabric to within ⅛in. of the fold, press the folds in with your fingers and tack temporarily to the frame, **2**. If the front corners are square, fold the surplus

fabric into a single pleat and tack it in place. With rounded corners, fold the fabric into a double pleat – one each side – before tacking, **3**. When the cover is wrinkle-free, hammer home the temporary tacks, then add an extra tack between them, so that they are spaced ¼–½in. apart, **4**. Trim off the excess fabric, then turn the chair upside down. Take a piece of bottoming and turn in about ½in. all round. Center it on the underside of the frame and attach it with tacks, at 2in. intervals, close to the folded edge, **5**. Fold in 3in. at one end of a length of braid. Insert a tack in the fold and tack the end of the braid to the chair. Spread adhesive along the braid and press it into position over the tacks, **6**, and secure the free end with adhesive and a temporary tack.

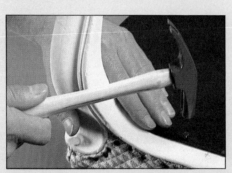

3 At the front corners, make a neat pleat and tack

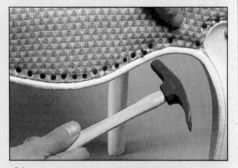

4 Insert extra tacks between the temporary ones, at ⅜in. intervals

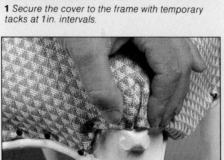

5 Tack bottoming to the underside of the frame

6 Glue a length of braid over the tacks and the raw edges of fabric

Re-covering a loose seat
Lay the fabric upside down on a flat surface. Center the stuffing on top with the fluffy side down on the fabric, then lay the seat centrally on top, also upside down, **1**. Fold the fabric around the frame along the back edge and temporarily tack at the center, on the underside of the rail. Working outward from the center, continue tacking at 1in. intervals, to within 2in. of the back corners. Smooth the fabric over the seat and attach it to the front edge in the same way. Repeat for the side

edges, checking that the fabric lies smooth on the top side. To neaten the corners, pull the fabric down hard diagonally, and tack the corner to the underside of the frame, **2**. Fold the extra fabric on either side of the tack into a pleat and tack into place. If there are any wrinkles, remove the tacks which are pulling too tight and re-tack. Trim the fabric to within ⅜in. of the tacks. Finally tack a piece of bottoming to the underside of the frame, as for a fixed seat. Turn in a small hem, center it over the pad, then tack it down every 2in.

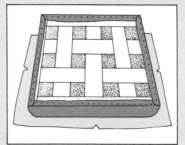

1 Center the stuffing on the fabric and place the seat on top

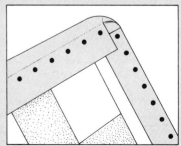

2 Tack the cover to the underside of the frame at 1in. intervals

Lighting

Types of light bulb ◇ Types of light fixture ◇ Suiting the lighting to the room ◇ Effects with lighting

Lighting needs to be both efficient and complementary to the contents of your home. If used well it can enhance, disguise, brighten, soften, highlight and reflect furnishings and decoration, while providing the right amount of light to see by.

Every room needs diffused general light to form a soft, shadowless backcloth. Sharper, directional light adds contrast and relief by creating dramatic highlights and shadows. For reading, writing, sewing or working, however, a specific bright light source is essential and must be planned for. These three types of light must be used in the correct balance for a harmonious effect.

Positioning fittings is as important as choosing the correct types and can affect the dimensions of the room and the effect of its contents.

Points to remember

◇ Position switches within easy reach of the doors.
◇ Do not exceed the maximum wattage recommended for the fixture.
◇ As a guide you will need 20 watts of light per square yard but dirty bulbs will reduce output.
◇ Fluorescent lights use half as much electricity as incandescent lights, but are more costly to install.
◇ Wall lights can make a room look smaller.
◇ Pendant lights can make a high ceiling seem lower.

For more information on wiring and electricity, see pp. 180-3.

Types of light bulb

Bulbs come in a variety of shapes and sizes. Most fittings take a pear-shaped bulb, but mushroom bulbs are designed for shallow fittings. Decorative shapes are made for chandeliers, wall lights and other special fittings. Larger bulbs are available for spotlights.

Finishes
Normal incandescent filament bulbs come in clear or pearl-white finishes and a few colors. Clear bulbs are best used with enclosed shades. Some directional fixtures use reflector bulbs which are partially silvered to concentrate the beam. Some are coated at the base to cast the light backward; others are coated behind the filament to project the light forward. Fluorescent tubes come in circular or straight form, in a range of sizes.

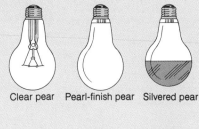

Clear pear   Pearl-finish pear   Silvered pear

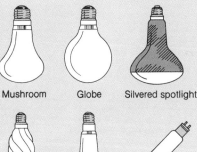

Mushroom   Globe   Silvered spotlight

Twisted candle   Pygmy lamp

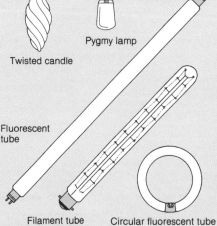

Fluorescent tube

Filament tube   Circular fluorescent tube

Light fixtures fall into two groups: directional fixtures, such as spotlights, which give out concentrated beams of light in specific directions; and diffused fixtures, such as pendants, which give a wide spread of general background lighting.

Pendant fixtures
Traditionally fixed to the center of the ceiling, these lights supplied light for every occasion in the past. Today, they form a useful back-up for more modern lamps and can be used with a dimmer switch and a rise and fall mechanism for use over a dining table. In confined areas, such as passages, hallways and stairs, pendants cast a useful general light and an attractive shade will add decorative interest. When fitted with translucent shades, pendant lights provide diffused lighting, but an upward or downward pointing opaque shade produces directional lighting. Pendant fixtures are available in many styles, including old-fashioned oil, gas and early light fixtures, and chandeliers. Shades for pendants come in glass, fabric, wicker, paper, wood, metal and other materials: and in a variety of shapes, including pyramids, cones, domes, bells, pleats and balls. Those with an enclosed base emit less glare than those with the bulb fully exposed. Pendant fixtures need to be wired up and attached to the ceiling with a ceiling fixture (see Job 161, p. 181).

Portable lights
Moveable lights include table and standard lamps and adjustable desk lamps. Traditional table and standard lamps with translucent shades throw a diffused light, while modern floor standard spotlights and desk lights all emit directional light for close work. The shape of the light shade will also influence the direction and intensity of the light beam. Desk lights can double as spotlights and if directed at a wall will cause the light to bounce off and spread into a diffused light. Desk lamps come in a variety of shapes, and with a stand or a clip-on fixing. Clip-on types save space on a crowded desk top. Standard and table lamps, like desk lamps, can simply be unplugged and moved to another part of the room or house. They also offer decorative flexibility, since the shade can be simply changed to suit new decoration or for variety and the base can be improvised from a bottle or jar.

Spotlights
Available in many shapes and sizes, these throw out directional light in wide, medium or narrow beams. The intensity of the light is determined by the type of bulb fitted: ordinary tungsten light bulbs for example give out a harsher light than internally silvered or crown silvered lamps. Spotlights can be wall or ceiling mounted, recessed into a ceiling, or, for more flexibility, they can be clamped on to bedheads, desks, workbenches or bookshelves, or clipped into a wall- or ceiling-mounted lighting track. Aluminum lighting tracks can be surface mounted or recessed into a ceiling or wall and wired to a single lighting point. Each track will then hold and power several spotlights. Each type of track is designed to carry compatible fittings, so be sure to choose the right ones.

Types of light fixture

Some, however, can be used for both. Directional fittings, for example, can produce background lighting if bounced off a light-reflecting surface. When choosing a light fixture, try to establish how much light it will emit, how much will be absorbed by the shade, what shape of beam it will give out, and whether it will shine upward or downward. It is always a mistake to buy a fixture merely because it matches the furnishings, particularly since many shades are changeable. Try not to pick a single fixture for the center of a ceiling, except perhaps for a small kitchen or bathroom— it will lack interest and will not flatter the furnishings. It is best to choose a combination of fixtures to create a good blend of general and specific light.

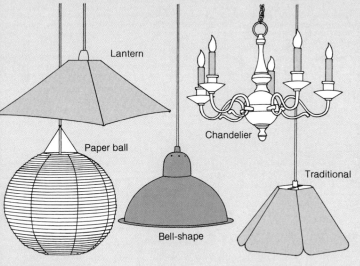

Lantern

Paper ball

Chandelier

Bell-shape

Traditional

Fluorescent fixtures
Although widely used in kitchens, fluorescent light can be useful for decorative lighting – concealed behind a curtain cornice to light the curtains, or fitted under a glass shelf to light ornaments. Fluorescent fittings, which consume very little power, are cheap to run and stay cool, so can be used in confined spaces. They also cast little shadow, so are useful in work areas. For an overall light source, fluorescent fixtures can be fixed above translucent panel suspended ceilings.

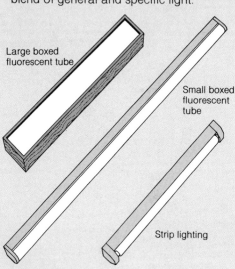

Large boxed fluorescent tube

Small boxed fluorescent tube

Strip lighting

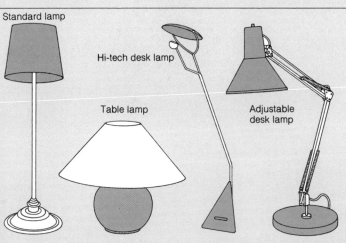

Standard lamp

Hi-tech desk lamp

Table lamp

Adjustable desk lamp

Wall lights
Traditional wall lights cast a diffused light, to be used instead of, or in addition to, a central pendant. They are best controlled with a dimmer switch and used in dark rooms, to illuminate dark halls and landings. Modern wall spotlights produce a concentrated beam of light which can be directed down on to a table or chair for specific work, or used to highlight a special decorative feature, such as plants or pictures.

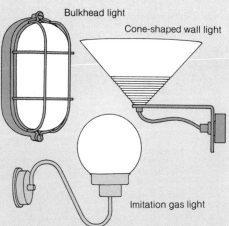

Bulkhead light

Cone-shaped wall light

Imitation gas light

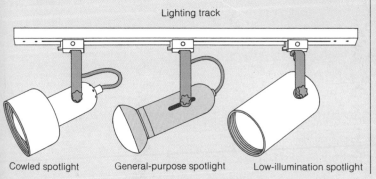

Lighting track

Cowled spotlight

General-purpose spotlight

Low-illumination spotlight

Uplighters and downlighters
Downlighters are square or cylindrical units, used to beam shafts of light downward from the ceiling. They can be fitted fully recessed into the ceiling, semi-recessed or surface mounted. Narrow beams highlight specific areas, wide beams provide more general lighting. Uplighters are fitted in reverse, beaming light up from the floor.

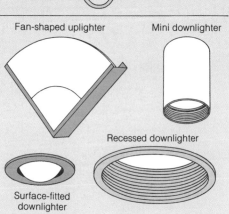

Fan-shaped uplighter

Mini downlighter

Recessed downlighter

Surface-fitted downlighter

Suiting lighting to the room

Different rooms have different lighting requirements to suit the conditions and the activities of the room. Living rooms, for example, need a soft combination of diffused, decorative and direct lighting, while kitchens need a brighter overall light for cooking. Evening meals are more relaxing in subdued lighting, so use diffused lighting and perhaps a dimmer switch or a pendant light in a dining room. In bathrooms and kitchens, ensure that all fittings are totally enclosed and have a shield or skirt to prevent anyone who is replacing a bulb from touching the metal bulb cap. If a small strip-light is to be used, ensure that it has a built-in switch and safety cut-out to isolate the holder when the tubular bulb is removed.

Hall and passage lighting

Dark, confined spaces need to be clearly lit with pervasive lighting from wall lights or down-lighters bouncing off the walls. Halls should also have a warm, welcoming glow from diffused but clear lights inside, and a porch light at the door.

Bedroom lighting

Most bedrooms need soft general light, with a switch by the door, and bedside reading lights positioned above or beside the bed, with easily reached switches. It can be useful to have lights inside closets: for example a side strip-light, illuminating the shelves from above. For a child's night light, use a dimmer switch or allow the light from a landing or an adjoining room to filter in.

Bathroom lighting

For general light, surface-mounted closed ceiling fixtures are best in most cases, especially plastic or glass types, which, unlike metal, are resistant to steam and condensation. Enclosed downlights or spotlights well out of reach of shower spray are also suitable. Fluorescent fixtures can be useful, especially if hidden behind a suspended ceiling or a cornice. In addition, you will need a light above a mirror. This should shine on to the face of the person in front of the mirror, not glaring on to the mirror itself. Remember that all lights in a bathroom should be out of reach of the shower spray.

Living room lighting

Greater variety of lighting is needed in a living room than in any other room in the house. You will need a combination of general, diffuse lighting, supplied by wall washers or a pendant; directional lights, such as spotlights on a ceiling track or down and up-lighters; and portable lights for specific activities. For reading, you will need a light shining from behind the chair; for working, a concealed light reflecting on to the wall or an adjustable light will be suitable. A light shining from behind will cast shadows. Rise and fall lighting is useful over a dining table and an indirect light near the TV set will make it less tiring to watch.

Staircase lighting

Stairs must be well lit to avoid accidents. It is best to angle the light from the side and to keep the light constant. Light-sensitive switches which automatically turn the light on when the natural light dims to a set level are useful for stairs.

Kitchen lighting

You will need both strong lighting for cooking, and more subdued lighting for everyday use and mealtimes. Dimmer switches can be useful for this purpose. Fluorescent tubes are the traditional way of lighting a kitchen. In a small room up to 65ft^2 a single tube mounted over a sink or working surface may be enough; in larger rooms, you will need at least two. They can be particularly effective under wall units, shining on to work surfaces. Adjustable spotlights offer good directional lighting over the stove or sink.

Effects with lighting

Lights can create illusions. A broad flood of light over a pale ceiling or wall gives an impression of height and space, while light directed on the floor darkens and lowers the ceiling. Localized pools of light make a room seem smaller and more cosy and help to highlight good features, while the resulting shadows can be used to conceal bad ones. Dark colors and heavy textures absorb light and therefore demand a stronger wattage – up to three times as much as a lighter surface. A shiny and pale surface on the other hand may reflect up to 75 per cent of the light.

Complementary lighting
A large, pendant light (above) emits good general lighting, but casts shadows in corners. An additional selection of spot and fluorescent lights helps to provide clear lighting for working surfaces, and brightens up alcoves and shelving.

Clusters of light
Bulbs or spotlights grouped together and reflected in a mirror (left) can create a dramatic multiplying effect, such as this stage-dressing-room style.

Localized uplights
Illuminating a plant (right), sculpture or ornament from behind with an uplighter produces a halo with subtle upshafts of softened light.

Pictures and mirrors

Pictures lend individuality to any room, but to look good they need to be well framed, well arranged and perfectly clean.

The easiest ways to frame a picture are to use a kit, to make a "frameless" (glass mount) frame, or to use a pre-fabricated frame. However, with care and patience, a beginner can make a frame.

Paintings, prints and watercolors should be arranged to form an integral part of the room and to harmonize with the furniture.

Mirrors too play an important part in the decor of a room, beyond their obvious uses as an aid to dressing, but they must be positioned carefully and the glass must be good quality.

Points to remember

◇ Always take valuable pictures to a professional restorer for cleaning and repair.
◇ Make sure that all pictures and mirrors are securely fixed to the wall to avoid accidents.
◇ Keep all pictures out of direct sunlight, electric light or heat, and do not subject them to rapid changes in temperature and humidity.
◇ Dust oil paintings regularly and protect prints and watercolours with glass. Keeping them clean will prolong their life.

Tools and equipment

The basic elements of a picture include wooden or aluminum moldings, 1/12in. thick picture glass, mounting cardboard and hardboard backing board. To fit them together, you will need turnbuckle clips or glazing points, and masking tape to seal the frame. When making a mount, use a sharp utility knife and a steel ruler. Use stamp collector's gummed hinges for attaching the picture to a normal mount, and adhesive tape for a window mount.

Making a frame
To cut accurate mitered (45 degree) corners, you will need a miter block and a fine-tooth back saw on wood and a fine-tooth hacksaw on metal. For assembling wooden frames, use pva wood-working adhesive and veneer pins to connect the four sides and a miter clamp to hold them. On metal frames, you will need epoxy adhesive to glue the corners, and screws to fix the frame to the backboard.

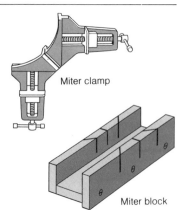

Miter clamp

Miter block

Types of picture frame

A frame should be chosen to suit the style of the painting, print or photograph it is to surround. Only oil paintings which are protected by varnish should be framed without glass. Premade frames come complete with glass and backing sheets. Framing kits usually come complete with a metal or plastic frame with pre-mitered corners, and clips, but without glass and board.

Wooden frames
Picture frames made from wood can be painted, varnished or gilded. If you are making a frame, a wide variety of special frame moldings are available. Carved and gilded moldings, for example, can be bought from picture-framing specialists and art stores. In many cases these suppliers cut the miters (the 45-degree corner angles) to size, so that you glue and pin the frame together. Hardware stores and wood yards supply simpler moldings, but will not cut miters.

Frameless glass mounts
The picture is sandwiched between a sheet of glass or acrylic plastic and a similar-sized sheet of backing board. The three layers are held together with simple metal clips or spring-loaded picture clips.

Metal frames
Polished aluminum is particularly popular for modern settings. However, it is best to buy these frames ready-made, since metal is difficult to work and join.

Old frames
Auctions and second-hand stores are a good source of picture-frame moldings. Over-large frames can be easily dismantled and cut down to size. If parts of a molding are missing, try casting a new section in plaster. Press dental impression compound on to a sound part of the frame. Remove it and pour plaster into it. When dry, glue the plaster shape to the frame.

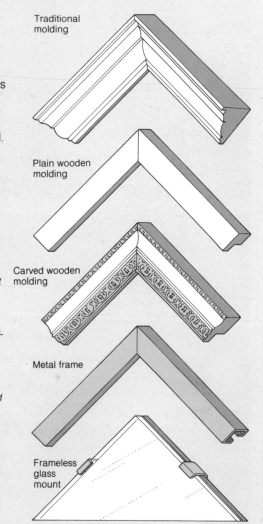

Traditional molding

Plain wooden molding

Carved wooden molding

Metal frame

Frameless glass mount

Types of picture hook

The fittings you use on the back of the frame or backing board depend on the weight of the picture. The type of fixing used on the wall is chosen to suit either a solid or a hollow wall. Both fixings, however, need to be compatible.

Fittings for lightweight pictures
For small pictures with moldings less than ¾in. wide, use D-rings, 1, inserted directly into the backing board. The picture can then be hung on a lightweight picture hook or screw. If the moldings are more than ¾in. wide, a screw eye, 2, can be fitted to either side of the frame, joined with nylon cord, pulled taut.

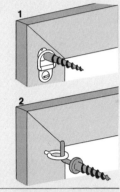

Fittings for heavy pictures
Heavier pictures need stronger fittings, such as picture plates, rings or battens, 2. Plates and rings are screwed to the thickest part of the moldings, on each side of the frame, about one-third of the way down. They can be linked with three-strand picture wire, twisted around the plate hole or ring and pulled taut, 1.

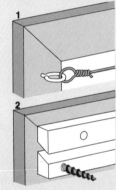

Solid-wall fixings
Solid walls will take picture hooks, which are fixed by hammering a thin masonry brad into the wall. Single hooks are suitable for lightweight pictures, 1, double-brad hooks for heavier ones, 2. If the wall is very hard, you may have to drill a hole, then insert a wallplug and screw.

Cavity-wall fixings
On cavity walls, insert an oval-head screw into a suitable wallplug, 1. You can hang the picture directly on to the screw head or hook the hanging wire over the screw head. Alternatively, screw a hook directly into a wallplug and hook on the picture fitting, 2.

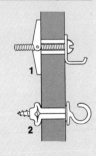

How to make a picture frame

To make a wooden picture frame, you will need four lengths of wooden molding. If the supplier has not mitered the corners for you, you will have to cut eight miters (45-degree angles) – two for each corner using a miter box and a fine-tooth back saw. So remember to allow for wastage when buying the molding. As a guide for calculating the length of molding required, add the combined length of the four sides to the width of the molding multiplied by eight, and add a further 2in. for cutting and waste. Once the mitered corners are precisely cut, they can be joined by glue and brads to form the frame. For a metal frame, the corners are mitered in the same way, but using a fine-tooth hacksaw.

Mitering the corners
Use a protractor to pencil in the 45-degree cutting guideline on the inside edge of the molding. Insert the molding in the miter block; the slots in the block will guide the saw to cut an accurate 45-degree angle, 1. Cut from the top face of the molding downward, working carefully to avoid splintering. Keep the blade perfectly in line and always ensure that you are cutting on the waste side of your guideline.

To cut the matching miter on the next piece of molding, angle the blade in the opposite direction. If the molding is thin, you may need to insert a piece of backing wood beneath the molding to raise it sufficiently for the saw to reach it at the base of the miter slot. This will also protect the wooden base of the miter box.

Check the angle of the mitered joints after cutting: if the two adjoining pieces do not form a perfect right angle, use a bench sander or "shooting board" to make adjustments (see below right). A shooting board can be made from a wide, straight board of wood with battens secured at exactly 45 degrees to the edge.

When both pieces of molding are trimmed to a perfect 45-degree angle, glue them together, to make a right-angled corner,

2. Then tap veneer brads into both moldings to secure the join. To hold the frame in position, while the glue sets, use a miter clamp which forms a true 90-degree angle, or Spanish windlass. A miter clamp is best, since it allows you to pin each corner immediately after gluing, 3. While one corner is in the clamp, miter the ends of the next pair of moldings. A Spanish windlass consists of four corner pieces connected by string, which is twisted around a nail like a tourniquet. With this arrangement, you will have to glue all the corners and tighten the windlass with the frame held flat, then pin the corners when the adhesive has set. If the miters set slightly out of position, break the bond and remake the joint. To check that the frame is square, measure the diagonals to check that they are equal. Finally, paint, stain, varnish or wax polish the frame.

Using a shooting board
Clamp the board to a work top and hold the molding against one of the angled battens. Smooth a plane across the mitered corner against the edge of the shooting board.

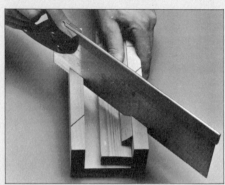

1 Saw the end of the molding to a 45-degree angle, using a miter block

2 When two moldings form a true right angle, glue them together

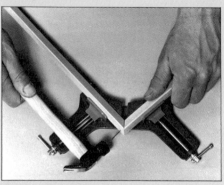

3 Hold the two pieces in position with a miter clamp, while the glue sets

154
Mounting a picture

Before framing, a picture is mounted on to a piece of cardboard. It may be stuck on to a cardboard backing, larger than itself; or attached to a surround, which forms a "window" for the picture, and holds it away from the glass. If a backing is being used, the picture is normally attached to it at the top corners, using two stamp collectors' gummed hinges or a pasted strip of tissue paper.

Making a window mount
Use a sharp utility knife and steel rule to cut an opening about ¼in. smaller than the picture, with allowance for a wider bottom margin. Lay the picture face up on a table, so that it just overlaps the edge. Lay the mount over the picture, and secure the back of the picture to the bottom of the mount with adhesive tape. Then turn both over and tape the top of the picture to the mount.

155
Framing a picture

A framed picture consists of five layers: the outer frame, a layer of glass, the picture, the mount and backing board. It is best to buy 1/12in. thick picture glass and ask the glazier to cut it to $\frac{1}{16}$-in. smaller than the frame, then cut your backing board to the same size. The mount is attached to the backing board with a hinge of adhesive tape along the top inside edge, to form an assembly of picture, mount and backing board. Before the glass is slotted into the frame and the picture assembly secured on top, rings, plates or eyes must be screwed to the frame or the backing board (*see Types of picture hook, p. 165*). The glass is secured to the frame with turn-buckle clips or glazing points.

Fixing the backing board
Lay the frame face downward, clean the glass with denatured alcohol, and slot it into the rabbet of the frame. Then lower the picture, mount and board assembly into the frame, ensuring that the picture is centralized, then secure the backing board. If you are using turnbuckle clips (screws with a swivel "tongue") screw them into each corner and the middle of the frame. If you have glazing points (wedge-shaped nails), press them against the backing board and tap them into the inner edge of the frame with a hammer, **1**, or the edge of a chisel. To seal the frame from dust and dirt, stick masking tape around the back of the frame, over the join between the frame and the backing board, **2**. This will also protect the wall from the sharp edges of the clips or sprigs. Alternatively, glue brown paper over the entire back of the frame, and, if necessary, trim the edge with a razor blade. Finally, if you are using cord or wire, secure it to the picture rings, plates or eyes and hang the picture.

1 Tap glazing points between the frame and the backing board

2 Seal the back of the frame with masking tape

156
Hanging a mirror

Mirrors are available framed, like pictures, or unframed with polished edges. The best are made from good-quality float glass, which is flat and free from imperfections. Bathroom mirrors need a well-silvered backing to resist the steam.

Framed mirrors are hung in the same way as a picture, although in a bathroom you may need to drill through a tile (*see Job 46, p. 52*). Unframed mirrors can be screwed to the wall, if you ask your glazier to drill four holes at each corner of the mirror. Undrilled, unframed mirrors can be mounted on to wooden backing board with mirror clips (which clamp the two layers together), or fixed directly to the wall with sliding clips.

Using a screw fixing
Hold the mirror up to the wall at the desired height, and make a pencil mark. Then mark where the screws are to fall in relation to the top of the mirror, using a carpenter's level. Drill the holes, and fit wallplugs. Insert round-headed mirror screws, with rubber spacer or faucet washers, to absorb irregularities in the wall and to allow air to circulate. Then hang the mirror on to the screws.

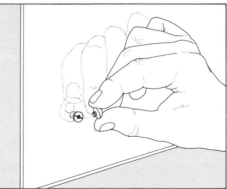

Fixing with sliding clips
A set of clips consists of two fixed clips, which support the bottom of the mirror, and two sliding clips, which secure the top. First drill holes for the bottom fixed clips. Insert wallplugs if the wall is solid, and screw in the clips. Rest the mirror on these and pencil its outline on the wall. Drill holes ½in. from the top and side edges and insert the sliding clips which grip the mirror.

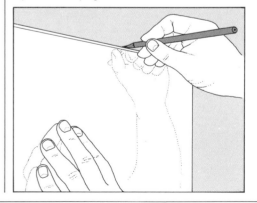

Arranging pictures and mirrors

For maximum impact and a harmonious effect, pictures and mirrors should be positioned with care. A special picture should stand on its own, provided it is not so small that it is lost in a large expanse of wall. Balance is as important as scale. It is not always a good idea to centralize a picture; it may look better offset but in harmony with a piece of furniture, for example. Smaller pictures often look best grouped together into a composite shape, but you can always try working out arrangements on the floor, before hanging them on the wall.

Mirrors can be both functional and decorative, but the positioning is crucial. A well-placed mirror can create the illusion of light and space, but it is usually wise to keep the bottom edge well above ground level.

Grouping pictures
Small pictures or photographs are often best assembled into a shape such as a pyramid or oval (right) or aligned with an imaginary line through the center of the collection. For the best effects, the individual images should perhaps be linked by a common color, style, shape or subject matter.

Creating space with mirrors
A dark, narrow corridor or a small, oppressive room will feel larger and lighter if a mirror is hung down the entire length of one wall (left). Full-length mirrored panels applied to closet doors, for example, can dramatically increase the sense of space.

Practical mirrors
Bedroom and bathroom mirrors, used as an aid to dressing and make-up, can in fact form an attractive focal point (above). Functional mirrors should be hung at a convenient height and can be positioned to link with a "back view" mirror on the back of a closet door.

Storage and shelving

Types of shelf material and support ◇ How to make a screw fixing ◇ Putting up shelves ◇ Types of storage

Well-placed storage and shelving units help to maximize the space in a home and will either conceal or display its contents. There are two basic types of shelving: a pre-fabricated adjustable shelving system to be assembled; and fixed shelves which you can build from raw materials. Fixed shelves can be attached to a wall or into an alcove. More complex home-made systems can be constructed with a wooden framework. These systems may be free-standing or secured to the wall. Storage units may also be fixed or free-standing and can be built from raw materials, assembled from a kit, or bought pre-fabricated.

Points to remember

◇ Shelf supports must be chosen for the load the shelf is intended to carry. Three average-sized paperbacks weigh 1lb, while three average-sized hard-backs weigh 2lb.
◇ Lumber yards will cut shelves to size if asked.
◇ Plan to fit built-in shelves after, not before decoration.
◇ If the carpet raises the back of a bookshelf, add a strip of wood under the front edge.
◇ The front edge of a shelf should not project more than 1in. beyond the end of its bracket support.
◇ Always fix shelves securely.

Tools and equipment

If you are buying an adjustable shelving system, you may need a hacksaw. If you have not bought your shelves pre-cut, or if you are building a wooden framework, you will need a small hand- or power saw. For boring holes, use a hand-brace and drill bit, or a power drill with a masonry bit for solid walls, and a twist drill bit for wood. Use 2in., 2½in. or 3in. countersunk screws of the correct gauge and wallplugs for solid walls, and cavity dowels or toggles for hollow walls. You will also need a measuring tape, rule and carpenter's level.

Types of shelf material

Particleboard, blockboard and plywood are the most usual materials for indoor shelving. Particleboard is readily available, reasonably priced and supplied in varying thicknesses, from ½in. to 1in. It is sold in standard widths, from 6in. upwards, to be cut to the required length. Veneered particleboard will provide extra strength. Plywood, blockboard or rough-sawn softwood is appropriate in a shed, garage or store room, while hardwood, when available, provides more expensive, high-quality shelving material. Metal is mainly restricted to pre-fabricated systems, but it is useful for heavy loads. Glass can be used for ornamental, lightweight display. Glass retailers supply standard stock sizes and will cut sheets to size and polish edges. A limited range of plastic shelving is also available.

Bearing weights
A shelf collapses because the material is inadequate for the load, or because the supports are not fixed securely to the wall. The shelving material must be the right type and thickness; the supports must be strong enough and spaced at reasonable intervals; and the screws should be long and thick enough to anchor the supports. The size is largely a matter of common sense, but the figures (below) give a guide to the maximum span between supports for medium loads.

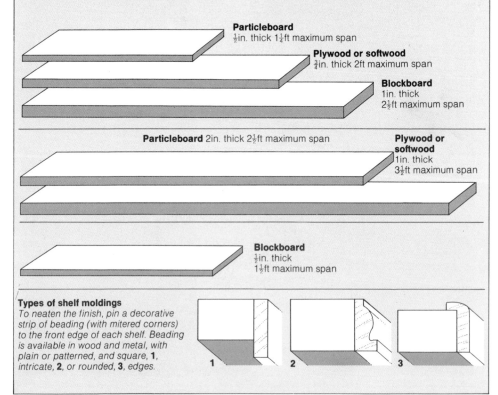

Particleboard
½in. thick 1¼ft maximum span

Plywood or softwood
¾in. thick 2ft maximum span

Blockboard
1in. thick
2½ft maximum span

Particleboard 2in. thick 2½ft maximum span

Plywood or softwood
1in. thick
3½ft maximum span

Blockboard
½in. thick
1½ft maximum span

Types of shelf moldings
To neaten the finish, pin a decorative strip of beading (with mitered corners) to the front edge of each shelf. Beading is available in wood and metal, with plain or patterned, and square, 1, intricate, 2, or rounded, 3, edges.

Types of shelf support

A variety of shelf supports is available for home-made shelving. For strong, fixed shelving, brackets or wooden and metal battens can be fixed to the wall. Some are suitable for a flush wall, others fit into an alcove. For lightweight, more adjustable shelving, pegs, dowels, plastic studs, clips and wire can be inserted into holes in wooden uprights. Fixed supports can also be used to make a built-in shelf system, and adjustable supports are useful for a free-standing unit. Alternatively, adjustable systems can be bought pre-fabricated, to be assembled at home. All these systems offer good support.

Wall-mounted fixed shelf supports

L-shaped brackets
These metal, steel or aluminum brackets come in 6-24in. sizes to fit standard shelf widths and are fixed to a flush wall. The front edges of the shelf should not project beyond 1in. of the bracket tip, so choose a suitable size and thickness.

Cantilever brackets
These metal rods are inserted into a hole in the wall and into the back edge of the shelf at each end. They are made of impact-resistant plastic and are molded to a high-tensile steel pin for extra strength. They come in 5in. and 7½in. sizes and fit at each end of the shelf.

Triangular brackets
These are only used for fitting a shelf in an alcove. The triangular section fits against the side wall and the shelf sits on the ledge.

Wooden battens
These lengths of wood are fixed to the walls to support the edges of the shelf and are also only suitable in a recess, since they have no supporting arm. The battens are usually 1in. × 1in., 1½in. × 1in. or 2in. × 1in., according to the load the shelf will have to support, and are cut to the required length. For a standard shelf, spanning a small recess and supporting a light load, you will need only two side battens. For wider spans and heavier loads, fix an extra (narrower) batten to the back wall.

Angled metal strips
These strips are "L-shaped" in cross-section and are used in place of wooden battens. They are cut to length with a hacksaw and secured to the side walls through pre-drilled holes. The shelf sits within the "L", so it is important that it does not fit too tightly against the wall.

Panel-mounted adjustable shelf supports

Pegs
These metal or plastic "pegs" or studs, which come in various shapes and sizes, slot into a hole in a wooden upright. The holes are spaced at equal intervals up the length of the upright and four pegs are inserted at each level to sit under each corner of the shelf for an invisible fixing.

Pegs for glass
Metal slotted pegs are designed to grip a plate of glass and are plugged into pre-drilled holes. Other types have a soft, felt pad for the glass shelf to sit on.

Dowels
Wooden dowels can be cut to length and simply tapped into snug fitting holes, at each corner of the shelf.

Invisible wire support
Holes are drilled in the uprights to hold the ends of a shaped length of ⅛in. galvanized wire. The ends of the shelf are grooved and slide over the wire which supports the shelf horizontally at each side.

Two-part clips
These metal clips support heavier weights. The socket part fits into an ¾in. diameter hole, drilled ½in. deep. The angled bracket then slots into the socket until it locks, and its other arm supports the shelf.

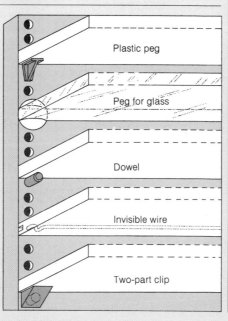

L-shaped bracket

Wooden batten

Triangular batten

Angled metal strip

Cantilever bracket

Plastic peg

Peg for glass

Dowel

Invisible wire

Two-part clip

Pre-fabricated adjustable shelving

These systems consist of aluminum uprights and brackets, and may include shelf material. Most systems are made in a satin, white or colored finish, and some come in anodized silver and gold, enameled black, brass or bronze. A limited range of wooden systems is also available.

Bookcase strips
An alternative adjustable metal system takes clips instead of brackets. The strips are usually available in 3ft lengths in bronze or zinc-plated steel. The strip is cut to size and four lengths are screwed to the sides of an alcove or to the side panels of a bookcase. For a neater finish, the strips can be rabbeted into side panels. Bookcase clips slot into the strip and come in a variety of shapes and sizes. Some are designed for heavy loads, some for glass shelves, and others for wooden shelves.

Uprights and brackets
*The uprights are available with regularly spaced square, oval, **2**, T-shaped, **3**, or double slots into which the brackets fit, allowing a wide choice of shelf heights. Alternatively, the upright may have a continuous channel, **1**, which allows the brackets to be fixed at any point. Both types are usually available in lengths ranging from 2½ft to 7ft and can be trimmed to size with a hacksaw. Those with a continuous channel are easier to fit, since it is not so critical that the two uprights line up perfectly, provided they are vertical. Some systems come complete with screws and wall-plugs; others recommend the size of screw needed to secure the upright to the wall. The brackets vary from 6in. to 2ft deep and should be chosen to suit the depth of the shelf. Brackets for the slotted system have lugs which hook on to the slots. Continuous channel brackets are usually L-shaped and come with a clip, which is locked with an integral screw.*

1

2

3

Basic technique

How to make a screw fixing

Most shelf supports need to be secured to a wall or panel by means of screws. The weight of the load will determine the size and strength of the screw, and the type of wall will determine the style of the fixing. For most shelves you will need 2in.- or 2½in.- or 3in.-long screws, according to the size of shelf. Likewise, you should choose a screw gauge suitable for the maximum shelf weight. No. 6 screws are adequate only for light weights, while No. 10 screws will support a heavily laden shelf. Use these two extremes as a guide for choosing a suitable gauge. Screws will not grip on their own in masonry or plasterboard, so in most cases, you will have to use some sort of wallplug (see *The Home Tool kit, p. 225*).

Fixing screws in solid walls
Choose a wallplug to match the screw size. Then, using a masonry drill bit the same diameter as the wallplug, drill a hole into the wall to the depth of the wallplug, 1. To prevent the drill bit slipping before you begin, make a small indentation in the wall by turning the drill manually. Plaster is not strong so be sure to penetrate deeper into the masonry. To avoid drilling too far, however, wrap some adhesive tape around the drill bit, the length of the plug away from the tip. Insert the wallplug into the hole, 2, and drive in the screw. The plug will then expand and the screw will be held securely in the wall. Take care, however, not to tighten the screw so hard that it breaks through the end of the plug. Do not drill holes near electrical switches or outlets or if you think pipes may run behind the wall; it could prove dangerous.

1 Drill a hole in the wall with a masonry drill bit

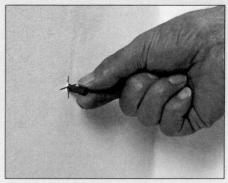
2 Push the wallplug into the hole

Fixing screws in cavity walls
A partition wall is too thin to allow a screw to grip sufficiently. Special "toggles" and expanding wallplugs are available to hold the screw in place. They are inserted into the wall, like a closed umbrella, 1, and when they no longer meet the resistance of the wall their "wings" open and anchor the fixing in position. Drill a small hole, just wide and deep enough to take the plug or toggle, and drive in the screw, 2, while maintaining tension by pulling back the fitting. This pressure will cause the plug or toggle to expand or open and so gives the screw a surface to grip on. If you have a partition wall with a wooden framework, it is best to drill and screw directly into the studs supports for a secure fixing. To locate the studs uprights, tap the wall and where it makes a dull sound, make your drill holes. If the studs are inconveniently positioned, screw on a batten to span two studs.

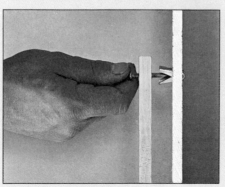
1 Push the toggle into a pre-drilled hole

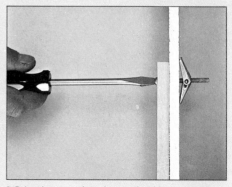
2 Drive the screw into the toggle with a screwdriver

Fixing screws in wooden surfaces
If you are attaching wooden side panels to alcove walls or putting up a wooden batten, you will need to make screw holes through the wood and into the wall. To ensure straight fixing holes, try drilling right through the wood and into the wall in one go. Using a twist drill bit, drill a hole slightly smaller than the screw. This will ensure that it grips well. Alternatively drill a pilot hole, then countersink the hole, 1. Insert a wallplug, tap it flush, then tap the screw into the end of the plug. When the end of the plug lies flush with the wall, drive in the screw with a screwdriver, until it lies just below the surface, 2. The countersunk screw can be covered with a wooden plug for an invisible fixing. Simply glue the plug into place, ensuring that the grain direction matches the surrounding wood. For larger holes, use a handbrace and bit, or a power drill and flat bit.

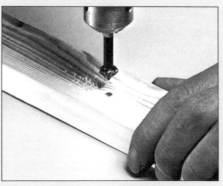
1 Use a countersink bit to widen the opening of the hole

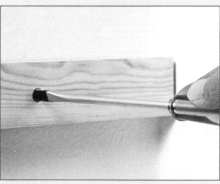
2 Drive the screw into the wood until it is countersunk

157

Putting up a fixed shelf

When you have decided how much weight the shelf is to bear, choose a suitable thickness and width of shelving and sufficiently sturdy brackets and screws. L-shaped brackets are the best for fixed shelves. For small shelves or if your wall is even, it is worth fixing the bracket to the shelf before screwing it to the wall. If your wall is uneven, or if the shelf is very long, it may prove easier to put the brackets on the wall first, then fix the shelf to the brackets. If the shelf is to bear a very heavy load, it is best to use cantilever brackets.

Fixing brackets to the wall
If you intend to add beading, pin a strip of wood or metal beading to the front edge of the shelf first. Then hold the shelf up to the wall with a carpenter's level on top, and when you have it at the correct height and level, mark the position of both brackets on the wall. Drill two holes in the wall for the first bracket, and when it is in position,

1 *Screw the second bracket to the wall in line with the first*

insert and tighten the screws, **1** (see Basic technique, p. 170). *Then repeat for the second bracket. With the two brackets in position on the wall, put the shelf on top, center it over the brackets and push it firmly against the wall. When it is in position, screw the first bracket to the underside of the shelf, **2**. Check that the shelf is straight, then screw the second bracket to the shelf.*

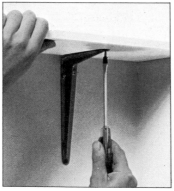

2 *Screw the bracket to the underside of the shelf*

Fixing cantilever brackets
Mark a horizontal line on the wall against a carpenter's level, to indicate the shelf height, then mark drill holes for the cantilever pins, taking care to position them the correct distance apart. Drill two $\frac{1}{4}$ in. diameter holes in the wall, $2\frac{1}{2}$ in. deep and at a perfectly horizontal angle. Insert the cantilever pins into the holes, and mark a second set of drill holes through the fixing holes. Remove the bracket, drill the holes and insert a wallplug in each. Replace the bracket and fix a screw through the fixing hole into the wallplug.

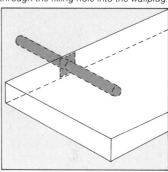

158

Fitting alcove shelving

Recessed shelving can be supported by wooden battens, angled metal strips or triangular brackets, which are fitted to the wall in the same way as L-shaped brackets. If, however, the walls are very uneven, it may be best to make two wooden side uprights to fit against the walls and fix the shelves to them.

Fixing battens
Cut three battens to length, one to span the back wall, and two for the side walls, each slightly shorter than the width of the shelf. Drill holes in the battens, every 2 in., then drill corresponding holes in the wall, along the horizontal line. Insert wallplugs and screw the battens into position. Place the shelf in the alcove and rest it on the battens. If the side walls are not perfectly straight, you will have to shape the side edges of the shelf to fit.

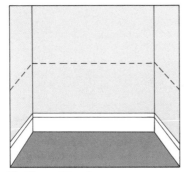

Marking out the alcove
Use a carpenter's level to mark position guides for the battens on each of the three walls at the height of each shelf. Measure the alcove width and cut the shelves to size.

159

Fixing adjustable shelving

Pre-fabricated systems are easy to assemble. The uprights are fixed to the wall, the brackets are slotted or screwed into position at the appropriate level and the shelves slide into place. When assembling the shelving, remember that the uprights must be fixed at the same height if the shelves are to sit level. If you need to cut the uprights to length, use a small hacksaw.

Securing the uprights
*Fix the first left-hand upright to the wall with one screw at the top and let it hang. Then use a carpenter's level to bring it into vertical line and mark drilling holes down the wall, **1**. Swing the upright aside to drill and plug the holes, then screw it into place. Clip a bracket to the left-hand upright, and use a shelf and carpenter's level to bring the right-hand upright into line. Clip on a parallel bracket, **2**, and when the shelf is straight, mark a fixing hole for the right-hand upright. Remove the shelf and brackets and screw the right-hand upright to the wall at the top. To align it, fix three shelves at the top, center and bottom, and mark drilling holes. Then drill, plug and screw as before.*

1 *Use a carpenter's level to align the left-hand upright*

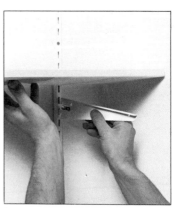

2 *Use a shelf to level the right-hand upright before fixing it*

Types of storage units

There are three basic types of storage system: fitted, free-standing and modular. Fitted cabinets have the advantage of maximizing storage space, while free-standing systems can be easily transferred to a different room or home and can be used as room dividers. Modular units may be free-standing or fixed, but those attached to the wall will support heavier weights than a free-standing unit. Many storage systems are available as a pre-fabricated kit to be assembled at home, but if you need to work to exact requirements, it may be best to build your own.

Before you start work on assembling a kit, it is best to check that all the parts, screws, block joints and cam joints have been included, and to spend a little time working out the construction principles, and the purpose of each element. It will then be easier to follow the instructions.

Modular units

Units built up from shelves, drawers and cabinets into complete storage systems offer flexibility and the choice of open storage for decoration and closed storage for protection. The system can be adapted or enlarged to suit your needs: some sophisticated designs even incorporate closets with sliding or louvered doors, drop-flap desk tops and glass doors. Two modules can be spaced apart to allow a shelf or desk top to rest on top, and a conglomerate of shelves and drawers can be arranged to produce boxed-in storage areas within the system. Free-standing modular units are easier to assemble than fitted ones, since they do not depend on the angles of the walls and corners. They can also be used as room dividers, though tall units should be weighed down at the bottom, to prevent toppling.

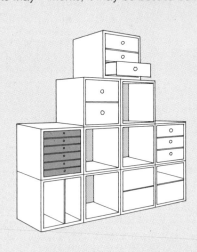

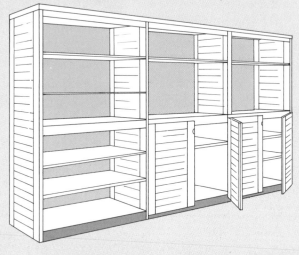

Built-in units

Fitted closets come in a variety of forms. They may be designed to fit into fireplace alcoves, to turn a corner, to span a bed or to bridge the gap between kitchen fixtures. It is vitally important to measure precisely before buying, since a fraction of an inch can make all the difference. If the cabinet is too big, you may have to call in a carpenter, if it is too small, you may be able to close the gap with a length of wood. Fitted cabinets must also be firmly attached to the wall, particularly if they are raised off the ground. Sliding, folding and up-and-over hinged doors and those with concealed hinges, help to increase the working or living space in a small area.

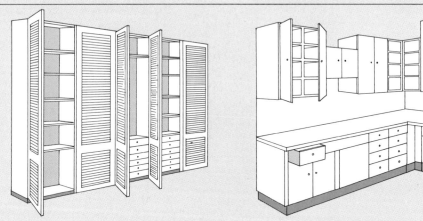

Free-standing drawer units

Drawers can be introduced into the house in one of three ways. They may be bought pre-fabricated, incorporated into a piece of furniture, such as a chest of drawers, or a kitchen storage unit; they can be bought as a kit, or they can be built from raw materials. Drawer kits come with side and corner pieces, and, in some cases, $\frac{1}{8}$in. thick white hardboard for the drawer bottom, and a front panel. You would use a three-sided kit if you wanted to supply your own front panel to match the rest of your furniture. Molded drawers, made from high-impact polystyrene, are also available and molded inserts can be added to create extra compartments.

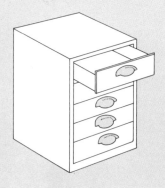

Using storage space

Every room offers more storage space than meets the eye. Under beds, sofas and window seats, over doors, beds and staircases, in corners, attics and cellars, and behind doors, there is usually space to be used. Storage units can be built around washbasin pedestals, to span alcoves and overhang beds; closets can be fitted to the full height of the wall, and extra shelves to be added to cabinets. Fold-away and pull-out tables and beds help to keep the living area of the room clear. Practical storage ideas can also be decorative, and it is worth improvising for individual effects. Everyday items such as shoes can be openly displayed on hooks, for example; and old tins, paint cans, and barrels make useful and attractive containers. Ideally, all storage and shelving systems should be versatile, so they can be moved to another room, extended, enlarged or adjusted to take different contents. Keep an eye open for the decorative possibilities of storage systems.

Using grids and hooks
Hanging racks and hooks provide convenient and easy-to-reach storage in a busy kitchen (below). They also make an inexpensive and attractive grid frame for clumps of herbs and cooking utensils (below). Wall hooks and rails likewise form an ideal storage system for tools.

Using attic space
The existing room shape will often suggest storage space. Alcoves, corners or the space created by the slope of an attic roof (right) can be transformed into attractive features, while housing books, ornaments or household items. Cellars and attics need to be warm and dry for storage.

Using window space
Light filtering through objects displayed on window shelves and sills adds interest to a simple arrangement (above). Window shelves also help to disguise an ugly view, but the window must be sealed.

Appliance fault-finding

Detecting basic faults
Mending small electrical
appliances ◇ Mending large
electrical appliances

Most electrical appliances give years of reliable, trouble-free service. But when they receive hard and regular use over the years, some breakdown is to be expected. Faults are always irritating, not least because we take smooth running for granted, yet many problems can be solved quickly and easily. Basic faults such as disconnected wires or dirty contacts can be corrected in a matter of minutes and it is always worth checking these as a matter of course before consulting a specialist. Some internal faults can be easily fixed when you know how to do it.

Points to remember

◇ Unplug any electrical appliance
◇ Buy and use only Underwriter's Laboratories (UL) listed equipment.
◇ Always operate and maintain appliances in accordance with instructional material supplied with it by the maker.
◇ Do not experiment. If you are not sure of the nature of the problem or solution, call in a professional. Remember that electricity can kill.

For more information on Electricity, see pp. 180-3.

160
Detecting basic faults

When an appliance stops working, it is usually a result of a lack of a complete electrical circuit. Somewhere between the service main in the home and the working portion of the device, a break exists through which electricity is not flowing. Check the basics before dismantling the device.

Checking power to the receptacle
If an appliance fails to function, the fault may lie in the household wiring rather than the appliance itself. Try another appliance in the same receptacle; a lamp is easy to work with, or if you have one, a tester. If the outlet has no power, check the other outlets in the room. If they work, the problem is a loose connection in the bad outlet, but if all of them are without power, the fuse or circuit breaker has blown. Find the source of the overload, correct it, and restore the circuit breaker.

Checking the plug
If there is power arriving to and exiting from the receptacle, then the problem may lie between the plug and the appliance. If the plug does not fit firmly into the outlet, the prongs may be bent or not making solid contact with the contacts in the receptacle. If the prongs are folded, insert a screwdriver between the layers and spread them slightly to improve contact. If they seem very dull in color, or tarnished, use a light sand paper to remove the oxide build up. Finally, if the plug can be opened, examine the wires from the cord and their connections with the terminal screws for loose wires or short circuits.

Checking the cord
If the plug is solid plastic, or the wires are firmly connected to the screws in the plug, examine the length of cord leading from the plug to the appliance. Any obvious signs of damage, such as cuts or blackened insulation signal that the cord must be replaced. If it seems in good condition, remove the case of the appliance to check the contacts that link the cord to the internal working parts. Each wire, including the green ground wire if present, must be firmly held in place without any loose strands.

Appliance	Symptom
Drip type coffee maker (gravity)	Coffee does not keep war
	Ready light does not work
Electric iron	Iron will not heat/control lamp is not lighting
	Iron will not heat/control lamp glows
	Iron overheats or underheats
Upright vacuum cleaner	Vacuum overheats/loss of suction
Cylinder vacuum cleaner	Loss of suction power
	Intermittent power
Toaster	Toaster will not heat
	Toast does not brown

Correcting faults in small appliances

Cause	Cure	Where to look
Failed keep-warm element	**Replace keep-warm element** Remove the base screws and pull off the rubber feet and bottom plate. Unscrew the nut holding the element guard and remove the old keep-warm element. Then remove the screws from the top unit, pull the casing and remove the reservoirs. Use long-nosed pliers to disconnect the lead wires from the terminal board and slide out the main element. Remove the retaining rod and separate the element from its pan. In some models, the entire heating arrangement can be replaced as a single unit. In others, the main and keep-warm elements are fitted individually. Specify the model number when you order a replacement. Reverse the procedure to reassemble the coffee maker.	Top unit Main element Keep-warm element Bottom plate
Failed light	**Replace light** Disconnect the leads from the terminals within the base. Push out the old light. Insert a new light and reconnect the terminals.	
Damaged cord	**Replace cord** Fit a braided, non-kink cord of the correct rating for the iron.	
Failed element	**Replace element** Locate the cover fixing screws and lift the cover off to expose the element. Disconnect the cord connections from the element and remove the element from the sole plate. Find an exact replacement for the element, fit it into position, reconnect it to the cord connections and replace the cover and screw it back on.	Cord connections Thermostat contacts Element Sole plate
Failed thermostat	**Replace thermostat** Thermostats are tricky to replace, so take it to a specialist.	
Failed drive belt	**Replace drive belt** Remove the cover plate from the front, then turn the cleaner over and remove the metal cover. Pry out the roller, slip off the old belt and fit a new one of the same type and size around the roller. Replace the roller and metal shield, turn the cleaner right way up and hook the new belt over the drive pulley, following the diagram on the casing. If there is no diagram, hook it on one way and if the belt slips off, hook it on the other way.	Drive pulley Drive belt Roller
Punctured hose	**Replace the hose** For a temporary repair, bind the hose with electrician's tape. For a long-term repair, remove the hose from its slot and insert an identical hose.	
Worn carbon brushes	**Replace carbon brushes** Take to a specialist.	
Failed element	**Replace the element** You will have to work carefully and methodically or you will upset the pop-up mechanism. Open the toaster and have a look at the mechanism, and if you can see how it works, unscrew the old element and fit a new one. If the toast will not pop up, you will have to take the toaster to a specialist since the mechanism is very intricate.	Element Pop-up mechanism
Faulty thermostat	**Replace the thermostat** Take it to a specialist or return to the manufacturer.	

Correcting faults in large appliances

Appliance	Symptom	Cause	Cure	Where to look
Electric range	Element will not heat	Faulty ring	**Replace element** Disconnect the range, then lift the cooktop and undo the box-like cover to gain access to the element terminal. Remove the screw on the element fixing plate, free it from the cooktop and disconnect the faulty element from its terminals. Fit the new element by reversing the operation. Call a professional for faulty controls or a failed grill.	Electric element
Gas cooker	Automatic lighter fails	Blocked burner pilot	**Unblock the burner pilot** Use a long pin to clear debris in the pilot jet.	
Dishwasher	Slow washing	Clogged drain screen or inlet holes	**Clear obstructions** Empty the perforated metal or plastic drain screen at the bottom of the cabinet. Then if the machine has a sprayer that sprays water into the cabinet, lift it off and clean it under a faucet to prevent the mineral deposits forming around the inlet holes. If inlet or outlet hoses have perished, replace as for a washing machine.	
	Dishes will not dry	Faulty blower or element	**Replace blower or element** Consult a professional.	Screen
Washing machine	Leaks	Perished inlet hose Perished internal hose Perished door seal	**Replace inlet hose** The inlet hose may perish if the faucets are not turned off when the machine is not in use. Turn off the main supply, remove the old hose and fit a new hose with new threaded couplers. Fit the couplers on to the supply pipe at one end of the hose and on to the machine inlet at the other. **Replace internal hose** To replace an internal hose, use a screwdriver to undo the worm drive or wire clamp holding the hose in place, and smear a little petroleum jelly over the spigots before slipping the hose into place. **Replace door seal** The door seal usually fits in a channel around the door. Remove the old one and press the new one into place. If the seal links the cylinder of the machine with the casing, leave the repair to a service engineer.	Internal hose
Tumble dryer	Over-heating/ slow drying	Build-up of lint in the lint screen	**Clear the screen** Lint and fibers collect in the screen, so try to clean it out every time the machine is used, or once a week. Other faults, including problems with the heat setting control, door switch or motor should be dealt with by a professional.	
	No power	Loose connection	**Check the plug and cord** Reconnect any loose cores.	Door seal
Spin dryer	Drum will not revolve/pump will not work	Faulty drive belt	**Fit new drive belt** Turn the machine on its side, unscrew the bottom plate and examine the drive belt. If it has become dislodged from its groove, adjust it into its correct position. If the old belt has snapped or worn thin, replace it. Match the length and thickness of the old belt, and stretch the new belt over the pulleys and fit them into the grooves.	
	Excessive vibration	Worn bearings	**Replace the bearings** Consult a professional.	Drum drive belt Pump drive belt

Home maintenance

Electricity ◇ Plumbing ◇ Heating ◇ Insulation
Roofs and guttering ◇ External walls
Weatherproofing ◇ Wood rot and infestation
Home safety ◇ Home security

It is tempting to leave home maintenance until things start to go wrong. But if you keep a regular check on the essential services of the house, and undertake necessary work at an early stage, you can hold down household and repair bills, increase the value of your house, and ensure comfort and safety in all weathers. This chapter maps out the electrical, plumbing and heating systems, details how they operate and gives instructions on simple upkeep and repair. It concentrates on the structure of the house, suggests how to solve problems such as damp, wood rot and infestation, explains the guttering system and gives advice on preventing fires, floods, accidents and burglaries. While major structural work and difficult installations are not included, the chapter covers all the important aspects of basic home upkeep – from fitting a light switch and clearing a blocked drain to insulating an attic and repairing stucco and siding.

Electricity

The electrical system ◇ Types of wire, cable, and fixture ◇ Fitting a ceiling light ◇ Wiring a light switch ◇ Wiring an outlet ◇ Wiring a plug Replacing a fuse

Electricity can kill. It is therefore essential to take great care in its everyday use, and to carry out all electrical work in the home to the highest possible standard. Never tackle any electrical task unless you know exactly how to go about it and understand fully what you are doing. If you are not sure about anything, employ a fully qualified electrician.

Before you start any electrical job, get to know the basic principles of how household electricity works. The diagrams on the opposite page show how electricity arrives in your home and how the wiring beneath the floors and behind the walls makes up the various different electrical circuits. Understanding these diagrams is important even if you do not want to replace the fixed wiring, because they show you why you should connect the wires in a particular way. Once you know why the system works in the way it does, you will be much less likely to make mistakes.

Points to remember

◇ Before working on the fixed wiring turn off the house's main disconnect, whether it be a lever, fuse or circuit breaker. Do the same for the circuit on which you are working.
◇ Leave a note on the service panel explaining to others what you are doing, so they do not reactivate the circuit.
◇ Double check that the circuit is dead by plugging in an appliance or by using a mains tester.
◇ Use cables, cords, plugs, and fuses of the correct rating for the circuits and appliances they serve.
◇ Always unplug any portable appliance from the power outlet before attempting to repair it.
◇ Always use good quality materials that conform to UL specifications and are marked as such.

Color coding for electric wires
In this section, the wires have been color-coded as: black for hot, white for neutral and brown for grounds and jumper wires. In a real cord, the ground is usually a bare copper wire; jumper wires are green, and hot wires may be red or black.

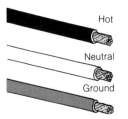

Hot

Neutral

Ground

Tips for care of plugs and cords

◇ Check all your plugs and cords at least once a year to ensure that they are not worn or damaged.
◇ Repair all loose connections and replace damaged cords. Do not attempt to splice worn, frayed or heat-damaged cords.
◇ Keep cords short.
◇ Keep cords away from heat sources such as stoves, heaters, or fires.
◇ Make sure that each appliance has a cord of the correct rating and that the total amperage of appliances attached to a circuit does not exceed its fuse rating.
◇ All permanent wiring must be installed with grounded cable.
◇ Every receptacle on a circuit must be grounded.

A guide to electrical terms

Amp Unit measuring the "amount" of current flowing in a circuit.
Circuit Complete, circular path to and from the power source through which electricity flows.
Conductor Substance, such as a metal wire, that can carry an electric current.
Earth or **ground** Pathway along which an electric current can flow safely to the ground if a fault develops.
Fuse also **circuit breaker** Protective device that cuts off the current if the circuit is overloaded or a fault occurs.
Live also **hot** The core of a wire or cable carrying current to where it is needed, or any terminal to which the live wire is connected.
Neutral The core of a wire or cable carrying current back to its source, or any terminal to which the neutral wire is connected.
Volt Unit measuring the electrical "pressure" driving the current around a circuit.
Watt Unit measuring the amount of power consumed by any electrical device.

Power consumption

The amount of electricity you use is measured in kilowatt-hours, commonly written "kwh". The number of kwh used is calculated by multiplying the rating of the appliance in kilowatts by the number of hours for which it is used. So a 2kw appliance used for half an hour consumes one unit of electricity ($2 \times \frac{1}{2} = 1$).

Common power ratings

Oven range	Food processor	Radio
4-8kw	*0·2kw*	*0·1kw*
Cooktop range	Water heater	Black and white TV
4-8kw	*4-5kw*	*0·25kw*
Refrigerator	Coffee maker	Color TV
0·7-1·2kw	*0·85-1·5kw*	*0·3kw*
Freezer	Vacuum cleaner	Music center
0·72-1kw	*0·25-0·8kw*	*0·5kw*
Clothes washer	Stationary heater	Light bulb
0·8-1kw	*1·6kw*	*0·024-0·2kw*
Clothes dryer	Portable heater	Room air conditioner
0·8-1kw	*1-1·5kw*	*0·8-1·6kw*

The electrical system

The fixed wiring in your home is the system of cables which carries electricity from the service entrance through the service panel and throughout the home. It must be of a correct rating and type for its task, and properly installed. Circuits are the portion of this system which run as cables from the service panel to sections of your home, or to specific appliances.

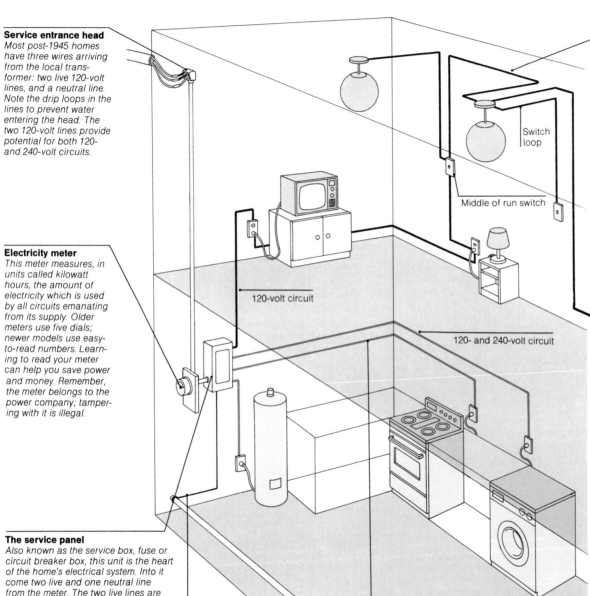

Service entrance head
Most post-1945 homes have three wires arriving from the local transformer: two live 120-volt lines, and a neutral line. Note the drip loops in the lines to prevent water entering the head. The two 120-volt lines provide potential for both 120- and 240-volt circuits.

Electricity meter
This meter measures, in units called kilowatt hours, the amount of electricity which is used by all circuits emanating from its supply. Older meters use five dials; newer models use easy-to-read numbers. Learning to read your meter can help you save power and money. Remember, the meter belongs to the power company; tampering with it is illegal.

The service panel
Also known as the service box, fuse or circuit breaker box, this unit is the heart of the home's electrical system. Into it come two live and one neutral line from the meter. The two live lines are fitted with a main disconnect, usually a fuse or circuit breaker of 100 to 200 amps. From it emanate the circuits which carry electricity to the home. Typically there will be a 240-volt circuit for the water heater, and perhaps another for the air conditioning, a 120/240-volt circuit for the range, and a number of 120-volt lines for the power and lights. Each circuit is protected by a fuse or circuit breaker of a particular amperage; never replace a fuse with one of a higher amperage.

Grounding electrode wire
The wire runs from the neutral bus bar in the service panel (which is directly wired to all the outlets, switches, and all grounded appliances) to a metal shaft in the ground. Deeply buried water pipes are commonly used as grounds. Some states require a special copper stake.

Switch loop

Middle of run switch

120-volt circuit

120- and 240-volt circuit

120-volt power circuits
The power that is supplied to the power outlets, lights and switches in the home is 120 volts, except for special circuits, which account for about five percent. Each circuit supplies, as a general rule, about eight power or lighting outlets. A circuit cable contains wires of a suitable gauge for carrying the required electrical load; typically, a 120-volt circuit is made up of a number 10 AWG wire (see p. 180), and runs for 70ft. The length of the line also effects its amp rating. Circuits are protected by fuses or breakers on the live line at the service panel. Three wires are contained in the cable; a black live line, a white neutral line, and a bare ground line (both the white and bare lines are connected to the neutral bus bar at the service panel). At each outlet, the live and neutral lines are connected to the fixtures to provide power to that outlet, and to continue their run. Outlets or lights in the middle of the circuit are called "middle of the run", those at the end are called "end of the run". When ceiling lights controlled by wall switches come in the middle of the run, a special system called a switch loop is used.

Special circuits
A number of special circuits are also distributed from the service panel. One may be a 120-volt line that leads to a transformer, which steps the power down to twelve volts, for a door bell. Another may be a 120/240-volt circuit which leads to an electric oven.

This appliance needs normal 120-volt power for its timer, but needs 240-volt power to supply the heating elements. These circuits consist of two live lines – usually black and red, and one neutral white line for the 120-volt line, plus a bare ground wire. If the service panel has circuit

breakers, this type of circuit will have two; one for each live line. Another special circuit may be a 240-volt line which leads directly to a water heater or air conditioner. These too will have two live lines, but no white; the live lines alternate as returns for each other.

Types of wire, cable and cord

The diameter of a wire conductor determines its current carrying capacity, and is measured by its American Wire Gauge number (AWG). Cables are insulated collections of wires which carry electricity to and throughout the house. Cords are flexible cables that link outlets with appliances. For safety, the correct conductor must be used in each different application.

Wires
Each wire has written on its side an AWG number and a set of letters which denote the type of insulation. The National Electric code has a table of ampacity ratings which specify which gauge of wire and which length should be used for specific situations. For example, 11 gauge wire can carry up to 20 amps safely for a distance of up to 35ft. The letter guide informs you where the wire can safely be used. For example, T stands for thermoplastic, plastic which covers a large temperature range, and W denotes a weatherproof rating. Be sure and get the proper gauge and insulation type for each job.

NO. 18 AWG
7 amps for doorbells, hi-fi speakers
NO. 12 AWG
20 amps standard 120-v circuits
NO. 10 AWG
30 amps 120-v appliances
NO. 6 AWG
55 amps 240-v major appliances
SPT or "zip cords" *light duty (lamps)*

Cables and cords
Multi-conductor cables range in size from "zip cord", to the large cables which carry electricity from the generator. Cables used around the home generally contain three wires: one bare wire, for the ground or earth circuit, and two wires in individual insulations. White-colored wires are used for the neutral or return line, colored wires (usually black or red) are used for the live line. As with individual wires, it is the collection of variables that determine which cable is suitable for a particular job; the wire gauge, number of wires, type of insulation, and flexibility. Check with the NEC chart or a qualified electrician before purchasing wire.

HPD or "Heater cord"; *wires in asbestos sheath*
NM, or Nonmetallic *sheathed cable for household circuits; paper and plastic insulation*
AC metal clad *paper and thermoplastic insulation*

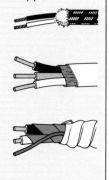

Types of electrical fixture

As well as simple fixtures and outlets, there are a number of fixtures that can make your electrical installation more flexible. Multiple (two-, three- or four-way) switches and outlets, dimmer switches, and timer switches are all quite simple to install in an existing circuit. There are also special outlets and plugs for stoves, dryers, and air conditioners.

Ceiling fixture
The basic fixture is bolted to a strap which is in turn bolted to a ceiling box.

Junction box
This is an outlet box with a solid cover containing only wire connections.

Light switches
As well as single switches, two-, three-, and four-way versions are available for controlling several lights.

Alternative light switches
Dimmers are popular in living rooms. Timer switches save money and help protect the home.

Single-pole switch | Three-way switch | Timer switch | Dimmer switch

Porcelain flange socket
This fixture attaches directly to an outlet box, eliminating the need for added cord.

Outlet boxes
There are many different boxes available in metal or plastic, and in square, octagonal, or extended shapes. Choose the box which best suits your situation by asking your electrical dealer for advice.

Special receptacles
120/240-volt appliances need special plugs and receptacles. Check for appropriate equipment in each instance.

Ground fault interrupters
GFI receptacles are expensive, but provide added protection against electric shocks.

Lamp sockets
These hold the bulb and are available with or without switches, depending on your needs.

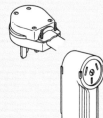

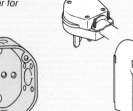

Estimating time

These times assume that the fixed wiring is in position and all you have to do is connect the cable and attach the fixture.

Lighting

Fitting a ceiling light
(1/4)-(1/2) hour

Fitting a fluorescent light
(1/2)-(1) hour

Wiring a light switch
(1) hour

Power

Fitting a 120-volt outlet
(1/2)-(1 1/2) hours

Wiring a 120/240-volt outlet
(1)-(1 1/2) hours

Rewiring a lamp
(1/2)-(1 1/2) hours

Fitting a plug
(1/4)-(1/2) hour

Replacing a fuse
(1/4) hour

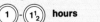

Tools and equipment

For everyday electrical repairs and emergencies there are several inexpensive items that should be stored near the service panel. The most important of these are: a flashlight, Lineman's pliers, a utility knife, a multi-purpose electrician's tool, insulated screwdrivers, electrician's tape, and the proper replacement fuses if your service panel is not equipped with circuit breakers.

A voltage tester, either in the form of a screwdriver or a neon bulb and housing with two leads, is also essential. A set of long-nosed pliers and wire caps of differing sizes will probably come in handy too. Larger scale repairs and extension work will require more specialized tools such as fish tapes and continuity testers.

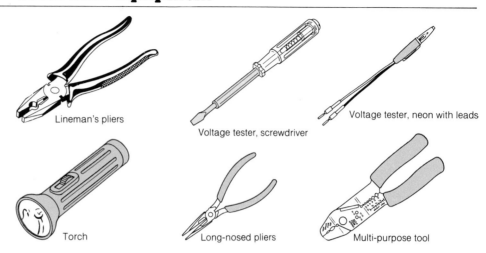

Lineman's pliers

Voltage tester, screwdriver

Voltage tester, neon with leads

Torch

Long-nosed pliers

Multi-purpose tool

161

Fitting a ceiling light

Outlet boxes for ceiling fixtures should always be connected securely to a joist or stud, either directly or by way of a hanger bar or furring strip. On large fixtures, either a bolt centered in the box (called a stud)

or a strap bolted to the box tabs will support the weight of the unit. The wires enter the outlet box through a knock-out section on its side or back, and are either directly screwed into the lamp holder (black wire to brass screw, white wire to silver screw) or they are connected by wire nuts to wires already attached to it (black to black, white to white). Tape this connection securely.

Mounting a ceiling light
First determine how the new fixture is mounted; is it a central-, strap- or direct-mounted unit? A direct-mounted unit has no wiring of its own. Connect the black house wire to the brass screw then the white wire to the silver screw and simply screw the fixture on through the box tabs. With a central- or strap-mounted unit, make sure that the box is the same

type or modify it. For a strap-mounted fixture attach a strap to the box either by way of the mounting tabs, or by using a locknut to secure it to a central stud. For a central-mounted unit, use a reducing nut or nipple to match the cap nut of the lamp. In all cases, connect the wires – black-to-black and white-to-white with wire caps of the correct size.

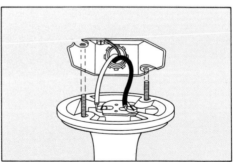

With a direct-mounted unit, insert the mounting screws in the box tabs and tighten

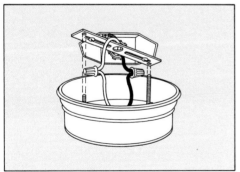

With a strap-mounted fixture, screw the strap to the box through the tabs

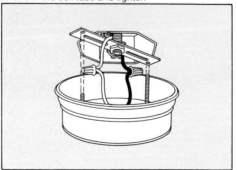

If the box has a central stud, connect the strap to it with a locknut

---

162

Fitting a fluorescent light

Despite their higher purchase price, fluorescent lights are far more economical than incandescents. They provide more light using less power for a longer period of time. To install them involves no special complications. You use a stud, nipple and nut system to secure it to the outlet box, and connect matching wires together using wire nuts and tape. Be sure to attach the ground wire to the metal case.

Installing a fitting
In the center of the back of the channel casing of the fixture you should find a pre-cut punch out. If it is of similar size to the outlet box's stud, use a stud and nipple nut combination. If it is a

larger cut out, use a strap mounted on the inside of the channel to hold the fixture to the ceiling. With both single and double bulbs, the wiring should be: white-to-white, black-to-black, and ground to channel.

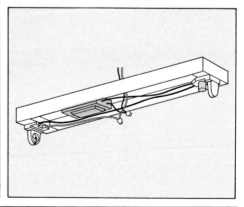

163
Wiring a light switch

The wall-mounted light switch is a sturdy piece of equipment; it will generally last up to twenty years. Thus the reason to replace it is generally for upgrading. Today the choice is wide: silent, dimmer, time-delayed or time-controlled switches and others. But whatever type you choose, it must have the same number of poles as the one you are replacing. Single pole switches provide single-location control for a light; three and four pole switches are used in gangs where more than one switch is used to control the same light. In this case, you must replace like with like. The number of wires in the switch box can range from three to eight, depending on its job. But in most cases, there are only three or four wires which have to be removed and replaced. If in doubt, tape and mark each wire as you remove it. Before inspecting any switch, you must turn off the circuit at the service panel.

Wiring a single pole switch
With the circuit off, remove the old switch from its screw mountings and pull the wires out to their full length, 1. With a switch loop wiring, there should be one black, one white with a black marking, and one bare wire. Cut the insulation off the last ½ in., twist the strands clockwise, and into hooks. Attach one wire to each screw, check for loose strands, and replace. If the switch has a grounding screw, connect switch, box, and bare wire using a jumper wire and a wire cap.

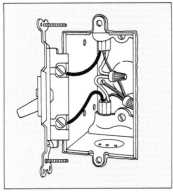

1 Pull out the old switch and extend the wires

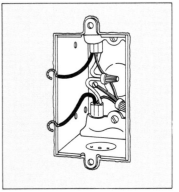

2 Strip a new section of wire, twist it into hooks, and connect to new terminals

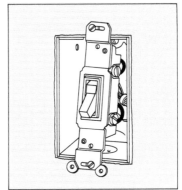

3 Attach ground terminal, box, and bare wire using a jumper wire

164
Fitting a 120-volt outlet

Every power outlet should have at least three wires connected to it; a black live wire, a white neutral wire, and a bare or green ground wire. Most outlets have six: a pair of each color. When replacing an outlet, always choose a grounded outlet with slots for three, rather than two prongs. After shutting off power to the circuit, remove the old receptacle. The new one will have five terminal screws; two brass, two silver, and one green. In either three or six wire configurations, attach the black wire(s) to the brass screws, the white wire(s) to the silver screws, and the bare one(s) to the green.

Wiring a 120-volt outlet
New receptacles have either terminal screws or push-in wire connectors which are easier to use. Strip the last ½ in. of the insulation without cutting wires (if there is enough wire, always use a freshly stripped area) and twist the strands clockwise, then into a hook, again clockwise. When the receptacle is mounted into a metal outlet be sure and connect a green wire from the green screw on the receptacle to the grounding screw on the outlet, using a wire connector. Check for loose strands, and tighten each screw securely.

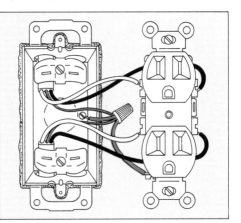

Middle-of-run outlets have six incoming wires

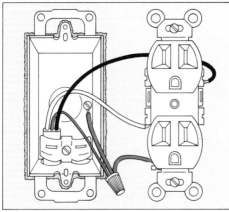

End-of-run outlets have only three incoming wires

165
Wiring a 120/240-volt receptacle

Electric clothes dryers, ranges, water heaters and air conditioners each demand their own circuit and special fittings; be sure and select the proper volt rating-120/240- or 240-volt, and proper amperage rating for your appliance. In each case, there is a need for two live wires, and a neutral or ground. In a 240-volt 30 amp receptacle, for example, both the black and white wires must be connected at the fuse box to live lines; the ground is bare.

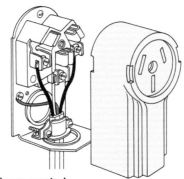

Wiring a receptacle
Connect the bare ground wire to the ground terminal in the receptacle and to the back of the box and fit the live wires to their terminals.

166
Re-wiring a lamp

If a table lamp is not working, it is best to find the fault by deduction. First change the bulb; then try another receptacle. Next, check the plug and cord for faults or loose connections. If these all fail to solve the problem, then it is best to fit a new switch socket, and at the same time replace the cord and plug if they are heat damaged.

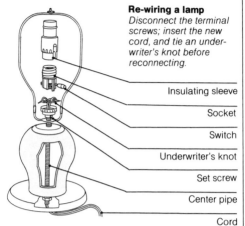

Re-wiring a lamp
Disconnect the terminal screws; insert the new cord, and tie an underwriter's knot before reconnecting.

Insulating sleeve
Socket
Switch
Underwriter's knot
Set screw
Center pipe
Cord

167
Wiring a plug

Always replace a plug if its body is cracked, broken, or charred. Flat cord or zip cord can be fitted with a self-connecting plug in a matter of seconds. Round cords, with either two or three wires, must be fitted to plugs with terminal screws. If these screws are coded, remember to connect the black wire to the brass-colored screw, the white to the silver screw, and the ground wire to the green screw. Do not forget to replace the insulating disk after wiring.

Connecting up a plug
With self-connecting plugs cut the flat cord squarely and clamp the plug's prongs onto it, 1.

With terminal screw plugs, feed the cord through the plug body, strip the outer casing, and tie an underwriter's

knot, 2. Strip ½in. of insulation from each wire, and twist the exposed strands together. Curl each wire clockwise, 3,

and wrap each around the appropriate screw terminal. Tighten the screws and replace the insulator disk, 4.

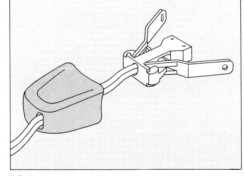

1 Self-connecting plugs come in many varieties. For use with flat cord, they are simple and quick

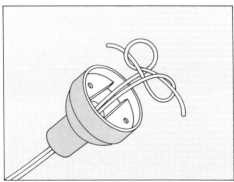

2 With screw plugs, feed the cord through the plug, strip the casing, and tie a knot

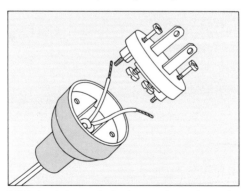

3 Strip insulation, and twist the strands together and in a curl clockwise around the correct screws

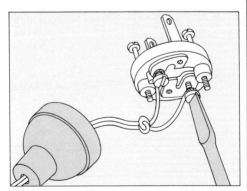

4 Tighten screws firmly, check for loose strands. If need be, re-wrap so no strands escape. Replace the disk

168
Replacing a fuse

If a fuse or circuit breaker blows, there is a fault somewhere in the circuit. You must make sure that the fault has been corrected before re-setting the breaker or replacing the fuse. Most circuit breakers have three position switches: on, off, and tripped. If the switch is tripped, switch it to off before resetting to on. Although some older homes are still equipped with cartridge or knife blade fuses, the most common fuse still in use is the plug fuse, or the tamper-proof plug fuse called Type S. Always replace fuses with the identical type and amperage rating.

Replacing fuses
Check the window in plug fuses to see if the metal strip has melted. A discolored window indicates a short circuit; a clear window and broken strip means an overload. Disconnect the main

switch, and while standing on dry ground or boards, grasp the outer ring of glass and unscrew it. Make sure that your replacement fuse is of the same amp rating. After replacement return the mains power to on.

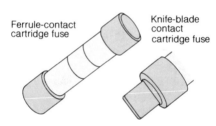

Ferrule-contact cartridge fuse

Knife-blade contact cartridge fuse

Type S fuse
These tamper-proof fuses have an adapter which will not accept fuses of the wrong rating. A 20-amp adapter will only accept a 20-amp fuse.

Normal   Overloaded circuit   Short circuit

Circuit breaker
These devices measure the electric resistance in live and neutral lines, and instantly shut off the circuit if even the slightest imbalance occurs. They provide extra protection against any dangerous current leakage.

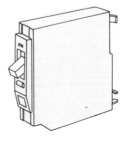

Plumbing

The plumbing system ◇ Types of pipe and faucet ◇ Tools and equipment ◇ Clearing a blocked sink drain ◇ Clearing a blocked main drain ◇ Clearing a blocked toilet ◇ Repairing ball and tank valves ◇ Installing and repairing faucets ◇ Curing leaks ◇ Plumbing-in a washing machine

The plumbing system consists of a network of pipes carrying hot and cold water around the home and taking waste material away. These pipes, together with the sinks, basins, baths and toilets they serve, usually need little maintenance. But when something does go wrong – whether it is a burst pipe or a blocked drain – a great deal of damage and inconvenience can result. With a basic knowledge of how household plumbing works, however, most of the necessary repairs are straightforward.

Modern pipes and fittings are easy to take apart and re-assemble, although repairs to old-fashioned iron pipes are more difficult and are best carried out by a professional. If you have old iron or steel pipes, it is probably best to get them replaced – copper and plastic are much easier to maintain.

You can avoid some problems by taking care of the plumbing in your home. For example, insulating pipes will reduce the likelihood of freezes and bursts.

The household plumbing system is divided into three distinct parts – the cold water system, the hot water system, and the DWV or drain-waste-vent system. Although the actual layout will vary

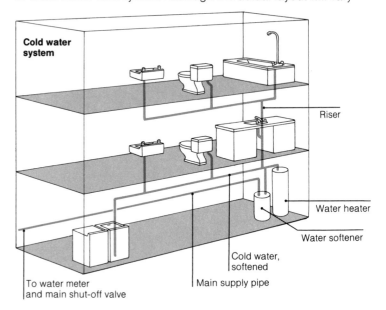

Cold water system

Riser

Water heater

Water softener

Cold water, softened

To water meter and main shut-off valve

Main supply pipe

The supply system
The collection of pipes which bring water from the public water main or a well, and on to all the fixtures of the home is called the supply system. This system must deliver hot and cold water at a steady pressure (40 to 50 lbs per inch in most areas) without spilling.

Immediately outside most homes the public water main is attached to a meter. Just beside the meter is the main shut-off valve for the home. If you cannot find yours, call the water company; it is essential to be able to shut down

the system in an emergency. From there, the main may go to a water softener, if one is fitted. From there it branches into two parallel networks; one which supplies cold water directly to the fixtures; and one which leads to the water heater, and on to supply hot water to the fixtures that need it. Many of these branch pipes have shut-off valves for particular fixtures.

Supply pipes that run horizontally have a slight pitch so that the entire system can be drained. Pipes that run vertically are called risers.

Points to remember

◇ Prepare yourself for emergencies by getting to know where the main and supplementary shut-off valves are so that you can turn off the water quickly.
◇ Tell other members of the household where the main and supplementary shut-off valves are so that they can act quickly if you are not there.
◇ Use a spring or pipe-bending machine to bend metal pipes, otherwise they will kink at the bend.
◇ After cutting metal pipes, rub the edges with a fine file to remove the burrs that may make joining the pipe difficult.
◇ If permitted by local code, replace iron and steel pipes with modern copper or plastic ones.
◇ When replacing pipe, check the type and size carefully – you may need adapters to join dissimilar materials or diameters.

Emergency action

If you have a water leak or a burst pipe, first turn off the water supply to stop flooding and then isolate the fault.
◇ With the main shut-off valve closed, you must turn off gas or electricity to the water heater and/or boiler.
◇ Drain the pipes by turning on all the faucets with the main shut-off valve closed.
◇ If you have hot water heat and must drain it, open the boiler drain first, then the

radiator valves; remove the air vent on the highest radiator so air can enter the system.
◇ If a water overflow approaches any electrical outlet, close the main disconnect for all the electricity in the house. Make sure that you are dry while doing this.
◇ To drain the system completely, close the main shut-off, open all the faucets, and, the drain faucet on the main if it is supplied.

The plumbing system

from home to home, most domestic systems work in the same way and once you understand the basic principles involved, you will be able to carry out simple repairs and maintenance. Remember that large parts of the system are hidden from view – water heaters are often in the basement, while the DWV system takes away the waste below ground.

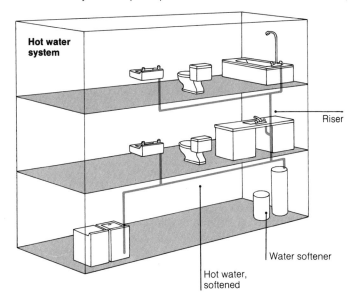

Hot water system

Riser

Water softener

Hot water, softened

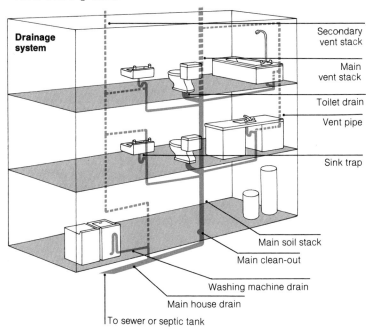

Drainage system

Secondary vent stack

Main vent stack

Toilet drain

Vent pipe

Sink trap

Main soil stack

Main clean-out

Washing machine drain

Main house drain

To sewer or septic tank

Older homes may have cast iron or steel supply pipes, but most modern installations use copper or plastic pipe of 1¾ in. internal diameter, or I.D. (I.D. is the accepted size measurement of plumbing pipes.)

The drain-waste-vent system
Like the electrical system, the plumbing system needs to be a complete circuit with supply and return lines. Every fixture that uses or provides water in the house – a faucet, a toilet, or a washing machine – needs a path to remove the water or waste. This system is called the Drain-Waste-Vent, or DWV system.

While providing a channel for removing liquid waste from the house, this system must also prevent gases which could rise from the sewer, from entering the house; and it must provide a pressure stabilization system which allows for the removal of waste without creating a suction effect. This is why there is a need for venting

The main drain leads the waste from the house to the sewer or septic tank; it may be accessible from the basement.

From it the soil stack rises vertically. Where these two join there is often a Y-fitting; this is the main clean-out, and can be used to clear blockages.

As the soil stack rises, branches lead off to the fixtures. Each fixture is equipped with a trap – most local codes demand that this be S- or P-shaped. Because of their shape, these traps are always filled with water, which prevents gases from coming up from the sewer and entering the house. At the same time the traps allow air to flow down during draining so that atmospheric pressure is maintained, and a continuous syphon effect does not develop. The branch waste pipes are gently curved, and pitched downward so that the waste drains by the force of gravity.

Besides drain pipes, vent pipes also enter the soil stack. These pipes provide a path for gases from each fixture to rise, and allow air to enter. Where the soil stack rises above the highest fixture, it is known as the main vent stack. It continues above the level of the roof, and is open at the top so gas can escape and air can enter.

A guide to plumbing terms

ABS Stiff plastic pipe used only for drains.
Auger A flexible spring-loaded metal cable that is used to clear blockages.
Closet bend Curved drain pipe that joins the toilet bowl discharge with the household drain system.
CPVC Plastic pipe that is used for supply lines and can carry hot water.
DWV Drain-Waste-Vent; the system of pipes and fittings which carries all waste to the public sewer or septic tank, and which allows for the venting of sewer gas.
Fitting Any device that connects pipes together, of any type, angle, material or size; or which connects pipe to a fixture.
Fixture Any device permanently attached to the water system – either supply or DWV – such as a sink, toilet, shower or washing machine.

Main clean-out Y-fitting near the bottom of the soil stack that can be opened for clearing.
Main drain Main drain pipe that collects waste from all the branch waste drains and delivers it to the sewer.
Main vent stack Central vertical drain pipe which carries gases from all other drain fixtures and passes the gases outside the home.
Trap Curved section of

fixture drain pipes that forms water seal which prevents sewer gas from exiting through the drain, and allows sewage and water through.
Valve Any device that controls the flow of material through a pipe.
Water hammer Banging noises caused by quick changes in water pressure. Shock absorbers prevent rapid pressure changes, noise, and damage.

Types of pipe

There are two basic types of pipe – supply and drainage (DWV). Supply pipes carry water to the faucets and fixtures in the home. DWV pipes carry water from waste outlets to the drains and the vents. Traditionally, pipes have been made from lead, cast iron, steel, and brass; but today, the use of copper and plastic, where allowed, is increasing.

Supply pipes and fittings
Steel, brass, and bronze have all been used for hot and cold supply lines, but today copper and in some areas plastic pipes are more widely used.

Copper piping is easy to cut and can be bent with a spring or bending machine. It is lightweight, non-corroding, and easy to assemble. Joints are usually soldered, not threaded; however, compression connections using threaded connectors are easily installed on rigid copper pipes. Copper piping is available in many diameters and it can be used for hot or cold supply lines.

Plastic supply pipes using CPVC plastic are semi-flexible, light, easy to handle, and very simple to join using solvent and push-fit connectors. Plastic has good thermal insulation properties (although it does need insulating in attics), and special fittings are available for connecting plastic pipes to other types.

Copper supply pipe

Steel supply pipe

PVC plastic supply pipe

Supply fittings

Drain-waste-vent pipes
Cast iron was the material most often used for DWV pipes until the introduction of plastic pipes. Cast iron is heavy, hard to join and subject to corrosion; and copper is too expensive to use in large diameter lengths. Plastics have largely replaced metal piping, although some local codes do not permit their use. Both ABS and PVC plastics are used and have the same properties, although they are not interchangeable. DWV fittings have gentle curves to keep waste flowing to the sewer. Fittings include clean-out plugs, traps and closet flanges.

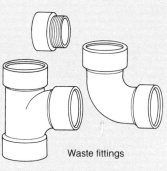

Copper waste pipes

ABS plastic waste pipe

Waste fittings

Types of faucet

Faucets are available in many different types and models. The older compression, or stem faucets, usually have washers and always have separate hot and cold controls. Newer stem models use diaphragms or cartridges rather than washers. A "mixer" which has only one handle to control both hot and cold can be a valve, cartridge, or ball type.

Valve faucets
These are washerless mixer faucets with a valve on each side, one for hot water, one for cold.

Ball faucets
These are washerless and long-lasting, though initially expensive. Like the valve faucet, the spout can swivel.

Cartridge faucets
Cartridges exist in compression and non-compression models. In the latter they may have metal sleeve or ceramic disk cartridges.

Compression faucet
With or without a washer, this traditional design comes with one control valve for both cold and hot.

Bath and shower faucets
These may be ball, valve or cartridge types. Some incorporate diverter valves for dual use of bath and shower.

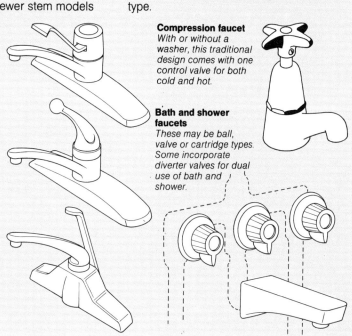

Estimating time

These times will vary according to your skill and experience, and, in the case of blockages, according to the seriousness of the problem.

Blockages

Clearing a blocked sink drain pipe

(1/4) **hour**

Clearing a blocked main drain

(1/2) **hour**

Clearing a blocked toilet

(1/2) **hour**

Toilet tanks

Repairing a ball cock

(1/2) **hour**

Repairing a tank valve

(1)-(1 1/2) **hours**

Faucets

Installing a faucet

(2)-(3) **hours**

Repairing a faucet

(1/4) **hour**

Pipework

Curing leaks

(1/4)-(3/4) **hours**

Plumbing-in a washing machine

(1 1/2)-(2) **hours**

Tools and equipment

For repairing metal pipes, you will need some or all of the following. For tightening or loosening fittings, you may need pipe, crescent and basin wrenches and a vise grip. For cutting you will need a tube cutter, an asbestos cloth and sandpaper. Solder or pipe jointing compound and fluoro-carbon tape materials are used for joining pipes; and an auger, and plunger are devices for clearing blocked pipes. A spring tube bender is also useful for shaping pipes. A working flashlight should always be close to hand. Plastic pipes need a special glue called solvent cement. Some repair work may demand more specialized tools.

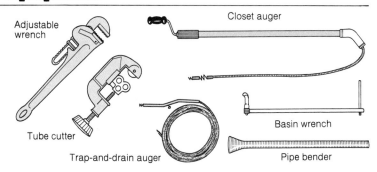

Adjustable wrench

Closet auger

Tube cutter

Trap-and-drain auger

Basin wrench

Pipe bender

169

Clearing a blocked sink drain

A plunger is usually the best solution if you have a blocked drain; chemical drain cleansers can cause damage to pipes.

Clearing a P-trap
Unscrew the clean-out plug, and use a stiff hooked wire to pull out any obstructions in either direction, **1**. If you do not find any clogs, use a pipe wrench to loosen the nuts which hold the trap in place, and re-move it. Use a trap-and-drain auger. Place it in the branch drain pipe, and while pushing it in, revolve the handle, **2**. Then remove the sink stopper and clear the sink drain pipe, **3**. Finally, clean out the trap, **4**.

Plungers use water pressure to force out the clog. Fill the sink halfway, and stuff a rag in the overflow before starting. Vase-line around the rim of the plunger ensures better contact. If that fails, check if the P-trap has a clean-out plug; if so, remove it and use a bent piece of coat hanger to try and pull out obstructions. Failing that, remove the trap and use an auger in the drain pipe, trap, and sink drain.

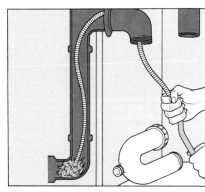

1 Using a pail to catch the debris, undo the clean-out plug, and use a wire to clear the trap.

2 Insert a trap-and-drain auger into the drain pipe and crank the handle

3 Remove the stopper and clean the sink drain pipe as well

4 Clean the trap thoroughly before replacing

170

Clearing a blocked main drain

Waste flows downward and toward the sewer, so any blockage is below the lowest clogged fixture. If all the drains are empty-ing sluggishly and odors permeate the house, the stack vent may be blocked. If fixtures on the top floor are clogged while those on lower floors are free, the upper stack is blocked. If fixtures on all floors are failing to drain, the problem may rest in the main drain. It may be easiest to reach from the main vent or soil stack; if not, you will have to open the main clean-out or a house trap. Have rags and a mop at hand.

Clearing the clean-out
Find the Y-fitting main clean-out near the bot-tom of the soil stack pipe and put a bucket under-neath it in case of flood-ing. Remove the plug with a wrench (turning counter-clockwise) and use a trap-and-drain auger to clear the ob-struction. Then flush it out with a hose. If the area is dry check the branch drain above it.

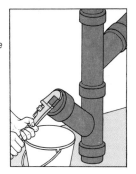

Clearing the house trap
If working at the main clean-out fails to clear the block check the U-trap below it. This is the last stop before the sewer. Open the plug nearest the outside line slowly. Water leakage means the block is there or below. Allow any water to drain out, then insert a trap-and-drain auger and try to break up the obstruction gradually.

171

Clearing a blocked toilet

If you have reason to believe that your toilet is clogged – do not flush it – that could cause an overflow. If, while flushing, you see that the bowl is not draining, quickly open the tank and close the tank valve to prevent more water from entering the bowl. Do not attempt to use chemical drain openers; they may harm the bowl's finish. The best solution for a clogged toilet, with either a front or back waste, is to use a cone-shaped plunger.

Unclogging a toilet bowl
With the bowl half full of water, fit the plunger and pump rapidly a dozen times. This should push the obstruction through the trap. If repeated applications fail to work, try using an auger. A closet auger is designed with a long handle to fit into the trap without harming the bowl's finish, but careful work with a trap-and-drain auger can also solve the problem. Insert the auger and turn the handle simultaneously to remove blockages deep in the toilet trap or closet bend.

Pump the plunger vigorously to dislodge the blockage

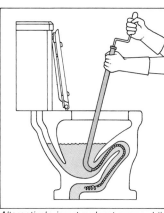

Alternatively, insert a closet auger while you turn the handle

Toilet fault-finding

◇ If the toilet keeps running, the problem is most likely in the ball cock assembly. Make certain that the float ball arm is not too high, and that the ball itself is not full of water.

◇ If the ball cock assembly is sound, check the tank valve assembly for a tight seal. Problems in flushing may originate here.

◇ If the bowl is not draining properly, use a plunger or auger to clear the trap and closet bend: do not attempt to flush the toilet until it is draining properly.

173

Repairing a tank valve

If the toilet continues to run after correcting the ball cock assembly, or if it has problems flushing, the problem may lie in the tank valve, or ball stopper and seat mechanism. Check it carefully.

Inserting a flapper and chain system
The plug used to stop the water in the tank entering the bowl can be a ball, half-ball, a disk or flapper; the last type is best. With the water on, check if the stopper is sitting firmly on the valve seat. If it is out of line, adjust the guide rod and lift wire assembly so that the stopper is directly centered over the valve seat. Check the valve seat itself; if necessary, *clean off the seat with steel wool to provide a better seal. If the stopper is in any way worn or cracked, remove it by unscrewing it and fit a duplicate. It may be possible to replace it with a chain and flapper system that fits your tank's fittings; these stoppers have fewer moving parts and are more durable. New toilets use all plastic parts with a different supply and flush system entirely.*

172

Repairing a ball cock

Toilets that are noisy or continue to run may have a defective ball cock assembly. Remove the tank cover and observe the action while flushing. If the noise begins when the ball cock opens, the problem may be a restricted water supply; adjust the shut-off valve below the tank to provide more water. If the noise continues, or if the water continues to exit the ball cock valve after the water level reaches the top of the overflow, check the ball cock.

Detecting the problem
If the float ball is not rising high enough, bend the float arm down slightly, so it shuts off earlier. If the float ball is not on top of the water, remove it, and shake it; if it sloshes, it has leaked and must be replaced. If the problem remains, the fault may lie in the washers of the ball cock itself. Turn off the water supply, and remove the cover. Remove the retaining pin or screw that holds the float mechanism to the valve, and remove the float and arm. Remove the plunger from the valve. Depending on the type, you will find either a plunger with a diaphragm or flapper valve below it, or a plunger with split and seat washers on its shaft. Remove and replace the flapper or washers, and reassemble the mechanism.

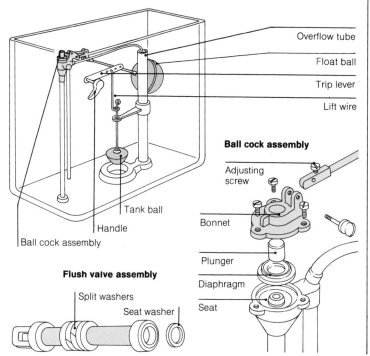

Overflow tube
Float ball
Trip lever
Lift wire

Ball cock assembly

Adjusting screw

Bonnet

Plunger

Diaphragm

Seat

Tank ball

Handle

Ball cock assembly

Flush valve assembly

Split washers

Seat washer

Bowl-refill tube
Trip lever
Chain
Overflow tube
Flapper

174

Repairing a leaky faucet

A faucet that drips from the handle or spout is annoying and costly. Most common faucets can be easily repaired. Start by turning off the water supply and draining the fixture. Compression or stem faucets have washers that may need replacing; to find the exact replacement washer, you must remove the old. Some washerless faucets have O-rings that can cause leaks as well.

Replacing a washer in a compression faucet
Remove the handle and packing nut to reveal the packing and stem. Remove these, and unscrew the washer screw that holds the washer in place and fit an identical replacement washer.

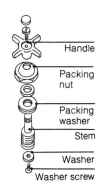

Handle
Packing nut
Packing washer
Stem
Washer
Washer screw

Replacing an O-ring in a valve faucet
If water leaks along the spout rather than from it, remove the spout by gripping the spout ring with vise grips wrapped in tape, and turning counterclockwise. Replace the O-ring.

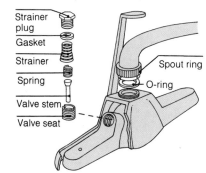

Strainer plug
Gasket
Strainer
Spring
Valve stem
Valve seat
Spout ring
O-ring

Tips for thawing pipes

◇ Before applying heat to a pipe, open a faucet so steam pressure can escape.
◇ Pipes can be warmed using a hot-air gun, hair-blower, or towels wrapped on pipes and soaked in hot water.
◇ Ice forms along lengths of pipe; spread heat and move it back and forth. Thaw out first the areas that are most likely to be frozen – uninsulated areas and bends.
◇ If the frozen pipe has obviously burst, turn off the water supply to the pipe before thawing it.
◇ Propane torches are quick but very risky; never use near wood or in attics.
◇ Thaw all pipes immediately upon discovery or a burst may occur.

175

Installing a faucet

To remove an old faucet and install a new one, it will probably be necessary to use a basin wrench to remove and replace the locknut and coupling nut. First disconnect the water supply and drain tap. Then insert the basin wrench from below, and remove the coupling nut then the locknut.

Attaching the faucet
Apply a little non-setting plumber's compound to the bottom of the new faucet before fitting the plastic bedding washer that lies between the faucet and the top of the sink. Put the faucet in place, fit a fiber washer on the tail from beneath, and replace the locknut. If fitting the faucet to a thin surface such as a steel sink surround, put a "top-hat" washer over the tail to act as a spacer before fitting the washer. Wrap the tail in fluorocarbon tape, and fit the coupling nut and a new fiber washer.

Cap
Handle
Packing nut
Stem
Seat washer
Washer screw
Valve seat

176

Curing leaks in pipes

Most leaks are caused by frost damage or corrosion. They may occur either in runs of pipe or at junctions. If the latter is the case, shut off the water supply, drain at the nearest fixture, and remove the pipes. Re-solder copper connections, or use fluorocarbon tape on screw threads and re-tighten. Compression joints can also be re-tightened and thus be made watertight again. Pinhole leaks in runs of pipe can be temporarily solved by inserting a toothpick into the leak and then taping over; but eventually all leaking pipe must be replaced, using pipe and connectors.

Mending pipes
Cure pinhole leaks with a toothpick and tape and control larger leaks with a piece of rubber and a hose clamp or two. For a permanent solution to the problem, cut out the affected pipe and insert a length of plastic pipe of the same diameter using straight connectors. Plastic pipe springs easily into place.

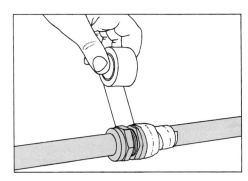

177

Installing a washing machine

Most washing machines must be connected to both hot and cold supply pipes. Shock absorbers, control valves and drain provisions will also have to be dealt with.

Connecting up
Locate and drain the hot and cold supply pipes nearest the machine and install a T-fitting on each. Run a pipe upward from each fitting and install shock absorbers. Run two pipes down from the T-fitting, install elbows and connect them to the machine's control valves and fit supply faucets. Connect the machine's flexible supply pipes to the valve with hose union nuts. Join the drain pipe with a branch drain, using a T-joint.

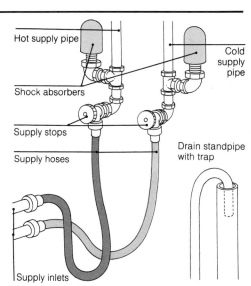

Hot supply pipe
Cold supply pipe
Shock absorbers
Supply stops
Supply hoses
Drain standpipe with trap
Supply inlets

Heating

Choice of fuel ◇ Types of central heating
Bleeding a radiator ◇ Curing a leaking valve
Replacing a radiator ◇ Balancing radiators
Installing a damper ◇ Flushing out a fluid
central heating system

Given the option, most people today would prefer central heating; it is more efficient, more versatile, and usually cheaper to run than an assortment of space heating appliances. Some systems can only be installed in new buildings; forced-air heating, for example, cannot generally be installed in finished homes. But hot water systems can be installed or improved in most homes. If you are planning a new system, assess your requirements carefully; some of the basic questions that need answering are: what type of fuel to use, what type of control, and the amount of heat and heat distributors you need. Fuels can range from solid fuels to oil, gas, or electricity; what is best for you depends on local availability, cost and storage facilities at your home. Control devices include timers, a central thermostat, or thermostatic valves for each heat distributor. The size and type of boiler depends on the amount of heat you need. Remember not to skimp at this stage; if you purchase a boiler with excess capacity, you will save expense later if you increase your home living area, and need additional heat. Heat distributors in a hot water system can be radiators or convectors; again, what is right for your home depends on its size, shape, and heating requirements. Consult a local heating engineer for advice. With a small amount of maintenance, most hot water systems will perform well for years. Minor repairs can be done without the cost of employing a professional.

Points to remember

◇ Plan a new heating system carefully, taking fuel costs, heating requirements, and possible extensions into account.
◇ Repair small leaks in hot water systems quickly; they will worsen if left unattended.
◇ Insulate hot water or steam pipes, or forced-air heating ducts to increase the efficiency and to lower the costs of the system.
◇ Flush out a wet central heating system once a year to remove any rust and add rust inhibitor to new water.

Choice of fuel

Central heating systems can be heated by gas, oil, electricity, or solid fuels such as wood or coal. Solid-fuel heaters need a large storage area, are messy, and demand much attention. Oil heaters, once very common and still seen, need large tanks and should have yearly professional maintenance, but are sturdy and easy to control.

Gas is generally the cheapest fuel and is very versatile. It can power a variety of boilers – including concealed back-boilers and compact, wall-mounted models. Gas makes no mess, does not have to be stored, and is easy to control. Electric-powered heaters need no flue, storage or clean up operations. They may be cheaper than gas.

Types of control

The versatility of any central heating system is affected by the amount of control you are given over the heat. You should be able to control easily both the temperature and the time period during which the system is operating.

Clock thermostats
Clock thermostats combine temperature control with the time control, allowing you to set different temperatures for different times.

Thermostats
These turn the heating system on or off in response to temperature.

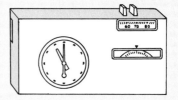

Thermostatic valves
With these you can set the temperature of each individual radiator in the house.

Estimating time

The times given for bleeding and flushing are for all the radiators in the system. The other times given are for repairing or replacing individual items.

Bleeding radiators
(½) hour

Curing a leaking valve
(¾) hour

Replacing a radiator
(1)–(1½) hours

Installing a damper
(½)–(1½) hours

Balancing radiators
(2)–(3) hours

Flushing out a fluid heating system
(1)–(2) hours

Types of central heating

A central heating system has a single heat source from which heat is distributed by a medium through a distribution net-work. The medium used defines the system. Fluid systems use hot water or steam through pipes to radiators or con-vectors; forced-air systems use air as a heating medium, and distribute it via ducts to vents in floors, ceilings, or walls.

Fluid-heat systems

A central boiler heats water, which flows to radiators or convectors. Here the water gives off heat, either by radi-ating the heat (radiators), or by the air circulating through hot vanes (con-vectors). A different set of pipes returns the water to the boiler to be reheated. Most systems have a pump that pushes the water around the network, but some older systems rely on the ten-dency of hot water to rise to create a flow.

To link the boiler and the radiators, small bore pipes of $\frac{1}{2}$ in. diameter are usually used. The flow pipe takes the hot water from the boiler to each radiator or convector inlet in turn. A second pipe is connected to all the out-lets of the radiators, and returns the water to the boiler.

Some older installations use a single pipe to lead and collect water from each radiator in turn. The drawback with this system is that only the first radiator receives water that is fully hot, so the other radiators have to be pro-gressively larger to give the same amount of heat.

A fluid system must be properly bal-anced for optimum effect; this means adjusting in-line valves or flow valves so that the correct amount of hot water arrives at each radiator for the heating requirements of each room.

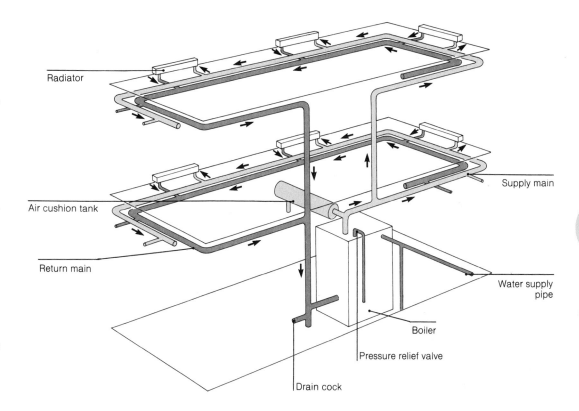

Radiator

Air cushion tank

Return main

Supply main

Water supply pipe

Boiler

Pressure relief valve

Drain cock

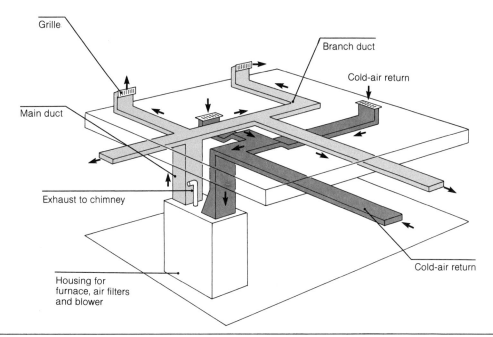

Grille

Main duct

Exhaust to chimney

Housing for furnace, air filters and blower

Branch duct

Cold-air return

Cold-air return

Forced-air systems

These systems use air as the medium to carry heat throughout the home. The most common type uses a central heater fired by gas, oil, or electricity, to heat the air which is blown by a central fan through ducts under the floors or in the ceilings and walls of each room. Most systems of this type need to be installed when the house is built, but modifications can upgrade this system. Insulating all the exposed duct work, if not already done, can save a great deal of energy and money.

Balancing a forced-air system is accomplished by manipulating the registers and dampers on each branch line to ensure that the heat is equal in all the rooms.

178

Bleeding a radiator

One of the most common problems with a fluid central heating system is a radiator that is not as warm at the top as it is elsewhere. This is usually caused by a build up of air in the system created by air dissolved in the water, or adding water to the system. If your radiator or convector is not equipped with automatic air valves, "bleeding" the system of air may rectify your problem.

Bleeding a radiator
Opening the air-bleeder valve at the top of the radiator or convector will allow the air to escape. Use the appropriate hex key or wrench. Be ready to catch

any escaping water. Close the valve as soon as water starts to escape. As you do this, the system will be topped up from the expansion tank. Bleed all radiators at the start of winter.

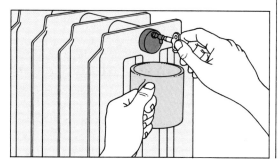

179

Curing a leaking valve connection

If there is a leak where the radiator is connected to the valve, try tightening the nuts linking the fitting to the pipe and the radiator. Use two wrenches;

Connecting a radiator valve
Close the valves at either end of the radiator using a small wrench for the return valve. Note how many turns are required to turn it off. Put a large, shallow container under the leaking valve and undo the coupling nut. As water flows out, open the bleeder valve slightly using a radiator key, wrench, or screwdriver. When the water has run out, clean the ends of the connector with steel wool, reassemble it and wrap fluorocarbon tape around the threads. Close the bleeder valve, and return valves.

one to tighten the nut, the other to brace the fitting as you work, so that you do not damage the pipework. If this does not cure the leak, isolate the radiator by closing the valves at either end; then open the connections. Clean any old sealant from the threads, wrap them with new fluorocarbon tape, and remake the joints. (*See Job 176, p. 189 for pipe leaks.*) If necessary, fit new connectors.

Unscrew the coupling nut of the leaking valve

180

Replacing an old radiator

Radiators sometimes leak along the bottom seam. If this is happening, corrosion has probably taken hold inside and you should replace the radiator. To

remove the old radiator, start by closing both the valves and disconnecting the radiator at both ends (*see Job 179 above*). Remove the radiator, and the old fittings as well. It may be worthwhile to replace it with a convector; ask a heating engineer for advice for your system. Do not attempt to replace it with a larger radiator, as your boiler may not be sufficiently powerful.

Fitting a new radiator
Maneuver the new radiator into position to align with the existing elbow valves and union nuts, 1. Screw the nut at each end on to the thread of the new connection and seal it with fluorocarbon tape, 2, then tighten the union.

nut. To fill the radiator, open the bleeder valve and the two valves at the bottom, 3. Use as many turns of the wrench to open the return valve as it took to close it. As the radiator fills, air will escape from the bleeder valve. Close this valve when water escapes.

1 *Align the opening of the new radiator with the union nuts on the risers*

2 *Connect the radiator to the inlet and return valves and seal with tape*

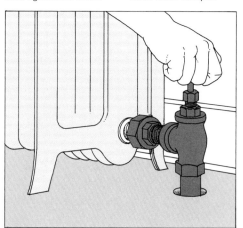
3 *Open the valves so that the radiator fills up with water*

181
Balancing a radiator

Inlet valves are one type of control over the heat output of a radiator; but if your system is equipped with flow or in-line valves you will find these more effective for evening out the heat from room to room. Located at the beginning of major branch lines, these valves act in the same way as dampers in a forced-air system, increasing or decreasing the flow of water from the boiler to the radiators. Most are easily adjusted using a screwdriver.

Balancing radiators or convectors
When the slot is parallel with the pipe, the valve is open; when perpendicular, it is closed. Set the valve between the two extremes, and make a mark to record the setting.

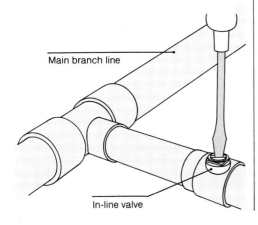

Main branch line

In-line valve

182
Flushing out a fluid central heating system

It is a good idea to flush and cleanse your entire fluid heating system before the beginning of each winter. This will remove any rust build-up, provide an opportunity to bleed each radiator, and allows you to add a rust inhibitor to the entire system. With the boiler cold, close the water inlet valve and open the boiler drain cock, and all the bleeder valves on all the radiators. Be sure the water flows to a floor drain.

Refilling the system
With the entire system empty close the drain cock, remove the pressure relief valve, and add a rust inhibitor. Replace the valve, and close all the bleeder valves. Open the water supply valve.

Watch the moving needle on the combination valve; when it matches the static needle (set when the system was installed) bleed the radiators on the top floor. Close the supply valve.

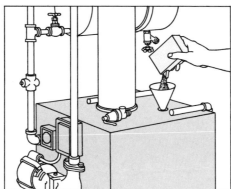

183
Installing a damper

In forced-air central heating systems, the device which balances the system from room to room is a damper in a branch duct. This is a metal plate which is fitted into the duct, and can be adjusted to allow more or less hot air from the furnace into a particular room. As a general rule, rooms closer to the furnace need less hot air, those farther away need more. If your system is equipped only with room registers, and you cannot balance the system effectively with them, you may wish to install dampers in the branch ducts. Start by locating the source of the branch duct.

Installing the damper
Open the duct on one of the seams that is accessible; some ducts snap apart, others have an S-clip. Measure the cross section of the duct. Cut a piece of tin ⅛ in. smaller than the opening. Buy two spring-loaded axle clips and a handle that

matches the axle. Install the spring clips in the exact center of the horizontal side of the tin plate. Drill two holes in the horizontal center of the duct to accept the spring clips. Insert into position, add the handle to the axle, and restore the duct to its branch.

Space heating systems

The term space heaters refers to appliances which are both heating elements and distribution points. Like central heating they may use gas, oil, solid fuel, or electricity to provide heat; unlike central heating systems, they may be portable, and are designed to warm only the room in which they are found.

Solid fuel and oil-fired space heaters need a permanent location, since they need a flue or chimney to carry noxious fumes safely outside; also, these heaters need a storage place for the fuel. Solid fuel heaters also need to be fed during operation. These heaters are not generally efficient; much of the heat may be lost up the chimney. Despite this, wood-burning stoves and fireplaces have made a come-

back in recent years. A series of pipes can be installed as a heat exchanger in some units; these draw cooler air from below, run them through the fireplace or stove, and back into the room. The tendency of hot air to rise creates a flow of air. In this way, 20 percent more heat from the same amount of fuel may be produced.

Propane space heaters are portable, clean, odorless, and, depending on local conditions, inexpensive to operate. Tanks can be rented, and if used responsibly, may last two to three weeks per filling. They must have a source of fresh air.

Electric space heaters are clean, safe, and can be relatively small. They can be fan-assisted, flat radiant heating panels, or small floor models.

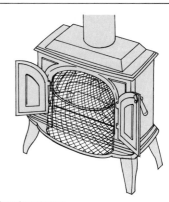

Wood burning stoves
Rustic and often handsome, wood burning stoves and fireplaces are popular; but they need a flue, storage place, and attention.

Insulation

Types of insulation material ◇ Reducing heating costs ◇ Lining and insulating a roof Insulating an attic ◇ Insulating pipes Types of weather stripping ◇ Insulating a basement ◇ Insulating floors and ceilings

Much of the warmth created by your heating system disappears through the walls, roof, windows and doors of your home. Insulation offers a way of saving some of this warmth, which in turn saves you money on heating bills. If your home has no insulation, you may be wasting three-quarters of the money you spend on heating. With proper insulation, it is possible to cut down on this loss by almost half.

You can insulate almost every part of the structure of your home. But some areas are responsible for a greater heat loss than others, and so are more important to insulate. Certain areas are also easier and cheaper to insulate than others. For example, it is simple and relatively inexpensive to insulate an attic, which might be responsible for up to one quarter of the entire heat loss. Windows lose less heat, and double glazing is an expensive form of insulation. Of course, your own insulation requirements will vary according to the type of home you live in. In general, the more outside walls you have, and the larger the area of the roof, the more insulation will be required.

Insulation can also save you money and trouble in the plumbing system. If you insulate your pipes, they will retain heat and will be unlikely to freeze and burst; and if you insulate your hot-water cylinder you will save money on heating water.

Points to remember

◇ Whichever part of the home you are insulating, leave some ventilation – otherwise you run the risk of condensation.
◇ Wear heavy gloves and a protective face mask when working with glass fiber insulation material.
◇ Make sure windows and doors are draftproof, but maintain an adequate air supply for fuel-burning appliances and to provide proper air turn-over in your home.
◇ Vapor barriers are designed to prevent dangerous condensation building up inside your walls; make sure your insulation is equipped with it, or be prepared to add it.
◇ Insulate water pipes wherever they are exposed.

Types of insulation material

A wide range of materials is used for insulation. Some of the most common materials are glass fiber and rigid polystyrene, which have excellent heat-saving properties and are made up in various forms. Some insulating materials are now backed with a foil vapor barrier, which reflects radiant heat. Foam cavity wall fillings need special equipment and should be installed by professionals. The effectiveness of each type of insulation material is measured by its rate of resistance to the flow of heat, known as its R-value.

Blankets and batts
Glass fiber and rock wool are the commonest types of insulation used. In thicknesses ranging from 1in. to 7in., these materials are placed between joists or studs in most new buildings. Blankets are sold in lengths of 16ft to 64ft, and in widths designed to fit between studs. Batts are identical, but in more manageable lengths of 4ft to 8ft. Both are usually backed with vapor barriers.

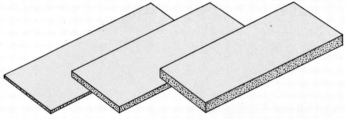

Rigid boards
Made from polystyrene or urethane, in bead or foam compressed sheets, these boards are available in widths ranging from 16in. to 48in. and from ½in. to 6in. deep. Like the blanket type they can only be installed in open, or new construction – to add them to old walls would involve removing the plaster or wallboard. While efficient insulators, they are less commonly used because of their flammability; most local codes require a covering of ½in. of fireproof material such as gypsum wallboard. Moreover, most come without a vapor barrier, which must be added. They are often used behind aluminum or plastic siding.

Loose fill
This material is inexpensive and easy to install. It can be spread in attics and raked to fill between the joists, or poured into areas that are hard to reach. It must have a vapor barrier laid down before being spread. Although cellulose insulates better than glass fiber, it must be treated with fire retardant. Loose fill settles, and if dampened, it shrinks, loses much of its insulating properties, and may lose its flame retardant qualities.

Foam
Foam is like loose fill in that it can be installed in otherwise inaccessible areas, but it must be installed by professionals. Urethane foams are effective, but also flammable.

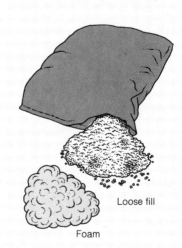

Loose fill

Foam

Reducing heating costs

The diagram below shows the proportions of heat loss for which the parts of a typical house are responsible. These vary for other types of buildings. Single storey units lose proportionally more heat through the roof and less through the walls, while a ground floor apartment has less heat loss through the ceiling than through the roof of a house.

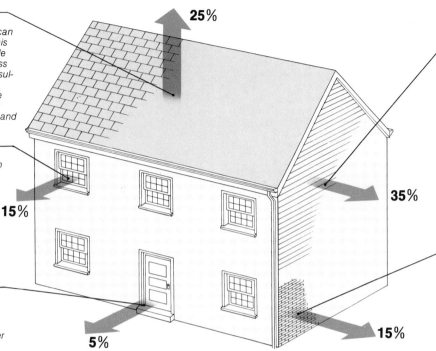

Roof and attic
As much as 25 percent of the heat can escape from an uninsulated roof; this can be cut to 8 percent by the simple effort of insulating the attic with glass fiber blanket material or loose-fill insulation. This installation is one of the easiest, and dollar-for-dollar may be the most cost-effective improvement you can make in saving on heating and cooling expenses.

Windows
Ordinary single-glazed windows can be responsible for losing 15 percent of the home's heat. This can be reduced to 5 percent by double glazing, but the cost of installation hardly justifies the saving on heat. You can save some warmth inexpensively by fitting weather stripping to window frames, and caulking the gaps around the frames.

Doors
Drafts under and around doors can cause a heat loss which you can reduce by making sure the doors fit well and have the necessary weather stripping properly fitted.

Walls
Potentially, the greatest heat loss can occur through the walls. They can be responsible for losing as much as 35 percent of the heat produced in the home. If you have hollow partition walls, the best method is to have the cavities filled with insulating foam by a specialist company. If this is not possible, you can line the walls with sheets of insulated plasterboard.

Underfloor area
Up to 15 percent of the heat can escape from under the floor. One of the simplest ways to cut this down is to fill gaps under the baseboards with caulk. Basements and cellars must be insulated as well.

Estimating time

The times for insulating roofs and attics are for a 10yd² area. Work out your own roof or attic area and increase the times accordingly.

Lining a roof
 hours

Lining and insulating a roof
④-⑥ **hours**

Insulating pipes
②-④ **hours**

Insulating an attic
①-② **hours**

Insulating a basement
 hours

184

Lining a roof

In an old house with an unlined roof, drafts and wind-blown rain can create problems. Lining the rafters with a polyethylene vapor barrier or foil-backed building paper can provide a seal against penetrating cold and damp.

Putting up the lining
Vapor barriers prevent condensation from entering the sealed insulation from the interior of the house, but older roofs may allow water to enter from outside. Before installing insulation in the attic or roof, line the underside of the roof with foil-backed building paper or polyethylene plastic. Cut sheets approximately 4in. wider than the distance between rafters, and with a staple gun attach them to the rafters, 1. Leave a space of about 1in. between the plaster and the slate or roof tile and nail runners, to allow for ventilation.

Before fixing the bottom of the strips, make sure that the plastic or paper extends to the eaves, and the vents there, so that any water that is blown under the tiles will run down the lining and drain through the vents in the eaves, 2. This will prevent a build up of water that will cause damage to the roof timbers. Make sure that there is an open vent through the eaves which extends up between the plastic and the tiles or roof material; this is to ensure ventilation, so that moisture will not be trapped against the roof and create rot causing structural damage.

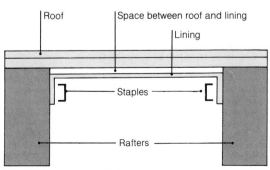

1 *Staple the sides of the lining to the rafters, leaving a space between the lining and the roof*

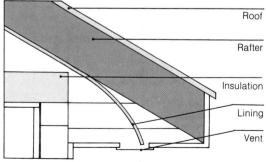

2 *Extend the lining into the vents in the eaves to provide a path for water to escape and air to enter.*

185
Insulating a roof

Lining a roof may prevent cold or damp from entering, but not heat from escaping. If you want to use your attic as a living space, then add insulation. With a lining in place, use blanket, batt or rigid board insulation. Glass fiber can be stapled in place with the vapor barrier facing down, or toward the heated area. Rigid board insulation may need an additional vapor barrier, and must be covered by $\frac{1}{2}$in. gypsum board or similar non-flammable material.

Fitting the insulation
With the lining securely in place, and after checking that the vents in the eaves provide air space between the lining and the roof battens that hold the tiles, add insulation. Blankets or batts often have foil vapor barriers that have extended edges, which can be used to staple the material in place. Alternatively, it may be easier to use garden bamboo canes or criss-crossed string to hold it in place, although this does not provide as good a vapor barrier. Rigid boards can be cut to fit between rafters and held in place by compression or small nails in the sides of the rafters, **1**. To finish, attach gypsum wallboard (required by many codes when covering rigid board, **2**). If the insulation did not provide a vapor barrier on the bottom side, add a sheet of polyethylene before covering with wallboard. Make certain the roof is well ventilated.

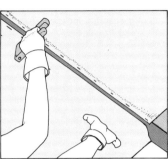
Staple blanket insulation to the rafters at 6in. intervals

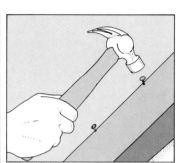
1 Secure rigid boards in place with nails driven into the sides of the rafters

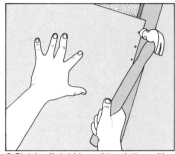
2 Finish off rigid board insulation with gypsum wallboard

186
Insulating an attic

Glass fiber and mineral wool in blanket form are the most popular materials for attic insulation because they are easy to install. Loose fill materials are also available, but need a vapor lining.

Before you start work, examine the roof timbers for signs of woodworm and dampness (see pp. 208 and 205) and take remedial action before fitting insulation. It is also a good opportunity to examine the wiring that leads to the ceiling fixtures, and to check the connections for loose wires. Then vacuum the loft. Use an industrial vacuum cleaner if one is available, and take care not to damage the plaster or plasterboard of the ceilings. When you are working in an attic, walk only on the tops of the ceiling joists. To avoid putting a foot through the ceiling, lay a few boards across the joists as temporary walkways. Protect your hands with plastic or rubber gloves when working with blanket insulation, wear a dust mask and slash holes in the new vapor barrier so as not to trap water between the layers.

Laying blanket or batt insulation
To lay blanket insulation, simply unroll it between the joists. Start from the eaves and work toward the center, with the foil side down. Join sections with butt joints. To cut the roll, use a straight-edge and a serrated knife, cutting on the vapor barrier side. Run *the insulation under all electrical wires, but do not cover incandescent lighting fixtures,* **1**. *Use non-combustible insulation to pack around chimneys that* are still in use. If possible, tack insulation to the attic hatch and around its frame, **2**; *these can be major heat loss areas. Save any scraps for pipes.*

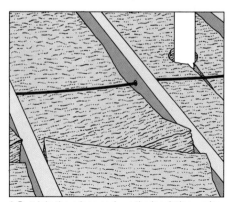
1 Butt join the edges and run the insulation under the electrical wires

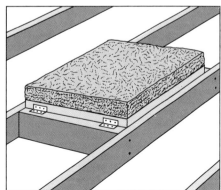
2 Tack insulation to the attic trap door

187
Insulating pipes

To help prevent freezing, insulate all exposed pipes in the basement, even downspouts. It is also worth insulating long runs of hot water pipes, especially if they are fitted under floors. This will keep the water hotter, and will prevent the waste that occurs when hot water in the pipes cools down quickly even when you have only drawn off a small amount at the faucet. Insulation can be a special electric-heated wire, molded foam casings, or just offcuts of blanket insulation, which are particularly useful at stopcocks, valves and corners. Do not compress it when installing; it loses its heat saving quality.

Fitting the insulation
Pre-molded foam insulation fits tightly around pipes, and may have adhesive or special fasteners to hold it in place. Offcuts of blanket insulation can be wrapped around pipes and fittings, *and secured with string or insulation tape; it is easy to use around corners and fittings. Electric heat tape is effective, but needs an outlet, and does not work during a blackout – when you most need it.*

Use foam insulation sleeves for long pipe runs

Offcuts of blanket insulation are useful for corners

188
Insulating a basement

Insulation in the attic can prevent heat from escaping; in the basement, it can prevent cold and damp from entering.

If your basement is the home for your water heater, duct work for your central heating, or long stretches of water pipe it is worth insulating them individually as well as the space itself. Besides covering the water pipes, wrap the water

heater on the sides and top, leaving free space around electric connections, or air vents if it is gas. Duct work should also be wrapped in blanket insulation, either using tape to hold it, or attaching the blanket to joists on either side. In both cases keep the vapor barrier facing out.

If the basement has a bare dirt floor, cover it using plastic strips. Roll it out overlapping each by at least 6in. Use sand or bricks to keep it in place.

If the basement is unused, insulate the ceiling with blanket material, with the foil side up, against the floor above.

Fitting the insulation
In an unused basement, use the same principle to fill the space between the ceiling joists as you did to fill roof joists (see Job 185, p. 196), but install the foil side up, and hold the blanket in place with bamboo or stiff wire. Never compress the material, since it lowers its insulation. In heated basements, attach furring strips to the walls, in a pattern to accept rigid board panels, with the width of the furring strips the same as the panels. Install the panels between the strips using the adhesive suggested by the panel maker. Attach gypsum wallboard to the furring strips when insulation is complete.

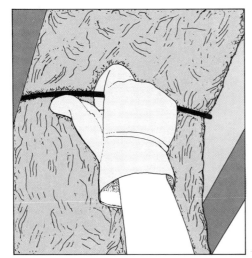

Secure blanket insulation to basement ceilings with stiff wire

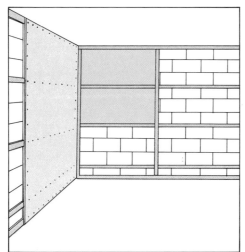

Install furring strips to the walls for rigid board panels

Types of weather stripping

Heat loss from drafts can account for up to 16 percent of the fuel bill. Double glazing can stop drafts from windows (*For more information, see p. 101.*) But it is best to fit weather stripping.

Hinged windows
For hinged windows (casement windows) there are numerous forms of weather stripping. For metal windows, a special vinyl gasket is available which can be secured with a compatible adhesive to the frame.

Wooden casement windows can be weather-proofed by using adhesive backed foam, spring metal (V-shaped strips which fit to the frames, and compress upon closure to form a seal), felt or rubber strips, or tubular vinyl or foam filled gaskets. For some spaces, with irregularly shaped gaps, caulking guns with silicone or polyurethane sealants can be used. These

expand and contract with changing conditions.

Double-hung windows
Nylon-pile strip, in a plastic or metal holder, is effective if tacked around the frame, so that the brush strip presses against the sliding sash. V-shaped metal or plastic strips work well for sealing the gap between rails where vertical sash windows overlap. Foam strips are also useful.

Doors
Drafts between doors and door frames can also be treated with weather stripping, provided that you use a durable type. Fit brush or tubular strips around the door frame. Position these so that the brush or soft tube touches the face of the door. For under-door drafts, treatments range from self-adhesive plastic strips to sweeps with one part fixed to the threshold and the other to the door.

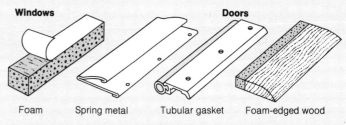

Windows   **Doors**

Foam   Spring metal   Tubular gasket   Foam-edged wood

Tips for insulating floors and ceilings

◇ The simplest method is to lay aluminum foil, or foil-backed building paper, beneath padding or foam-backed carpet.

◇ Insulate a cold solid floor by laying polyethylene sheeting and polystyrene slabs, covered by a tongue-and-groove particleboard.

◇ Insulate a wooden floor with fiber insulation board covered by hardboard.

◇ If you do not want to raise the height of a wooden floor,

insulate it by taking up the floorboards and inserting either glass fiber blankets or rigid boards.

◇ Cover gaps between baseboards and walls with beading.

◇ If there is no access to the floor above the ceiling, insulate with material fixed between battens and cover the battens with paneling (see Job 96, p. 85).

◇ Use thermal board for a heat-saving ceiling.

Roofs and gutters

Equipment ◇ Types of roof covering ◇ Replacing a slate Replacing a shingle ◇ The guttering system ◇ Clearing a blocked gutter ◇ Clearing a blocked downspout Repairing a sagging gutter

The roof is one of the most important parts of any building. If you keep it in good condition, it will protect your home from wind and rain, preventing damp getting into the rooms below and rot establishing itself in the timbers. Because of their exposed position, roofs often need repair. Asphalt shingles easily get damaged and the covering of flat roofs starts to crack.

The guttering system, important in keeping rainwater away from the walls and stopping penetrating damp, should also be kept in good repair. Basic roofing repairs such as replacing split shingles are not difficult. But it is essential to pay attention to safety.

Points to remember

◇ Always take care when working at a height – never try to cut corners to save time.
◇ Wear soft, rubber-soled shoes that give a good grip.
◇ For work on a roof, use a roof ladder or a wooden chicken ladder – never walk directly on a slate or tile roof surface.
◇ Work in good weather – avoid wet, cold, and windy conditions, when it is easy to slip and lose your balance.
◇ Ask someone to hold the ladder steady.
◇ Support ladders with strong boards to stop them sinking into the ground.

Equipment

To gain access to roofs and gutters you need a regular metal or wooden ladder and possibly, a roof ladder. Choose a double or triple extending ladder. A triple extending ladder is easier to store and to erect single-handed. Aluminum alloy ladders are lighter than wooden ladders. The treads should be wide enough for comfort and positioned so that they form flat surfaces when the ladder is at the correct angle. At the top and bottom of each section there should be rubber safety grips so that the ladder cannot slip.

Roof ladders are essential for work on all roofs except the flat type. They are often made of lightweight aluminum alloy and have small wheels that enable the ladder to be pushed up the roof to the ridge. Choose one that just fits the distance between the top and the eaves. They can be rented, or you can convert a sectional ladder to a roof ladder using a bolt-on wheel-and-hook set.

A useful alternative to the metal roofing ladder, especially when you are working on fragile roofing materials such as slate or asbestos, is a wooden chicken ladder. This consists of a long board about 12in. wide fitted with horizontal wooden strips that support your feet. It should be fitted with wooden hooks at one end, so that you can secure it to the roof peak.

Using ladders
Place the ladder at the correct angle to the wall. For every 9ft of height up the wall, it should be 3ft away from the base. If the top of the ladder has a stay, allow for this when positioning it. Stand the foot of the ladder on firm, level ground. If the ground is soft, put it on a thick wide board. Anchor the base of the ladder to a stake driven firmly into the ground.

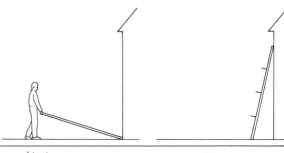

Securing ladders
On a smooth or slippery surface, block the base of the ladder with a wooden batten (right) or attach rubber pads to the feet (far right). On a concrete surface, for example, rubber pads will take up slight irregularities in the surface and make the ladder stable.

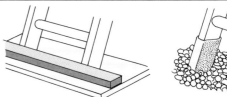

Roof attachments
To fit a roof ladder, push the wheels up the roof towards the ridge. Then invert the ladder and check that the roof hook is secured firmly over the top of the ridge (right). If you are using a chicken ladder (far right), anchor it to the ridge of the roof with hooks. The wooden board will protect the slates from damage and the cleats act as footholds. Other roof attachments available from tool rental companies include an angled seat board, which provides a seating platform while you work, and toe-board jacks which are nailed to the roof and hold a foot-supporting plank in position.

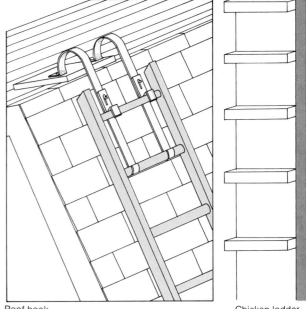

Roof hook   Chicken ladder

Types of roof covering

The main materials used for roofing are shingles and slates, which are used on pitched roofs; and felt, which is used on flat roofs.

Slates are often used for roofs on older houses, but they are usually too expensive to use on new roofs. A slate roof in good condition will give excellent service. New slates are still available for repairs, and secondhand slates in good condition form a cheaper alternative. Imitation asbestos-based slates are also suitable both for repairs and for replacing a complete slate roof, to keep it in the same style as the original. There are variations in slate sizes, so measure a slate from your roof before buying replacements.

Shingles can be made either from asphalt or wood, Asphalt shingles come in strips about 3ft wide. Each strip is made up of two or three shingle tabs, divided by cut-outs. Asphalt shingles are flexible, and therefore easier to repair than wooden types.

The advantage of wooden shingles is that you can repair an individual piece – you do not have to replace a whole strip. One problem with these shingles is that moss often grows on them and this encourages rot. You should scrape the moss away and treat the affected area with wood preservative.

Flat roofs, such as those often built on home extensions, are often covered with felt. This material is also sometimes used on sloping roofs.

Slate roof construction
Each slate is fixed by two nails to the wooden sheathing, which is nailed to the rafters. To ensure that the covering is waterproof, alternate rows of slates are staggered, and each row overlaps by half the one below it. At any place on the roof there are therefore at least two thicknesses of slates.

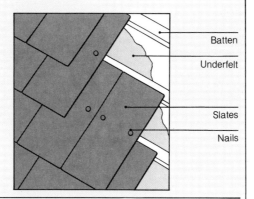

Batten

Underfelt

Slates

Nails

Asphalt shingle roof construction
The wooden rafters are covered with sheathing, which takes the form either of wooden boards or sheets of plywood and gives a strong support for the other roofing materials. The sheathing is covered with overlapping sheets of roofing felt and the shingle strips are nailed in overlapping courses on top of this.

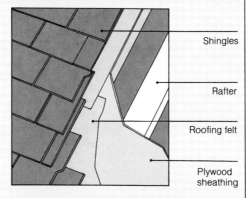

Shingles

Rafter

Roofing felt

Plywood sheathing

Wood shingle roof construction
This type of roof is constructed in a similar way to an asphalt shingle roof, except that the shingles themselves come in individual pieces rather than in strips.

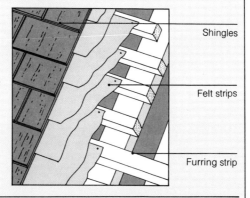

Shingles

Felt strips

Furring strip

Flat roof construction
On flat roofs the felt is usually attached in three separate layers, bonded together with tar or asphalt. The first layer is nailed to the sheathing and the subsequent layers are bonded to it. Flat roofs are usually finished with light-colored stone chippings that reflects much of the sun's heat.

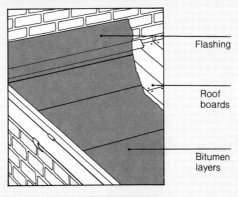

Flashing

Roof boards

Bitumen layers

Estimating time

These times assume that ladders and other access equipment are in position. The times for repairing flashings and clearing gutters are for a 10ft run.

Roofs

Replacing a slate

(¼) **hour**

Replacing a shingle

(¼) **hour**

Repairing flashings

(¼)-(2) **hours**

Gutters

Clearing a gutter

(¼)-(½) **hour**

Clearing a blocked downspout

(¼) **hour**

Repairing a sagging gutter

(½)-(1) **hour**

Safety tips for using ladders

◇ Always use well-maintained equipment for roof and gutter work.
◇ Use a ladder stay to hold a ladder away from guttering and prevent it from slipping sideways – never lean a ladder directly on a gutter.
◇ Make sure that a ladder is resting at the correct angle before climbing it.
◇ Make sure that the foot of a ladder cannot move before climbing it.
◇ As soon as you reach the top of a ladder, tie it using rope to a large eye bolt fixed in the wall or fascia board.

189

Replacing a slate

Remove any broken pieces of slate with a slate puller. Slide it up under the broken slate and move it to the one side until you can feel the fixing nail. When you tug the puller downward, the barb on the end will hook around the nail, pulling it out of place or cutting through it. Repeat the process on the other nail, and then pull out the remaining broken pieces of slate.

To secure the new slate in position, a strip of lead about 10in. long and 1¼in. wide is nailed to the roof sheathing and then bent back up over the lower edge of the slate.

Fixing the slate
After removing the old slate, 1, cut a strip of lead to the right length and nail it between the two slates in the row below using a 2in. aluminum or galvanized nail. The nail should pass into the wooden sheathing to which the lower row of slates is fixed, 2. Then push the replacement slate into place and line it up with the others in its row. Secure it in place by bending the protruding end of the lead strip up and over the lower edge of the slate. Double over the end so that the lead strip is not easily flattened by melting snow sliding down the roof.

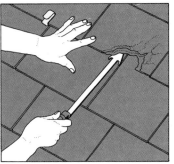

1 Using a slate puller, take out the old pieces of slate

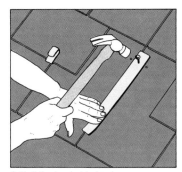

2 Nail the lead strip in place

Tips for repairing flat roofing

◇ To recondition an old roof, scrape off the stone chippings, deal with any serious cracks or blisters, and re-coat the whole roof.

◇ Prepare an area for repair by scraping away the chippings and drying out the area using a hot-air gun.

◇ After preparing a cracked area, press down the crack with a wooden wallpaper roller; paint the area of the crack with asphalt roofing cement. When this has dried, nail a patch of 15 pound roofing felt over the repair. Overlap the edges of the repair by at least 2in. Cover the edges of the patch and the nail heads with roofing cement.

◇ If the roof is covered with chippings, paint the repair with roofing cement and sprinkle chippings over the surface of the roof while it is still wet.

◇ If there are blisters and bubbles, make two cuts at right-angles across the center of the blister, turn back the edges, and treat in the same way as a crack; the edges will overlap slightly, because the blister will have stretched the surface of the felt.

190

Replacing a split shingle

If a wooden shingle is badly split or damaged, you should replace it immediately, to stop moisture getting into the roof timbers and causing rot. First remove the old shingle. Use a mallet and chisel to split the slate into narrow pieces. Then work these from side to side until they are free of the nails. The next stage is to get rid of the nails, which are concealed beneath the shingles above the one you have removed. The easiest way to do this is with a slate puller, which you slide under the shingle. If you do not have a slate puller, use a long hacksaw blade.

Fitting a new shingle
After removing the old shingle and nails, fit a new shingle about ½in. smaller than the space you need to fill – this will allow for expansion. Tap it into place using a hammer, and protecting the shingle with a wood block. Line it up with the other shingles in the row and secure it with galvanized roofing nails. Cover the nail heads with roofing cement.

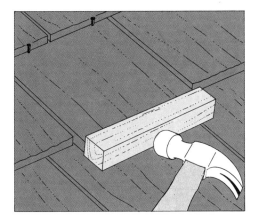

191

Repairing flashing

Flashings seal the joints where a roof meets a brick wall. Traditional flashings are made of sheet lead or zinc, and the top edge is usually tucked into the brickwork. If this pulls out, leaks can occur. Rake out the old mortar, tuck the flashing back into place, holding it firm with lead strip, dampen the joint, and press fresh mortar into place. If there are tears, cracks, or holes in the flashing, clean the areas with a scratch brush, paint the surrounding areas with flashing-strip primer, and when this has dried, fit self-adhesive flashing strip to cover up the holes and create a waterproof seal.

Badly corroded flashing is best replaced with a self-adhesive strip. This involves preparing and priming the surface carefully first.

Fitting self-adhesive flashing strip
Remove the old flashing and clean the brickwork with a scratch brush. Repoint the brickwork if necessary (see Job 195, p. 202). Paint a band of flashing-strip primer where the new flashing strip is going to be fitted. The band of primer should be about 5in. wide on the roof and 7½in. wide on the wall. When the primer has dried, press down the first band of flashing strip, so that it overlaps the roof by about 5in., with a 2½in. overlap on to the wall. Then apply a second strip, to cover the primer on the wall and overlap the turn-up of the first strip. Use a wallpaper seam roller to flatten bubbles and creases.

The guttering system

The basic system consists of gutter channeling, attached so that it falls slightly toward an outlet. This is connected, by means of a spout top fitting, to a downspout that discharges onto a paved area or splash block. Sometimes another pipe is fed into a downspout by means of an open-ended, funnel-shaped inlet called a hopper.

The most common material for guttering is plastic. Copper gutters are also made and some homes have wooden gutters. There are three different methods of hanging gutters. Some are secured with a strap nailed to the roof, some are nailed directly to the fascia, and some are held by a spike that is nailed through a tube into the fascia.

Downspouts are also made in a number of materials. The most common types are aluminum, copper, and galvanized steel. Some downspouts screw onto the outside of the gutters, others are designed to fit smoothly inside.

Gutter and downspout sizes vary according to the area of roof they drain. It is important that gutters and downspouts are large enough to deal with heavy rainfall. A generally adequate size for guttering is about 5in. across, with downspouts $3\frac{1}{2}$in. in diameter. If you are uncertain about which size to use, consult the manufacturer of the systems you are considering. Guttering usually comes in 10ft lengths. Allow a drop of $\frac{1}{2}$in. for every 10ft of guttering.

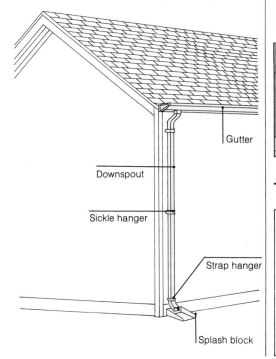

Gutter

Downspout

Sickle hanger

Strap hanger

Splash block

192

Clearing a blocked gutter

If a gutter is overflowing or there is a severe water leak from a downspout, there may be a blockage in the gutter, or in a downspout. Start by clearing out the gutter. When you have done this, pour a bucket of water from the stop end and check that it drains quickly. This test may highlight other faults, such as leaking joints. After clearing a metal gutter, let it dry and apply two coats of fibered asphalt cement to the inside.

Scraping out the debris
When cleaning out a gutter, work from the downspout outlet to the stop end, to prevent debris being pushed down the spout. Use a garden trowel, or, to make the job easier, cut a scrap of hardboard or plywood to the shape of the gutter to act as a scraper.

193

Clearing a blocked downspout

Place a tray under the downspout outlet to catch debris. Clean the top of the spout either by removing it or with drain-cleaning wire. Probe upward through the spout outlet. Clear the straight sections with bamboo canes.

Removing a blockage
Try clearing the spout top by pushing a trap-and-drain auger down from above. This may force debris down, so put a container at the bottom.

194

Repairing a sagging gutter

The most likely cause is that the fixing nails have corroded and worked loose. Or the aluminum strap may be damaged. The solution is to put in new gutter fixing nails or a new gutter strap.

Replacing a strap
Remove the slate and the broken end of the old strap and attach a new piece of aluminum. Nail the end of the new strap to the roof. Replace the slate.

Tips for repairing leaking gutters

◇ Clean an aluminum gutter thoroughly with steel wool before applying epoxy resin. Add two coats of fibered asphalt cement to fill a small hole.

◇ With larger holes, clean the gutter, add a layer of fibered asphalt cement and then cover the hole with two layer of aluminum foil. Cover this with another coat of fibered asphalt cement to complete the repair.

◇ If a metal gutter has a very large hole or tear, replace the affected length rather than trying to fill the hole.

◇ To repair wooden gutters, cut out any rotten wood, treat the area with a preservative, and fill the hole.

External walls

Repairing stucco ◇ Repairing siding ◇ Pointing a wall Dealing with wall stains

Brick and wood siding are the most common materials for external walls. They all vary greatly in their appearance, although they can be disguised by the addition of stucco or siding. Most people prefer to leave large projects involving external walls to a professional, but there are a few smaller jobs that are quite straight-forward. The most useful of these are pointing – repairing the mortar joints in brickwork – and patching up areas of stucco and siding.

It is also easy to paint external walls. Brick and stone walls are usually attractive without painting, but painting can considerably improve the appearance of a rendered or stucco wall. It is important to prepare the wall carefully (by brushing off stains and loose material, filling holes, and applying primer) and to use a paint that is suitable for exterior masonry.

Points to remember

◇ For a small area of pointing buy ready-mixed dry mortar.
◇ Before pointing or repairing stucco, scrape out all the loose material and dirt.
◇ Brush water into the joints before pointing – otherwise the moisture will be sucked out and the pointing will crumble.
◇ Keep the mortar mixture fairly dry – it should not run out of the joints.
◇ Never wash walls covered with mineral deposits.

Estimating time

All these times are for working on 10 square feet of wall – multiply them to get a time for the repair you want to carry out. If the repair is high up, you will also need extra time to set up a ladder safely.

Repairing stucco hours

Repairing siding hours

Repointing hours

195

Pointing a wall

Old mortar that is cracked and loose will let in rainwater and cause dampness on interior walls. If only a small area of your brickwork needs repointing, do it yourself with a mix of one part masonry cement and three parts fine sand. Add a little water, but keep the mix on the dry side – if it is too runny it will be weak and will run down the wall causing stains. So it is worthwhile waiting for about five minutes to allow the mix to firm up before starting to repoint. First cut off loose rendering.

Applying new mortar
First chip away the old mortar using a slim cold chisel, 1, to a depth of ½ in. Avoid damaging the bricks. Clean all the flaking pieces of mortar and dust from the cracks with a scratch brush. Before repointing brush out the joints with water, 2. This will ensure that water is not sucked from the mortar by the dry bricks, causing it to crack or crumble again quickly. Using a pointing trowel, cut off rounded slices of mortar, and press these into the vertical joints, 3. Trim off excess mortar with the brick jointer, 4. Match the finish with the original pointing. It may be flush, slanted, v-shaped, concave or raked. When you have completed the vertical joints, tackle the horizontal ones. In hot weather keep the joints soft for a few days by spraying water on them to stop them crumbling away quickly.

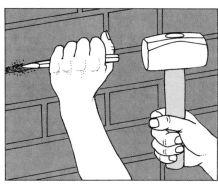

1 Clear out the old mortar, including all the crumbling material and debris

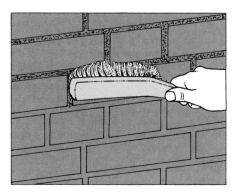

2 Brush the joints with water immediately before repointing them

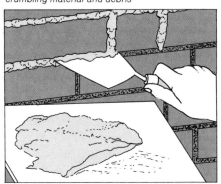

3 Point the vertical joints, then the horizontal using a trowel to apply pieces of the right size

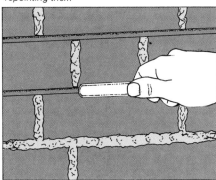

4 Remove excess mortar and shape the joint with a brick jointer

196
Repairing stucco

If your stucco is cracked, clean out the crack with a scratch brush and widen it at its deepest point with a putty knife so that it will hold the repair better. Then moisten the crack, and repair with a mix of one part masonry cement and three parts fine sand. Finally add mortar pigment and keep the repair damp for two days.

With a larger area of damaged stucco, you should chip the surface away until you get to a firm, undamaged area. Then make a patch, applying the stucco mix in three coats. You may have to repair the chicken wire that supports the first coat.

On both types of repair, it is often difficult to match the color to the original stucco. It is usually easiest to give the whole wall an overall finish coat.

Patching stucco
After chipping away the defective stucco, examine the chicken wire and repair if it is damaged. Then dampen the patch area and apply the base coat, pushing it through the wire and building it up to within ½in. of the surface, 1. Scarify the surface, when it starts to set. Keep the first layer damp for two days, then put on the second coat, to within ⅛in. of the surface. Keep this damp for 2 days and leave it for a further 4 or 5 days before dampening the stucco again and applying the finish coat.

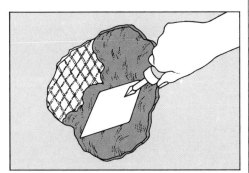

1 Apply the base coat with a trowel until it lies ½in. below the surrounding wall

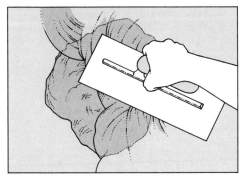

2 After applying a second coat, leave it for a week before adding a finishing coat

197
Repairing siding

Wooden siding often cracks or splinters and it also subject to rot. If a small section of siding is damaged, it is quite easy to cut out part of a board and replace it. If a whole board is badly cracked or rotten, it is best to take it out and replace it with a new one.

The easiest siding to repair is the type made from simple overlapping beveled boards. Tongue-and-groove and shiplap siding boards can also be replaced in the same way, but you will need to cut the tongue or lap off the board to make it easier to fit.

Taking out a section of siding involves forcing wooden shims under the damaged piece so that you can cut it out with a backsaw. Cut away the nails by pushing a hacksaw blade between the boards and use a keyhole saw to cut away the wood beneath the board above. You should then be able to chisel out the damaged section of board and fit the replacement piece.

To keep out water it is important to finish off carefully. Use wood putty to fill the gaps at each end of the board, and apply wood sealer before painting the board the required color.

Replacing a damaged section
Drive wooden shims under the section you want to remove, 1, and start to cut through the board at both ends using a backsaw, 2. When you have cut the lower part of the board, split it along its length with a chisel, so that the lower section falls away. Finish cutting away the upper part of the board with a keyhole saw. This allows you to cut the board where it is covered by the siding above. Next, push a hacksaw blade up under the overlapping siding to cut away the nails that are holding it in place. You should now be able to take out the remaining part of the board. Slide the new piece into position, hammer it home, using an offcut to protect the new piece, 3, and nail it to the siding above and below, 4. Finally fill the gaps with wood putty.

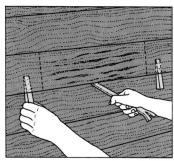

1 Insert shims behind the damaged section, using a prybar as a lever

2 Cut through the board at each end with a backsaw

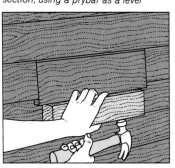

3 Knock the new board into place by hammering against a wooden offcut

4 Nail the new board securely in position

Removing stains

The most common stain found on brickwork and stucco is efflorescence, a light, powdery deposit consisting of mineral salts from the bricks or mortar that are drawn to the surface. Remove the deposit by cleaning with a scratch brush. Then apply neutralizer, or a mix of one part muriatic acid and four parts water.

To remove dust from stucco and brickwork, brush on a stabilizing solution and leave it for 24 hours to dry before painting the wall. Small areas of dirt on a wall can be removed by scrubbing with clean water.

If you have a wall that is water-stained, you should first eliminate the cause of the dampness and let the wall dry out. Then seal the wall with alkali-resistant primer to make sure that the stain is not visible through a new coat of paint.

To clean wooden siding, hose it down to remove surface dirt, and brush off any stubborn marks. (*For information on rot, worm and termites, see pp. 208-9.*)

Waterproofing

Defenses against dampness ◇ The causes of dampness ◇ Estimating time ◇ Waterproofing a basement ◇ Preventing a leak ◇ Types of condensation control

Any home that is not well maintained is a potential victim of dampness. The roof, walls, windows, and doors are battered by the wind and rain; the floors and walls can be attacked by rising moisture from below ground; and inside the house the plumbing pipework represents another potential source of dampness. The result can be anything from spoiled decorations to a very damp environment, which can cause poor health for the occupants of the home and major structural damage as the wood starts to rot. Another source of dampness in the home is condensation, moisture that gets trapped in a room and cannot escape. It is often produced in a building that is well insulated and heated, but poorly ventilated.

House foundations and basements are both places where damp can build up. Where possible, protect foundations by digging drainage ditches to divert water away from your home. To prevent seepage, patch wall cracks and apply patching mortar with a waterproofing additive. There are other ways in which you can protect your home from dampness. Many of the potential problems are in parts of the home that are not normally noticed – for example, the tops of chimney stacks and the guttering system. It is essential to keep these areas in good repair, and many of the jobs involved, such as keeping the gutters unblocked, are quite simple. The difficulty is being aware of the causes, so that you can make repairs in good time.

Points to remember

◇ Keep gutters clear and in good repair to avoid leaks and penetrating moisture.
◇ Examine regularly the condition of chimney stacks, pots, and flaunching.
◇ To avoid condensation, ensure that ventilation is adequate, particularly if your home is well insulated.
◇ Check the condition of your roof by examining it from inside the roof during heavy rain.
◇ Keep air spaces clear of all obstructions to ensure good sub-floor-ventilation.

Defenses against dampness

It is often possible to keep moisture away from the foundations and basement of your home by digging drainage ditches. If your house is on sloping ground, these should be positioned so that they intercept water flowing downhill and take it around the house. When a ditch is not practical, or when dampness persists after you have patched cracks in a wall, install plastic sheeting in a trench dug around the foundations to prevent moisture getting in. The trench should be about 2ft deep and 4ft wide, and you should coat the wall with asphalt before putting in the plastic sheeting. In cases where the dampness is caused by deeper cracks in the foundations, it may be necessary to dig down to below the level of the crack and put in drain tiles to take the water away. But foundation repairs can be expensive and you may prefer to fit a sump pump.

Installing plastic sheeting
First dig a trench around the house walls and coat the brickwork with a layer of asphalt. Next press plastic sheeting against the asphalt and along the base of the trench. Fill the trench with rocks and cover with a surface layer of soil.

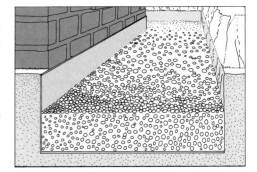

Using drain tiles
Install drain tiles on top of a gravel layer in a trench, dug to a level deeper than the wall cracks and sloping away from the house. The trench should continue about 12ft clear of the house, to carry the water away.

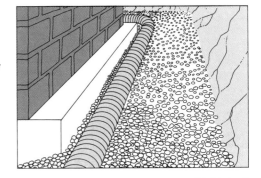

Fitting a sump pump
The pump should be installed in a hole at the point in the basement where water tends to collect. A bed of gravel at the base of the hole will prevent the pump getting jammed with mud. Water discharges through a pipe, which should be on the side of the house where the drainage is most efficient.

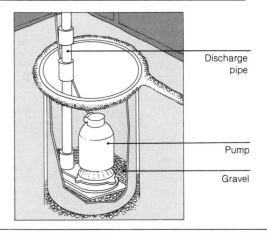

Discharge pipe

Pump

Gravel

The causes of dampness

A damp patch in a room can usually be linked quickly with a nearby structural fault. For example, a wet patch at the top of a wall in an upstairs room may be caused by a leaking gutter or downspout, while a stain on a wall near a window could be caused by rain being blown through a gap between the frame and the wall. But sometimes a damp patch inside the home is some distance from its cause on the outside of the building. For example, water leaking through a crack in a roof tile can drip onto the roof timbers and run along for several feet before dropping onto the ceiling below.

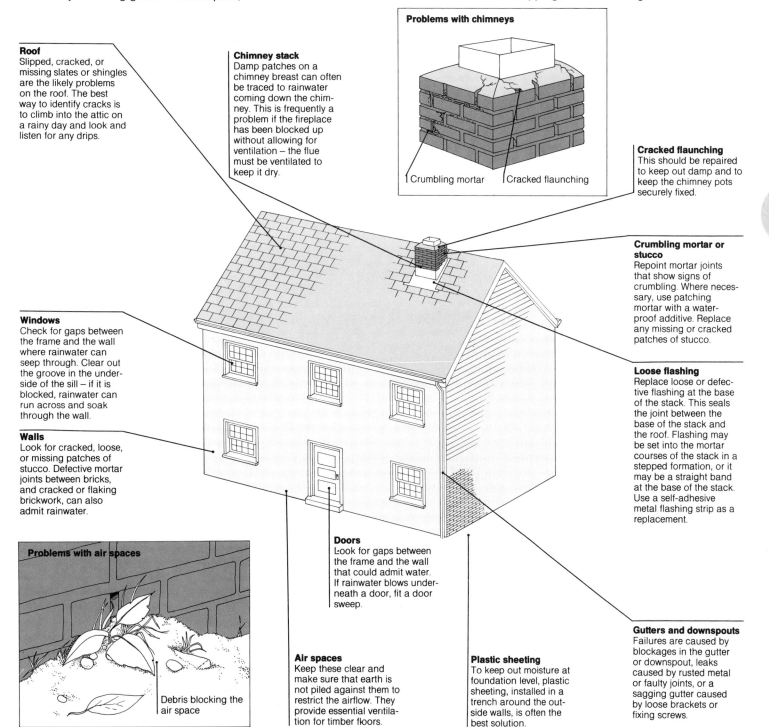

Problems with chimneys

Crumbling mortar   Cracked flaunching

Roof
Slipped, cracked, or missing slates or shingles are the likely problems on the roof. The best way to identify cracks is to climb into the attic on a rainy day and look and listen for any drips.

Chimney stack
Damp patches on a chimney breast can often be traced to rainwater coming down the chimney. This is frequently a problem if the fireplace has been blocked up without allowing for ventilation – the flue must be ventilated to keep it dry.

Cracked flaunching
This should be repaired to keep out damp and to keep the chimney pots securely fixed.

Crumbling mortar or stucco
Repoint mortar joints that show signs of crumbling. Where necessary, use patching mortar with a waterproof additive. Replace any missing or cracked patches of stucco.

Windows
Check for gaps between the frame and the wall where rainwater can seep through. Clear out the groove in the underside of the sill – if it is blocked, rainwater can run across and soak through the wall.

Walls
Look for cracked, loose, or missing patches of stucco. Defective mortar joints between bricks, and cracked or flaking brickwork, can also admit rainwater.

Loose flashing
Replace loose or defective flashing at the base of the stack. This seals the joint between the base of the stack and the roof. Flashing may be set into the mortar courses of the stack in a stepped formation, or it may be a straight band at the base of the stack. Use a self-adhesive metal flashing strip as a replacement.

Problems with air spaces

Debris blocking the air space

Doors
Look for gaps between the frame and the wall that could admit water. If rainwater blows underneath a door, fit a door sweep.

Air spaces
Keep these clear and make sure that earth is not piled against them to restrict the airflow. They provide essential ventilation for timber floors.

Plastic sheeting
To keep out moisture at foundation level, plastic sheeting, installed in a trench around the outside walls, is often the best solution.

Gutters and downspouts
Failures are caused by blockages in the gutter or downspout, leaks caused by rusted metal or faulty joints, or a sagging gutter caused by loose brackets or fixing screws.

198
Waterproofing a basement

When cracks occur in basement walls they can let in water from outside. In many cases you can fix the cracks from the inside, although sometimes it is necessary to make the repair on the exterior of the wall.

Patching a stationary crack
Start by widening the crack, using a cold chisel, until it is about 1in. across. Make sure that the crack is clear of loose pieces of concrete. A scratch brush is ideal for cleaning out this sort of crack. Next coat the inside surfaces of the crack with patching mortar before filling it. If the patch is not effective, dig down to the exterior wall and fill and seal from the outside.

Patching a moving crack
For a small crack, clean the opening and the surrounding wall with detergent. Cut a piece of fiberglass cloth so that it covers the crack and overlaps at least 2in. onto the wall all the way around the opening. Apply a coat of asphalt sealer to the wall and stick on the patch, covering it with another coat of sealer. If the crack is a large one, fill it to about half its depth with mastic sealer and finish off with patching mortar.

Filling a floor-wall crack
Widen the crack and dry it out with a propane torch. Then put in a strip of mastic joint sealer next to the wall. Next half-fill the hole with epoxy resin. Finally fill the rest of the crack with mortar. If this fails to keep out the damp, you may have to fit a sump pump.

First determine whether the crack is moving or stationary. Put marks on the wall on each side of the crack and measure the distance between them. If the distance is still the same after two weeks, the crack is stationary. Stationary cracks can easily be patched with mortar. But moving cracks require different treatment, using fiberglass cloth or mastic joint sealer to allow for the expansion and contraction.

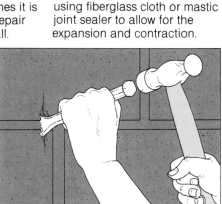

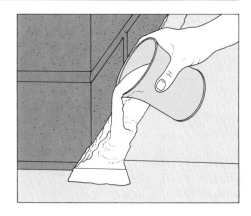

199
Preventing seeping in a basement

Dampness in a basement is not always due to cracks or holes in the wall. Sometimes moisture seeps through the walls and an overall waterproofing treat-

Keeping out seepage
Moisten the wall before applying the mortar. Then, using patching mortar mixed with a waterproofing ingredient such as latex or silicone, put a 1in. layer on the wall. Work from the base of the wall upward. Before the mortar has completely set, cover the surface with a coat of waterproof cement paint. Use a stiff brush to work it into the mortar.

ment is required. Waterproof paint might be the answer, but sometimes it is necessary to coat the interior walls and floor with patching mortar.

Seepage frequently occurs through dirt basement floors. A covering of polyethylene plastic will keep out the moisture, but a more substantial, concrete barrier is required if the basement is in use.

200
Plugging a leak

When water is flowing in a continuous stream through a hole in a basement wall, you should drain the water away into a bucket and block the hole to stop further leaks. You can

start to repair the hole while water is still coming out. You do this by using dry, hydraulic cement to support a piece of rubber hose, which is inserted into the hole to carry away the water. When the water has drained away and the rubber hose is no longer needed, the hole is plugged with another piece of cement.

Stopping a flowing leak
*After chipping away any loose concrete around the hole, insert a length of rubber hose to take away the water, **1**. Fill the hole around the rubber hose with dry hydraulic cement and, when it has set, pull out the hose and fill the remaining hole with a plug of hydraulic cement, **2**. Hold the cement in place for two or three minutes.*

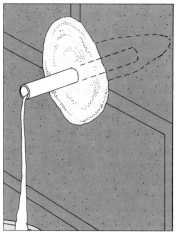

1 Insert a rubber hose into the hole to drain out the water

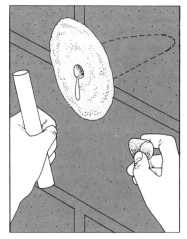

2 Remove the hose and stop the hole with a plug of cement

201
Preventing condensation

If dampness in a basement is not coming from a leak or seepage it might be due to condensation. It is easy to find out whether the water is originating outside or inside the basement. Tape a piece of aluminum foil to the wall. If moisture builds up on top, suspect condensation. If the top surface is dry, but moisture has continued to collect behind the

foil, then it is probably seepage.
Condensation is caused when there is too much humidity in the air or when there is a large temperature difference between the air inside the basement and the wall. Excess humidity can come from a basement shower, washing machine, or dryer, or it can be formed when there is poor ventilation. If you cannot remove the source of the humidity, install a dehumidifier or heat exchanger, improve the basement's ventilation (this will also compensate for any temperature difference), or seal the walls.

Installing a vapor barrier
In an unpaved basement or crawl space you can make an effective vapor barrier by installing strips of polyethylene plastic. Attach the end of each strip to the wall about 2in. above the floor using duct tape. You should also tape the strips together at the point where the wall meets the floor. Overlap the strips of plastic by about 6in., and weight down the overlapping edges with rocks or bricks.

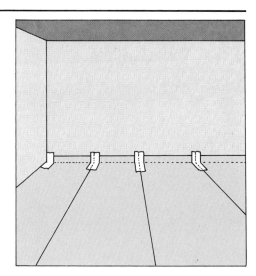

Types of condensation control

The key to curing condensation is to get the right balance between heat and ventilation in the home. But it is important to cut down the sources of condensation. Avoid kerosene heaters and unflued gas and oil heaters; reduce steam by covering saucepans and turning off the kettle as soon as it has boiled; and if possible avoid drying laundry inside the home.

Heat exchangers
A fresh-air heat exchanger removes stale air from a room and replaces it with fresh air from outside. But it does this while retaining about 70 percent of the heat in the room. The outgoing and incoming flows of air are separated by a network of barriers as they pass through the unit. The effect of this is to remove the moist air from the room and replace it with dry air, so that condensation is reduced.

There are two basic types of fresh-air heat exchangers. The smaller type looks like a window air conditioner. It is cheaper, uses only about one-tenth of the electricity used by an air conditioner, and can cope adequately

with the heat-exchange requirements of one room. If you have several rooms that need a heat exchanger, you may find it worthwhile having a large, central unit installed.
Dehumidifiers
When condensation is a serious problem, use a dehumidifier. This is a machine that works rather like a refrigerator. It draws warm, damp air over a cold coil so that the water condenses, and then passes the air over a warm coil so that it is warmed again as it passes back into the room.
Range hoods
These deal with cooking smells and steam very efficiently. There are two types. One extracts the steam directly

to the outside air, the other filters the air and recirculates it into the room. Some models offer a choice between recirculation and extraction.
Ventilators
An open fire needs adjustable ventilators – ideally situated on either side of the hearth and fitted in the floor. With a solid floor, the ventilator should be fixed over the door leading to the hall.
A timber floor also requires ventilation. Air spaces are set in the walls for this purpose and they should be kept clear at all times. Blocked fireplaces should also be ventilated with an air space or a grille.
Thermal insulators
Lining cold walls and ceilings with

sheets of expanded polystyrene before wallpapering will eliminate condensation. Thermal insulating plasterboard, cork tiles, or tongue-and-groove edged boards will have the same effect. Special anti-condensation latex paint is also available. This absorbs moisture when the humidity is high and releases it later when the air is drier.
Windows
Double-glazing with sealed units will solve the problem, although other types of double glazing may produce misting between the panes. (*For more information about curing condensation with double glazing, see p. 101.*) The best solution may be to increase the ventilation by fitting a fan or vent.

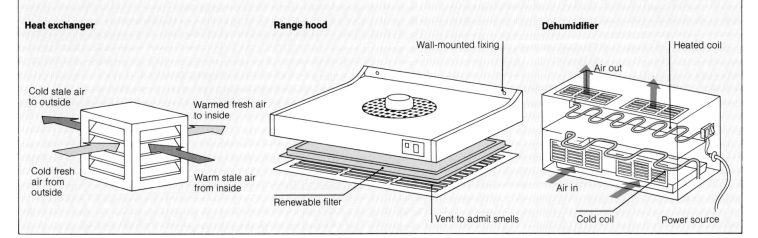

Heat exchanger
Cold stale air to outside
Cold fresh air from outside
Warmed fresh air to inside
Warm stale air from inside

Range hood
Wall-mounted fixing
Renewable filter
Vent to admit smells

Dehumidifier
Heated coil
Air out
Air in
Cold coil
Power source

Wood rot and infestation

Types of rot and infestation ◇ Treatments for rot and woodworm ◇ Treating wet rot

Rot and infestation are the enemies of wood. Both, if left unchecked, can destroy woodwork completely. Where structural timbers are concerned, the damage can be far reaching and very expensive to put right. So if there is any evidence of rot, woodworm, or termites in your home, you should take steps to eradicate it immediately.

There are two types of wood rot – wet and dry. Both are caused by fungi that originate in wet timber. The signs of rot vary from rapidly growing fungal threads to timber that breaks up in a pattern of squares.

Woodworm is the general name for a number of wood-eating beetles, of which the furniture beetle is the most common. Other common beetles are the powder post beetle, which can reduce timber to powder, and the house longhorn beetle, which can spend as long as eight to ten years eating away a piece of wood. Evidence of an attack is provided by the holes from which the beetle larvae emerge. Termites can be found in lumber anywhere. They are difficult to detect, but they often make earth tunnels, about $\frac{1}{2}$ in. wide, between supplies of timber.

Rot and infestation need not be serious problems if they are diagnosed and treated in time. It is possible to deal with small, isolated attacks yourself, provided that you are sure to treat or replace all the affected timber. But if the infestation has taken hold and spread, you will need a specialist exterminator.

Points to remember

◇ Keep attics, basements, and other parts of the home made of timber well ventilated to cut down the risk of rot.
◇ Make sure that tiles, slates, shingles, gutters, and downspouts are all in good repair, to keep out penetrating damp.
◇ Watch out for rot around leaking pipes.
◇ Treat small areas of wet rot yourself.
◇ Treat timber infestation quickly – if the damage is extensive, call in a specialist exterminator.
◇ Treat all the timber that has been attacked, paying particular attention to the dry-rot fungus.

Types of rot and infestation

Rot or infestation may not be immediately apparent because they tend to start in places that cannot be seen – in concealed timbers beneath floorboards, in cellars, and in attics. But once you examine timber, the signs of infestation are obvious.

Dry rot
Attacks of dry rot usually originate in areas that are damp and poorly ventilated – floor joists, basements, and under sinks are common places. First, matted fungal strands appear, which develop a silver-gray skin possibly tinged with streaks of lilac or yellow. A texture like cotton batting forms, followed by a pale gray, corrugated fruiting body resembling a pancake and surrounded by rust-red spore dust.

Because the attack usually starts in a hidden place, the first sign you notice may be a musty smell or the sight of the cotton-batting-like material appearing from below floorboards, baseboards, or wall paneling. Once you have exposed the area, the dry rot will be obvious. The timber that has been attacked will become dark brown and cracks will have developed, breaking up the surface into squares. If touched, the wood will crumble easily.

The danger with dry rot is that it will transfer from wet to dry timbers. It does so because it is able to produce water-carrying roots that can be up to $\frac{1}{4}$ in. in diameter. These roots can travel anywhere, even through brickwork, until they find dry timber which they can dampen to provide ideal conditions for growth.

Wet rot
The areas where dry rot can develop – wherever there are damp, un-ventilated timbers – may also be prone to wet rot. This form of rot has yellow-brown streaks or patches, accompanied by string-like strands that grow in a fern shape on lumber or damp plaster. The wood becomes brownish-black and cracks along the grain, though criss-cross cracking is sometimes possible. In timbers such as window frames and doorsteps bubbling paintwork is sometimes the first clue to wet rot. Though equally serious, wet rot is easier to treat than dry rot, because it is always found in damp timber. But if you have wet rot, you must remember that a dry-rot attack may be developing nearby.

Termites
Looking rather like ants, but with thicker, untapered bodies, termites are active during early spring and fall. Some species stay above ground, while others hide under the wood surface. When they find a nesting site in a piece of lumber, they discard their wings, so, if you find termite wings, quickly call in a specialist exterminator.

Dry rot
Furred, corrugated and smooth fungal growths are the tell-tale signs.

Wet rot
Wood attacked by wet rot develops streaks, then darkens and cracks.

Termite attack
Subterranean termites dig along the grain, others work across it

Treating rot and infestation

Using a wood-repair system

The initial cause of rot is dampness somewhere in the house structure. The first thing to do is to cure the cause of the dampness (*for more information, see pp. 204-7*); there is no point in treating rot until the cause is removed. Once this is done, act quickly to treat the rot.

Treating dry rot
Dry rot can have a devastating effect on a building, and treatment should be carried out with the utmost care and efficiency. If structural timbers have been affected, it is usually safest to leave the job to a specialist firm.

Timber should be cut away at least 3ft beyond the edge of the dry rot. If water-carrying roots have passed through the walls, plaster and mortar joints must be hacked out. If dry rot is discovered below the floorboards and in the joists about 6in. of soil may have to be removed. As soon as the affected area is cleared, the debris should be taken away and burned. If this is not done, red spore dust could recontaminate the property. Surface spores and strands can be destroyed using a propane torch.

The treatment itself involves spraying a fungicide over the affected areas and 6ft beyond. Two coats of fungicide are required, the second applied after the first has dried. New timber should also be coated, and sawn ends dipped in timber preservative for a few minutes before fixing.

Roots in the walls are killed by drilling downward-angled holes, about ½in. in diameter, on both sides of the brickwork. They should be 7in. deep and drilled at 30in. intervals. The holes should be filled with fluid, which eventually soaks into the brickwork.

Any replastering should be done in three coats. The middle coat should consist of zinc oxychloride plaster ¼in. thick. If walls are not replastered, they should be covered with two coats of zinc oxychloride paint.

If only a limited area of wood has been damaged by wet rot, eradicate the rot and repair the timber using a commercially available wood-repair system. This should contain a wood hardener, a filler, and preservative tablets to prevent further decay. A small area takes only 1 to 3 hours to treat.

Eradicating wet rot
Begin by digging away the worst of the rotten wood and then brush quick-drying wood hardener over the entire area, 1. Rebuild the shape of the wood with filler, 2, and finally drill holes into the surrounding wood and insert the preservative tablets, 3.

1 *Apply wood-hardener over the affected area*

2 *Fill the hole, putting on the filler with a putty knife*

3 *Drill holes in the wood to take preservative tablets*

Window frames
Wooden window frames are susceptible to rot, especially at the joints between the uprights and the lower rails.

Sub-floors
Look out for rot when sub-floor ventilation is poor. Termites can also be a problem in joists and floorboards.

Roof timbers
If the roof has been leaking, rot may have taken hold here. Termites also attack roof timbers.

Kitchens
Rooms, such as kitchens and bathrooms, where condensation is a problem are often susceptible to rot.

Door frames
Rot as a result of rising damp can occur here.

Downspouts
Leaking downspouts can cause penetrating damp, which creates conditions ideal for both wet and dry rot.

Treating wet rot
Where there is a large amount of damage, it is best to leave treatment to a specialist firm. First, any rotten timber should be cut out and the surrounding wood treated with two liberal coats of dry-rot fluid or wood preservative. New timber should also be treated with preservative (see Job 202, right). Small areas of damage can be repaired with wood filler. Where only a small amount of wood has been affected, you can make good the damage with a wood-repair system.

Treating termite infestation
Subterranean termites are the most difficult to deal with, and you should call in a specialist exterminator to eradicate them. This will involve creating a chemical barrier around the house, so that the termites cannot get to the earth and therefore die of thirst. Non-subterranean termites are easier to eradicate because they usually attack smaller areas of wood. If the timber is still sound, injecting a chemical to kill the termites will solve the problem. But damaged timber should be replaced.

Treating woodworm infestation
If there are small holes in the timber surface, and signs of light-colored dust around them, suspect a woodworm attack. Clean the wood and brush or spray it with woodworm fluid. Wear old clothes when you are applying the fluid. If you find woodworm in the attic, treat all the attic timbers. You need not treat the other timbers in your home, such as the floorboards, unless they too show signs of woodworm. If the damage is extensive, call in a specialist firm to carry out the treatment.

Household safety

Emergency action ◇ Types of fire-fighting equipment ◇ Danger areas in the home Children and home safety

Safety in the home is largely a matter of common sense. If you keep your electrical and gas installations in good repair, take steps to prevent fire, and make sure children are not able to reach any of the potentially dangerous items (from cans of bleach to boiling saucepans) in the home, you will avoid most accidents. But you should also be prepared for the unexpected. Find out how to turn off your electricity and gas supplies, and read the instructions on emergency action (see right) for gas and fire emergencies.

Points to remember

◇ Get to know the positions of your main gas and water supply faucets and the main electrical disconnect, so that you can turn them off in an emergency.
◇ Only use fire extinguishers approved by UL standards.
◇ Never drape clothes over a heater, or leave them where they could fall on to the appliance.
◇ Always keep radiant heaters at least 1yd. away from curtains and furniture.
◇ Make sure that flues and chimneys used for gas and wood-burning appliances are kept clear of soot and debris.
◇ Keep heaters where they cannot be knocked over by children or elderly people.
◇ Turn kerosene heaters off before refilling them.
Electricity
◇ Check your electrical equipment regularly, or have it checked by a qualified electrician.
◇ If you have small children in the house, cover receptacles with tape or spring-loaded flaps.
◇ Ensure that all electrical equipment is correctly grounded.
◇ Use cord correctly, do not trail it across floors; run it under carpets, or staple it to walls or floors.
◇ If the floor is damp, stand on a rubber mat or dry wooden boards while you work.
◇ Have electric blankets serviced every two years by the manufacturer.
◇ Keep electric blankets uncreased.
Gas
◇ Take prompt action if you smell gas (see right, top).
◇ Have gas appliances serviced regularly.
◇ Always have gas appliances professionally repaired.
◇ If you run a gas line yourself, make sure all connections meet code requirements.

Emergency action

If you suspect a gas leak
◇ Extinguish all flames including cigarettes.
◇ Open doors and windows.
◇ Turn off all gas taps.
◇ Check whether an unlit appliance has been left on.
◇ Check whether a pilot light has blown out.
◇ Do not operate electrical switches.
◇ If you suspect a leak, test for it using a fairly strong solution of concentrated dishwashing liquid; this will bubble where the gas is leaking. Call the gas company.
◇ Have repairs carried out straight away by a gas fitter.
◇ If an obvious source of the leak cannot be found, turn off the entire supply at the gas meter and call the gas emergency service.

In case of fire
◇ Get everyone out.
◇ Close all the doors behind you.
◇ Call the fire department.
◇ If anyone is still in the building, tell the officer in the first fire engine.
If you are trapped in a room
◇ Check the temperature of the door handle – if it is hot, the fire is probably burning on the other side, so do not open the door.
◇ Use blankets or mats to prevent smoke from entering under the door.
◇ Even in a smoke-filled room, 2in. to 3in. immediately above the floor will be clear of smoke.
◇ Go to the window and shout for help – do not jump, wait for rescue.

Types of fire-fighting equipment

Small domestic fire extinguishers are useful, but they have a limited capacity, so they should be used promptly. For this reason it is worth installing a smoke alarm to warn you quickly of any fire. These alarms are battery-operated and can be mounted unobtrusively on a ceiling.

One of the most useful pieces of equipment is a fire blanket. Keep one in the kitchen, where it is ideal for putting out a fire of burning fat. Turn off the heat, cover the pan with the cloth, and allow the pan to cool before taking it outside. Never use water on a pan of burning fat or oil.

Fire extinguishers
*Water extinguishers, **1**, are used for combustible materials such as wood and paper, but not for fires involving electricity, fat, or oil. Water comes out of a nozzle on the end of a hose, which should be directed at the base of the fire and kept moving across the burning material. Damp down the embers to prevent re-ignition.*
*Dry powder extinguishers, **2**, which have a stubby nozzle can be used on all fires, particularly those involving oil, fat, and electricity. Choose one with at least 2lbs of powder. Direct*
the jet of powder at the nearest edge of the fire and drive the flames away from you with a quick, sweeping action. The material can be removed with a vacuum cleaner, although you should discard contaminated liquids and clean electrical equipment thoroughly before you attempt to use it.
*Vaporizing-liquid extinguishers, **3**, have a horn-shaped nozzle and can be used on any small fires, particularly electrical fires. The extinguisher should weigh at least 1½lbs. It is used in the same way as a dry-powder extinguisher.*

Danger areas in the home

Certain areas of the home are more prone than others to accidents. Most people know that the kitchen (see bottom of page) presents many potential dangers, but there are other parts of the home where accidents can easily happen if you allow them to do so. But by simply thinking in terms of safety and using items in the proper way, you can avoid most accidents. The important areas are electrical and gas equipment, which should be serviced regularly, and open fires.

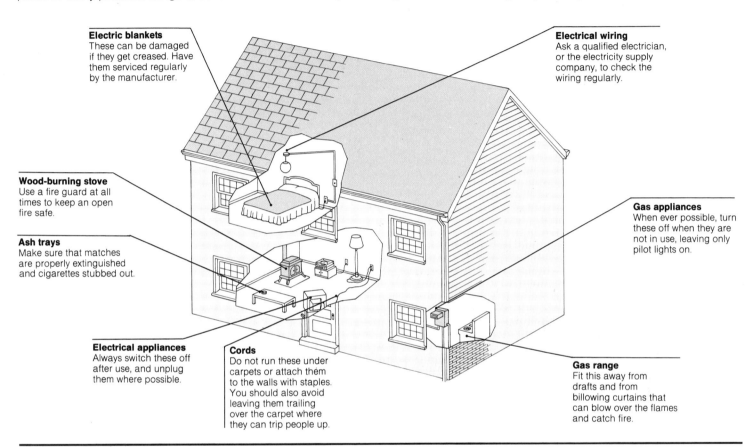

Electric blankets
These can be damaged if they get creased. Have them serviced regularly by the manufacturer.

Electrical wiring
Ask a qualified electrician, or the electricity supply company, to check the wiring regularly.

Wood-burning stove
Use a fire guard at all times to keep an open fire safe.

Ash trays
Make sure that matches are properly extinguished and cigarettes stubbed out.

Gas appliances
When ever possible, turn these off when they are not in use, leaving only pilot lights on.

Electrical appliances
Always switch these off after use, and unplug them where possible.

Cords
Do not run these under carpets or attach them to the walls with staples. You should also avoid leaving them trailing over the carpet where they can trip people up.

Gas range
Fit this away from drafts and from billowing curtains that can blow over the flames and catch fire.

Safety in the kitchen

More accidents occur in the kitchen than in any other room in the home. This is mainly because kitchens are busy places that are full of potential hazards to children, such as hot oil, sharp knives, and jagged tins. So it is important to take special precautions in the kitchen, especially if you have young children. Design the kitchen so that hot oil and pans of boiling water do not normally have to be carried across the room. Keep knives well out of reach of children, whether on a wall rack or in a drawer. If possible, keep young children out of the kitchen using a safety gate on the door, especially when you are preparing or cooking food. Teach children safety habits from the beginning.

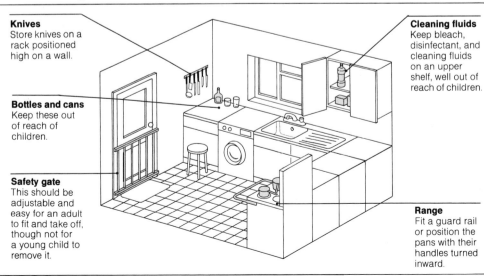

Knives
Store knives on a rack positioned high on a wall.

Bottles and cans
Keep these out of reach of children.

Safety gate
This should be adjustable and easy for an adult to fit and take off, though not for a young child to remove it.

Cleaning fluids
Keep bleach, disinfectant, and cleaning fluids on an upper shelf, well out of reach of children.

Range
Fit a guard rail or position the pans with their handles turned inward.

Security

Preventing burglary ◇ Types of window lock
Types of door lock ◇ Fitting a mortise
deadlock ◇ Types of alarm system

Being burgled is always a disturbing experience. It is disruptive enough to lose valuables which can be replaced with insurance money, worse to lose items of sentimental value. But the cruellest aspect of burglary is not necessarily that things are stolen. You may be the victim of vandals who smash ornaments, slash upholstery, empty food and drinks around your home, and daub the walls. The effect of this on even the most stable personality can be devastating.

You may think that you have nothing worth stealing. But a thief will not know this before breaking in and may vandalize your home in anger and frustration at discovering nothing worth removing.

There are two main ways in which you can protect your home from intruders. The first is simply a matter of thinking in terms of security and following a number of simple procedures – such as locking the door when you leave the home, canceling deliveries if you go away, closing windows when the house is empty, and leaving on lights and a radio when you go out in the evening. The second way in which you can make your home more secure is by fitting extra equipment, such as window locks, better door locks, and even alarm systems and security grilles. If you do both of these things, you will greatly reduce the risk of your home being burgled.

Points to remember

◇ Lock all doors and windows at night and when you leave your home unoccupied.
◇ Cancel deliveries to your home whenever you go away.
◇ Leave lights on when you go out in the evening.
◇ Fit secure locks to both doors and windows.
◇ Simple window catches and cylinder-rim night latches on doors do not give adequate protection against break-ins.
◇ Avoid louver windows or glue the glass panes securely to the metal fittings.
◇ When buying an aluminum door, ensure that it has a good lock – it is almost impossible to fit a replacement.
◇ Make sure upstairs windows are secure – particularly if they are accessible by climbing up a tree, a downspout, or an extension to the house.

Although it is impossible to make your home absolutely secure from the most determined thief, you can protect yourself and your possessions by following a few simple procedures. Mark valuable items with an ultra-violet pen, or an engraver, make a note of SS numbers, and take photographs of valuable items. Do not keep valuable papers such as house deeds in your home, and make sure that you are properly insured.

Security devices
There are several items that you can fit to your doors and windows to improve the security of your home. Mortise deadlocks should be fitted to the doors – the simple night latch found on most doors is not adequate as it can be forced very easily. On windows, locks should also be fitted. In addition, it may be worthwhile installing a burglar alarm or, in a high-risk area such as a basement window facing on to a street, a security grille or bars.

Care with keys
Do not leave any identification on your keys and avoid carrying keys in a purse or handbag that may contain some form of identification. Even if a lost key is returned, a copy may have been made. If you lose a key that is marked with your address, the only solution is to change the locks or lock mechanisms. Do not be lured from your home by a call, purporting to be from the police, telling you to collect your lost keys. As you go out the caller may let himself in.

Dealing with callers
Beware of confidence tricksters. Old people, in particular, should be on their guard against callers who say they are from organizations such as a local department or a charity. Many such ploys are used to gain entry to homes, and even if nothing is removed on the first visit, thieves can call again to take specific items. You should leave a strong door chain in place while you establish the callers' identity, if possible telephoning their office to check on them.

Another common trick is for one caller to keep you talking at the front of the house while someone else enters through the back door.

203

Fitting a mortise lock

A mortise deadlock is the most secure type of lock and it should be fixed to all outside doors. It fits in a slot cut in the door. When locked, the bolt shoots into another slot in the door post, and the mechanism locks the bolt in position so that it cannot be forced out. The most secure types come with a beveled spring latch and a deadbolt.

Fitting this type of lock involves cutting slots in both the door and the door post. If you are working on a door that is hanging in its frame, wedge it open or ask a helper to hold it steady. First mark the lock position carefully, using the lock itself as a guide. The best way to cut the slots is to remove the bulk of the wood with a hand brace containing a large-diameter bit. The slots can then be finished off with a chisel. Once the lock slot is the right size, a hole should be cut through the door to accept the key. Then the lock can be fitted and the hole for the edge plate cut. Fit the edge plate using long screws to ensure a secure fixing to the door post.

Preventing burglary

Glazed doors
There is an added security risk with any glazed door. It is worthwhile changing to a door made completely of wood, but if you want to keep the glass, replace it with strengthened glass (see p. 95) or fit a grille or bars.

Doors
A solid hardwood door fitted with a mortise deadlock is best in terms of security. Lock all doors at night and whenever you leave your home unoccupied. Do not leave door keys where they can easily be found. Avoid such places as on a string attached to the back of the letter-box, and under a paving stone, brick, flowerpot, or doormat. When moving into a new home, it is worth changing the locks.

Doorstep evidence
Items such as milk bottles, newspapers, and letters near the front door give a clear sign that a house is unoccupied. Notes left for tradesmen are also clues, so cancel all deliveries verbally whenever you go away.

Lights
You can also ask your neighbor to help by coming in each day to switch on and off lights and perhaps a radio or television set, to make the house look as if it is occupied. Alternatively, use a time switch to turn lights on and off. Light-sensitive switches, which turn on one light when it gets dark and turn it off again after a set time, are also available.

Windows
Fit window locks and keep all your windows locked at night and whenever there is no one at home. Lock even small windows – burglars will push a small child through an open window who can then open other windows or doors.

French doors
Because of their large area of glass and the way they fasten together in the middle, French doors are difficult to secure. Hinge bolts on both sides and mortise rack bolts in the middle will make them much more burglar-proof.

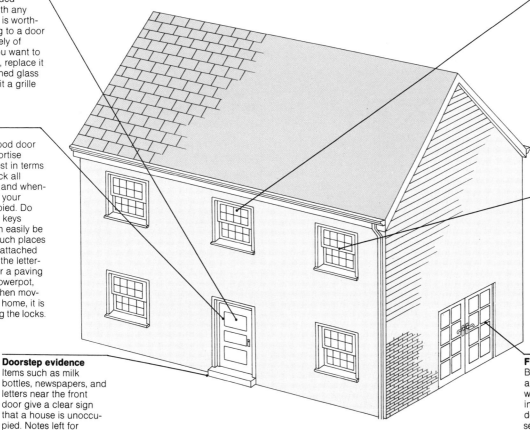

Cutting a mortise and fitting the lock and edge plate
Begin by marking the fitting position carefully, using the lock as a guide, 1. With the door held firmly in position, drill a series of holes with a hand brace using a ½in. bit. When you have drilled all the holes to the required depth, use a chisel to cut away the remaining wood, **2**, and insert the body of the lock to check that it fits. When it does, mark the size of the lock's face plate on the edge of the door and cut a rabbet with the chisel. Next cut a hole for the key, **3**. You may need to use a keyhole saw to extend the hole into a slit of the right shape for the key. Once more, check that the lock fits and that the hole is in the correct position. Finally, mark the position of the edge plate on the door post, cut a slot in the same way that you did for the lock, and fit the plate, **4**. It is important to fit the striker plate as securely as possible.

1 *Use the lock itself when marking its position on the door*

2 *Cut away the waste wood with a chisel*

3 *After drilling the key hole, check its position by inserting the lock*

4 *Fit the edge plate to the door post*

Types of window lock

Windows provide a common route of entry and any that are accessible from the ground, via a tree, or by climbing on to a roof, should be well protected. Burglars do not normally climb in through broken glass. If they break glass it is usually in order to open a window or door through which they can then gain entry. To stop this happening, fit window locks. Some are clearly visible and so act as good deterrents. The most useful types of lock are described in the table on the right.

You should always remove the keys from window locks, but it is advisable to leave them nearby. Put them where they cannot be reached or seen by a would-be intruder, but where they can be quickly found from the inside in an emergency such as a fire.

A range of devices is available for locking the two halves of a double-hung window together, or to prevent either half being moved. The types include wedge locks, sliding window locks, screw, and sash locks. When choosing from this range, make sure that you buy locks that fit the width and thickness of the window frames, and remember that some types allow you to leave the window locked slightly open, for ventilation.

In a casement window that opens with a crank handle, you can simply remove the crank handle so that the window cannot be opened. But a locking latch, which can be fitted in place of the old latch handle offers much more protection.

French doors present other security risks that can be overcome with bolts. Mortise rack bolts should be fitted to the top and bottom of the part that closes first; and a double cylinder deadbolt for the one that opens first.

Type		Window	Fitting method	Notes
Wedge lock		Wood double-hung	The lock is fitted to the top of the lower sash and the strike plate to the bottom of the top sash.	The dual strike plate system allows the window to be locked while slightly open.
Locking latch		Metal casement	If replacing an old latch with a locking one, the new latch fits into the slot in the frame and is fastened with sheet metal screws.	When buying the latch, you will need to specify whether it is to fit on to the left- or right-hand window.
Sliding glass window screw		Sliding glass windows	Slots into vertical or horizontal track. A thumb-screw prevents the window sliding.	These are quick and easy to install and need no tools.
Rod lock		Wood double-hung	A rod hole, 2⅜in. deep is driven through both sashes, avoiding the glass. The lock body is screwed to the top rail of the bottom sash, so that the rod fits into the hole.	A second rod hole can be drilled a little higher, to allow for ventilation.
Horizontal sash lock		Wood double-hung	The locking section is screwed to the top rail of the lower sash; the hook section is screwed to the bottom rail of the lower sash.	The horizontal lock faces away from the glass, affording greater security.
Vertical sash lock		Wood double-hung	Same fitting method as for horizontal sash lock.	Like the horizontal sash lock, the lever indicates when the window is locked.
Ventilating window bolt		Wood double-hung	Same fitting method as for horizontal sash lock.	The bolt will hold the window closed or in a ventilating position.
Sliding window lock		Sliding glass or metal window	The lock slots on to the track and the grip prevents the window sliding.	Quick and easy to install and no tools required.
Clamp-on window lock		Sliding aluminum window	Clamps on to the sliding window track.	A simple key clamps the lock on to the track.

Types of door lock

Outside doors provide a common route of entry for intruders and should be well protected with locks and bolts. On the front door two locks are needed – an automatic deadlocking latch to hold the door closed while you are at home, and a mortise deadlock to keep it secure when you are out. The most important feature of a deadlock is that when the key has been turned, the bolt is immobilized so that it cannot be forced back out of the door jamb. The dead-locking latch and the mortise deadlock will provide extra security if they are placed some distance apart on the door. The best positions are one-third of the way from the top and one-third of the way from the bottom of the door. Do not rely on a simple night latch to protect an outside door. It is very easy to force from the outside.

When choosing any door lock, always ask for a five-pin cylinder and always use wood screws of a good length. Short screws may be dislodged if a forced entry is attempted.

Back-door protection

Burglars are more likely to attack a rear door than the front door, so this too should be well protected. Fit a mortise deadlock with a handle.

For extra security, the back door should also be fitted with bolts. Fit one near the top and another near the bottom of the door frame.

Outward opening doors pose another security problem. The hinges are exposed, so that it is easy to knock out the hinge pins and force the door open. You can solve this problem by fitting two hinge bolts on the hinge side of the door, one a third of the way from the top, the other a third from the bottom. With this type of fastening, a fixed bolt engages in a hole cut in the door frame, so that the door cannot be lifted off its hinges.

On garage doors, in addition to a regular lock, it is worth fitting a long bolt which can be secured with a padlock. On overhead garage doors, drill a hole through the track and fit a padlock and repeat on the other track.

Type	Door	Fitting method	Notes
Double cylinder rim lock	Wood front door	Screws to the back of the door. The cylinder fits from the outside. The strike plate fits on the door post, and aligns with the rim of the lock case.	It can be operated by key from the inside and the outside. For extra security use long screws.
Cylinder night latch	Wood front door	Screws to the back face of the door. A box to take the fastened bolt is screwed to the door post.	This type of fastener can be easily opened by an intruder. It should only be used as a latch in conjunction with a deadlock.
Deadlock door guard	Front door	The deadbolt fits into a slot chiseled in the door edge and the door guard is surface mounted. A strike box is screwed to the door post.	It is operated by a key from the outside and a button handle on the inside.
Deadbolt lock	Wood door	Fits into a slot chiseled in the door edge. The lock cylinders fit on to the central shaft and the strike plate fits into the door post.	Double cylinder types which are controlled by a key both inside and out are the most secure.
Mortise dead lock	Wood front door	Fits into a slot chiseled in the door edge. A slot for the bolt must also be made in the door post.	This combines a dead bolt and spring latch for high security.
Key-in-knob lock	Wood door	Fits into a slot chiseled in the door edge. A spring latch connects to a strike plate mounted on the door edge.	Can be easily opened by an intruder.
Sliding door lock	Sliding aluminum window	Screws to the top and bottom of the fixed frame.	A key-operated bolt prevents the door from sliding or from being lifted off its track.
Double bar lock	Door that opens outward	Strikes are bored into the door frame on each side for the bolts.	The lock is operated by a knob on the inside or a key on the outside.

Other security equipment

There are several items that you can fit in addition to window and door locks to improve the security of your home. Door viewers and door chains can protect you when answering the door to unknown callers. The various security grilles and bars that are available offer protection from all but the most determined thief and are particularly useful in areas where the risk of criminal activity is high. Viewers and chains are easy to fit. Bars are best fitted by a professional.

Door chains
A simple chain may deter some burglars, but since it is only as strong as its securing screws, it is not difficult to force most chains by kicking the door. But door chains do have some value and if you are going to fit one, use long screws rather than the small ones that are often supplied. Chains should also be fitted in a way that makes it impossible for someone on the outside to reach through the gap and take the chain off. Some chains are lockable and some models also incorporate an alarm.

Door viewers
A simple barrel tube containing a one-way lens giving a panoramic view allows you to identify callers before you open the door. Buy a viewer that is the right length for the thickness of the door. Fitting is simple. A hole is drilled through the door and the two halves of the viewer are slipped through and screwed together.

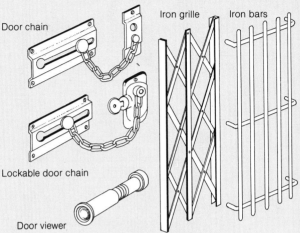

Door chain

Lockable door chain

Door viewer

Iron grille   Iron bars

Grilles and bars
Mild steel bars can be fixed externally or internally. If they are used externally the ends of the bars should be embedded 2in. to 3in. deep in the brick or woodwork. Inside, bars should be attached to a flat metal frame which can be bolted to the brick or woodwork around the window. The bars themselves need to be strong enough to withstand forcing. A locksmith will be able to advise you on your own particular requirements, but you will usually need bars at least $\frac{1}{2}$in. square or $\frac{1}{2}$in. in diameter spaced at intervals of 5in.

Most security grilles are made to measure by a locksmith. They are made from expanded metal mesh welded to a steel frame which is bolted to the inside wall. Scrolled grilles, fixed in the same way, are more attractive but less secure.

Types of alarm system

Further protection for your home can be provided by a burglar alarm system. You should fit an alarm in addition to window and door locks. It will not stop someone from breaking in, but it may make them go away quickly or alert you to the fact that your home is being broken into.

An alarm system operates from a central control panel and works from the electrical supply or from a battery. Usually, you set the system to operate as you leave home. There is a delay of about a minute to allow you to set the alarm and leave, and there is a similar delay to let you switch it off when you return. Many systems also incorporate a second switch, located in a hidden position inside the house, from which the alarm can also be operated.

A common problem with alarms is that they often sound by accident – because they have been set incorrectly, because they have been activated by children or animals, or because the wind has blown open windows or doors. An alarm will only be effective if you and your neighbors always take it seriously.

Magnetic alarm systems
With the most elaborate alarm systems, the wiring connects to a series of magnetic contacts attached to doors and openable windows. One half of the contact is fixed to the window and the other half to the frame. If the window is opened the two parts separate, the electrical contact is broken, and the alarm bell on the outside of the building is instantly activated.

As a second line of defense against an intruder who manages to get in without sounding the alarm, magnetic contacts can also be fitted to internal doors. In addition, alarm-activating pressure pads can be installed under the carpet at points where a burglar is likely to walk.

There are many magnetic alarm systems available, some of which you can fit yourself. They are not difficult to put in but care must be taken to conceal all the wiring, pressure pads, and magnetic contacts.

Infra-red alarm systems
Another type of alarm system, which you can fit instead of, or as well as, a magnetic type, uses infra-red rays to throw an unseen barrier over a wide area. Similar alarms are available that use ultra-sonic waves and microwaves. The bell sounds when the barrier is broken. Some of these alarms can be triggered by drafts and normal air movements, although the best models are far more dependable.

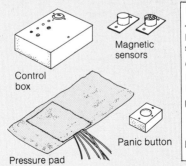

Magnetic sensors

Control box

Pressure pad

Panic button

Key
◆ Magnetic sensors
● Panic buttons
▬ Pressure pads
▭ Control

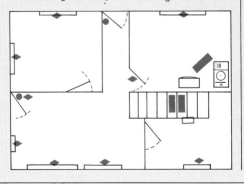

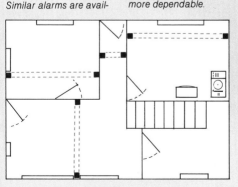

The home tool kit

Workshop equipment ◇ Measuring and marking tools
Cutting tools ◇ Hammers, nails, tacks and brads
Screws, screwdrivers and wallplugs ◇ Drills, chisels
and planes ◇ Scrapers, sanders, putty knives
and trowels ◇ Brushes, rollers and paint pads
Pliers, pincers and wrenches

A comprehensive, all-purpose home repair tool kit is essential
if you plan to tackle your own home improvements. This
chapter specifies the recommended tools for a basic home
tool kit and catalogs them according to function. Together
with identification photographs, you will find information on
how to use individual tools, the range of sizes and designs
available, and advice on caring, storage and safety. You may
need to supplement this basic kit with more specialty tools
as you progress to more complicated jobs.

Workshop equipment

A workshop or working area – whether a shed in the garden, a corner of the garage, or simply part of a room in the home – is the ideal place to store the tools needed for home maintenance and improvement. The basic essentials for a work area are good light night and day, plenty of storage space, a work bench, and a vise or clamps to hold the work steady. The area should be free of dampness. A number of socket outlets just above bench height will be needed for power tools, and in the winter, heating will be needed. A fire extinguisher positioned near the door is a worthwhile safety precaution in the workshop.

A fixed workbench with closets or shelf space below is ideal for one end of the workshop. Bench-mounted tools, such as a drill stand or a small grinder,, can then be permanently mounted. It is useful to fix a vise to one end of the bench. If you do not have the space for a permanent workbench, a free-standing, folding bench is very useful and easily stored.

Benches

Folding bench
The portable bench incorporates full-width jaws that act as a vise. The bench can also be used as a simple table, trestle, or saw horse. The folded size is 30in. × 28in. × 7½in.

Workbench
This sturdy bench is fitted with a vise and includes storage space for tools. A useful size is 60in. × 24in. × 32in.

Vises and clamps

Woodworker's vise
Lumber and other materials need to be held still when they are being sawn, drilled, or otherwise prepared. A bench-mounted vise is ideal for this. The best type for general purpose is the woodworker's vise. Some types are permanently mounted to the bench; others can be clamped on and removed when necessary. The jaws are usually 7in. or 9in. wide, with an opening capacity of about 9in.

Clamps
These are used to secure objects to the bench when you are working on them. The most common are C-clamps, very versatile clamps with a large adjustable screw. The strongest types have ribbed malleable iron or dropped forged-steel frames. The fully open sizes range from ¾in. to 12in.

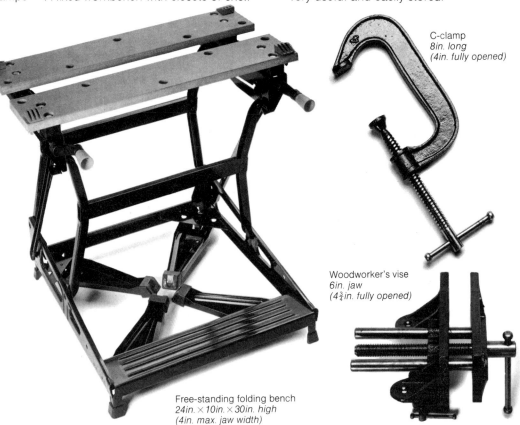

C-clamp
8in. long
(4in. fully opened)

Woodworker's vise
6in. jaw
(4¾in. fully opened)

Free-standing folding bench
24in. × 10in. × 30in. high
(4in. max. jaw width)

Workshop storage

Hand tools
Store in accessible racks. Use plastic or wire tool-hanging clips fixed on to sheets of perforated hardboard, or make your own wooden racks.

Saws, hammers, and pincers
Hang on simple racks made by driving nails or dowels into battens fixed above the bench. Most will hang over one peg, but hammers have to span two pegs.

Chisels, files and screwdrivers
Store in a simple rack. Nail a strip of plywood, about 75mm wide, to the top edge of a wooden batten that can be attached horizontally to the wall. Drill holes in the plywood so that the blades of the tools pass through, and the handles are supported.

Power tools
Cover bench-mounted tools with cloths. Store portable tools in lockable closets or on shelves. Keep the cords wrapped around the tools when not in use.

Cutters, blades, and tool attachments
Drill and brace bits are best stored upright in wood blocks drilled with holes of suitable sizes. If you have a large number of drill bits, store them in a cabinet with small drawers made of clear plastic, to allow the contents to be seen.

Hardware
Store nails, screws, nuts, and bolts in jars or labeled cans. One method is to fix the lids of screw-top jars under shelves, allowing the glass jars to hang down with the contents clearly visible. Cutlery-type wooden trays or plastic drawer units can also be used. Adjustable shelving is useful for storing larger materials and paint cans. Various size plastic trays, some with covers, which hang in slots on a wall-mounted board are also available.

Measuring and marking tools

Accurate measuring and marking is essential. It is particularly important in woodwork, but is also vital in decorating and other work. The most useful measuring and marking tools are: a good retractable measuring tape, a steel ruler, a try square for marking right angles, and a good quality carpenter's level. Treat these tools very carefully – if they are damaged they will become inaccurate. Check them regularly for accuracy, and store them in a dry place. Buy the best quality measuring and marking tools you can afford. Make sure that wooden and metal parts are firmly attached.

Tapes and rulers

Flexible steel tape
Probably the most useful measuring tool, this can be used for sizing many different materials. Tapes are available with both metric and standard markings, or standard only. Buy one with a thumb lock. A top sight is also useful. This is a plastic window in the case which allows an internal measurement to be read off directly, without it being necessary to add the width to the dimension shown on the tape. The most useful all-round length is 10ft.

Steel ruler
This is a very precise ruler for measuring and laying out work. It is marked with exact standard measurements, usually down to $\frac{1}{32}$in. Although unmarked steel straight edges are available, you can use a steel ruler as a straight edge for cutting and marking. Lengths range from 6in. to 6ft.

Folding ruler
This can be used in confined spaces where it is difficult to use a one-piece ruler. Traditional folding rulers are made of boxwood, but modern folding rulers are often made of engineering plastic. The most common type is a four-section ruler, although there are also steel rulers with a single fold. Lengths range from 1ft to 6ft.

Leveling tools

Carpenter's level
This tool is used to determine whether or not a surface is level. It should be as long as possible. When the surface is horizontal, the bubble in the tube should fall between the two lines. There should also be tubes for checking verticals, and some method of adjusting the tubes. It is useful if the body of the level is cut away, so that you can read the tube either above or below eye level. The best modern levels have aluminum or plastic bodies. Sizes range from 3in. to 6ft.

Plumb bob
This is a useful aid for marking vertical lines. It is a torpedo-shaped brass or steel weight used with a chalked line to mark verticals on a wall, particularly when hanging wallpaper. Weights available range from about 1½oz.

Squares

Try square
Essential for marking square ends across a length of wood, there are both traditional try squares with a rosewood stock at right-angles to a tempered steel blade, and modern designs with a plastic stock. On the best try squares, the blade extends into the stock and is firmly riveted to it on both sides. This makes it less likely that the square will go out of true. Both inside and outside edges form a 90-degree angle. Sizes range from 6in. to 1ft.

Combination square
This is a very versatile measuring and marking tool, which can be used as a steel ruler, try square, miter square, and level. It consists of a steel ruler, clamped in a square head, which is often fitted with a level tube. It can check levels, the depths of mortises, and angles. The usual blade length is 1ft.

Marking tools

Marking knife
For precise marking, use this knife instead of a pencil. It has an angled steel blade, which is ground and sharpened on one side only, like a chisel. A trimming knife can be used when a marking knife is not available. The flat side of the blade can run against a try square or a rule. The usual size is 6in.

Marking gauge
Use this gauge for marking lines parallel to the edge or end of a piece of wood or board. The line is marked by a steel point fixed close to the end of a bar, on which an adjustable clamp can be locked at the required distance from the point. The clamp is locked in place by a metal screw on the side. On some models, there is a graduated scale on the stem. This shows the distance from the stock to the point. Sizes range from 6in. to 10in.

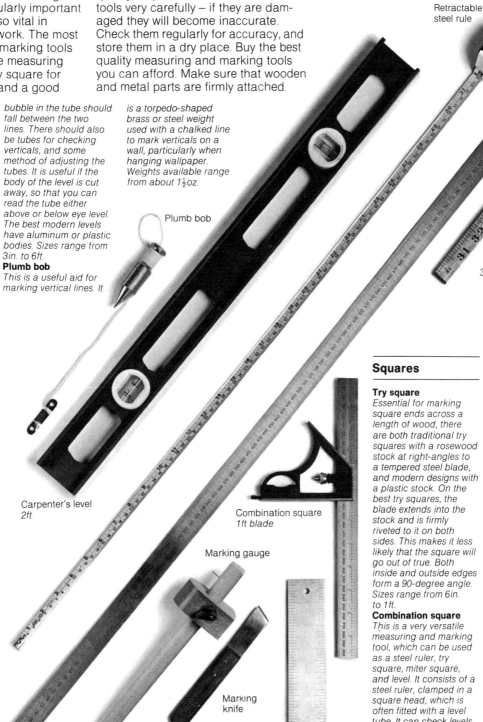

Retractable steel rule

3ft steel rule

3ft folding wooden rule

Plumb bob

Carpenter's level 2ft

Combination square 1ft blade

Marking gauge

Marking knife

Try square 8in.

Saws and other

Saws are the most versatile cutting tools, particularly for cutting wood. They come in a variety of types and sizes. Items such as scissors and trimming knives also perform many useful functions.

Saws have very sharp teeth. The size of these affects the fineness and speed of cut – more teeth give a finer but slower cut. Saws are sold according to the number of teeth per inch on their blades.

When using a saw, grip it firmly. Support the wood and start the cut by drawing the blade backward in an upright position. Saw steadily and rhythmically, using the full length of the blade, and only apply pressure on the down stroke. Keep your shoulder in line with the blade and support the waste end to prevent splitting.

General-purpose saws

Panel saw
This all-round handsaw is used to cut large planks, boards, or panels to size. It has cross-cut teeth, and the most useful size has a 21in. blade and 9 teeth per inch. The most common length is 21in.

Cross-cut saw
With a larger blade than the panel saw this tool is ideal for cutting lumber across the grain. The usual length is 2ft with 8 teeth per inch.

Rip saw
The chisel-shaped teeth have their edges almost at right-angles to the length of the saw. This enables the teeth to cut quickly along the grain of the timber. The usual length is 26in. with 5½ or 6 teeth per inch.

Back saw
This saw has a straight, rectangular blade with a stiffened back. It is used for cutting wood accurately, especially when making joints. Lengths range from 8in. to 12in. with about 14 teeth per inch.

Saws for intricate cutting

Coping saw
The coping saw can make curved cuts in thin wood and plastic. The blade is narrow and has very fine teeth. The rectangular frame keeps the blade tight, and the tension is regulated by turning the handle. It can be adjusted to cut in any direction by turning the blade pins. The usual length is 6in.

Fret saw
For cutting tight curves in wood, plastic and glass fiber, the fret saw is ideal. The blade is under tension in the 12in. deep frame. It is 5in. long and is set to cut on the down stroke.

Keyhole saw
This saw can cut small holes in places such as keyholes, where the saw frame makes using a coping saw impossible. Its simple handle clamps on to the narrow, tapering blade. Blade lengths range from 5in. to 15in., teeth from 7 to 10 per inch.

Saws for cutting metal

Hacksaw
For cutting metals and plastics, use a hacksaw. Modern types have a pistol-grip handle and an adjustable bow frame to accept different blades. These are fitted with the teeth facing forward. The latest blades have hard teeth, but have none of the brittleness of

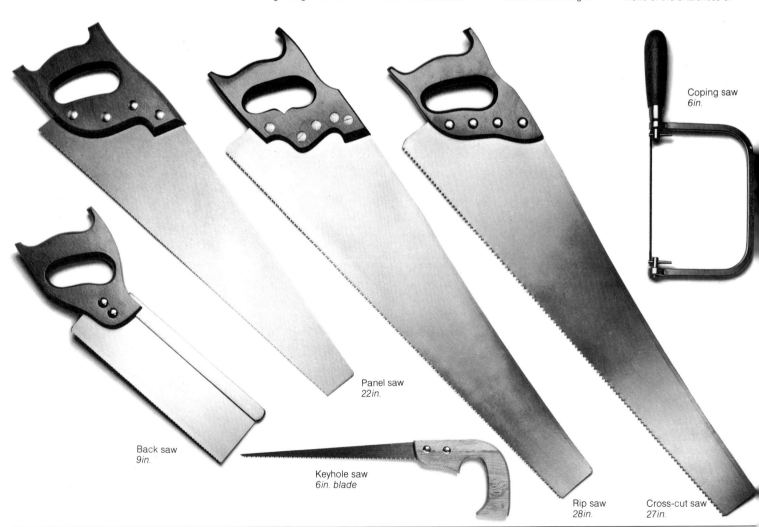

Coping saw
6in.

Panel saw
22in.

Back saw
9in.

Keyhole saw
6in. blade

Rip saw
28in.

Cross-cut saw
27in.

cutting tools

old-style hacksaw blades. Hacksaws are available with 8in. to 16in. blades with from 14 to 32 teeth per inch.

Junior hacksaw

This saw is ideal for cutting metal and plastic in confined spaces. The traditional type is made from a one-piece spring-tension frame. To fit a blade, insert one end into the frame slot, then press this against the edge of a bench to fit the other end. The usual length is 6in. with 32 teeth per inch.

Power saws

Saber saw

A versatile power saw, the saber saw will make straight, curved, or scroll cuts in wood, man-made boards, metals, plastics, and many other materials. Saber attachments are available for some power drills, but self-powered sabers are better balanced and more powerful. The straight, narrow blade is about 4in. long and moves up and down at about 3,000 strokes per minute. Some saws are single speed, while others offer a slower speed of 2,400 strokes per minute, which is ideal for cutting plastics and metals. There are also continuously variable speed models which will cut as slowly as 500 strokes a minute. Some models have a pendulum blade action, which increases the speed of cut and also allows the saw to cut thicker metals. Different blades are needed for cutting different materials.

Circular saw

This power saw is useful for fast, straight cutting of wood, man-made boards, plastics and laminated boards, sheet metals, thicker soft metals, masonry and ceramic tiles. Special blades are required for some materials. The circular blade revolves at between 3,000 and 5,000 rpm. Upper and lower blade guards should be fitted for safety. Circular-saw attachments are available for power drills, but some drills are not really powerful enough to drive them adequately. Common blade diameters are 5in., 6in., 7in. and 9in. Maximum cutting depths range from $1\frac{3}{8}$in. for the smallest blade size, to $2\frac{1}{2}$in. for the $7\frac{1}{4}$in. blade. As a safety precaution, all circular saws should be fitted with upper and lower blade guards before connecting to the electricity supply.

Other cutting tools

Scissors

General-purpose scissors are particularly suitable for work with fabrics and for decorating. Paper-hanger's scissors for wallpapering are available in 10in., 11in. and 12in. blade lengths.

Utility knife

One of the most useful general-purpose tools, the utility knife can be used for many tasks, including cutting soft floor tiles, trimming wallpaper, and scoring lines on most materials. Replaceable, razor-sharp blades are held in an easy-grip handle. The handle is often in two halves, which should be separated to change a blade. This also provides a place for storing the blades.

A range of straight, curved and keyhole-shaped blades is available.

Powered saber saw

Portable circular saw
5in. diameter blade

Fret saw
6in.

Junior hacksaw
6in.

Scissors
5in. blades

Hacksaw
12in.

Utility knife
5in.

Range of blades

Hammers

There are several types of hammer that can be used for a number of different jobs, from tapping in a tiny brad to breaking up concrete. They are generally sold by the weight of their metal heads. The heavier the head, the more pressure you will get. A 10oz hammer is a useful, easily handled average weight for the majority of jobs. A claw hammer is the most useful general-purpose hammer, while a cross-peen hammer is good for tapping in small brads. Sledge-hammers are necessary for work on masonry, and wooden mallets are often useful in carpentry.

When using a hammer, hold it firmly at the shaft, watching the nail carefully. Regularly sand down the hammer's face to ensure that the head does not slip. Be careful when selecting hammers; inexpensive tools may seem attractive, but often they will not stand repeated use.

General-purpose hammers

Claw hammers
This is ideal for inserting and pulling out nails. The "straight-claw" hammer can be used to lever up floorboards. Claw hammers are available with shafts of wood, glass fiber, or steel, in weights up to 2 lbs. They often have easy-grip, shock-absorbing rubber sleeves. The claw should taper to a fine "V" so that small brads, as well as large nails, can be extracted.

Ball peen hammer
This type of hammer is used for metal working. The flat face is used to drive chisels and punches, while the ball is useful for shaping metal. It is often used with a rivet set to rivet two plates together. The hammer has a wooden handle and head weights up to 16oz. are available.

Pin hammer
A lightweight version of the cross-peen hammer, the pin hammer is used for delicate work such as knocking small brads into picture frames. It is available in head weights of up to 4oz.

Specialized hammers and mallets

Club hammer
Used for heavy-duty work, this hammer is ideal for demolishing walls or for driving bolster chisels. Wear gloves and goggles when doing this type of work. The sledge-hammer is a larger version of the club hammer and can be used two-handed.

Tack hammer
This is used mainly to drive in upholstery tacks, although some types also have claws for extraction. The head is usually magnetized so that tacks can be held and accurately positioned. The hammer is available in weights up to approximately 7oz.

Mallet
There are several types, but a carpenter's mallet is the most useful, especially for driving chisels. Carpenter's mallets come in head widths up to 7in.

Sets and pin pushes

Nail sets
Nail sets are used with a hammer to drive nail heads below the surface. They are available with tip diameters of $\frac{1}{16}$in. and $\frac{1}{8}$in.

Pin push
A pin push is used for driving thin pins without a hammer. The pin is placed in the magnetized barrel and is driven home by pumping the spring-loaded handle.

Nail set $\frac{1}{16}$in. diameter

Pin push No 14-16 pin gauge

Claw hammer 20oz

Small claw hammer 6oz

Ball-peen hammer 12oz

Tack hammer 4oz

Club hammer 3 lb 5oz

Wooden mallet 5in. head

Nails, tacks and brads

Nails provide permanent joints for holding together materials such as wood. An extremely strong joint can be made if the right type of nail is used correctly.

A wide range of nails is available, suitable for many different tasks, ranging from woodwork and roofing to upholstery. Nails are specified by their name and their size. This can be given in inches or in "pennies", abbreviated to the letter "d". As the length increases, so normally does the thickness.

Nails are usually driven straight in. But if they are hammered in at an angle, they will be less likely to be pushed out, giving extra strength.

As nails can split wood, drill small pilot holes in delicate work, or nip off the nail points to blunt them. Nailing near the end of a piece of wood can cause a split.

Common nails
For rough construction work and frame-making, plain steel or galvanized nails give the required strength. Lengths range from 1in. to 6in.

Box nails
These are similar to common nails, but thinner. They are useful when the strength of the common nail is required, but where a true common nail would split the wood. Sizes from 1in. to 3½in. are produced. Smaller wire nails have the same design.

Finishing nails
These are useful for jobs where appearance matters. The head can be driven below the surface, and the nail is unlikely to split the wood if inserted with the larger side

parallel with the grain.

Roofing nails
With rings on their shanks and extra-large heads, these nails are specially designed to secure roofing materials. Sizes range from ¾in. to 1¾in.

Drywall nails
Used when installing gypsum board, drywall nails have flat heads that lie flush with the board surface.

Dome-head tacks
Small, decorative tacks with bright, domed heads are frequently used in upholstery work.

Brads
Similar in shape to finishing nails, brads are shorter and thinner. They are very useful for joining moldings and attaching thin sheets of plywood to wood frames. They are

also ideal for making picture frames. They are available in both plain and non-rusting steel in lengths ranging from ½in. to 2in.

Plasterboard nails
These have slightly concave heads, designed to dimple the surface of gypsum board.

Masonry nails
These can be driven directly into brick or concrete walls. Large masonry nails are produced for heavy work, while smaller nails can be bought for tasks such as hanging pictures. Masonry nails are available in sizes ranging from 1in. to 4in. Square-section and fluted types are made as well as the regular round nails.

Steel tacks
With plain heads, smaller than those on upholstery tacks, these are used mainly for securing carpets.

Staples
Wire staples can join wire to wood and are particularly useful in fence construction.

Flooring nails
Traditional flooring nails are large and strong with heads that are easy to drive beneath the surface. Annular-ring nails can also be used for flooring. Their grooves give extra grip.

Blued plasterboard nails
These come in various colors, so that when driven into plasterboard, the heads are hidden.

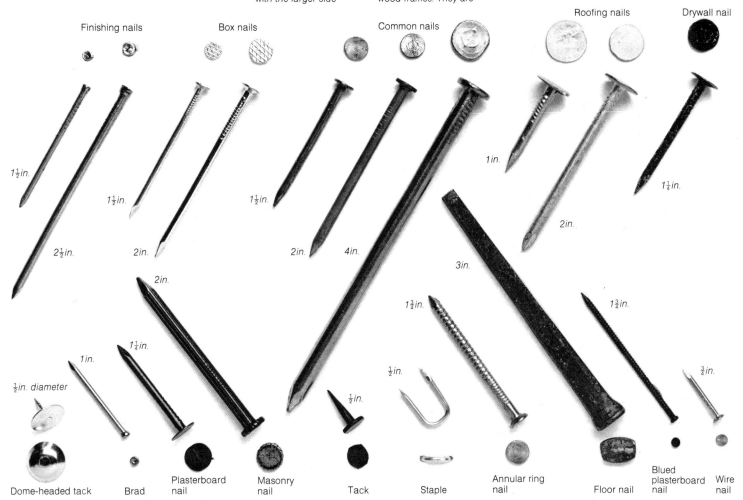

Finishing nails · Box nails · Common nails · Roofing nails · Drywall nail

1½in. · 1½in. · 1½in. · 2½in. · 2in. · 2in. · 2in. · 4in. · 3in. · 1in. · 2in. · 1¼in. · 1¾in. · 1¾in. · 2in. · 1¼in. · 1in. · ½in. diameter · ½in. · ½in. · ¾in.

Dome-headed tack · Brad · Plasterboard nail · Masonry nail · Tack · Staple · Annular ring nail · Floor nail · Blued plasterboard nail · Wire nail

Screwdrivers

Screwdrivers are essential for everyday maintenance and construction tasks around the home. Three or four different sizes will probably fit most of the screws used, but there are two types of screw head – single-slot and cross-head – so you will need six to eight screwdrivers in your home tool kit.

When using a screwdriver, make sure that the blade fits well in the screw head and keep the tool vertical. A ratchet, or pump-action, screwdriver is easier and faster to use, but you need to keep one hand on the shank to stop it slipping. The traditional bulbous screwdriver

handles in wood or plastic are comfortable to grip and less likely to cause blisters than other designs. Sets of screwdriver bits can be bought with a single handle, often with a ratchet mechanism. Store screwdrivers in a drawer or hanging in a rack, and sharpen single-slot screwdrivers on an oilstone.

General-purpose screwdrivers

Single-slot screwdrivers
There are several different designs for ordinary single-slot screws. The tips are flared and may be tapered on the sides, while the handles may be rounded, fluted, or rubber-covered. Blades vary in length, but generally, the larger the tip, the longer the blade. A range of tip widths will be required to fit the usual screw gauges. Use a $\frac{3}{16}$in. tip for No. 4 and No. 6 screws, a $\frac{1}{4}$in. tip for No. 8, a $\frac{3}{8}$in. tip for No. 10, No. 12 and No. 14.

Cross-head screwdrivers
Various patterns of screws are available and it is important that the tips fit well to give a good grip. Otherwise the screws will get damaged and be difficult to remove. Of the different patterns, the Phillips screwdriver is the most useful. It is available in three sizes, 1, 2, and 3 point.

Stubby screwdrivers
With their short blades, these are ideal for use in confined spaces. They are available in a range of tip sizes in both single-slot and cross-head styles. You can also get them with a T-bar for extra leverage. The usual blade lengths are 1in. and 1$\frac{1}{2}$in.

Ratchet and impact screwdrivers

Ratchet screwdrivers
The advantage of these tools is that they allow you to drive in a screw without altering your

grip. They are available in single-slot and cross-head styles. A thumb slider control changes the action to drive clockwise or anti-clockwise as well as to remain fixed in one direction. Ratchet screwdrivers are available in blade sizes from 3in. to 6in.

Spiral-ratchet screwdrivers
These pump-action screwdrivers are designed to work by pressure on the handle, giving a very fast action to the spiral grooves along the length of the blade. For final tightening the screwdriver can

be locked to give a standard screwdriver action. The spiral can also be locked closed, to give a simple ratchet action. This type of screwdriver has a chuck, allowing different bits to be fitted. Blade lengths range from 9$\frac{1}{2}$in. to 2ft.

Offset screwdrivers
These give more leverage to drive screws in inaccessible places. The blades are made of steel and cranked in shape, with the ends forming the screwdriver tips. They are double-ended, and suitable for cross-head or single-slot screws.

Blade sizes range from 3in. to 6in.

Impact drivers
Use these for freeing seized screws and nuts. You strike the handle with a hammer and the mechanism creates pressure to free a tight fitting. The most common size is 5$\frac{1}{2}$in.

Electrical screwdrivers

Electrician's screwdrivers
These have thin blades with parallel tips, so that they can turn a screw at the bottom of a hole. The handles are well insulated in heavy-duty plastic and some blades are insulated in a plastic sleeve. Blade sizes range from 3in. to 10in.

Continuity tester
This is used to test electrical currents. It has an insulated blade and handle, and features a neon bulb which lights up if the blade touches a live terminal.

Screwdriver bits

Power screwdriver bits
These are used to drive screws with electric drills featuring variable-speed controls. Single-slot and cross-head bits are available and they have hexagonal shanks to give a non-twist grip in the chuck. Some single-slot bits can slip, so it is best to choose bits with a sliding sleeve to hold the screw in the slot.

Screwdriver bits
These bits are used in a hand brace to tighten or free large screws. They are often reversible, with different-sized blades on each end. Single-slot and cross-head types are available.

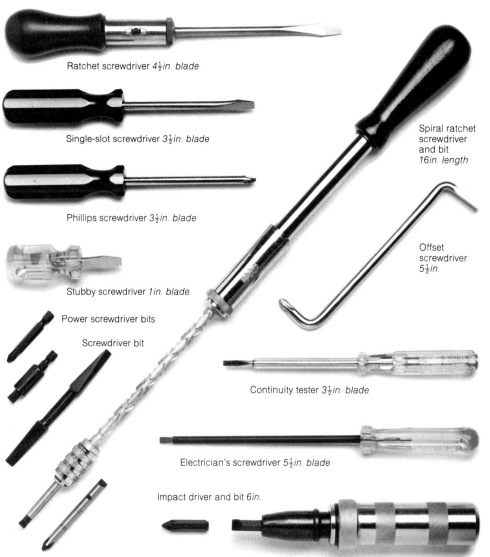

Ratchet screwdriver 4$\frac{1}{2}$in. blade

Single-slot screwdriver 3$\frac{1}{2}$in. blade

Phillips screwdriver 3$\frac{1}{2}$in. blade

Stubby screwdriver 1in. blade

Power screwdriver bits

Screwdriver bit

Spiral ratchet screwdriver and bit 16in. length

Offset screwdriver 5$\frac{1}{2}$in.

Continuity tester 3$\frac{1}{2}$in. blade

Electrician's screwdriver 5$\frac{1}{2}$in. blade

Impact driver and bit 6in.

Screws and wall plugs

Screws produce really firm, strong joints between pieces of lumber. They are used in high quality woodwork, and are the best choice when components may have to be dismantled. Joints are stronger with screws than nails because the turning action draws the pieces together.

It is important to choose screws of the right length. If possible, use a screw that is three times as long as the thickness of the wood being attached. But make sure that the screw is not so long that it will pierce the reverse side of the work. A screw that is too thick may split the wood. As a general rule, a screw should not exceed 1/10th of the width of the wood. If you are fitting a hinge, the screw size will be limited by the size of the holes in the fitting.

When using screws, keep them a distance of five times their diameter from the side edge of the wood and ten times their diameter apart.

Screws

Flat-head screws
The heads of these screws lie flush with the surface. They are used to join pieces of wood and for fittings such as hinges. Flat-head screws are available both as straight-slot and Phillips types. Lengths range from ¾ in. to 5½ in., and gauges from 2 to 20 in straight-slot. The range in Phillips is similar, though the sizes available may vary from store to store. The usual materials are plain steel, plated steel, and various corrosion-free metals.

Round-head screws
The heads remain above the surface. These screws are used mainly for attaching metal fittings

to wood. Both straight-slot and Phillips types are produced.

Oval-head screws
These attractive screws protrude slightly from the surface, while the lower part of the head is counter-sunk. They are usually made from steel or brass.

Drywall screws
With this type the thread runs the whole length of the screw. This makes it ideal for man-made boards and soft wood. Lengths range from ½ in. to 1¾ in.; gauges from 4 to 10.

Lag screws and bolts
Square- or hexagonal-headed lag screws and bolts can be used when extra strength is required. Turned with a wrench, they are available in sizes from 3½ in. to 6 in.

Anchors and toggles

Solid-wall anchors
A wide range of anchors is made which allow you to insert wood screws into solid masonry walls. After drilling a hole in the wall with a masonry bit, the anchor is inserted and the screw driven into place. Anchors made of lead, plastic, and nylon are available for a wide range of screw sizes.

Hammer-driven anchor
Designed for attaching items to hollow walls, this type is inserted with a hammer. The bolt is then tightened, and the metal shoulders expand in the wall cavity to give a secure fitting.

Hollow-wall anchor
This anchor is inserted

through a hole drilled in a hollow wall. It has metal shoulders that expand as you turn the bolt.*

Gravity toggle
Because its mechanism relies on gravity, this toggle can only be used for making fixings to vertical surfaces. The toggle is passed through a pre-drilled hole in the wall and its bar swings down to form a right-angled fixing. The bar falls away and is lost if you remove the bolt.

Spring toggle
The twin arms of this type of toggle are pushed through a pre-drilled hole and spring apart in the wall cavity. As with the gravity toggle, the fixing is lost when the bolt is removed.

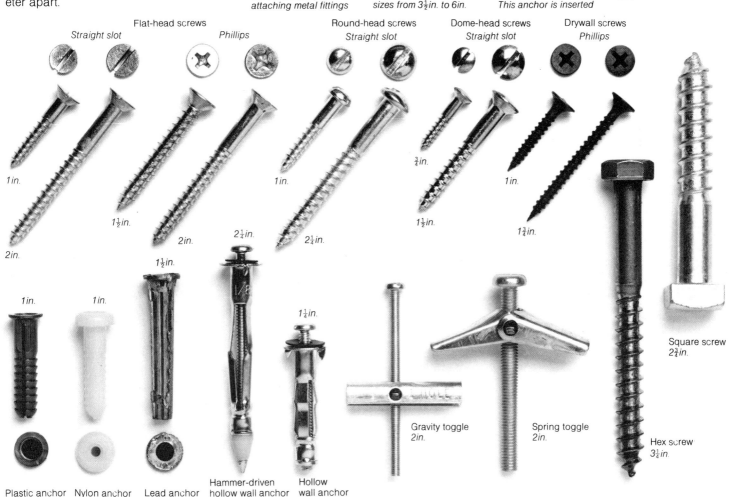

Flat-head screws
Straight slot   Phillips

Round-head screws
Straight slot

Dome-head screws
Straight slot

Drywall screws
Phillips

1 in.

1½ in.

2 in.

2¼ in.

1 in.

2¼ in.

¾ in.

1½ in.

1 in.

1¾ in.

2 in.

1½ in.

1¼ in.

1 in.

1 in.

Square screw
2¾ in.

Hex screw
3¼ in.

Plastic anchor   Nylon anchor   Lead anchor   Hammer-driven hollow wall anchor   Hollow wall anchor

Gravity toggle
2 in.

Spring toggle
2 in.

Drills

Drills can be used to make holes in a variety of materials, such as wood, masonry, and plastic. The simple hand drill is slow, but it is easy to control and is essential when no electric power is available. It is easy to use and can make holes in both wood and metal. But for masonry work you will need either a breast drill or an electric drill, while a push drill is required for plastics. Hand drills are not expensive, but only a limited range of bits is available for them, mostly for drilling into wood.

Electric drills are more expensive, but quicker and much more versatile. With the correct bits, they can make holes in almost any material, and a variety of attachments, such as sanding disks, can also be fitted for specific jobs.

Both hand and electric drills need even, steady pressure, otherwise you will get jagged-edged holes. It is worth the extra expense of buying good quality bits, as these will stay sharper and be less likely to break during use.

Drills and braces

Hand drill
Used to drill holes in wood and metal, this drill is operated by a handle and cranked gear wheel, which gives variable speeds for different materials. More modern designs have enclosed gears, so that they do not get dusty. Some models have a detachable side handle which can be used when extra grip is needed. The chuck takes twist drill bits up to $\frac{5}{16}$ in. in diameter.

Hand brace
To drill large-diameter holes in wood, use a hand brace. This turns by means of a rotating frame that applies sustained power to the drill bit. With the appropriate bit it can also drive and withdraw screws. Different sizes of brace are available, and the best types have a ratchet action so that the brace can be used in confined spaces.

Breast drill
This is a larger version of the hand drill and it can make holes in wood, metal, and masonry. It has a curved, saddle-shaped plate, which you can lean on for extra pressure.

Push drill
This is a pump-action drill for making small-diameter holes – usually pilot holes for screws in wood. It takes bits, called drill points, which range in size from $\frac{1}{16}$ in. to $\frac{3}{16}$ in.

Electric drill
An electric drill can be used on a variety of materials. For general hand-held use, choose a drill that offers 350-500 watts power with at least two speed settings. The most common chuck capacities are $\frac{3}{8}$ in. or $\frac{1}{2}$ in., and the latter is also the largest hole that this type of drill can make in steel. Additional features available on electric drills include a high-speed hammer action that is very useful for drilling hard materials. A reversing switch is also available on some models. Attachments, such as sanders and scratch brushes, are made to fit most models.

Drill bits

The part of a drill that actually makes the holes is called the bit. A limited range of bits is available for hand drills and there is a much more varied range of bits for electric drills. The range includes twist drill bits for drilling wood and metal; dowel bits for wood; masonry bits; countersink bits; auger and spade bits for making large holes; and screwdriver bits.

Hole borers

Scratch awl
This tool is used to make starting holes for screws.

Gimlet
With its spiral shaft, this can also be used to make starting holes.

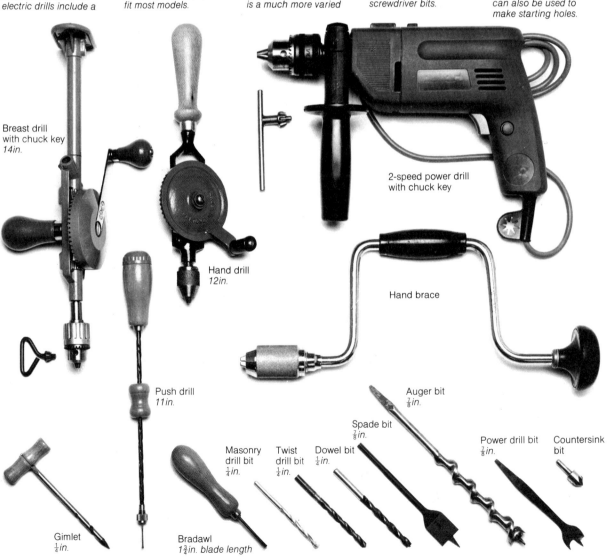

Breast drill with chuck key 14in.

Hand drill 12in.

2-speed power drill with chuck key

Hand brace

Push drill 11in.

Auger bit $\frac{7}{8}$ in.

Spade bit $\frac{7}{8}$ in.

Masonry drill bit $\frac{1}{4}$ in.

Twist drill bit $\frac{1}{4}$ in.

Dowel bit $\frac{1}{4}$ in.

Power drill bit $\frac{1}{8}$ in.

Countersink bit

Gimlet $\frac{1}{4}$ in.

Bradawl $1\frac{3}{4}$ in. blade length

Chisels and planes

Chisels are wood-shaping tools, useful for paring and chopping out areas of wood to take hinges and other fittings. All new chisels need honing on an oilstone to sharpen them for easy use.

For the best finish, chisel either with, or at right-angles to, the grain of the wood. Use a wooden mallet to tap chisels with wooden handles; with hard plastic handles, an ordinary hammer can be used.

Planes are used for slicing off unwanted pieces of wood, shaping and reducing wood to size, and also for smoothing wood. The longer the piece of wood you are planing, the longer the plane you should use. Before planing, check that the blade is sharp and that its edge is parallel with, and just protruding from, the sole plate. Work with the wood grain.

Plane blades can be sharpened, but this is a skilled job, best left to a professional. For this reason, rasp planes, with replaceable disposable blades, are increasingly popular.

Chisels

Bevel chisels
This is the most versatile type of chisel. Blade widths of $\frac{1}{4}$in., $\frac{1}{2}$in., $\frac{3}{4}$in. and 1 in. are the ones most commonly used. The blades' taper-ing edges enable the chisel to cut in confined spaces, such as the undercuts in dovetail joints and in shallow hinge recesses. Since this type of chisel is designed for lightweight work, if a mallet is used, tap it only lightly.

Plain chisels
Available in widths from $\frac{1}{8}$in. to 2in., these chisels feature stout blades with straight sides. They are much stronger than bevel chisels and can be hit harder with a mallet. Their uses are limited, but they are good for chopping out mortises and making frames for partitions.

Cold chisel
This strong steel chisel is ideal for removing mortar from brickwork before pointing. It can be hit with a hammer and widths from $\frac{1}{2}$in. to 1in. are available.

Brick chisel
This chisel can be used for a variety of levering tasks, such as taking up floorboards, and for cutting masonry. Lengths from 7in. to 8in. are produced.

Honing equipment

Oilstone
This is used for honing chisel and plane blades. It is available in coarse, medium, and fine grades and also as a combination stone; fine on one side and medium on the other. Oilstones should be kept in a box and oiled before use. Hold the blade at 30 degrees to the stone and work it back and forward.

Honing guide
A very useful wheeled gadget, the honing guide helps to keep the chisel or plane blade at the correct angle when it is being honed. The blade is clamped in the guide, which is then moved to and fro on the oilstone.

Planes

Smoothing plane
This is used for smoothing wood on smaller jobs. The sole plate is usually $9\frac{1}{2}$in. long. It should be used with care on long pieces of wood.

Jack plane
The sole plate of the jack plane is 14in. long, making it easier to plane a flat surface. It is a useful all-round tool.

Block plane
This small plane, with a sole plate $5\frac{1}{2}$in. to $7\frac{1}{2}$in. long, can be used with one hand. The blade is set at a shallow angle with the bevel uppermost for smoothing end grain.

Rabbet plane
The broad cutting blade of this plane allows it to be used for smoothing up to an edge and for the shoulders of large joints. The sole plate is $9\frac{1}{4}$in. to 13in. long.

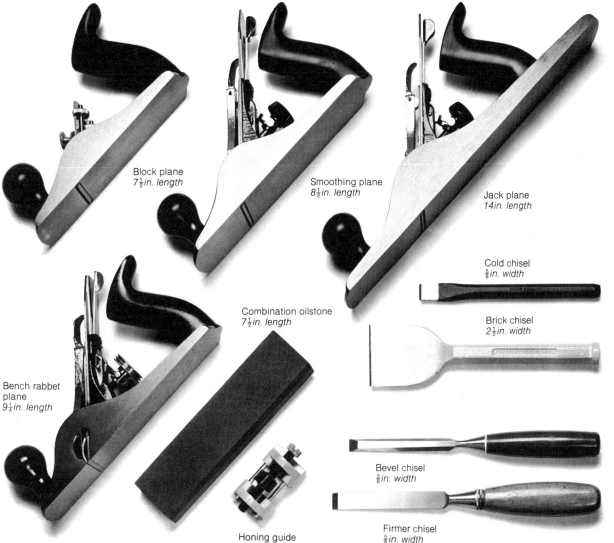

Block plane
$7\frac{1}{2}$in. length

Smoothing plane
$8\frac{1}{2}$in. length

Jack plane
14in. length

Cold chisel
$\frac{5}{8}$in. width

Bench rabbet plane
$9\frac{1}{4}$in. length

Combination oilstone
$7\frac{1}{2}$in. length

Brick chisel
$2\frac{1}{2}$in. width

Bevel chisel
$\frac{3}{8}$in. width

Honing guide

Firmer chisel
$\frac{5}{8}$in. width

Scrapers and sanders

Paint scrapers are useful for removing old paint, in conjunction with paint-stripping solution. Old wallpaper can also be stripped after it has been liberally soaked in warm water or stripping solution. A simple upward motion is all that is needed. Shavehooks can remove flaking and softened paint from wooden moldings. Gas blowtorches can strip off layers of paint but should be used with care because of the fire risk. Hot-air strippers are far safer.

Sanders are invaluable for smoothing surfaces. But some surfaces clog the abrasive, so wet-and-dry types are produced, which can be used wet and wiped down. Whenever using abrasives on wood, work in line with the grain. Abrasive papers are available in grades from coarse for rough work, to fine for finishing, and are graded numerically. The higher the

Scrapers

Paint and wallpaper scraper
This is the most versatile scraper. Use it to remove old, softened paint and dampened wallpaper. Scrapers with wide blades are suitable for large areas; narrow blades are useful for window frames. Blade widths range from 1 in. to 5 in.

Shavehook
For removing softened paint from wooden moldings around doors and windows a shave-hook is best. A drawing action should be used. Shavehooks are available with a choice of three different blades: triangular, pear-shaped, and a combination blade with straight, convex, and concave edges.

Window scraper
Use this to trim excess, dried paint from window panes. It has a standard trimming knife blade fixed in a plastic handle. When using a window scraper, start flush with the frame and scrape downward.

Hook scraper
Also known as a Skarsten scraper, this tool can be used for fine cabinet finishing or heavy-duty scraping. A range of interchangeable blades (straight, convex, concave, serrated, and double-ended) are produced, together with two handles allowing you to use the tool with either one or two hands. You work by pulling the tool toward you. Blades are available in 1½ in. to 2½ in. widths.

Abrasive papers

Sandpaper
This is used to finish wood roughly. It wears quickly but is inexpensive. It is often called "sandpaper", because of its yellow color.

Garnet
A hard, sharp abrasive, garnet is made from the semi-precious red stone. It is ideal for wood finishing. It is fairly long-lasting and is available in finer grades than sandpaper.

Silicon carbide
This is often called "wet-and-dry paper". It can be used wet to prevent clogging when rubbing down painted surfaces. It can also be used to clean metals.

Emery
This black abrasive is available with paper or cloth backing. It has a slow-cutting action and is used mainly to clean and polish metal. The cloth-backed type is long-lasting and ideal for cleaning pipes.

Tungsten carbide
This very sharp, hard abrasive is expensive but long-lasting.

Sanding block
This is a cork or wood block around which you wrap a sheet of abrasive paper. You can buy a sanding block or make one from a piece of wood.

Other sanding equipment

Sanding attachments
These can be fitted to an electric drill. Sanding disks are the most common type. Attached to a flexible rubber backing pad, and mounted in the drill chuck, the disk is used to sand wood, metal, and plastic. The main problem with this type is that it produces swirl marks. Wire wheel brushes have a gentler action and do not produce swirl marks. Foam-drum sanders consist of an abrasive belt, wrapped around a foam drum mounted in the drill chuck. They are used on flat and curved surfaces.

Power sanders
Finishing or orbital sanders are the most widely used type. A strip of abrasive, moving at high speed in a series of tiny orbits, gives a fine finish on wood and painted surfaces. Belt sanders are powerful machines that can be used to sand wood and metal quickly. They are more expensive than orbital sanders, but sand in a straight line.

Rasps and files

Files
These are used to smooth metal and wood, to remove burrs and other irregularities, to enlarge and finish holes, and to sharpen some cutting tools. Files are available in a range of degrees of coarseness. A number of different shapes are also produced, from slender, slim taper files to flat and half-round designs.

Rasps
Used mainly on wood, rasps are also effective on plastics, aluminum, and lead. They are available in a range of different cuts, and in flat, round, and half-round shapes. Rasp teeth are coarser than file teeth, so they slice off slivers of wood easily.

Surform tools
These are hollow rasps with handles. They have steel blades with sharp-edged holes which can cut wood away rapidly. The blades can be replaced very easily.

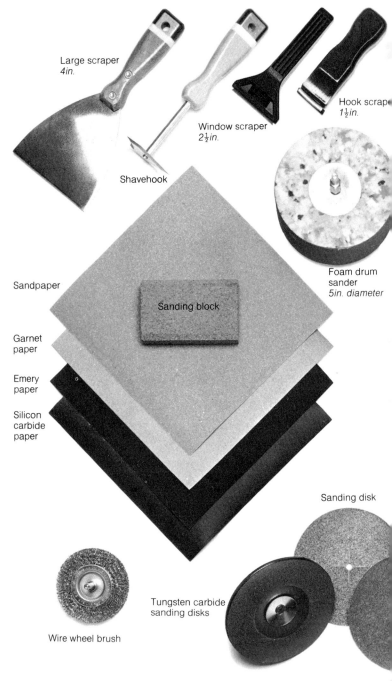

Large scraper
4 in.

Window scraper
2½ in.

Hook scraper
1½ in.

Shavehook

Foam drum sander
5 in. diameter

Sandpaper

Garnet paper

Emery paper

Silicon carbide paper

Sanding block

Sanding disk

Tungsten carbide sanding disks

Wire wheel brush

number, the finer the paper.

Files and rasps can be used to shape metal and wood. Round files can enlarge holes in metal, while triangular files can sharpen saw blades. The file cuts on the forward stroke, so apply even pressure. Chalk the file's teeth before use, to prevent clogging, or brush the file with steel wool during use. Most files are sold without handles, so you should buy these separately.

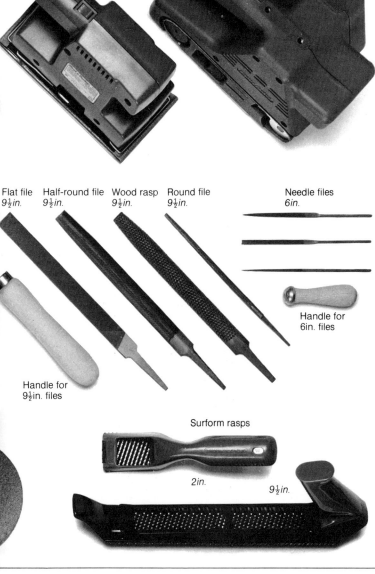

Orbital sander

Belt sander

Flat file
9½in.

Half-round file
9½in.

Wood rasp
9½in.

Round file
9½in.

Needle files
6in.

Handle for
6in. files

Handle for
9½in. files

Surform rasps

2in.

9½in.

Filling and plastering tools

Filling knives are useful for general repair work. The most common type has a wide, flexible blade to spread filler into holes in wood or masonry.

Trowels are essential for mixing, shaping and applying mortar. Different types are available for different functions – a rectangular trowel for applying plaster; a pointed trowel for brickwork. Keep all metal trowels lightly oiled to prevent them from rusting.

Fillers

Putty knife
Used to spread fillers in wood or plaster, this has a flexible blade, so that filler can be pushed into holes and cracks. The edge of the blade can be used to score cracks and clean out loose material. Narrow-bladed knives are useful for shaping and smoothing putty when glazing windows. Wider blades are useful for applying drywall tape. Blade widths range from 1in. to 4in.

Plastering and bricklaying tools

Brick trowel
The traditional trowel for applying mortar is available in blade lengths of 6in. to 12in.

Pointing trowel
This slightly smaller trowel is used for applying mortar and repairing joints between bricks. Blade lengths range from 3in. to 8in.

Brick jointer
Jointers give the right finish to mortar joints between bricks. Blade

lengths range from 5in. to 12in.

Plasterer's trowel
This is used to apply and smooth plaster on walls and ceilings. Sizes range from 4in.×10in. to 4¾in.×11in.

Wooden float
For a fine, matt finish on the surface of skim plaster, cement mortar, or concrete. The usual size is 5in.×11in.

Hawk
A hawk is used to hold small amounts of plaster or mortar when working. Sizes range from 10in. square to 14in. square.

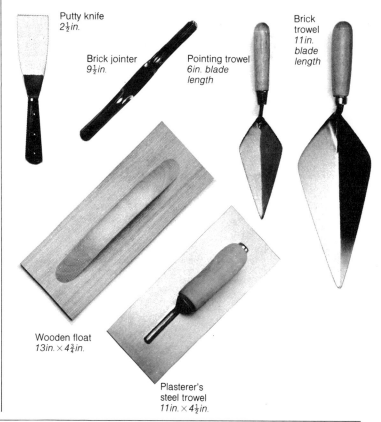

Putty knife
2½in.

Brick jointer
9½in.

Pointing trowel
6in. blade
length

Brick trowel
11in.
blade
length

Wooden float
13in.×4¾in.

Plasterer's
steel trowel
11in.×4½in.

Brushes

For top-quality results it is vital to use good brushes. The best are made with boar's bristle. When choosing a brush, a good guide to quality is price – the more you pay, the better it should be. A top quality brush will also be less likely to shed bristles. Look for a good length of bristle and a bulky filling. The bristles should flex without spreading too much and spring quickly back into place when bent back.

Artificial fiber bristles tend to be smooth and not as springy as true bristles, so they do not hold paint as well as those made with natural bristles, and tend to leave brush marks on the surface. But good quality nylon brushes are very hard wearing and, if their bristles are tapered and textured, can hold latex paint very well.

Paint brushes

Flat brushes
Use these to apply alkyd or semigloss paint or varnish to woodwork. When working, do not overload the brush: apply the paint in even strokes. Sizes range from $\frac{1}{2}$in. to $4\frac{1}{2}$in. Use $\frac{1}{2}$in. and 1in. brushes for small areas and intricate work, and 2in. and 3in. brushes for larger areas, windows and doors. For walls and ceilings, if you do not want to use a roller, a 4in. or $4\frac{1}{2}$in. brush will give quick coverage. To prevent new brushes shedding hairs and spoiling new paint, flick the brush and rub it along a rough surface, until all the loose bristles have come free.

Cutting-in brush
The slanting angle of the bristles enables you to take the paint neatly right up to an edge, such as the glass in a window frame, a baseboard or a door panel. The usual width is $\frac{3}{4}$in.

Foam brushes
These are an inexpensive alternative to pure or synthetic bristle brushes. They do not shed hairs, they are light to use, but do not produce such a good result. They require no cleaning and are simply thrown away after each job. They consist of a plastic handle which extends into a shaft, covered with a foam pad. A range of sizes is available.

Wall brushes
Large versions of flat brushes, these are used mainly for painting walls and other large areas instead of a roller. They are available in a wide range of sizes, particularly between $4\frac{1}{2}$in. and 12in. The larger sizes can be heavy and tiring to use for long periods, so it is best not to overload these. Some wall brushes have a wide stock into which the bristles are set in two or three rows of round bunches. This type of brush is particularly suitable for stippling paint on to rendered walls.

Wallpaper brushes

Smoothing brush
This is used for smoothing down wallpaper when it is being pasted to a wall. The brush should be used from the center of each strip of wallpaper outward to remove air bubbles and creases. The brushes are available in sizes between $7\frac{1}{2}$in. and 10in.

Wallpaper paste brush
A special brush, with synthetic bristles, is available for applying wallpaper paste. An ordinary wide wall brush is quite adequate for this job. To remove traces of paste before it dries and hardens, soak the brush in warm, soapy water.

Other brushes

Scratch brushes
These brushes are used for cleaning metal and masonry surfaces before decorating them. They may also be used for scoring the surface of washable wallpapers prior to soaking them. Some types have a metal scraper attached to one end to aid the removal of loose flakes. Power-tool attachments are also available that perform the same function. Several shapes are made, including small brushes for confined spaces.

Wallpaper pasting brush 5in.

Foam paint brush 1$\frac{3}{8}$in.

Foam paint brush 2in.

Foam paint brush 3in.

Wallpaper smoothing brush 7in.

Cutting-in brush $\frac{3}{4}$in.

Paint brush 1in.

Paint brush 2in.

Scratch brush 11in.

Wall brush 4in.

Rollers and paint pads

With a roller you can apply paint quickly to large areas of wall and ceiling. Rollers are used in conjunction with a paint tray – you fill the tray with paint and load the roller from it. Apply the paint carefully, taking care to avoid splattering. When buying a roller, make sure the roller sleeve can be removed from the handle assembly for cleaning. Clean the roller well after use.

Paint pads are easy to use, and will cover large, flat surfaces quickly. They apply paint smoothly, do not spatter very much, but are not very versatile. With the larger pads, it is often possible to insert a brush handle into the pad handle, for easy painting above arm's reach. It is difficult to clean pads after using oil-based paints, so it is best to confine their use to water-based paints and the type of easy-clean oil-based paints that can be removed with hot water and detergent.

Rollers

Paint rollers
Ideal for painting large areas quickly, rollers tend to give a slightly more stippled finish than either brushes or pads, but, unlike pads, are not confined to use on flat surfaces. Short-pile rollers are best for smooth surfaces, while those with longer pile can be used for textured surfaces. Many rollers splatter paint during use, but this is less of a problem with lambswool and nylon pile types than with foam rollers. Most rollers are about 7in. wide. When using rollers, a paint tray is also required to enable you to load the paint evenly. Foam rollers are the cheapest and they are best used with water-based paints. Mohair rollers have short, fine pile, suited to applying oil-based paint to give a gloss finish.
Lambswool and nylon pile rollers are ideal for applying latex paints. The longer the pile, the deeper the texture of the paint surface.
Textured foam rollers give attractive finishes with self-texturing paint. A range of patterns is available.

Seam roller
This small hardwood roller is used to press down the edges of wallpaper before they dry out. It should be used firmly, but without pressing so hard that all the paste is forced out to give a weak seam. After use, you should wipe the roller and wallpaper to remove surplus paste. Seam rollers are available in hardwood and plastic, in sizes ranging from 1in. to 2in.

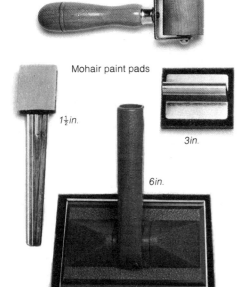

Wooden seam roller
1½in. roller width

Mohair paint pads

1½in.

3in.

6in.

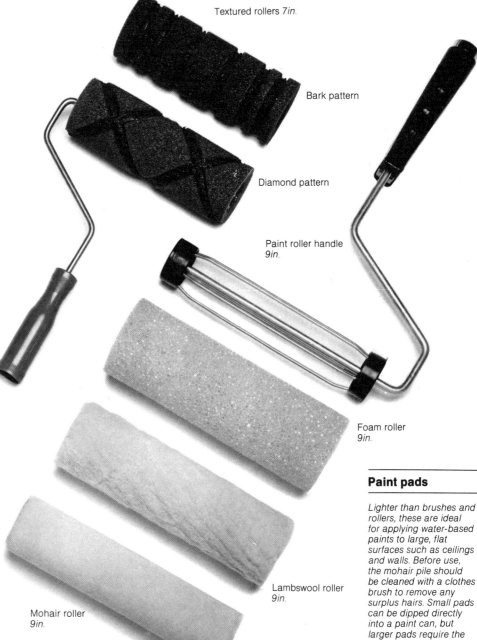

Textured rollers 7in.

Bark pattern

Diamond pattern

Paint roller handle
9in.

Foam roller
9in.

Lambswool roller
9in.

Mohair roller
9in.

Paint pads

Lighter than brushes and rollers, these are ideal for applying water-based paints to large, flat surfaces such as ceilings and walls. Before use, the mohair pile should be cleaned with a clothes brush to remove any surplus hairs. Small pads can be dipped directly into a paint can, but larger pads require the use of a tray. Sizes range from 2in. × 1in. to 8in. × 3½in.

Pliers and pincers

As well as cutting and shaping wire, pliers can be used for a wide variety of holding and gripping tasks. When using pliers, hold them firmly, keeping your palm away from the pivot, which can pinch your skin as the jaws close. Pliers can also bend sheet metal. The sides of the jaws should align with the bending line to produce a neat bend. The side cutters on many pairs of pliers will cut soft wire.

Use pincers to pull out brads and nails. Grip the body of the nail as closely as possible to the surface of the wood and protect it with a small piece of hardboard next to the nail. Lever the handles to one side so that the jaws roll over the hardboard, and the nail emerges. Grip the nail again lower down the shank and repeat.

General-purpose pliers

Lineman's pliers
Suitable for general-purpose work, these pliers have serrated jaws for gripping flat objects, and curved jaws for gripping rods. There is a side cutter for cropping soft wire and usually one or two hard wire croppers near the pivot. The handles sometimes have plastic insulation. Sizes range from 5in. to 10in.

Flat-nosed pliers
For the long reach needed to grip thin sheet metal and small objects, use these lightweight, flat-nosed pliers. Sizes available range from 4in. to 7½in.

Specialized pliers

Electrician's pliers
These are used to grip, bend, and cut electrical cable and cord. They are the same design as Linesman's pliers, but always have insulated handles. Sizes range from 6in. to 8in.

Needle-nose pliers
Also known as long-nosed pliers, these are used for handling small objects and cutting small wires, especially in confined spaces. They are lightweight and have narrow, tapering jaws with fine serrations for a good grip. A range of different jaw shapes is available. Sizes range from 4½in. to 8in.

Slip-joint pliers
These are particularly useful for holding pipes. They combine the functions of pliers and wrench and are invaluable when an adjustable, long-handled tool is required. Channel lock pliers have four or six adjustments that allow the jaws to grip

Wire strippers 6*in.*

Long-nosed pliers 6*in.*

Needle-nose pliers 6*in.*

Tack lifter 7¼*in.*

Prybar 18*in.*

General-purpose pliers 6*in.*

Slip-joint pliers 6*in.*

Lineman's pliers 6*in.*

Carpenter's pincers 8*in.*

Multiple slip-joint pliers 9*in.*

Multi-purpose tool 8½*in.*

Plier type tile cutter 8*in.*

tightly to suit the size of the object. Slip-joint pliers are also available with bent or narrow jaws. Sizes range from 5in. to 10in.

Other equipment

Carpenter's pincers
These are gripping tools for pulling out nails and brads. The heads are rounded and polished so that they will roll easily on the surface as the nail is being extracted. Sizes range from 6in. to 10in.

Tack lifter
For quick extraction of tacks and small nails, use this screwdriver-like tool. It has a curved, V-notched blade which slips under the head of the tack. The handle is pressed down to lift the tack. Sizes range from 6¼in. to 8in.

Prybar
The large claw at one end of the bar allows you to lift large nails, such as those securing floorboards. The flattened end of the bar can be used to pry up boards. The length of the bar gives good leverage.

Wire strippers
These remove insulation from the ends of electrical cord and cables. Various styles are available, but they are all adjustable for different thicknesses of wire. The traditional type has spring-return handles and V-notched, high-tensile blades, adjusted by a side-locking screw. Sizes range from 6in. to 8in.

Tile cutters
Plier-type tile cutters have an angled face, so that the tile breaks evenly on either side of a scored line. Tile snips allow you to remove small pieces of waste material from the edge of a tile.

Wrenches

Wrenches are tools for loosening and tightening nuts and bolts. Fixed open-ended or "plain" wrenches are easy and fast to use. Enclosed or "box-end" wrenches are stronger, but less versatile. Both types are available in a variety of sizes and can be used for many jobs, from working on electrical and plumbing fittings to servicing domestic appliances.

Adjustable wrenches will fit a wide range of nut and bolt sizes. They are normally open-ended with one movable jaw, set at an angle to the shaft, operated by a screw, although there is also a limited range of adjustable box-end wrenches. Adjustable wrenches are particularly useful for making plumbing joints with compression fittings and for fitting faucets.

General-purpose wrenches

Open-ended wrenches
These are the most common and versatile wrenches. They will slide on to a nut or bolt from the side, and they are faster to use than box-end types, although not as strong. They can also be used on pipe joints where it is impossible to use a box-end type. They are available in many different sizes, which vary according to manufacturer.

Box-end wrenches
Slower to use but safer and stronger than open-ended wrenches, these grip more tightly. The ring of the wrench has either 6 or 12 points which link with the sides of the nut or bolt. A 12-point wrench can be used on both hex-agonal and square bolt heads. Box-end wrenches are available in many different sizes, varying according to maker.

Combination wrenches
These versatile wrenches have a box at one end and an open-ended jaw at the other.

Multiple wrenches

Multiple box-ends
Intended only for light-weight work, the ends contain a selection of five different-sized rings.

Adjustable wrenches
These are particularly useful in plumbing work. Several different designs are available but most are bulkier than the same-sized open-ended or box-end wrenches. But they are weaker and should be used care-fully. They fit a wide range of nut sizes

Monkey wrenches have a fixed jaw and a rack. Sizes range from

6in. to 18in.
Crescent wrenches are adjusted by a worm screw in the handle. Sizes up to 24in. are available.

Adjustable box-end wrenches are also avail-able. They feature a metal shaft with two pivoting heads, which tighten against the shaft as you turn the wrench. With this design, you do not have to remove the wrench between turns. Sizes up to $8\frac{1}{2}$in. are produced.

Other wrenches

Pipe wrenches
Similar in design to adjustable wrenches, these are used for grip-ping pipes and rods.

Footprint wrenches have an adjustable pivot and grip the pipe when the handles are squeezed. Lengths up to 20in. are available.

Stilson wrenches are very strong, have spring-loaded jaws, but may damage the pipe. Sizes range from $\frac{5}{8}$in. to 8in.

Vise-grip wrench
Often known as a Mole grip, this wrench has a locking device that allows it to grip flat or circular metal objects very firmly. The jaws are controlled by an adjust-ing screw, and extreme force is applied when the handles are closed. Designs with straight and curved jaws are avail-able in sizes ranging from 5in. to 12in.

Basin wrench
This is used on nuts, such as those under a sink, that a conventional wrench will not reach. It has a moving-jaw head which turns by means of a bar. Sizes are avail-able for fittings up to 2in. wide.

Stilson pipe wrench *18in.*

Basin wrench *10in.*

Newbey wrench *9½in.*

Combination wrench $\frac{11}{16}$in. $\frac{5}{8}$in.

Crescent wrench *10in.*

Open-ended wrench $\frac{5}{8}$in. $\frac{9}{16}$in.

Crescent wrench *8in.*

Adjustable box wrench

Vise-grip wrench *8in.*

Multiple box-end

Box-end wrench $\frac{11}{16}$in. $\frac{5}{8}$in.

Index

Acknowledgments

Authors acknowledgments
The authors would like to thank the following for their contributions to the book:
David Holloway, Mike Lawrence, Christine Parsons, Yvonne Rees, Tony Wilkins.

Dorling Kindersley *would like to thank the following for their invaluable help in producing this book:*
Vic Chambers, Tod Norman, Jonathan Hilton, Cathy and Fred Gill, Jon Bouchier, Dominic Neville, Giles Neville, Jackie Giles, Elizabeth Whiting, Tony Wallace, Denise Weaver, Mike Trier, Tim Shackleton, Corinne Ashby, Judy Berman, Michael Upshall, Gill Aspery, Sophie Mitchell, Michael Stowers.

Photography
All photographs by Jon Bouchier except:

Key t = top, b = bottom, l = left, r = right

Elizabeth Whiting Associates
15tl, tr and b, 21br, 30, 31, 34tl and tr, 46t, 47b, 58b, 67, 71b, 103, 107, 163, 167bl and br, 173t and br

Camera Press
46b, 47t, 58t and c, 59, 71t, 87, 108, 155, 167t, 173b

"Coverplus" (Woolworths)
15rc

Demonstrators
All demonstrations by Dominic Neville except:
Giles Neville pp. 48-55
Jackie Giles pp. 26-7, 42-3

Illustrators
Les Smith
Kevin Maddison
David Ashby
Kuo Kang Chen

Suppliers
The following kindly loaned or supplied tools and materials for use in the book:
Ajax Flooring Co Ltd., London SE4

Black and Decker Ltd., Maidenhead, Berks.

Buck and Ryan Ltd., London WC1.

Amtico, London W1.

Artex Ltd., Newhaven, Sussex.

Copydex Products Ltd., London WC2.

David Douglas (Carpets) Ltd., London SW8.

L. G. Harris & Co Ltd., Bromsgrove, Worcester, Worcs.

ICI Dulux Paints Ltd., Slough, Berks.

Knobs and Knockers, London W1.

On the tiles, London SW6.

Arthur J. Sanderson & Sons Ltd., London W1.

Sphinx Tiles Ltd., Newbury, Berks.

Uniroyal Ltd., London SW1.

Vigers and Blackmur Ltd., Barking, Essex.

Welpac Hardware Ltd., Barking, Essex.

Wicanders (GB) Ltd., Crawley, W. Sussex.

Wimbledon Woodcraft, London SW19.